NEW VISION FOR MANAGEMENT EDUCATION

LEADERSHIP CHALLENGES

NEW VISION FOR MANAGEMENT EDUCATION

LEADERSHIP CHALLENGES

PETER LORANGE

President IMD
The Nestlé Professor
Lausanne, Switzerland

2002

Pergamon
An imprint of Elsevier Science

Amsterdam – Boston – London – New York – Oxford – Paris
San Diego – San Francisco – Singapore – Sydney – Tokyo

ELSEVIER SCIENCE Ltd
The Boulevard, Langford Lane
Kidlington, Oxford OX5 1GB, UK

First edition 2002

Library of Congress Cataloging in Publication Data
A catalog record from the Library of Congress has been applied for.

British Library Cataloguing in Publication Data
A catalogue record from the British Library has been applied for.

ISBN: 0-08-044034-7

♾ The paper used in this publication meets the requirements of ANSI/NISO Z39.48–1992 (Permanence of Paper).
Printed in The Netherlands.

Contents

Acknowledgements

Numerous persons have contributed to this book. Gordon Adler has done an outstanding job, editing the manuscript several times and discussing many key issues with me. He deserves my warmest thanks.

I also received important inputs on earlier versions of the manuscript from Dr George Bain, Vice Chancellor, Queens University of North Ireland; Professor Kaj Sköldberg, Stockholm University; Professor Ingemar Ståhl, Stockholm School of Economics; and Professor Jacques Marcovitch, Rector, University of São Paulo.

The ideas and issues discussed in this book have been developed together with colleagues at IMD. Many have contributed substantially, and it would be impossible to single any out. However, two exceptions need to be made. I have had the privilege of working with Professor James Ellert, Senior Associate Dean of IMD, on the leadership tasks of IMD for many years, always leading to constructive results, many of them reflected in this book. In addition, I have been co-operating with Professor Bala Chakravarthy for more than twenty years, involving many discussions on strategic leadership within business schools. I also had a chance to have extensive discussions with Mr Knut Haanes. Thank you, Knut.

Catherine FitzSimons did an outstanding job typing and pre-editing several versions of this manuscript. Eva Ferrari and Annette Polzer also gave good support. Thank you to all.

Peter Lorange
Lausanne, December 2001

Preface

Doing business is more complicated and demanding than it has ever been. The competitive environment for today's corporation is changing fast. Economies are opening, and new customers are cropping up in the world's heavily populated and fast-growing regions. Many businesses are facing global competition. Demographics are shifting. Expectations are changing and so are consumer behaviours. As a result, more often than not, executives need to see their businesses in a global context. Even the managers of regional or local businesses have to run their firms as if they were global. The pace has accelerated — speed is everything.

At the same time, mergers, co-operative arrangements, network-based organisational arrangements, and a plethora of new competitive structures in certain industries are changing the competitive rules of the game. Especially where a new breed of entrepreneurs is redefining the rules of the game in their industries, new corporations are springing up fast. To make matters even thornier for executives, not only are the rules of the game changing, but the changes themselves are different from region to region and from country to country.

Classical players are left scratching their heads. Various actors, playing the role of "integrator" of other actors' inputs in the chain, are redefining the roles of the other players in the traditional value chain. The new emphasis is on service — the "software" side — rather than on the more traditional production of "hardware" components, concrete and steel.

Further characteristics of all this change are massive outsourcing, downsizing of activities, and radical reengineering. To be able to move faster and adapt more quickly, organisations are stripping themselves down to the essentials, farming out their superfluous activities. The rate of creation of new jobs in the centre (defined as "wholly owned activities") may stagnate, while the growth in new jobs elsewhere in the value chain may increase exponentially.

In addition to this mounting speed, competition and complexity, government scrutiny of business is on the rise. More than ever before, stakeholder activists are voting their values. More stringent ethical norms for business practice are gaining acceptance. Calls for sustainable development are growing louder.

Finally, the express train of the technological revolution keeps on rolling. Telecommunications, computers, multimedia and information-handling, network-based working style and communications — all have served to flatten out and make more "virtual" the hierarchical corporations of the industrial evolution.

What do all these changes mean for corporations as they head into the new millennium? Of course they have to respond to company-, business- and industry-specific transformations, and remain more alert than ever before to what they mean. They need to exploit new opportunities, and defend their positions. Above all — and this is perhaps the biggest change — they need to learn.

Why is learning paramount? Because the modern corporation cannot afford to take a defensive position. To be passive is to fail. Successful corporations see change as an *opportunity* to redefine the way they do business, to dream up innovations that generate growth and profitability. Their executives spot opportunities that nobody else sees. Regardless of the industry, today's winning organisation is dominated by ad hoc projects and initiatives, many of them virtual. Entrepreneurial initiatives set the tone and shape the agenda. Timing matters. Take Hewlett-Packard, for instance. At HP, missing the planned completion of the development process by three months can mean the death of the project.[1] Global business teams — executives from key markets — have to work together to develop and expand business faster than they could using traditional approaches, and present a common face to customers, from Dallas to Beijing, and from Helsinki to Cape Town. Team members may come from all over the world — it is a global market for talent. Old hierarchies are ceding to flat, de-layered organisational structures. Having a human team that can learn faster and adapt more appropriately creates a definite strategic advantage.

All these shifts put an extraordinarily heavy demand on the people in an organisation. In the past, leading corporations could secure their success by perhaps drawing on their sheer size, their sheer economic muscle, the sheer magnitude of their market presence and market shares, and/or the sheer excellence of their proprietary technologies. Today, these old advantages bring little unless strong people work at the centre of the organisation. Today, human capital is king.

But having strong people isn't enough. The corporation needs high quality people who can learn: every single member of the organisation has to have an open mind, an ability to adapt, and a willingness to learn. These abilities go hand in hand with flexibility: all members need to be flexible in what, why, how, and when they learn. The corporation can strengthen this flexibility. How? The people responsible for determining what needs individuals and organisations should acquire — typically top managers — must assess their company and human resource needs in a highly flexible, proactive manner. Rather than increasing their people's specific learning (of course, that remains important, too) they must work to increase their managers' and employees' ability to learn.[2] And this means, consequently, that the learning agendas of firms are likely to change dramatically. Or, as van Baalen and Moratis said, "So, what are these challenges facing business schools in the new, knowledge intensive, network economy? Since knowledge has moved to centre stage in a network economy, one of the essential elements of value creation now is (organisational) learning and, hence, education."[3]

Clearly then, the centrepiece of all these change agendas is human resources. He who accumulates relevant human capital faster than his competitors will win the "marathon of learning". How a firm invests in its human resources is perhaps the most critical strategic decision today. In the past, critical strategic decisions were typically about major capital expansion projects, research and development, and acquisitions. But today, critical strategic decisions have much more to do with *how* to "invest" in one's organisation so that the relevant capabilities are at hand when needed. Although these decisions are less of a financial burden than many of the more classical strategic decisions just mentioned, they are just as important.

Consider, for instance, what happens when a firm is thinking about investing in a new plant as part of a decision to expand capacity. Nestlé's pet food business in Japan serves the point (keep in mind that Nestlé is not only the largest food company in the world but also number one in pet food).[4] Simply put, Nestlé decided not to invest in a new plant in Japan. Instead, the Swiss company "invested" in a network of executives who developed a logistics approach for the business. The emphasis was put on people — serving the customers, i.e., a strong revenue-generating side. Orders were filled by sourcing the various pet food products from plants elsewhere in the Nestlé system: Australia, Thailand, and the United States. The company put heavy emphasis on logistics, planning so that the various containers with pet food went directly to the customer. This cut transportation costs. The overall result was that, rather than investing in a new plant, Nestlé invested in a network, and reaped large gains in its returns. The investment process became a creative process, built around new people competencies and focused on sourcing planning, creative revenue generation and logistics.

If a firm invests in a huge new plant as part of a decision to expand capacity, but it can't run the plant or sell what it produces in new markets, the investment will be for naught. As in the Nestlé case just cited, it is the *people* that secure the return on investment. It is not hard to imagine that even if Company "A" and Company "B" make identical return-on-investment calculations, the greatest returns will accrue to the one with the best people backing up the investment.

When firms execute large, complex projects, integrate acquisitions, or roll out the benefits of a particular research and development finding, it is always the people that make the difference.

Change, adaptation, learning, the quality of the human capital of a corporation — all are linked. So the need for corporations to learn is greater than ever before. Clearly, top management must concern itself increasingly with the human element of any major strategic decisions: *Do we have the most appropriate team in place? Where are the executives we can draw on? How can a new team be mobilised which is as strong as at all possible?* The list of such people-related considerations is probably limitless, but the bottom line is finite and clear: the only viable strategic approach for today's modern corporation is to view its human capital as *the* key strategic resource, and the *only* way to build up this invaluable resource is through learning that matches the corporate agenda.

The modern business school can play an important role here, assuming that it can provide *relevance*, that it can be a meaningful learning partner to the modern corporation facing the challenges outlined above. To assure that its offerings meet the shifting needs of choosy corporate clients, the business school, first off, has to have strong leadership, which will be recognisable in the school's choice of direction. Obviously, a business school cannot be everything to everyone. So the school needs to cruise the areas on the strategic chart where it aspires to be a value-creating partner to business, i.e., it needs to practice the dictum that "strategy means choice". And if one accepts the premise that a business school's strategic direction can *be* managed — I most wholeheartedly do — the choice of the Dean will be critical. Somebody has to be willing to raise a hand and say, "I'll take it on."

The problem is, academics all too often view business school management tasks as onerous burdens. Unattractive routines that pull them away from research and teaching. Nevertheless, I would like to think that, with some of the ideas in this book and the collective published wisdom of other business school leaders, combined with my conviction that anyone who takes on the task of managing a business school is doing "something of importance", business schools will continue to be able to attract the necessary leadership talents to get the administrative tasks done. Not just done, but done better than ever before. This will probably mean answering the call for a new leadership approach, one that can develop and improve the value-creating substance that must be at the core of the modern business school so that it can serve as a learning catalyst to the business organisations it serves. Because, as I have already argued, today's needs for organisational learning *are* different; they call for a different business school which, in turn, requires developing new leadership approaches and a new leadership focus.

The business school for the new millennium is a breed apart. In the remaining chapters of this book, you will find models, guidelines, examples, both good and bad, for managing that special breed. This book is grounded in hands-on experience. It is based on over thirty years' association with business schools-cum-academic institutions. It draws on my association as a faculty member of two leading US business schools, the Sloan School of Management (MIT) and the Wharton School (University of Pennsylvania), and on my somewhat shorter tenures at three European business schools: IMD, the Stockholm School of Economics, and the Norwegian School of Management. At Wharton, the Norwegian School of Management, and IMD — the schools from which I will draw most of the examples in the book — I have had various administrative roles, including serving as President of the latter two. I have thus, to a greater or lesser extent, taken part in what can be seen as the task of establishing a strategic direction in these institutions.

Experience has taught me that academic direction setting is never clear-cut. It is complex, and often rife with dilemma and even controversy. In fact, in the three decades since the 1970s, a number of widely respected management thinkers have tried to tell us how best to set direction (i.e., manage) our business schools. They *cannot* be managed, some have claimed. They *can* be managed, but only loosely, others have argued. They can be perhaps "steered", but they can't be managed, at least not in the way we think of when we talk about "managing" a corporation, even others have said. For these writers, the business school is heavily bureaucratic, about as responsive to the market as a great ship under full sail, coming about with ponderous slowness. To them, managing a business school strategically is impossible.

So it should come as no surprise that, all too often, academic institutions view management ideas and practices with scepticism, if not outright disapproval. "Unfortunately, management in education is still a concept that stimulates a negative reaction from many academics. As a result, organisations in higher education tend to neglect management concepts and practices."[5]

In thinking about the ideas in this book, discussing them and debating their merits, and reading around the subject, I discovered that even those who agree with me that you can set strategy and manage the business school seem to believe, however, that whatever strategy the school sets will be — must be — driven by a heavy focus on research, but with a curiously simple conception of what research means, in this case, classical, academic, and steered toward one, and only one, valued outlet — the refereed journal.

In *New Vision for Management Education — Leadership Challenges* you will learn why I believe all of these thinkers miss the mark. I will call for a more multi-faceted value creation — research, yes, but more broadly defined and together with several other value-creating outputs. Taking a wider perspective, I will argue in *New Vision for Management Education — Leadership Challenges* that the modern business school *can* be managed strategically, certainly better than the simple, evolutionary, laissez-faire, hands-off way of most academic institutions. The obvious question is, of course, how. How should academic institutions most effectively set strategic direction? How can they best create value? These two questions underpin the explorations in this book. Above all, I will try to answer the timely questions: What characteristics does a modern business school need to *have,* and what does it have to *do* in order to succeed?

In trying to answer them, I will range across the entire organisation and over time. And in so doing, I will assume that an academic institution such as a business school *can* be managed strategically — i.e., that it is meaningful to talk about a deliberate process of strategy-setting and implementation for it, and that innovation is critical for survival and growth. Business school success does not have to be left to lucky accident. I will further assume that setting strategy in a business school implies choice. And that is also means developing people, projects, partners, and processes. Setting strategy will therefore require innovation which, in turn, requires resources, space ("room to manoeuvre") that further implies choice. Value creation in a business school consists of helping clients with discovery, knowledge development, and learning activities.

The arguments of the book rest on two fundamental assumptions. The first is my belief in the market: the business school must measure the *relevance* of its offerings by the *response from the market.* This is, in itself, not a trivial task. Keen judgement is needed to maintain a "responsible market focus" — to know *how* to respond to the market while also upholding the basic values associated with the academic profession. The second assumption of this book is what I believe to be the vital role of the Dean or the President (I equate the two here). It is the Dean, or President, I believe, who mainly through *recruiting and working with faculty* and *selecting critical projects* must align institutional and personal agendas.

Robert Joss, Dean of the Graduate School of Business at Stanford University, claims that managing a big business school is "one of the most demanding jobs imaginable, requiring academic leadership, managerial skills, and money-raising flair".[6] My purpose here is to show how the Dean can meet these demands. I will explore the best ways for business schools to stake out and implement strategic direction. If you are interested in how business schools for the new millennium can be run according to sound strategic management principles, read on.

Introduction

From the beginning of this book, I will argue that the modern business school *can* be managed, and that it *should* be managed in a way that entails setting and implementing a deliberate direction ("strategy"). The dynamic business school is a reality today, and the management approaches and suggestions outlined in this book are feasible, but demanding. The process of setting realistic strategic direction is not necessarily easy. Setbacks and frustrations will mark the way. Putting each element of the strategy into practice involves keeping a clear focus and a clear sense of priorities. After all, "strategy means choice" — balanced choice! And, *simplicity* will be critical to make the strategy work! However, despite these difficulties, there seems to be significant potential increase to the value-creation capabilities of many modern business schools. An auspicious sign. And this book is meant to help all stakeholders in the business schools of today to realise that potential. Throughout, I will draw heavily on examples from my many years of experience as an academic administrator, and later Dean; previously at The Wharton School and the Norwegian School of Management, and now, since 1993 as President of the International Institute of Management Development (IMD) in Lausanne.

I call the school that follows the path outlined in the following pages the *dynamic business school*, the route it takes, *dynamic*. As you will see, it is dynamic in the sense that it is flexible, and adapts quickly to the needs of its learning partners/customers. It seeks direction proactively, always working to develop new knowledge that complements what I call its "adaptive thrust". Further the dynamic business school's faculty members are entrepreneurial: the school gives them the "space to do their own thing" and they use it to take their own initiatives. Administrative, "catalytic" efforts from the top should drive the school to develop a stronger overall portfolio dimension, also dynamically. The book will show how this top-driven effort might look. And it will demonstrate that the Dean's work complements the other inputs in the direction-setting of the school.[1]

As you will see, the strategic direction of a dynamic business school thus results from a combination of forces. Bottom-up, entrepreneurial inputs combined with top-down leadership inputs. This interplay of forces, in that it changes over time, must be seen in a dynamic context. Sometimes, for instance, this will mean that it responds more strongly to the adaptive needs of the school's clients — what I call its learning partners; at other times, it spots and takes relatively more advantage of opportunities for "proactive, directional leaps". The top-down portfolio balancing will thus also take on a different character depending on this changing mix of proactive versus adaptive bottom-up initiatives.

The balance between these forces is extremely important and will be explored in the book. It is the checks and balances that lead to the solid strategic direction of the business school, and it is an appropriate ongoing balance that ensures a continuing solid strategic direction. As I will argue — and demonstrate — all members of a business school's team have to recognise this. The various dimensions must find a healthy modus vivendi. One of the aims of this book is to show how to find it. A strategy that flows out of a "win/lose" power play among various stakeholders is unhealthy.

Key questions for the academic administrator-cum-practitioner may be: How can the findings of this book be generalised to other business schools, to academic organisational settings more generally, and to other professional organisations? What general value do the propositions put forward in this book have? For instance, can business schools that are not private, independent, self-governing schools like IMD also be managed along the lines I have laid down? Can other types of professional schools, academic departments, and even university faculties be managed this way? Finally, to what extent might various types of brain-driven professional organisations, such as management consulting firms, borrow from this approach to management?

Further, among the many questions I will address in this book is the extent to which we can draw on management concepts already developed elsewhere — theories for strategy, leadership, organisation, etc. — or whether, as some scholars suggest, the academic setting is so different that few more general theories and applications apply. Mittlehurst asks the question this way: "Are models and images of leadership developed in other contexts of relevance to academe, or is there something distinctive about the nature of leadership in the academic context? Where in the academic environment might leadership be identified and how might it be developed?"[2]

As I will argue in more detail, the most important question, perhaps, is whether the organisation has the financial clout to support the market-oriented adaptation and services outlined in this book. Financial health is a critical condition for more market-oriented educational value creation. Many of the suggestions in this book for adapting to the learning partners' needs are probably applicable to a wider range of business schools and consulting firms, provided that they have the financial means. This probably means that a primary "customer focus" will have to be on executive development, a segment with customers who typically have the ability and willingness to pay whatever customer focus costs.

The book's suggestions may, however, be less appropriate for schools that offer primarily undergraduate, ordinary MBA and Ph.D. programmes. These market segments clearly have less financial upside. Such schools would normally, therefore, need some government support. Regrettably, however, this type of support often means a diminishing of the pressure on the business school to adapt. Still, as long as a reasonable part of the tuition fees would come from the individual, a quasi-market situation could be maintained. It could be further enhanced by having a so-called voucher system, as proposed by Professor Milton Friedman of the University of Chicago.[3] Under such a system, the government would give out vouchers that students would use to pay for an education at the school of their choice.

Perhaps some academic disciplines would be unable to expect payment at all — classical archaeology or theology come to mind. While some possibilities exist for introducing pressures for adaptation in a university setting *in general*, market orientation in some areas simply could not be taken to the extreme proposed in this book. Still, terms like "service university"[4,5] (Tjeldvoll) or "entrepreneurial university"[6] (Clark) are becoming more and more popular and underscore the notion and implied value of a market orientation. It must be recognised, however, that market mechanisms have limits, practically, as well as ethically, and sensible judgement must be applied to the question of how far one can go.

The applicability of the ideas in this book depends on the extent to which the learning partner seeks cross-disciplinary, eclectic learning support (as opposed to being served more traditional, disciplinary-based, functionally focused learning inputs). A typical business school can serve undergraduates most effectively by exposing them to basic disciplinary fields and giving them the basic foundations of business. A similar, heavy disciplinary base would also prevail in most MBA and Ph.D. programmes. As a natural consequence, many business schools are, therefore, organised along functional departments, each with its own disciplinary offerings. While such "traditional" schools would be in positions to serve the above-mentioned undergraduate, MBA and Ph.D. student segments well, they might not, on the other hand, be in a good position to serve the more advanced, managerially focused students or leading executives. Thus, many business schools may be limited in their ability to follow the cross-disciplinary value-creation proposition outlined in this book.

So, which schools should pursue a cross-disciplinary focus to a greater extent than prevails today in academic institutions? As already implied, those various professional schools within the university that focus on serving end-user groups in society, as well as business schools with an ambition to serve the executive sector in an unique way, could adopt a broader, cross-disciplinary focus.

During relatively stable times, the Cartesian approach to learning — and hence, teaching — in specialised ways might be quite appropriate. By learning the various foundation pieces *first*, students would *then* be able to put them together for a holistic understanding. However, with the explosion of knowledge we are seeing today, the Cartesian approach is probably less appropriate than ever before. Keeping a holistic view is critical. The challenge in this context, however, is to keep a holistic view of one's *learning*. A good analogy is what happens when children create views of a particular phenomenon they are trying to learn about. Children try to put together a *holistic* view of the situation or phenomenon, and then "redraw" their holistic view as more information comes in. This process matches what a business school does when it provides a curriculum (a "sequence") of increasingly detailed, cross-disciplinary snapshots of a given business or management phenomenon.[7,8,9] This iterative approach calls for more cross-disciplinary learning, a fundamental reorganisation of business schools, other professional schools, and academic departments. Again, one of the aims of this book is to help with that fundamental reorganisation.

Of course the ideas in this book are not applicable solely to dynamic business schools. A cross-disciplinary approach is also valid for other types of brain-driven service organisations such as consulting firms. While many consulting firms specialise in specific functional areas, and do not take a cross-disciplinary approach, a number of outstanding general management consulting firms have many "cross disciplinary" features. For instance, they often follow a particular industry view that provides eclectic value creation to the management of this same industry.

Central is the question of whether the organisation or structure of an institution matters in the degree of its ability to be market-oriented. As the short case at the end of Chapter 1 will show, IMD is an entirely independent organisation that has chosen to have no academic, disciplinary departments. This allows the school to more easily pursue academic value creation from a cross-disciplinary platform. The school is an integrated, cross-disciplinary body of knowledge that allows for adaptation in the small *and* in the large. It makes no portfolio tradeoffs between organisational units in the classical sense, such as, for instance, would be the case when shifting the relative emphasis among various academic departments. Rather, the possible portfolio tradeoffs could be among, say, eclectic project initiatives that relate both to teaching and research regarding such issues as: open versus in-company programme balance, geographic coverage/balance, balance between various types of programme offerings —

leadership, change, new business development, etc. The book will explore these issues fully.

Many business schools face different tradeoffs than the ones above, particularly if they are organised along academic department lines. In such cases, market-oriented factors drive the tradeoffs, and the value-creation approach in this book would only apply to a limited extent. The organisation into departments would create an institutional portfolio tradeoff focus, *not* a market-driven portfolio tradeoff focus. Similarly, universities are typically organised in autonomous departments. Here too, when an institutional focus takes the upper hand, the ideas in this book would have limited applicability at best.

For business schools that are part of larger universities, where funds typically flow from the business school to the university, and where strong academic regulations govern the business school from the centre (tenure is a good example), the approach in this book cannot be applied to the fullest extent either. Governance strictures will set limitations on the market-based tradeoffs! I would hope that the spirit of this book would still remain useful, however, in that it could serve as a reminder *always* to maintain a focus on creating academic value that is more consistent with the true needs of the learner — a market perspective should always prevail!

It makes sense, before exploring the ideas, approaches and suggestions in this book, to reconsider the market-based value-creation challenge facing today's business school from three complementary standpoints: retrospective, a reconsideration of a current perspective, and more speculative. Start with the first — the retrospective standpoint. Much of this book will focus on how to adapt the business school to a changing environment, how to come up with processes and structures that allow the business school to stay relevant. The discussion, in general terms, will cover the following strategies for evolution of the business school:

- From being fundamentally disciplinary/axiomatic to becoming more of a *market oriented, eclectic, pioneering oriented, value-creating organisation*;
- From being fundamentally a collection of individuals to being more *based on teams* as the fundamental provider of academic value creation;
- From primarily basing its value-creation delivery on serving individuals to becoming more of a *learning partner to organisations*, such as business firms;
- From fundamentally being a school that adapts to the new realities to a school that also *more proactively shapes the agenda of the future*.

Taking the current perspective, we need to reconfirm that we are in the middle of a technological revolution that does, indeed, fully apply to the educational sector. This means embracing virtual learning technology, seeing network reality as a central part of a school's life, loosening up the borderlines between the business school's organisation and the other co-operative entities in the network, such as corporate universities, learning partners, other business schools, other professional organisations, etc. Thus, today's perspective is a networked, technology-driven one, allowing value creation to take place in a much more multi-faceted way than ever before. Today's perspective builds on the retrospective argument of adapting to new realities; the adaptive challenge today is, however, heavily based on the new technology, the new network reality.

Putting on the more speculative glasses, we can also reflect on what this book is trying to say about the future, the challenges that will, in all likelihood, face those business schools that want to preserve relevant academic value for many years to come. I argue throughout the following fifteen chapters that the future is likely to push schools to have an even greater focus on bringing their human capital to the market, which may include its core competencies, the power of the talents of the faculty members, and the dynamic capabilities of this pool of talents to renew and strengthen itself and to stay ahead. Of course, all organisations face this challenge. The issue of outsourcing, for instance, as I will consider in some depth, will play an increasingly significant role in providing an approach for many corporations to its own intellectual-value maintenance. Perhaps business schools will become more providers of a total support package to corporations, in effect having a contract with them to stimulate and develop their intellectual competencies. More and more, the work context for all of this will be virtual, perhaps with the classical business school campus serving as an occasional meeting place. The business school will thus interact with corporations to a larger extent than ever before as network organisations.

An interesting prospect will be the metamorphosis the business school may go through. I maintain that there will be more reliance on smaller faculty-based sub-groups that take care of building up their own know-how. Further, the individual faculty member will increasingly have a rather flexible role, and a wider choice of ways to create value, including membership of flexible teams. More likely than not, the business school will become more of a meeting place where members of various flexible teams get together to deliver value for corporate networks. Perhaps the school will be more of a "meta-planner", a "meta-orchestrator", and will draw on various semi-autonomous faculty teams on a more or less formal basis. These teams might be responsible for their own learning and research, and might, perhaps, even be able to handle this challenge in different, flexible ways. Just imagine a networked business school, more fluid and flexible than its traditional counterpart, that allows individual faculty members to be much more self-selective about what they want to do! A fascinating and promising prospect!

Needless to say, the emphasis on market-based values that I have tried to vigorously present in the following pages will then become even more important. As I will argue, the network-based school will have to have a clear focus on key values: eclecticism, cross-disciplinary value creation, innovation, teams, adaptability and flexibility, and the value of a sense of ownership in the members of the network. A network will, of course, not stay together over a longer period of time unless there are some centripetal forces holding it together. This is the key role of the values, the "glue" in the prospective network-based business school that I believe will — indeed must — come.

In the final analysis, perhaps a *change in spirit* matters most when business schools ask themselves how best to provide for the needs of their clients — to live up to a market focus. Above all, this book tries to outline what such a change in spirit truly involves. As such, it is meant to inspire all whose calling and responsibility it is to manage academic institutions strategically.

Chapter 1

Setting Strategic Direction in the Business School: The Essential Balance

Executive Summary

Managing a business school strategically is possible. But setting the strategic direction in the modern business school is markedly different from setting strategy in corporations, because its "product", value creation, is intangible. The role of the Dean (or President), though vital, is inherently different from that of the CEO; he does not have the same power. Although a corporation and a business school are not run in the same way, there is no less of a need for the school to set strategic direction. It must make the strategic choices necessary to respond to the market. It must make sure to achieve an internal balance and to create the kind of value the customer expects. This opening chapter proposes four approaches to strategy in business schools that should ensure that the main missions — research, teaching, and citizenship — of the school are operationally carried out: the adaptive business school, *the* proactive business school, *the* entrepreneurial business school, *and the* rationally managed business school. *The implications of each of the four approaches for the school and its leadership are discussed. The idea of a dynamic business school — a school that balances all four approaches — is presented. Three key strategic choices involved in keeping the balance are discussed:* acknowledging economies of scale, mediating through networks, *and* solving clients' unique problems. *This chapter further provides an overview of, and a framework for tackling, the most important, general issues confronting anyone given the brief of managing, i.e., setting the strategic direction of, the modern business school. To illustrate these first ideas and establish a reference point for the book's further discussions, the chapter closes with an extended broad example of value creation from the International Institute of Management Development (IMD) in Lausanne, Switzerland.*

Strategic direction setting *can* take place in the modern business school. For the leadership of the modern business school, setting strategy means juggling many concerns, managing many forces, and making many difficult choices along the many paths to value creation. It means choice, for as the old saying goes, "strategy is choice". It means living with the tension between short-term and long-term strategic needs. It means never being able to fully bridge the "gap" between a reactive, adaptive strategic focus and a proactive, visionary strategic focus. The business school must formulate a dual strategy, with all of the trade-offs and choices discussed in this chapter.[1,2]

More specifically, as this chapter will show, strategic direction setting must be the clear outcome, I believe, of several tradeoffs between bottom-up entrepreneurial *and* top-down leadership tradeoffs, proactive vision *and* adaptation to the client's focus. A variety of carefully chosen research and teaching activities can reconcile the inherent tradeoffs — a top-down portfolio strategy is called for. In other words, when those in the school charged with the mandate to lead, be it Dean, President or a team setting the strategy, they simply need to select those activities that take the best advantage of increasing economies of scale and counterbalance the ones that are most susceptible to decreasing economies of scale.* A specific choice of strategic issues must be brought into play, since these tradeoffs impact them: choices having to do with decreasing economies of scale, increasing economies of scale, and specialisation.

The output of the strategy can be described in terms of the *people* the business school emphasises, the *processes* these people follow in pursuing their strategies, the *projects* they choose to work on, and the choices the strategic *partners* have taken. The most critical question, however, may well be: How do the leaders of the modern business school amass enough clout — you may say power, influence, resources, and authority — to *lead?* If they can, and they follow the strategies and ideas in this book, they *can* define a strategy for the school, and then make that particular strategy stick. But let us begin with a cursory review of the seminal ideas on the topic since 1980.

---

* The normal label used for the person heading a business school would be the "Dean". Other labels are Principal (as in the case of the London Business School), or Director General (INSEAD). However, when the business school is a free-standing institution, not part of a larger university, I prefer to use "President", as is the case at the Norwegian School of Management and at IMD. This signifies that the senior officer of the institution is indeed the "top of the pyramid", in that he does not have the president of a university above him.

Managing the Business School: Traditional Views

In the last two decades, several path-breaking works have answered the question of whether academic institutions, including the business school, can set strategic direction, and if so, how. Their answers make a good platform from which to start our exploration of strategy setting and launch our examination of the central example in the book, IMD, on which some of the shaping ideas are based.

In their 1973 book, *Leadership and Ambiguity*,[3] Cohen and March offer eight metaphors of leadership for the corporate university President. They conclude that the anarchy metaphor is most appropriate. "Each individual in the university is seen as making autonomous decisions", they claim.

> Teachers decide if, when, and what to teach. Students decide if, when, and what to learn. Neither co-ordination (except the spontaneous mutual adaptation of decision) nor control is practised. Resources are allocated by whatever process emerges but without explicit accommodation and without explicit reference to some super-ordinate goal. The "decisions" of the system are a consequence produced by the system but intended by no one and decisively controlled by no one.[4]

This view of the university as little more than "organised anarchy" is more or less similar to the famous "garbage can model"[5] and offers precious little guidance in managing a university — or a business school, for that matter — in such a way that those entrusted with leadership can actually set strategic direction, Deans and Presidents, for example.

Lord Dahrendorf, who spent many years as head of the London School of Economics, fundamentally believes that academic institutions cannot, and should not, be managed strategically.[6] He echoes the idea that academic institutions are, at heart, intractable, and cannot be managed. "A university neither wants nor needs to be run — basically, it runs itself, by way of its own mysterious 'internal channels'." He goes on to suggest that "interference with the usual channels", which I take to mean "management intervention", should be reserved for "extreme situations".[7]

Similarly, Cohen and March,[8] in their analysis of a number of academic institutions, seem to conclude that a laissez-faire approach is the best way to manage strategically. Proponents of this approach sing, "let it be". They take the now-infamous "garbage can" approach. According to them, the institution should be allowed to evolve incrementally, largely with impetus from the bottom.

Not an advocate of the anarchy approach, Keller claims that, although the leaders of academic institutions can set strategic direction, the position of the institution in the flow of "historical forces" plays a key role, and may, in fact, severely limit strategic direction setting. Keller further suggests that the setting of strategic direction is a matter of *balancing* several viewpoints, forces, and contextual dimensions. Nevertheless, he clearly believes that academic institutions are somewhat more malleable under the guiding hand of the administrator. He comes up with a strategic-planning model that rests on six postulates of academic strategy.

> Since the fundamental aim of strategic planning is a Darwinian one of linking the forward direction of your organisation with the movement of historical forces in the environment, the two critical areas for analysis are one's own organisation and the environment. You need to look inside and outside. And in each of these searches there are three elements.[9]

Looking inside, Keller sees three chief concerns for the leader of an academic institution:

1) Traditions, values, and aspirations;
2) Strengths and weaknesses: academic and financial; and
3) Leadership: abilities and priorities.

Not satisfied to look inside, Keller finds what he calls "external dimensions", which include:

1) Environmental trends: threats and opportunities;
2) Market preferences, perceptions, and directions; and
3) The competitive situation: threats and opportunities.

Keller seems to imply that the setting of strategic direction is a matter of balancing several viewpoints, forces, and contextual dimensions. He claims that, although the leaders of academic institutions can set strategic direction, the position of the institution in the flow of "historical forces" plays a key role, and may, in fact, severely limit strategic direction setting.

In his book, *The Organisation of Academic Work*, Blau seems to go one step farther by actually outlining a *role* for bureaucracy and structure, the need for which he appears to accept from the start. "Academic institutions have the difficult responsibility of providing an administrative framework for creative scholarship." He does warn us, however, that this may make academic institutions "susceptible to the ill effects of bureaucratic rigidity".[10] Blau sees bureaucracy coming into conflict with scholarship at times. "Several bureaucratic features of academic institutions have deleterious consequences for educational performance", but not for research performance, since "research can be separated from an institution's administrative machinery while education is intricately enmeshed in it".[11] Blau thus recognises that setting the direction of research may be somewhat "easier" than setting the direction of other value-creating activities, most notably teaching.

In his recent study of what creates successful, dynamic "entrepreneurial universities", Clark pinpoints five organisational "pathways of transformation".[12] His five pathways model is a good starting template for characterising an effective strategy for a business school. Clark starts with what he calls the "strengthened steering core", which embraces central managerial groups *and* academic departments. He includes the "expanded developmental periphery", which would encompass outside organisations and groups. Clark adds the "diversified funding base", and also designates a "stimulated academic heartland". This corresponds to the academic values and belief systems. And lastly, he refers to an "integrated entrepreneurial culture" — i.e., the people and the processes they follow to create value.

James Duderstadt, in *A University for the 21st Century*, sees four groups of forces driving change in academic institutions: financial imperatives, changing societal needs, technology drivers, and market forces. But yet, he reminds us of the need to differentiate professional schools from the typical core of the classical university. "There are some important differences," he says,

> because most professional education requires an ongoing relationship with the world of professional practice, professional schools tending to be closely coupled to the needs of society. Professional practice and service are usually expected components of the activities of both students and faculty. Further, since professional schools are so tightly linked to practice, these schools tend to respond much more rapidly to changes in society. Good examples are provided by the dramatic changes that have occurred in medical and business schools in recent years.[13]

Professor George Bain, Vice Chairman of Queen's University, Belfast, and formerly Principal of London Business School, has addressed the issue of developing a strategy founded on "balanced excellence", a balance between academic pursuits and providing relevance for practitioners.

I believe that professional and similar schools are most likely to be successful if they pursue a strategy of balanced excellence. A school with balanced excellence eschews dichotomy or dilemma thinking: the tendency to believe that the choice between any two objectives must be mutually exclusive. It optimises rather than maximises. It places a strong emphasis on rigor and analysis and does not see any fundamental conflict between these qualities and relevance and practice. The "basic" and "applied" aspects of its work are closely related and are used to link theory to practice. Hence most of its teaching and research are concerned not only with obtaining a deeper understanding of fundamental social or physical relationships, but also with providing a better basis for decision-making by managers and other policy makers.[14]

Bain makes the further point that balancing both academic and what he calls "vocational" excellence is not only critical for the overall success and quality development of an academic institution, but also difficult.

Arguably, no business school has so far achieved "balanced excellence". Indeed, many are not interested in doing so; they prefer to maximise either the academic or the vocational. Of those which are interested, Harvard, Northwestern, Stanford, and Wharton have probably come closest to the goal. Achieving balanced excellence is not easy. It involves managing a high level of complexity.

Or, according to Simon,

A professional school administration — the Dean and senior faculty — have an unceasing task of fighting the natural increase of entropy, of preventing the system from moving toward the equilibrium it would otherwise seek. When the school is no longer able, by continual activity, to maintain the gradients that differentiate it from its environment, it reaches that equilibrium with the world which is death. In the professional school, "death" means mediocrity, and inability to fulfil its special functions . . . organising a professional school . . . is very much like mixing oil with water: it is easy to describe the intended product, less easy to produce it. Left to themselves, the oil and water will separate again. So too will the disciplines and the professions. Organising, in these situations, is not a once-and-for-all activity. It is a continuing administrative responsibility, vital for the sustained success of the enterprise.[15]

Creating Value in Four Ways

What should we take away from all this theory? If you believe, as I do, that academic institutions, most particularly the business schools of the next millennium *can* and *should* be managed, and that academic leaders play a pivotal role in setting and implementing a deliberate direction for the school, you must not only reject some of these ideas, but also ask how to incorporate the ones you accept into a coherent blueprint for managing the business school. It is clear, of course, that setting and implementing the strategic direction requires a clear focus and sense of priorities. So, it is the *way* academic leaders focus their activities *inside* the academic institution that matters.

Since it is the strength of the *individual* academic players, with their own agendas, that drives any direction setting, setting strategic direction happens in a highly individualised way, person-by-person. Also, it *is* possible to rally all the individual forces in a business school to consensus around a particular strategic direction, although they are de facto highly dependent on the evolutionary context, values, and key environmental factors. As Keller and Blau imply, with proper sensitivity and within limits, setting academic direction might just be possible after all. Procedures, rules, and structures drive academic organisations, which are, by nature, bureaucratic. This endemic bureaucracy limits choice in all other aspects of academic value creation, perhaps especially teaching. Although other value-creating activities such as research may get done, even in a relatively undirected academic setting, all the other sources of value creation may be weakened.

While the aforementioned authors describe limitations or constraints (with the possible exception of Keller and Clark), they fail to value the academic leader explicitly. A Dean's authority is typically much more limited and tenuous than that of a corporate executive. The Dean is appointed by the university President or Chancellor. It is not a tenured position; he serves at the pleasure of his bosses. But the Dean interacts with *his* faculty, many of whom have tenure. They do not need to please the Dean, and there is ultimately relatively little a Dean can do to force faculty members to do things they do not want to do. Thus, the Dean's job has been likened to that of Speaker of the House — his effectiveness depends on the ability to build coalitions and to persuade faculty members, with their own independent bases of authority and power, to join together in a common effort.

Respecting the assumptions above, and using the modern business school as an example, I will argue that academic leaders *can* play a pivotal role in setting and implementing a deliberate direction for the school. The Dean and some combination of faculty and staff *can* set a strategic direction. Academic institutions need to set strategy in order to enhance their capacity to create value. I will proceed on the assumption that setting and implementing the strategic direction requires both a clear focus and sense of priorities. And I will further assume that a well-developed sense of building coalitions, creating a power base through managing stakeholders — individuals and groups, and most notably faculty — is essential. Thus, it is the *way* academic leaders focus their activities inside the academic institution that matters most.

The key success criterion for a business school is to *create value*. Creating value, which is essentially the mission of the business school, means emphasising:

- *research* — creating new knowledge about management and the role of business in the economy and society;
- *teaching* — disseminating knowledge for individuals to learn; and
- *citizenship* — service to the community.

The most effective way to set strategy is to heighten focus on the various ways business schools can strive to create value. If you make a lifetime of looking closely at business school programmes, as I have, you will make out four ways business schools have traditionally aimed to create value. For the sake of clarity, I call these four approaches (strategies would be another name) adaptation, proactivism, entrepreneurialism, and rational leadership. Think of each way as a focus on a particular aspect of the school's value-creating processes. For academic leaders to set strategic direction effectively they must worry about creating value, through research, teaching, and citizenship, in each of these four ways; doing well in only one, or two — such as research only — is inadequate. The most effective way to set strategy overall is for the leadership to become not only aware of, but actively pursue, the four ways and their interplay, and in so doing, to maximise the school's value for clients. A given business school may choose one, or a combination of a few, but ultimately, tomorrow's top business school will need to use elements of all four approaches to create a dynamic strategy.

Setting this dynamic strategy will be a matter of balancing the four approaches. And this will mean that the ideal direction for any academic institution (if we can speak of an "ideal") will consist of getting the right tradeoffs among proactive vision *and* adapting to the clients' needs, through bottom-up, faculty entrepreneurialism and top-down leadership. All these approaches will have to be brought into some sort of balance, and the Dean, together with the key stakeholders, will have to manage this balance by making strategic choices. Thus, the strategic direction of the school at any point in time will reflect only a temporary balance of forces and, therefore, of power. And so, the school's strategy will change over time as the balance of internal forces shifts.

The Adaptive Business School

The *adaptive* business school sets its direction and adjusts to the changing needs of its students or its clients, e.g., companies, alumni, business executives interested in continuing education. To create value, it will be *driven by the market*, which is a major challenge. IMD, for instance, is seeing a lot of demand from key clients for increased emphasis on leadership to facilitate more internally generated growth in their companies, for example, more development of new business opportunities and more focus on entrepreneurial drive in large, established corporations. Further, IMD is fielding a lot of demand for more emphasis on effective implementation in making these growth opportunities a reality, which calls for a different organisational culture, via cross-functional teams and more emphasis on cross-cultural compatibility. IMD has responded in part by modifying its open programmes to reflect these emerging needs, in part by offering more tailored programmes that directly address these needs, and in significant part by both trying to hire new professors with an interest in these areas and stimulating the present professors to undertake more research into internally generated growth.

If a business school cannot adapt to the needs of the students or clients, it will be unable to generate the resources it needs for long-term sustainability. Nevertheless, as important as the adaptation challenge may be, it is too one-sided, since the school only adjusts to the changing needs of the student or client — *after* the fact. By taking an adaptive approach too far, for example, the business school becomes no better than a reflection of the thinking of its leading clients. And further, by trying to be as adaptive as possible, the business school is always trying to keep up with the thinking of its leading clients. Intellectual leadership thus becomes a matter of intellectual cloning or catching up. Needless to say, when it comes to academic value creation this cannot be all.

In effect, by taking a purely adaptive approach, although the school may have a strategic direction, spear-headed as it is by the students or client firms themselves, the process of setting strategy may be rather passive. As such, even though listening to one's learning partners is one critical aspect of direction setting, merely being adaptive is inadequate. Still, caution should be exercised before downplaying the adaptive dimension. It could be dangerous to change the core curriculum or research agenda too quickly in response to demand shifts in the job market that may turn out to be temporary, or to make changes that simply respond to the latest corporate management fad.

And the Proactive Business School

A *proactive* business school seeks the direction it needs to take, "senses" where to go, and gets there ahead of its clients (and other business schools!). In concrete terms, this means making sure that its directional ("strategic") moves ultimately meet the needs of students and clients, not merely by adapting to their needs post facto, but by actually leading change, leapfrogging ahead. It means *driving the market!* [16]

A good example is the so-called networked organisation, where competence rests largely in some key brain-driven know-how, which develops the organisation's commercial value. Consider for instance a company, such as British Airways, that sees its key value added as the ability to organise a route scheduling system, built around the BA brand. To own aircraft, even to operate ground bases, etc., might be seen as critical for British Airways, but these are activities that could still be outsourced. Based on a view of which will be preferred segments of travellers to focus on, say, various business people, and on what geographic areas business is most likely to grow, say, US/Europe, the company would be relatively free to develop this business. The marketing for such an organisation might increasingly take place via Web-based technology or e-commerce marketing. Proactive steps, such as developing sleeper seats in business class, can thus be rapidly taken.

For a school such as IMD, it is important to think proactively about how the e-commerce-based global network organisation of the future might look. The school should ask: What competencies do we need to add, hopefully sooner rather than later, to be able to lead this type of organisational development? What would be the intellectual inputs from a business school such as IMD in "showing the way" towards a more networked, more e-commerce-driven business reality? IMD is following a number of research activities to build these competencies. As an aside (and for later discussion), we are finding that recruiting faculty members who might be interested in these activities also represents a major challenge.

Interestingly, other scholars, such as van Baalen and Moratis, for instance, consider IMD as a good, perhaps even path-breaking, example of a network business school:

IMD can be considered as a true network business school. Not only does it use learning methods that reflect network learning — learning through communities — it also deploys advanced learning technologies. Next to learning, IMD's organisational structure and its organisational arrangements clearly reflect network structures. These networks include IMD's Learning Network, network with corporate universities, research networks, IMD faculty and department networks, and IMD's Alumni Network.[17]

One tricky part of the strategic levelling act is balancing the proactive strategy with the adaptive. Both dimensions — to be led as well as to lead — have merit, but in a complementary manner. Too much relative focus on being proactive can lead the school to "jump the gun" with an insufficient revenue base; too much relative focus on being adaptive, on the other hand, can lead to milking the market dry, so as to live on borrowed time.

Needless to say, the ability to connect to today's needs of your major learning partners/clients and, at the same time to catalyse them to look forward is a critical challenge. At IMD we are talking with a leading airline about this. On the one hand, the airline corporation has a need today, as the industry consolidates and markets get tougher, to develop better synergies among its various organisational entities. Improved overall culture, one might say, should lead to more efficiency, more cost savings and above all to a strengthened ability to offer an integrated air travel product to the airline's full-paying clients. Thus, IMD is working to offer programmes that will help the airline *adapt* to its needs. At the same time, the airline company is very interested in the prospect of e-commerce, the prospect of "lightening" its balance sheet by outsourcing, and thus strengthening the capability it might have in the longer run to create a higher return to its stockholders. We are introducing such configurations into our programmes.

The key, however, is to find an equilibrium so that the immediate take-home value for the participants is not being "diluted" by these more futuristic considerations. I would argue, however, that even when in balance, the singular proactive approach falls short of optimal value creation. It is simply not enough to have a great vision for the future and to expect that leading corporations will pay for it. After all, leading corporations need to strengthen their own immediate organisational effectiveness to create stockholder value. To have a focused, selective drive towards leading change, towards leading one's learning partners into a better future will be important. The key is to be realistic here, and not to be unilaterally carried away with the longer-term futuristic potential needs, which will always remain untested. Shorter- and longer-term focus go together. The strategy must focus on both the future and the immediate — both today. Crucial as this balance of adaptation and proaction is, it still misses an important additional way to secure optimal value creation, namely the bottom-up/top-down interplay between the faculty and the Dean.

Also, the Entrepreneurial Business School

Any attempt at optimal strategy setting must include unleashing the value-creating power of the faculty — it must tap into their entrepreneurial spirit (hence the name for this approach: entrepreneurialism). Two IMD examples should show what I mean.

In recent years, a group of IMD faculty members have been very interested in developing an international management competence further. They see this as a way to add concrete value to the more general concept of creating internally generated growth competencies. Further, this international competence lent itself to a better understanding of how to manage the international human resource function, again, to strengthen internally generated growth. All of these activities were driven by the individual insights and desires of specific faculty members. In fact, they led to an entrepreneurial focus within the more general accrual of internally generated growth-driven leadership capabilities.

The second example stems from the interest of a few faculty members in further strengthening the understanding of how to use modern, computer-based technology as part of generating business value. Their pursuit led, among many insights, to a much more concrete understanding of what modern networked organisations might look like, and what the critical leadership challenges might be. In both cases, this new, more entrepreneurial approach enriched IMD's already proactive value-creation culture.

The *entrepreneurial* business school represents an essential, but still partial, element in setting strategic direction optimally. No one would argue that the individual initiatives of faculty members cum entrepreneurs are unimportant in the effective strategic management of a business school. In the effective strategic management of a business school, the Dean and the other stakeholders can neither downplay, nor ignore the significance of faculty entrepreneurs. In fact, the effective business school unleashes its faculty members' energies, tweaks their willingness to take on initiatives and spearhead "pioneer" and "rapid expansion" teaching and research activities, which build on the individualistic drive of each faculty member, so deep-rooted in academic life. The key here is, indeed, to create proactiveness, through research-based discoveries and pedagogical teaching innovations.

Yet, to countercheck the entrepreneurial forces, a team approach to creating value in the business school is also necessary. To ensure effective adaptability, students or clients benefit most from the co-ordinated activities of a true faculty team. The same holds true for research efforts: eclectic teams of faculty members, working together on a cross-disciplinary basis, are the best hope for value management, or generating any other academic insights. This "team" oriented faculty must bring a balanced portfolio of talents. To find his place within the broader portfolio-strategy context of the business school, the entrepreneurial faculty member, to be effective alone and/or as a team member, must possess a sense of maturity and breadth. The faculty team can only have its full strength when its members are compatible. Ultimately, this compatibility not only helps ensure creativity and proactive thinking, it also serves the learning partners better by adaptation. Perhaps we need to invent the label "team-based entrepreneurialism" for blending these bottom-up faculty-driven initiatives into a cohesive overall strategy for the school.

...And the Rationally Managed Business School

Despite their importance, the *entrepreneurial* elements of a business school are not a value-creating panacea. A business school's Dean or President must, to a certain extent, manage from the top, must in effect project a well-defined role. This must include playing the role of the orchestra conductor, working to improve the conditions of the faculty and staff, prodding here, motivating there, making sure that conditions are right in the orchestra so that the musicians can give themselves fully to their performance. To be a source of encouragement, to add support, and to provide positive feedback will thus be a part of the Dean's strategic agenda — a key implementation task!

But the Dean, like the conductor, also plays the catalyst so that a clearer, more deliberate direction can result. This will include a portfolio focus, a vision for "how things fit together", for what the school should and should not do. In my experience, individual faculty members may see value in adding a particular programme that may not fit well into the school's portfolio, or match well with what the leadership believes should be the school's strategy. A particular strategic initiative may indeed be interesting, but still not fit into a *particular* school's vision of itself.

At IMD, various faculty members are strongly interested in developing regional programmes, say, offered in China, Korea, or Singapore. The school's strategy on the other hand portrays IMD as "the global meeting place". The school as a whole sees its key challenge in bringing executives to IMD from the various regions, including Asia, so that the broadest spectrum of leaders from all over the world can learn from each other at one global meeting place. Thus, while particular programme suggestions may make good sense on their own, they may not fit well in an overall portfolio notion of what makes sense for the school as a whole. Hence, the leadership faces the challenge of encouraging individual faculty members to see the poor fit between idea and the school's portfolio, without thereby being discouraged that their own entrepreneurial growth desires might thereby need to be re-channelled.

Let me give another example, namely, the offering of additional open programmes within the school's portfolio of open programme activities. Again, a particular faculty member might want to offer, say, a programme that is primarily function-oriented, pitched towards relatively inexperienced executives. The programme idea may make perfectly good sense on its own. But seen within IMD's portfolio strategy, however, the programme may make less sense. It diverts the school's marketing resources into programme areas that are not part of the school's mainstream portfolio, which is pitched more towards general management programmes for more senior executives. Again, the Dean's challenge is to gently "orchestrate" an understanding of the reasons the programme doesn't fit. In other words, the Dean's job is to facilitate the process of selection. The task is to manage it through top-down vision, not to be merely a glorified adding machine of bottom-up initiatives. Such orchestration is not a matter of judging whether programme suggestions are "right or wrong", but rather a matter of making sure all teaching and research activities dovetail neatly into the school's portfolio strategy.

A school thus managed can be thought of as *rationally managed*. By rational, I mean that the portfolio strategy requires the leadership to take a rational view of what fits and what does not fit in the palette of programme offerings. Managing rationally is thus a matter of making impartial decisions about additions to the programme portfolio, without getting persuaded to encourage research and/or teaching activities that might be highly interesting and promising on their own, but which would not fit the school's overall portfolio vision. The issue is therefore to keep a portfolio focus and not to let "all blossoms bloom"; hence our notion of rational portfolio management.

Still, our picture of managing dynamic business school success as merely a matter of a conductor providing input, energy and focus from the "podium" does not give a full picture of the value creation process for which I am arguing. Input from the top can only be part of a more full-blown value-creation process. As noted, actual strategic direction thus emerges from balancing the bottom-up and top-down forces. This balance is what, in all likelihood, will determine the

The Actor Dimension

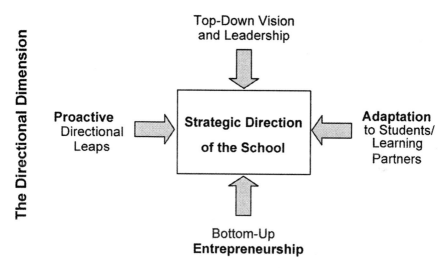

Figure 1.1: Forces with an impact on the strategic direction of the school.

ultimate "focus", or strategic direction of the school. Remember, however, that tenured faculty will often have their own resources; some faculties, alumni, companies, and potential donors are more powerful than others. If the business school is part of a university system (IMD is not), the university may make its own claims on the business school's resources. Business school Deans often find themselves clashing with university Presidents and administrators over control of their financial resources. Business schools are often the most profitable operations on campus, and revenues generated by them are at times diverted to fund the activities of less prosperous schools and departments. Important internal dynamics thus have an impact on this top-down/bottom-up balance. To have a realistic chance to create a certain power balance, the Dean must bring his own resources, coalitions, and connections to the table.

For the sake of further clarity at this stage, Figure 1.1 illustrates in two dimensions the four approaches to setting strategy forces described thus far.

The directional dimension sets out the strategy of the business school's research and teaching activities. It is a function of the need to respond to the various customers, i.e., to adapt. It is also a function of the proactive vision of the faculty members, and thus their interest in pioneering and rapidly expanding into new directions, i.e., more of a strategic leapfrogging dimension. The paradox is that a better strategic direction will most likely emerge out of the tradeoffs or sources of positive tension between the two types of directional input illustrated: one might say, market leading *and* market led.

The other axis of the model shows two complementary actor dimensions. On the one hand are the important entrepreneurial inputs by the faculty members, working both alone and in teams, creating what one might call "bottom-up input". These influence the strategic direction of the business school, both by shaping the proactive, so-called "leaps", and by shaping the school's adaptation to the needs of its learning partners. A top-down vision and leadership dimension, driven by what the choices the Dean/President feels the business school *should* make in setting its strategic direction to develop an overall portfolio, complements the bottom-up forces. The top-down force counterbalances the bottom-up entrepreneurship dimension, so that the emerging direction results from a balance of these forces. Or, as Cyert states:

> To survive the difficulties ahead, colleges and universities must have more foresight in management. But, at the same time, universities must maintain their decentralised form and capitalise on the entrepreneurship and idea-generating abilities of the faculty. Thus, there needs to be more active and decisive campus leadership — but it must seek and include faculty contributions.[18]

All in all, the strategic direction of a business school can best be depicted as a combination of the forces described above and illustrated in Figure 1.1 that reflect a temporary balance of power at any point in time. Both the bottom-up, entrepreneurial input, as well as the top-down leadership input, are likely to change over time. So are the adaptive needs of the learning partners as well as the opportunities for proactive, directional leaps. The relationship between different coalitions of forces changes. Clearly then, the actual strategy of a business school at any point in time is the result of the power shifts and inter-active forces among key stakeholders — individuals and groups — along the four dimensions in the Figure. And keeping the dynamic balance among them is extremely important.

The Dynamic Business School

To set strategic direction effectively, academic leaders must worry about creating value in each of the four ways so far described; to do well in only one, or two, is inadequate. Further, they need to see strategic direction setting as a matter of balancing the four approaches. And this will mean that the ideal direction for any academic institution (if we can speak of an "ideal") will consist of getting the right tradeoffs among proactive vision, adapting to the clients' needs, bottom-up faculty entrepreneurialism, and top-down leadership. Even once these approaches have been brought into balance, the Dean or President will have to keep them in balance by making strategic choices relating to economies of scale and specialisation, people, projects and processes.

If we accept that value creation in a business school requires the balancing act just described, then I believe the overall richness of the value creation can be better captured by the term *"dynamic business school"*. My use of the word "dynamic" to describe the process by which the modern business school can best create value is no coincidence. The word "dynamic" acknowledges the need to adapt dynamically to the needs of the students, learning partners, and customers. It suggests that the balance must not be static. It also implies, I believe, that the school must lead in the development of new knowledge in order to complement its adaptive thrust. The temporary shifts in the balance of power among the key stakeholders activate this. Its direction, to use my earlier term, must develop proactively. This will only be possible when an administrative, catalytic effort from the top spearheads the dynamic development — here the Dean or President must play a role.

This may all sound good in theory, but the ideas in this book are for practitioners, and must pass the test of applicability. Finding the equilibrium I've pleaded for is a tricky, oft-labyrinthine task fraught with hidden dangers and dead-ends. And once you've got all the forces into a steady state, keeping it may be even more difficult. Any successful business school really is a dynamo, and like the early electric generators, it is a highly charged machine. Setting strategic direction by making explicit strategic choices, though they form the basis for creating the balance, entails tradeoffs. And tradeoffs mean setbacks and frustration, due above all to the multitude of competing needs and concerns that stakeholders in an academic institution typically debate. Nevertheless, after sixteen years as a business school administrator, I believe that it is always possible to increase the value-creation capabilities of the modern business school significantly.

How the Balance May Shift

Consider just a few ways the "dynamism" within the dynamic balance can dissipate, and the forces go out of balance. The school's strategic direction can result from, say, one force having a disproportionately strong influence. It is all too easy, for instance, for a business school to proceed by letting the bottom-up entrepreneurial forces get "free play", with the Dean or President playing the role of a "non-existent" figurehead. Or, alternatively, what if the Dean, playing a dominant, top-down role, focuses heavily on one kind of value creation at the expense of the other three? What if the post facto adaptive forces take over? Or, lastly, what happens if the school's direction comes out of proactive directional leaps, without any counterpoints?

It is the checks and balances among the forces that lead to the solid strategic direction of the business school, and it is the ongoing dynamic development of this balance that ensures it. All members of a business school's team need to recognise the importance of this ongoing balance. A healthy strategy will not develop from a "win/lose" power play among various stakeholders. The strategic context for the business school should evolve out of a healthy modus vivendi among the various dimensions. And leadership authority has to be firmly lodged in one place; otherwise, there can be no really co-ordinated attempt to establish and implement a coherent strategic direction. Static balance, on the other hand, could very well lead to nothing better than organised anarchy.

Think about the relationships of coalitions of forces, of power balances between key stakeholders, a little further. Imagine the example of a school whose financial situation is weak, characterised by real budgetary problems. A relative power shift towards the Dean may occur; the perceived crisis indirectly strengthens his hand. He may use the added power to tighten up the school's portfolio strategy, cancelling or diminishing research and/or teaching activities that do not readily fit in, and likewise rejecting new faculty proposals. The Dean will have the power to put the house in order by adding more of a clear adaptive focus, and the faculty will *not* have the power to push for more "expensive", innovative, proactive initiatives.

Ponder another situation, where the school enjoys great success, with a string of positive achievements behind it, and with a productive faculty in place that mostly focuses on disciplinary-based research and teaching. A new Dean has just arrived — he wants to push for more emphasis on executive education. This emphasis would call for more cross-disciplinary faculty co-operation to address the adaptive needs of the corporate learning partners. It might also call for inclusion of this form of teaching in the faculty workload equation, to further add strength to the adaptive thrust. The problem that the Dean might run into, however, is that the faculty may not want more emphasis on executive education; they may prefer to stick to the well-defined thrust of the disciplinary norms of the classical academic model. This conflict may be further exacerbated by tension between an MBA programme built on the pillars of separate academic disciplines and a more cross-disciplinary executive education department. Can the Dean then still move some of the key faculty stakeholders in his direction? Can he redirect discretionary resources for new cross-disciplinary initiatives? Can he appoint more "open-minded" department chairpersons? Most importantly, can he convince key faculty groups that the *future* relevance of the academic value creation of the school might benefit from such a proactive shift? We do not know the answers in full; to formulate them, the Dean will need clear, visionary and persuasive leadership abilities.

Looking at another example, consider a possible power balance tension between two faculty groups — say, finance and marketing. The finance group may have a heavy disciplinary focus, around a clear set of well-defined axioms. The marketing group, on the other hand, turns out to be more eclectic, perhaps even with a more managerial bent. The finance group clearly wants to maintain an adaptive thrust on its disciplinary base. The marketing group wants to experiment more with developing new thrusts to lead the market. But, is such a proactive shift without risk implications for individual faculty members? During the tenure decision process, for instance, it would typically be much easier for the finance group than for the marketing group to successfully argue its case. After all, it would have well-established, axiomatically set norms to refer to, making it easier to judge what might be performance worthy of tenure, i.e., sticking to the norms of tradition! Again, the Dean can intervene, putting his authority behind some of the promising but unorthodox tenure cases, thereby influencing the proactive/adaptive balance. A typical Dean can only do this sparingly, however; he must pick his battles carefully.

Keeping the Dynamic Balance: Three Ways to Create Value*[19]

But what about the strategic task of the Dean? How can he further define the dimensions that should guide the development of a portfolio strategy, beyond a healthy proactive/adaptive balance? Setting strategic direction, managing the focuses that have an impact on the value-creating portfolio of activities of the dynamic business school, "keeping the balance", is necessarily difficult. The balance does not come out of itself, of course. Explicit strategic choices are not only necessary; they form the basis for creating the balance. These choices entail tradeoffs.

* I have drawn extensively from the ideas of Stabell and Fjellstad in this section.

Bringing my exhortations down to the level of operations, I would claim, for the practitioners among my readers, that the dynamic business school can be "operationalised" by following any combination of *three* fundamental strategic implementation options for creating value. Although I intend to explore them more fully in the rest of the book, they belong here, at the beginning, since they must rest at the centre of any tradeoff debate. As you will see, it is impossible to be as fully committed to each of the three at the same time as you could be if you put only one at the centre of your value-creation principles. They deal with how to create value through activities that yield decreasing and/or increasing economies of scales and/or specialisation.

Acknowledge Economies of Scale (Mass Production) to Create Value

When you lead a business school, you cannot escape the business reality of "mass production". You must acknowledge economies of scale. The laws of the economies of scale are paramount: the more students you have, the fuller your classrooms, and the nearer you are to fully-booked seats, the more efficiently you can run your teaching. The larger your research budget, the more efficiently you can carry out your research. Many academic institutions follow the light of mass production wherever it leads them — to the point at which the more customers they get, the *lower* the cost to serve the last customer, and the *lower* the cost, the lower the price they can charge to their last student/customer. There is little "upside" to this strategy.

Most of classical academic value creation, in essence, is exposed to the pheno-menon of decreasing economies of scale. One could say that the academic busi-ness is the "poor man's way of doing business". Professors essentially make their time available, standing in front of the students in the classroom to deliver teach-ing value. The number one resource limitation is therefore the professor's time. When he has taught the number of sessions his capacity allows for, then there is no more room for revenue generation, at least not from his efforts. This business model clearly lacks an "upside" (decreasing economies of scale prevent it).

The same is true with conventional research, which again focuses above all on the capabilities of the individual professors. When these professors provide value creation through their research output — typically highly personalised — the time limitations of each professor set the upside limits. Again decreasing economies of scale tend to lead to an asymptotic maximum for how much research and teaching an academic institution, being a sum of professors, can deliver. Beyond a certain level, size per se is therefore not a highly critical factor.

Admittedly, with greater size, the financial burdens of one's fixed installations can be spread over more activities. The utilisation of fixed assets, however, is typically less critical in academia than the utilisation of the intellectual power of the faculty and research staff. We typically do not get economies by adding additional professors and research staff; it is more of a straight additive function, with a decreasing economies-of-scale effect taking place.

Mediate Through Networks to Create Value

Another way to operationalised strategy setting is "mediation through a network". A school following this approach brings together students-cum-customers who add value to one another and to the institution. Thompson calls this approach the "mediating industry".[20] In essence, you create value by putting people together — creating clubs. The more customers you get in your network, the *higher* the value for the last customer who joins, and the higher you can set the price of your services.[21] The larger network always beats the smaller networks — the members are basically partners in a club, not individual partners. Here, you do *not* want to create value by isolating each member, say, through having key accounts for each. Rather, you want to have all members participate in each key activity; this way, you create value via key activities for all members. The interesting feature of this approach is that it may lend itself to *increasing* economies of scale. The *more* you do, the better it goes, and so the school can benefit from some "upsides" here. After a school has "invested" in a network, the network becomes more and more "valuable" the larger it is, with the potential of an increasing return on investment.

IMD, with its strong emphasis on its network of Partner and Business Associate firms, increasingly takes this approach. By emphasising more and more the use of computer-based technology, so that the executive members who are part of IMD's network can "attend" sessions in cyber space, i.e., by physically being in their offices but still being part of the school's research briefings, its so-called "discovery events", increasing economies of scale come into play. Using interactive technologies, the business school can create the conditions to get a large group of executives working together on a particular issue, with a rather fixed investment in faculty's time and other preparatory efforts (creating the Web sites, configuring software, finding appropriate material, etc.). Adding new members to a virtual network of this sort is "free". The school makes the effort up front, and as long as it sticks to a reasonable level of activities, few limitations restrict the size of the network.

The largest opportunities to achieve increased economies of scale clearly build on the explosion we are seeing in multimedia technologies, particularly in their applications to learning. Imagine developing case studies for corporate universities that will use them for distance-learning. Such cases would involve developing a particular set of problems that students can access via modem, cable, or satellite on the Web. By clicking on the screen, the student could find all necessary background information, underlying facts, "live" testimonials by key executives involved in the decision, facts on competitors, etc. A business school could be compensated for developing this type of learning material each time an executive "clicks" on the case.

DaimlerChrysler corporate university has seven thousand "students", and can use such a case quite extensively; so, to sponsor the development of such online case material, the auto maker does not have to make a large investment per student. Although the investment to develop such a "case" might be high, the school faces an interesting value-creation equation — the greater the number of people who "click" on the case, the more income it receives. When the school is further able to work with several corporations to support their corporate universities, allowing for swapping of cases among them, assuming of course that there is no direct competition among the corporations involved, interesting applications become apparent and significant increasing economies of scale come into play.

Another example is The Wharton School, which has launched a very ambitious network project called "Wharton Direct". Wharton Direct involves working on the Web on a synchronous basis, with real time access across the world for participating executives. Executives sign up for this network service from wherever they are around the world. They get top-of-the-line lectures by Wharton professors, and a chance to talk back and forth about the lecture topics. So far, Wharton offers limited possibility for the participating executives to talk to each other directly about these problem-solving issues, but that will probably come. Interestingly, with the difference of time zones around the globe, executives have to get up in the middle of the night to take part in a live, virtual session. Nevertheless they do. Most virtual networking efforts have thus not been truly synchronous, but rather asynchronous, instead allowing the participants to log in to the network when it suits their schedules to post their questions and comments in chat rooms. Clearly, this represents an increase in convenience, but also a likely decrease in quality, in the sense that the direct interactive dimension is lost. One interacts with network inputs from the centre which is already old. Nevertheless, Wharton Direct is a bold example of what a global network can do.

Pioneered at the Norwegian School of Management is another network consisting of 15 regional campuses.[22] Here, the centre of the network is its academic hub institution in Sandvika, outside Oslo, which is structured more or less like most quality-driven business schools, with a rather large professorial staff undertaking classical research and applying the findings to teaching. These experiences are then the basis for standardised programme developments. In addition, the school has developed fifteen regional entities all over Norway, largely staffed by local business people, but with a small professional full-time core of learning co-ordinators/administrators. The various course curricula are developed centrally at the core of the network, and with teachers-cum-executives receiving training in delivering these courses. Here an increasing economy of scale effect is present — the efforts from centralised course development can be broadened considerably through decentralised offerings to give much more economic benefit. In addition, a computer-based learning network further increases economies of scale via distance learning, developed and co-ordinated centrally, but offered to the individual students operating out of the fifteen regional campuses. The Norwegian School of Management thus serves as an example of networked value creation focused on the basic learning level of individual students, as opposed to the network of executive development focus of IMD.[23,24]

The choice of focus for one's network, i.e., of membership in the network — Wharton with individual executives, IMD with corporations, the Norwegian School of Management with individual undergraduates — creates an effective flow of information for understanding problems, and by so doing, creates a team of people who work on them in an ongoing loop. The Wharton direct network members work on what typically concerns an individual executive in his/her ongoing learning. The IMD network members typically work on problem-oriented issues facing their corporation, and which allow themselves to be further tackled via informal benchmarking in the network. The Norwegian School of Management network members work on individual learning facing the undergraduates, i.e., more on acquiring basic knowledge. Common for all, however, is the interaction among the members of the network for realistic problem solving, learning as you go, evolution of learning as further insights yet are unearthed as part of this dynamic interactive network-based learning process.

Solve Clients' Unique Problems to Create Value

The third approach to creating value is so-called "unique problem solving". It is based on solving unique problems that the customer cannot solve himself. Much sponsored research follows this mode. Asymmetric information is at work here — the expert, with his renown, versus the customer. Much of the so-called "problem solving" amounts to the expert helping the client to reach the best understanding of the problem possible, and hence, the most accurate diagnosis. The customer often solves the problem himself.[25]

As an example, think about the development of a vision for a corporation. Typically, this entails a process that brings a relatively small group of the corporation's top executives together to go through a number of issues in a "visioning" process to discover, or create, their own vision. One of the faculty members acts as a "catalyst". The process is uniquely focused on the given corporation. The faculty member(s) involved become compensated for their time as catalysts rather than as deliverers of classroom inputs.

A similar approach involves "think-outs" where members of a corporation come together to work on a particular strategic issue. Here also the professor(s) act as catalysts, rather than deliverers of classroom content. In this case, as in the previous visioning example, there will of course be little or no increased economies of scale beyond a certain routine, perhaps, that the professor develops in supporting any visioning process or problem-solving process that he can use with any corporate client. The limit is on the professor's time (a decreasing scale effect).

Doing benchmarking for a consortium of firms is another kind of unique problem solving. Since benchmarking has to do with mapping best practices in various areas, it also involves networking, bringing several participating companies together to benefit from the research work. Here we have both a consortium effect and increasing economies of scale. Interestingly, the business school can combine such a benchmarking exercise with virtual learning technology, by setting up interactive discussions on the benchmarking results, and thus adding further value to the process. The professor might at the margin be involved in the elaboration of the benchmarking results vis-à-vis individual consortium member companies, in an activity we might call "consulting on the Web". While benchmarking and networking clearly provide increasing economies of scale, the potential attraction of offering tailor-made quasi-consulting to individual companies could create a huge potential faculty resource need.

While unique problem solving is clearly not driven by increasing economies of scale, but rather, typically, is characterised by decreasing economies, it is still an interesting business equation. The value on offer typically has a unique, high value for the learning partner who, therefore, may be more willing to pay a high premium for it. By bringing together the relevant sets of data, allowing the participating executives to "see it" from their own point of reference, the customer often solves the problem himself. Here is the essential value creation in this case. The quality of the benchmarking, the way it is put together, and the structure of the data represent true value creation.[26]

Choosing Among the Three Options

To set strategy, how should a business school choose among mass production, mediating through networks and solving its clients' unique problems? The most critical decision is between the value creation in the classroom versus the value creation in networks, between issues/problems the school should answer/solve and the issues/problems others (clients) should answer/solve, either on their own or with one another. Clearly, a good part of a school's value creation will always be based on actual learning in the classroom, with the decreasing economies of scale consequence that we have discussed so extensively. No doubt, this kind of value creation is likely to remain the bulk of academic value creation for most schools for many years to come. The issue, however, is how much of modern technology-based, network-based value creation a school can add, thus creating a new balance with a stronger component of increasing economies of scale.

In choosing the relative emphasis among the three options for shaping the school's portfolio strategy, the Dean faces several constraints. One will be the power balance equation — the stakeholder coalition puzzle — already discussed. The Dean may have no other option, for instance, than to continue a focused emphasis on mass production. Another key factor will be the school's existing capabilities. Are not the choices themselves affected, even significantly, by the school's existing capabilities to create and exploit economics of scale and/or specialisation, as well as its desire to be both adaptive and proactive in responding to customer demand? There is a clear feedback loop between a school's existing organisational capabilities and the strategic portfolio choices the Dean can make among potential areas of emphasis.

For instance, the Dean may want to create a network with a designated group of corporations-cum-learning partners. His problem might be, however, that his faculty may *not* be in a position to "deliver" the cross-disciplinary managerially focused input that this would require — discipline-based fragmentation is the source of limitations on the capabilities of a typical network, and the Dean must thus be aware of this. For instance, a faculty with a strong focus on undergraduate and MBA-level teaching, backed up by a strong axiomatic research tradition, may simply have neither the interest, nor the capabilities to engage in unique, cross-functional problem solving, based also on much interaction with business executives. Again, the Dean must realise that his options may be limited, at least in the short run, if he wants to emphasise unique problem solving in his school's portfolio strategy.

Another important factor is the maturity of the marketplace itself, which may also highlight the balance of the critical decision between the problems the school should solve and the problems others (clients) should solve, either on their own or with one another. It should be noted that, in this world of expert problem solvers, customers may be referred to each other. The key is to choose the school's area(s) of problem solving. This choice creates an effective flow of information for understanding problems, and by so doing, creates a team of people who work on them in an ongoing loop! Stabell and Fjellstad describe this cycle of strengthening the school's own capabilities by choosing in what arenas to engage.[27]

The Dean's Way to Look at Strategy: Considering Actor-Conditioned Outcomes

Setting strategy in the business school actually means making a number of choices. Each choice involves the various tradeoffs described earlier: proactive direction setting *and* adapting to the needs of students and/or partners, bottom-up entrepreneurship *and* top-down leadership. Setting the strategic direction of the business school means tradeoffs within *both* the actor dimension *and* the directional dimension, as depicted in Figure 1.1. But it also involves choosing among activities that require significantly different, and equally important strategic choices, each of which is related to decreasing and increasing economies of scale, and specialisation.

Movement in one strategic direction or another is only possible when these forces are slightly *out* of balance — that is, when power and authority are clearly lodged in the hands of one person or group willing to use them to push things in a particular direction. Hopefully, there is the possibility of what I call "controlled dynamics", which happens when one of the forces is sufficiently stronger than the others to make a strategic move, albeit in a slow and controlled manner.

Perhaps one of the limitations of many past discussions about strategic outcome has been that "outcome" is merely meant as the *content* of the strategy, i.e., the strategic choices and deliberations leading to specific content issues. But another, perhaps more useful way to look at strategy setting in a business school is to consider the resulting *outcomes* of the strategic direction-setting process.

The strategic outcome will also have process outcome implications, i.e., the major working process implications associated with the given strategy. For instance, if a particular strategy were aimed at adjusting proactively more quickly to certain environmental conditions, an important process outcome would be setting up various working processes within the school to facilitate more rapid proactive adjustment (as opposed to more bureaucratic slow-downs). Figure 1.2 illustrates this. Note that a strategy can be manifested as its projects — its content — as well as its processes. As such, the outcome of the strategic projects *and* processes is a valid representation of a strategy — one of the two alone provides a partial, incomplete view only.

To reiterate an earlier point, we need to squarely include the various actors involved in the strategic outcome, particularly those affected by the strategy — professors and staff alike — since they "carry" it. Included should also be the customer actors, the learning partners, which might include corporations, students, and/or network participants. A question for the Dean now is whether he can assess his outcomes and his actors — actual and desired. He must take inventory in order to develop a plan for strengthening his hand and to develop stronger coalitions for (hopefully progressive) change. One might ask whether radical changes in the operation of the school are used by the Dean to try to significantly shift the balance of strategy-setting power in his or her direction. For the Dean modelling the interaction between strategic outcomes and the actors involved may be a key here.

We see from Figure 1.2 that the four dimensions — people, partners, projects, and processes — can be fitted into two dimensions. To have an impact on the strategy — to create a slight imbalance through controlled dynamics — the leadership needs to ask questions that pertain specifically to how to have an impact on these "dimensions".

In the "involved actor dimension", the relevant questions for the Dean may be:

- **People:** What are the types of people who need to be attracted to the institution to enhance the strategy? Are there some areas of competence that would be especially desirable to look for in new professors to enhance the strategy — say, within *change management* or *leadership* — for instance, to facilitate the boosting of research and executive development to top-level executives? Can we spot younger, high-energy professors who have a higher propensity for taking some personal risks, to try something new, as opposed to squarely fitting into well-developed axiomatic traditions? Can we attract more senior professors to play more deliberate proactive change roles? Their evolving interests for high-level managerial problems may now be strong

INVOLVED ACTOR DIMENSION

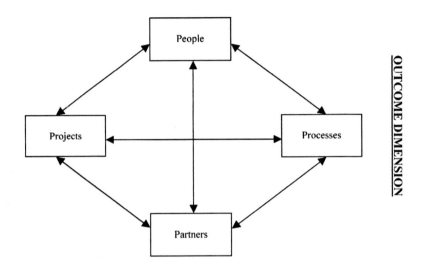

Figure 1.2: A four-part actor-conditioned strategic outcome paradigm.

— they have already proven that they can get tenure and do classical axiomatic research!

● **Partners**: Which are the learning partners that I, as the Dean, *want* to involve, i.e., those that can have the most impact on our school when we work with them and learn from them? For instance, can we proactively attract companies to work with that are truly leading edge, custodians of best practice — as opposed to saying yes to any company that knocks on the door? Can we similarly attract companies to our network that *mean* to work with us as *learning partners,* as opposed to seeing us as merely another subcontractor? How can the students we attract to our MBA programme be assessed also from a leadership potential dimension, and not only based on scholastic records and test scores? Perhaps a more proactive classroom dynamic might result?

For the "strategic outcomes" dimension, it should be noted that the factors interact greatly with the involved actor dimension factor. One set of factors is clearly dependent on the other, in a dynamic interplay. Possible strategy-setting questions for the Dean may include:

- **Processes**: What guiding principles do the people in the organisation follow in order to create the academic work? And if they do not help move the organisation in the desired strategic direction, how can they be modified? For instance, might it be that ending tenure or choosing to hire more contract faculty without tenure would enhance a more flexible, cross-discipline strategy intended to serve leading "best practice" corporations more effectively? There is no doubt that the Dean would need to exercise much persuasion to institute such a change, drawing on the positive new demands posed by the school's leading learning partners. Along the same vein, should academic departments be consolidated — or even eliminated — to more readily facilitate the now called-for cross-disciplinary learning input? What about faculty compensation? Can the Dean compensate the faculty to a significantly larger extent through bonuses, based on actual contribution? The Dean may develop both a scheme for profit sharing and a performance-based bonus, to effectively bring the faculty more in line with the strategy.
- **Projects**: What projects are being chosen? On what does the Dean want to focus? The portfolio vision of the school clearly comes into play. The Dean's most critical task is thus to develop a plan for how to influence people, partners, and processes in order to impact the choice of projects in a more realistic, more effective way, so as to pursue the portfolio strategy.

Since he "owns" the portfolio strategy, the Dean is thus important, but he will of course understand that this strategy is the outcome of more or less explicit coalitions among actors. Increasing his power base, he might do a lot however, by influencing people, the partners, processes, and therefore the projects. Indeed, the Dean may do a lot through controlled dynamics in order to have an impact on coalitions and power balances that shape the strategies of the school. He can help tip the power balance through sensible faculty appointments, through emphasis on working with desirable learning partner companies, through modification of various processes, to name a few. A considerable part of a Dean's effectiveness is likely to rest on his ability to utilise to its fullest this *indirect* way of managing for strategic progress, to make controlled dynamics a natural way for him to work.

Creating Value: The Case of IMD

At IMD, academic value creation draws on elements from each of the three value-creating archetypes and, for each, an appropriate balance between proactive and adaptive perspectives, with the faculty and the Dean involved in the process. We draw on different approaches for different parts of our programmes.

Our MBA and most of our publicly offered executive education programmes, for instance, feature mass production value creation. The larger the programme, the more the class is filled up, the better! The critical strategic choice here is which niches to focus on for effectively achieving volume, and also how much to expand without sacrificing quality. The key strategic choice for academic value creation is which activities to involve all partners in — and how to attract the most interesting firms as learning partners.

Value creation through networking is demonstrated clearly through IMD's Learning Partners network. We developed our so-called learning network of Partner and Business Associate firms, which physically came together a dozen times a year to participate in "discovery events" around our latest research topics. An important strategic choice here is the choice of research to put on the discovery events agenda. We then extended the original network to include virtual networking using available multimedia technology. From this base, we developed virtual learning content: virtual cases, virtual presentations, discussions in chat rooms. The balance has thus gradually shifted from value creation via professors in the classroom to value creation via professors working in networks. This balance, however, remains fluid. I expect relatively more influence on network-based value creation in the future.

Further, there is the choice of teaching programmes that are de facto networking events, where one learns perhaps just as much from one's student colleagues as from the professor. Our *Orchestrating Winning Performance* (OWP) programme is a good example. OWP is a short but intensive exposure to state-of-the-art thinking on the latest management issues for all members of the network. But what really sets OWP apart is that it breaks with most executive education traditions. It allows participants to "design" their own programme, so they can tailor it to their needs and their organisations. The participants may follow participant "streams" in line with their own interests. Every single IMD faculty member takes part — each offers a session based on their latest research and newest teaching materials. The totality of this is a dynamic menu of offerings from which the participants can choose. Participants get the faculty's most recent insights into the realities that are shaping the international business environment. OWP uses time efficiently — participants get the equivalent of a two-week programme, but only have to be away from the office over a weekend and four working days.[28] There is virtually no capacity limitation, so some economies of scale come into play. This is a great financial plus. The large number of participants ensures intensive networking and implies a richer, more diverse learning experience for the participants, and for the faculty. The larger the OWP class, the better; the larger the networks, the better. Smaller sub-networks may even co-operate among themselves, thus creating even more powerful meta-networks.

Making the right choice of additional activities for the network members is essential. Supporting consortia of what are known as corporate universities in various ways may produce interesting activities, with a sharing of pedagogical materials for virtual delivery. This is becoming an increasingly important part of IMD's activity portfolio. However, support of individual network members as if they were key accounts does perhaps not represent value creation in a truly effective way. Rather, creating a consortium of co-operating corporate universities — of course from non-competing owner firms — provides for the opportunity to share in the use of the developed materials more broadly. If the school gets paid in terms of a user fee, this again creates an interesting upside.

In our world of expert problem solvers, the best strategy for the business school may be to refer customers to each other. In an active network, value does not necessarily flow from the school to each participant. Rather, executives from the participating network companies may develop contacts among themselves, and therefore provide value to one another. In essence, "sub-networks" develop among the various "peripheral nodes" in the network. In truly successful networks, this value, based on sharing among participating firms, can be very positive. The bulk of the value, in other words, will probably shift from interaction between the centre (the school) and the various nodes (participating network members) to direct interaction among the nodes themselves, i.e., learning among executives themselves with the business school simply providing the overall network infrastructure.

High pricing is essential — the business school mobilises the best resources for the most critical problems that come to its door; it avoids routine. The key is to choose the school's area(s) of problem solving. I have already elaborated on how IMD is working on this, i.e., primarily via its learning partnership network, where it has created links with more than 140 corporations which are either "Partner" members or "Business Associate" members. The cost is SFr. 100,000 or 50,000 per year respectively — a flat fee rather than a fee for attending as if it was a class. IMD's research steers the agenda for the IMD network activities. We are presenting our research to the participating companies. So it follows that

IMD's network does not have one clear direction, but is rather multidisciplinary, with a relatively heavy emphasis on a variety of leadership issues.

The so-called Partner firms that pay twice as much as the Business Associate members can send up to four participants to each briefing session; business associates can send two. In addition, the Partner firm gets support for specific problem solving and the "catalytic services" mentioned above. Here, IMD's involvement is meta-planning of these companies' internal learning activities and specific problem-solving workshops, visioning activities, etc. Price and quality go together, and characterise such network activities at IMD.

When it comes to creating value by solving unique problems, IMD decides which few areas of competence it wants to represent, thereby offering unique value to companies both for tailor-made programmes and for specific research. IMD's knowledge of general management, with emphases on creating a global portfolio, effective implementation, and change management, all in cross-cultural management situations, is such an area of specialisation. Of course, the further "trick" is to choose client firms that can enrich IMD's knowledge in these areas, and avoid ones that neither need nor allow for this specialised focus.

Given these choices, then, how has IMD actually set its strategy? And how has it aligned its organisational resources behind its strategy? The key lies in the process of balancing the focus between the Dean and the faculty. At IMD this process has two essential elements. First, there is an open, ad hoc discussion at least once a year, re-addressing IMD's portfolio strategy. During these "retreats", examples of key issues include:

- Should we have an MBA programme and, if so, how large? Answer: Yes, but a small one, with one class section only, allowing IMD to innovate fast, aggressively, bringing in new ideas, often based on our research — in fact, shortening the cycle between discovery and market adaptation! Much emphasis is thus on the proactive side of the value creation!
- What should be the ideal approximate balance between open programmes, tailored in-company programmes, and emphasis on the network? Answer: Roughly one-third of each, for now, as the shared intention, with the network presently much smaller, but with the shared intention to increase it!

A second key underlying factor, therefore, driving these portfolio discussions is the concern for IMD's economic situation, with a proper balance between proactive drive and adaptive focus, and a proper mix of "eggs in several baskets". Since IMD is a free-standing, self-owned institution, this becomes a particularly important concern for all.

There is a tacit agreement concerning the overall portfolio vision. As for the particular programme initiatives, the faculty members are the drivers, as individuals and in small groups led by a professor in the role of programme director. The faculty programme directors typically pick their own teams of faculty, based on their assessment of which colleagues can deliver the most relevant input in this instance, and with whom they feel comfortable working. Within these teams, there are usually strong debates concerning the balance between a proactive and an adaptive emphasis. The Dean plays a rather limited role in these tradeoffs, beyond appointing the programme directors and occasionally vetoing new programme initiatives that fall outside the portfolio vision. He also keeps tabs on the pattern of workloads, so that some professors do not end up being totally overworked while others freeload.

Are there special circumstances related to IMD's context that may make setting the strategy an easier process of balancing forces? Are there circumstances that could make it easier at IMD to align its organisation to pursue its strategy? I believe so: the answer is IMD's free-standing status, as independent from any university. Not only does this independence put tangible pressure on everyone to contribute to the economic well-being of the institution, everyone must think market, to help find a realistic balance between proactive and adaptive. The Dean is in fact also the President. This means he does not operate within the often shaky "appointed" context in which most Deans live. The faculty does not enjoy tenure, leaving everyone with a perhaps largely self-imposed "pressure" to deliver. In addition, there is no academic title hierarchy — everyone is a "professor". Why have titles when the faculty, both senior and junior, will be called upon to work in cross-disciplinary teams? Finally, there is no departmental structure; the faculty is organised as one team. Again, this enhances the flexibility to adapt cross-functionally. With a faculty of 50, this works. With a larger faculty, one might have to live with departments, but only a few! All of these factors contribute to a more pragmatic, even strategic, balancing process, I believe.

Chapter 2

Providing Relevant Corporate Learning

Executive Summary

The most important asset of today's corporations is human capital, and large corporations are rapidly becoming the most important clients of the modern business school, which now needs to think of its students as "clients" or "learning partners". The key task of the business school is providing relevant learning, research-based, tailored programmes that provide corporations with activities that help them directly meet their business challenges. For the business school, delivering such tailored programmes entails being able to adapt to its clients' needs, organising internally to deliver the most relevant learning possible, developing an optimal portfolio of clients, and ensuring that it has the right mix of competencies to deliver and to manage these tasks. All of this will require the school to manage three "delivery gaps" — the tailored delivery gap, the relevance gap and the consistency gap — and implement a purposeful strategy that keeps these gaps as small as possible. Managing these gaps involves looking back, defining a vision, getting the right organisational structure in place and managing cash flow.

Today, more and more often, the most important clients of the modern business school are large corporations. These leading companies see change as a chance for their executives to redefine the way they do business, find innovations that feed growth and profitability, and take advantage of opportunities others miss. It is critical for them to mobilise faster than ever before. All of this requires learning, and so these corporations are looking to business schools to be "learning partners".

In their book *The Silicon Valley Edge: A Habitat for Innovation and Entrepreneurship*, Lee, Miller, Hancock, and Rowen argue that the innovative atmosphere of Silicon Valley, with its creation of many new successful corporations, stems at least in part from its interactive "symbiosis" with Stanford University. The authors further argue that Stanford's quality is at least to some extent a function of its being closely linked with the Valley's highly innovative business environment. Thus, they see Stanford and the Silicon Valley as a two-way learning network, critical for success both ways, with the learning based on a functioning set of two-way links. They further argue that linked network learning is an important way to think about learning as taking place between *actors*, such as between corporations and the university, among corporations themselves within Silicon Valley etc., in contrast to learning as primarily leading to progress as a totally *internal* process within the firm, such as what seems to be advocated by Chandler when it comes to Japanese corporations. The keys to making such networks work include keeping an open mind, avoiding all but a minimum of formal organisational structure, taking advantage of physical proximity, and building complementary brain trusts, such as between corporations and academe.[1,2,3]

But no matter how the school sets and implements its strategy, whether or not it follows any of the ideas outlined in Chapter 1 or the ones above, no matter how it finds and holds the "dynamic" balance necessary for success, it will, above all, have to help corporations succeed in the tougher business environment of the early new millennium — by becoming a "learning partner". In a short time, the business school will have gone from being a closed organisational entity, a relatively "closed system" if you will, to becoming an open organisational entity, an "open system" that is essentially a part of its own clients' organisations. The positive value of such close, open co-operation, argues Herbert Simon in "The Business School: A problem in organisational design",

> can be an exceedingly productive and challenging environment
> for fundamental researchers who understand and can exploit
> the advantages of having access to the real world as a generator
> of basic research problems and a source of data.[4]

Using the example of INSEAD, Jean-Louis Barsoux underscores the value for the business school of such close co-operation.

> Proximity to business has marked the culture of the school,
> sometimes giving it a slightly schizophrenic feel. For example,
> INSEAD professors are unusually sensitive to their course evaluations, such attentiveness to customer feedback is closer to the
> norms of business than to the satisfying model that tends to

pervade in academia. In a more general sense, rubbing shoulders in business has instilled an emotional intensity, a capacity for renewal and an addiction to growth, which are more typical for commercial concerns than of academic institutions. Opportunism and entrepreneurialism are words one rarely associates with educational establishments but which are recurrent features of INSEAD's development.[5]

In *Higher Learning*, Derek Bok notes that benefits accrue to both the business school and its faculty by opening up to the practitioner.

> Universities can make a distinct contribution to the professions while helping faculty members to remain in closer touch with the world of practice. In many cases it is the quality and diversity of the students and their manifest desire to learn that do the most to persuade universities to move in this direction. As business schools have discovered, the experience and interest of seasoned practitioners and the chance to help them fill important professional roles are opportunities too attractive to pass by. . . . Competitive enterprise may bring improvements in a quality of instruction that will spread beyond continuing education to benefit the entire curriculum.[6]

An entirely new agenda is opening up for the business school — as a learning partner. So it is no coincidence that, to an increasing degree, business schools are putting items on their research agendas that directly benefit companies. Traditional academic research is becoming less significant as business schools work to create learning activities tailored to the needs of their corporate clients. The key challenges for the modern business school that aims to become a learning partner are: seeing the modern business school students as "clients" and learning partners and adapting to their needs; building the right competencies; and developing an optimal portfolio of clients. Creating full value for the school's learning partners will entail, as we shall see, addressing and managing what I call the "three delivery gaps". Above all, to reiterate the message of Chapter 1, it will entail understanding the critical conditions for managing any business — in this case, the business school — in a purposeful manner by following a deliberate process of setting and implementing strategy.

Create Value by Knowing Who Your Clients Are

In the past we typically talked about "students" as the primary beneficiaries of the value creation in a business school. Students were individuals who attended business school programmes. Today, however, these "students" may be teams, divisions, whole institutions that not only attend programmes at the school but also work with the business school as partners on specific projects. So today we need to broaden the term "student" to "client".

A "client" may be an individual who actually learns through taking part in various learning activities at the business school as an individual (I prefer to call them "learning partners"). But a client may also be an institution, a corporation, that sends a number of its executives to a business school. As such it is a corporate learning partner. Either as an individual or as a corporation, the client pays for what it gets.

In a simple sense, for a business school, success depends on the ability to provide relevant learning (i.e., "value") for its clients. This value has to be high enough so that it matches whatever the clients have to pay to get it. Both the learning content and support have to meet the expectations of each and every client. For those who have to sign the cheques for the tuition fees, the value for money equation has to balance. The upshot of all this is that the business school has to adapt to its customers' needs.

Consider a typical example. Many companies have been saying that they can only afford to have their executives attend a business school for short periods — the old MBA programme is far too long. Too long, also, is the traditional and relatively long executive development programme. Further, many companies maintain that their executives need more action-oriented learning. Their executives should be able to take their learning home, apply it and benefit from it directly, on the job. Many of these executives will be young.

IMD has responded to these specific corporate needs and demands in several ways. One example is the *Building on Talent* (BOT) programme, which brings the students to IMD first for two weeks and then, several months later, for one more week.[7] There is plenty of distance-based learning in preparation for the programme, allowing the participant to master more basic materials at home while still working. Between the two IMD sessions, the participants work on particular strategic projects in their own companies and get feedback from IMD professors via the Web. BOT is relatively short, and modular, and allows students to apply their learning on the job between IMD sessions. Virtual learning lets clients learn the basics at home, and thereby not miss valuable work time. Geared towards fast learning, rather than the deeper, slower study typical of the MBA track, BOT meets the express needs of a younger group of talented executives from IMD's client companies.

In the past, as already stated, the typical clients of business schools were individuals who took their undergraduate and/or executive development programmes at a given business school, and decided on their own which programmes to attend. The schools set the curricula, without interference, and without having to demonstrate their direct relevance to the corporate world. The classical MBA curriculum comes to mind. Here, the student typically went through semester-long courses on various functional topics, built around the axiomatic knowledge of that given function. The learning took place in a typically Cartesian fashion: the student came to each topic sequentially. Little, if any, integration among topics took place. Individuals studied on their own, with little group or project work, and little synthesis. This was clearly an efficient way to provide business school *teaching*, but it was probably a very inefficient way to provide meaningful *learning*. The business school organised its courses more or less independently, and with little or no co-ordination among courses, along the lines of the specific discipline for which the faculty members were recruited. To a greater or lesser extent, individual tuition fees balanced the economic equation for the business school. Fortunately, when the bottom line came out red, government sources, proceeds from endowments, and donations provided the much-needed, and often considerable, funds.

Today everything has changed. The students, clients, and "learning partners" — whatever name you choose — have changed. And the concept of human capital as the strategic asset of a corporation has become a reality. For the modern corporation, with its progressive, new teams of fast-learning executives, change is an opportunity to redefine the way it does business, to come up with business innovations that feed growth and profitability. Change is a chance for its executives to see, and then take advantage of, opportunities that are not obvious to competitors. It is critical, therefore, that management be able to spot opportunities faster than others, and mobilise its own resources faster, to "go for" these opportunities. Firms have to make an extraordinary effort to adapt their products and services in ways that require them to stretch their imaginations far beyond previous marks.

The implications for the modern business school are clear: leading corporations come looking for "partners" in the race for imaginative ideas. For many leading business schools, the firm has become the major client/learning partner. Again, IMD serves as a case in point. The Lausanne-based school has approximately 4,000 students per year. Only 85 are MBAs, but even here, 30 percent are sent by their companies; 70 percent come on their own initiative. In the long *Programme for Executive Development* (PED) only approximately 10 percent of the students make the decision to attend; firms send the vast majority. In almost all IMD programmes, the vast majority of the students are sent by their companies. It is thus clear who the major client is. While IMD is perhaps extreme, for most schools the trend is the same.

Although business schools will keep serving undergraduates and graduate students, they are likely to be doing so less than ever before. The classic business curriculum of the future will come to business students with the imprint of the corporation. What is the consequence for business schools of this shift in student needs and expectations? Simple: more and more, the world's large corporations are driving research-based academic delivery. Corporations pay (often handsomely) for the schools' services, and the schools alone — without the benevolent outstretched palm of the government — are responsible for their own economic viability. This trend is likely to continue since, as noted earlier, many of today's business schools have been getting resources from the government sector, often with little or no questioning of the academic value they offer. The result was exclusive, self-centred business schools rife with complacency. Nowadays, the very notion of governmental support is being called into question.

It is safe to assume that society will not foot the bill for them any more, at least not on a large scale. After all, the public fairly asks, "Why should the public sector underwrite business school expenses in return for exclusive, one-way, non-adapted teaching?" "Where's the return on investment of society's resources?" Many countries and government agencies are putting a cap on, or even cutting government funds for higher education in general, and business schools specifically, which further galvanises the links between corporations and business schools.

The successful business school, therefore, must be able to serve the learning partner, with its executive clients, in ways that create significant tangible value. To do this, they must understand the adaptive pressures that their corporate learning partners and their executives face every day in turbulent, acutely competitive markets. The business school itself has got to find ways to strengthen its intellectual capabilities to be able to serve this new breed of learning partner, for whom the right knowledge may mean the difference between profit and poor house. But how is the modern business school supposed to accomplish all this?

Create Value by Adapting to Your Corporate Clients' Needs

If we start with the assumption that a business must be served in as *relevant* a fashion as possible, we must reject the classical position that traditional axiomatic academic research alone makes for a successful business school. While academic research is important, a number of other factors — all admittedly related to the research activities, albeit often more loosely — are at least as significant, if not more. These include how the school goes about adapting to its clients, how it understands the needs of those clients, how it organises itself internally in order to adapt to and serve those needs, and how its critical decisions inform its process of adaptation and progress.

Understanding the corporate clients' needs, having a clear understanding of the situation of the firm, the school can design a tailored set of proposed learning activities — at IMD we call them a "menu" — to meet the needs of the client. The learning activities menu is custom-made, driven by its particular circumstances and geared to its *business* needs. Make no mistake about it — we are talking about delivering tailored education at the business school level.

Once the school knows what its clients want and need, it somehow has to muster the right competencies to be able to teach the knowledge the learning partner needs. These so-called "competencies" are nothing more than the aggregate knowledge and expertise, combined with the pedagogical skills of the faculty members. Not only does the business school need individuals with unique expertise and outstanding teaching skills, it needs faculty who can work both as a team with one another (not a trivial undertaking in itself), but also with the school's corporate learning partners. In other words, the school needs faculty who believe in, are highly skilled at, and truly dedicated to, learning partnerships. This goes far beyond the traditional requirements of research, publication, and effective "university service".

To best serve its current and future corporate learning partners, the modern business school needs to find ways to consistently manage the full array of client needs. Each set of tailor-made "learning menus" becomes an integral part of the school's value-creation process. Taking on partnerships that upset the balance or mix of the school's competencies too radically, or that require time and manpower on projects that cause it to lag or be unable to evolve along with the evolving needs of its corporate clients will simply not work. Over time, the school must maintain consistency in faculty, programmes, and capabilities — as all of this relates to a desired portfolio of learning partners.

The major managerial challenge for the leadership of a business school will be to meet three challenges: meeting the clients' needs, having the requisite competencies, and developing an optimal portfolio of clients. More specifically, the school needs to address and systematically manage (i.e., "minimise") what I think of as the three "delivery gaps": the tailored delivery gap, the relevance gap, and the consistency gap. If the school addresses these three gaps properly, its success should be largely assured.

Managing the Tailored Delivery Gap

First, the school has to ask if there is a sufficient match between the specific needs of a given learning partner, with its individual executives-cum-clients, and the corresponding tailored service the school provides. You can think of the difference between what the client needs and what the school can actually offer as the "tailored delivery gap". There are three ways to think about this potential match. Consider the open programmes a business school offers. Here the question is to what extent the topics offered are in line with the needs of the executives-cum-clients from a typical learning partner firm. A particular need might be leadership and general management. Developing an international competence might be another. A third set of needs might be to build specific functional capabilities of one kind or another. For the business school in this case, the key to assessing the gap would be to assess whether the open programme portfolio meets the typical needs of busy executives in leading firms. Clearly, some executives need one thing; others have different needs. The key is to have a palette of open programmes that more or less meet the most critical needs.

You can think about the tailored delivery gap another way, too. The school can ask how well its in-company programmes (those that the school designs specifically to meet the needs of a particular client) meet the specific demands of a given firm. Here, we would expect the gap a priori to be small, or not to exist at all, since the school will ostensibly be delivering, or trying to deliver, on a specific request from a specific firm. We would, in effect, be surprised if there wasn't a good match.

Delivery shortfall usually has to do not only with the school's inability to provide the relevant, substantive inputs, but also its inability to integrate the variety of issues covered in the programme into a whole that matches how executives typically see a competence, i.e., a competence that represents a synthesis of various inputs, rather than various specific know-how competencies on their own. Thus, effective delivery is also a function of effective programme design know-how, as well as of pedagogical delivery by the faculty. Holistic thinking is perhaps the most critical characteristic for being able to deliver successfully.

Another tailored delivery gap exists in research. Most commonly, research follows axiomatic, discipline-driven traditions. When a business school delivers this sort of research to practising executives, there will again typically be a gap. The problem is that the research that focuses on a particular discipline can often be too narrow to meet the needs of practitioners. What the executives need are pieces of synthesised knowledge, often through combinations of more specific disciplinary research inputs. What the school's researchers often deliver, in contrast, and all too typically, are bits and pieces of more specific knowledge that do not merge easily into the accumulated, practice-oriented knowledge inside the heads of busy executives.

Needless to say, I believe that business schools can manage the delivery process to lessen the gaps, and even eliminate the non-tailored delivery altogether. How? By focusing on the relevance of the open programme portfolio mix, by providing synthetic designs for one's tailored programmes, and by orchestrating the sharing of research that focuses on creating more holistic knowledge out of the otherwise narrow, disparate chunks of research.

To keep the tailored delivery gap narrow, the school simply needs to understand the needs of its learning partners and honestly assess its own ability to design and deliver programmes that meet those needs. The hard part of managing the evolution of what the school delivers is to remain consistent with, and relevant to, the evolving needs of its corporate partners. Think about an example: a learning partnership that seems to be highly successful, with little or no tailored delivery gap. Imagine that the company in question has subscribed to a tailored programme aimed at developing particular growth strategies to help the firm generate more aggressive, internally generated growth. This programme might well have strong elements of "seeing opportunities before they are obvious to everyone else", and "focusing on the team-based implementation of such opportunities by creating flat, non-hierarchical, implementation-based project groups".

As the relevant know-how of the firm gradually builds, to some extent, we hope, as a direct result of the given programme, the content of the original programme may become less and less relevant. Here is the irony. The know-how the business school is transmitting is no longer as pertinent as it was when the company entered the programme (a direct result of its success). What was new is now old hat. A tailored delivery gap may thus develop as a consequence of the gradual increase of the clients' knowledge flowing from the programme itself. Thus, as the programme progresses, modifications become necessary — for example, focusing more on international opportunity-seeking or implementation in international, cross-cultural groups. Another way to look at this is to think of maintaining a low tailored delivery gap in a dynamic context as "managing a relevance gap".

Managing the Relevance Gap

Seen in terms of "relevance", the difference between the actual ability of the school's faculty to deliver a tailored programme for the learning partner and what it needs to be able to deliver is essentially a "relevance gap". Here's an example.

Fast-moving firms typically assume that business strategies have to be highly dynamic. Such strategies, they believe, must at the least adapt to the pace of change in business. As the CEO of Nestlé, Peter Brabeck, said in a recent interview in the Harvard Business Review, "if we cannot change at least as fast as our business, we will clearly fall behind and rapidly go out of business".[8] It follows that what is relevant will change over time. So the modern business school must constantly update its programmatic efforts and their delivery in order to manage the relevance gap. As a small aside, another way to think about the challenge a business school faces as it tries to keep its relevance gap as small as possible, is that the partner's needs change as a result of working with the school. This effect appears similar to Heisenberg's uncertainty principle[9] which states the fact that the very process of measurement alters what is being measured. To extend the metaphor, it is very difficult, if not impossible, to assess or "measure" a company's strategy without in some way affecting that strategy. Similarly, the needs of one's learning partners will change due to the fact that you are involved in a learning partnership context with this client.

Here, faculty ability implies not only the ability to provide the relevant subjects, industry analyses, and historical background, but also the ability to teach it ("deliver" may be a better word, since it involves a wide variety of learning activities). The question of whether there is a gap here thus has direct bearing on what competencies a school needs to develop in order to stay relevant for its learning partner. To prevent a relevance gap, the school has to manage its competence base. It has to line up different mixes of faculty to cover its programmes as they evolve.

For example, faculty members must keep informing each other, working *with* each other, so that they stay co-ordinated in their evolving work with the client. In practice, however, it is easy for this not to take place. Some faculty may, for instance, be good at updating and revising their inputs, while others may be less good. Over time, a relevance gap may grow, because the totality of the faculty co-ordinate their efforts less and less relatively to the evolving needs of the client.

Managing the Consistency Gap

The difference between what the corporate clients need and what the business school can deliver is another important gap. I call it the consistency gap. A good match may, for instance, exist between what a company wants and what a school is delivering, i.e., the tailored delivery gap is small. There may be a good evolution of what is being delivered relative to the client's emerging needs, i.e., the relevance gap is narrow. Still, over time the client's learning may outstrip the business school's learning, and thereby create a gap — again, a sort of relevance gap. This would simply imply that the school over time may not have the competencies that it now needs to support the client. After many productive years of working together, the co-operation may wind down, or end, because the school no longer has sufficient competence. One could say that the assumptions behind the learning partnership have changed in such a way that the school simply cannot respond.

One can argue that one of the school's roles might be to manage the evolution of the learning partnership in such a way that the relevance gap never develops. This might involve a process analogous to that one might find in marketing, namely, where a company tries to drive the market, as opposed to being "market driven". Thus, the school may want to try to drive the evolution of a learning partner's needs so that new levels of competence become internalised, rather than being driven by needs that might come up which the school cannot respond to.

To ensure that this consistency gap doesn't grow too wide, the school needs to regularly review what competence base it needs in order to stay on top. How can it serve its key learning partner clients in an even more proactive way? How can the school meet current client needs, stimulate its own evolution and, at the same time, anticipate the future needs of current and future clients? In other words, how can the school best figure out what it will one day need to be able to do, so as not to create a widening gap over the long term. While the relevance gap addresses adaptation on a small scale, the consistency gap concerns adaptation on a large scale.

Managing the tailored delivery gap is a matter of ensuring a direct, immediate match between what the learning partner/student expects and the school's promise of programme delivery and implementation. The school must be able to demonstrate that it *understands* what the key demands are. The relevance gap entails securing an actual match between the school's capabilities and the learning partners' requirements. In this way, it can realistically provide tailored services for a number of clients and students on an ongoing basis, thus teaching to create value, and establishing a learning partner activity-pattern that is in tune with the day-to-day needs of the clients and its students. The consistency gap is about the more fundamental issue of how the school's overall capabilities should evolve so as to be able to deal with the anticipated evolution and emerging adaptive needs of today's leading corporate clients. As I have already suggested, it is critical that the school drives the build-up of its own competence, and is not being driven by the needs of its learning partners only. Needless to say, the school needs to be both competence driving and competence driven; for the business school, this is not an "either/or". A balance must be struck.

Managing the Three Gaps by Deliberate Process

To create full value to its learning partners, the business school needs to manage all three gaps. Clearly, therefore, no school can afford not to have a deliberate process of managing these gaps, of setting and implementing strategy. But what are the critical conditions for managing a business school in a purposeful manner? Successful strategic management of the emerging business school rests on the simple — and obvious, but all too often overlooked — fact that the business school cannot do everything or be all things to all clients. Strategy means *balanced* choice. The problem is, finding the "balanced way" among these forces can be like passing an iron bar through a magnetic field. Consider three short examples of how difficult it can be.

When it comes to a tailored delivery gap, a school will always feel pressure to add more and more programmes and offerings to its portfolio of programmes. In this way, in theory at least, the school will be able to cover more and more diverse needs of most of its current and potential learning partners. The problem, of course, is that no school's resources will allow for such a proliferation of programme offerings. The question, therefore, is what would be the optimal portfolio, keeping an eye both to present and anticipated needs, both to securing future revenue streams and maintaining the present ones.

Similarly, when it comes to finding a balanced strategy for managing the relevance gap, it is clear that a business school's various programmes need to be modified and updated, so that programmes stay relevant. At the same time, it is simply impossible to update everything at every point in time. This again would devour too many resources. Again, the key is to find a balance between updating programmes for future position and upgrading programmes to secure the immediate results from current activities.

Last but not least, managing the consistency gap is a matter of balance. On the one hand, a business school will want to develop competencies for the future; at the same time, all competence development draws on resources. The trick is to find a balance between using one's present competence base and developing a proactive competence base for positioning the school to be a future thought leader. As you can see from all these examples, the question of *balance* is critical. To talk about the "right" strategy is myopic — it is the right balance that makes all the difference.

Managing the Three Gaps to Keep the Balance

In light of the overarching importance of managing the three delivery gaps, and the obvious difficulty of doing it well, what is the school to *do*? First, the institution needs to take account of where it has come from, that is, how it has adapted to both the market and its clients' needs in the past. Think about this as being led by one's markets, being adapted to the particular needs that the present learning partner companies ask for. Or think about this as being sensitive to the needs to secure the school's cash flow through having a portfolio of value-creating activities that today's learning partners appreciate, ones that are now commanding a value for which customers are willing to pay. This is analogous to the process by which sociologists try to understand "average needs" as represented by the market, being a combination of the requirements that have been built up over the past years, a kind of looking back.

This looking back can be useful, but it isn't enough. To keep the dynamic balance the school needs to fashion a clear vision of its strategic direction. In order to maximise the clients' benefit and appreciation well into the future, the leadership must ascertain where the institution should go. Try to imagine this as "driving the market", in contrast to the earlier "being driven by the market".[10] The challenge in this vision-making is anticipating what your learning partners/clients will need in the future, in order to position your strategy to be able to deliver it. If you foresee, for instance, that your learning partners will need to emphasise the flat, networked organisation more heavily in the future, you may want to build competencies, through research and programme redesign, that emphasise insights into working in teams, cross-cultural effectiveness within teams, dealing with control issues, among others. The key, to use my earlier words, is to lead the market, lead the development of the needs of one's learning partners, as opposed to being led by one's learning partners and the market. This involves articulating the vision with sufficient clarity for the institution to set its strategic priorities, and then invest its resources optimally.

While the Dean (or Board, or top administrative team) may lead the institution's retrospection, may even spearhead the effort to articulate a vision, and thereby be a "catalyst" in its thrust to drive the market, strategic articulation and leadership cannot come from the top only. A great deal of the strategic input will flow "bottom-up". Without using "bottom-up" pejoratively, I mean that the faculty members, with their research initiatives and teaching strengths, represent the major dimension of the strategy. I would argue, in fact, that faculty will shape and fuel the strategy. Indeed, academic value creation stems, in general, endemically from the initiatives of individual faculty members, working alone. Although it can happen that when faculty members work together, individual initiatives lead to further value creation, the basic driving force is the individual motivation of each faculty member. The force is fuelled by research initiatives, pedagogical initiatives, etc., all of which amount to bottom-up critical input that shapes the strategy.

In the absence of full faculty commitment, there is no point whatsoever in talking about the Dean, or any other administrative body, making, shaping, defining, or setting strategy. Once again balance is essential. "Bottom-up" initiatives are, by definition, individualistic and partial; the faculty should not be allowed, or even expected, to hold sway. The school needs to think about its strategy as not merely the sum of bottom-up individual faculty members, but as a deliberate *portfolio* of initiatives that somehow fit together. It may be that the school is weighing certain areas of competence, or certain areas of teaching more heavily than others. It may be that, by considering the link between individual academic value-creating initiatives, the school (i.e., those responsible for direction-setting) can come up with clearly articulated strategies for how these initiatives might reinforce, or "create synergies" with each other. Clearly also, the availability of resources in the school will call for some sort of priority setting; hence, once more the importance of a clear set of top-down portfolio strategies. Again, we see the need for a strategy that balances, in a positive symbiosis, the bottom-up initiatives and the top-down portfolio vision. To achieve a better overall portfolio balance, the "top-down" leadership and "vision setting" mentioned above should perhaps take a lead in fashioning the school's overall portfolio. From observing the leadership (or lack thereof) in many institutions, it seems to me that the biggest challenges can be found in instilling sufficient vision and what I like to call "overall portfolio perspective".

Implementing Strategy: Putting it All Together

Once the leadership and the faculty have articulated a vision, someone has to decide where to put in the priorities so the school can use its scarce resources optimally. Of course, no success is possible unless the institution has at least some discretionary resources, some "space to manoeuvre". Businesses might call this "intentional over-staffing" in order to have enough resources for building new business through research and development, additional market research and long-term market promotion, additional business-model analysis capacity, etc. The same is true in academic organisations. The professors must, above all, have time for research. Enough teaching resources must be available so that each professor has a reasonable teaching load, not only a reasonable overall teaching load, but also a sequence of teaching activities that "chops up" his agenda as little as possible. To have enough faculty to allow for this type of planned "co-existence" between research and teaching is therefore critical.

Unfortunately, many academic institutions suffer from being too thinly staffed. Faculty teach too much and time for fundamental research is too scarce. Having sufficient slack must also include having enough other resources, too, which often includes research associates and funds earmarked for research. The key is to have enough people *and* funds to be able to spearhead the part of the strategy that involves what I like to call "building the future today". If you don't have room to move, there are no choices to be made, and talking about a change of direction is futile. All too often, resources may just be too tight. The faculty is overloaded with day-to-day teaching activities, research assistance and funding are scarce, and free classrooms are unavailable for new programmes. To reiterate: the modern business school must have enough "play" in its human and research resources to be able to effectively, meaningfully, work today for today *and* for tomorrow. Without this "looseness", changing the strategic direction will be impossible. But flexibility and room to adapt are not only a matter of the absolute level of availability of resources. Creating "space" is also a matter of developing an internal structure that allows for fundamental adaptation. Critical in this respect are getting the right departmental structure in place and managing cash flow effectively.

Departmental Structure: Creating Room to Move

Traditionally, academic institutions have been organised around academic departments that tend to mirror the axiomatic research traditions carried out by those members of the academic institution who fit into given departments: finance, marketing, organisational behaviour, strategy, production, etc. Clearly, this structure has advantages. For one, faculty members from different fields can interact. Second, tool-up costs for further research within narrowly defined academic areas are relatively low. Further, given the fact that various faculty members might play more or less interchangeable roles within the common functional field, offering teaching programmes along strict functional dimensions is relatively easy.

The weaknesses in this approach are obvious, however. Having many small academic departments tends to stifle the choices of how to redistribute resources. Given that one's clients-cum-learning partners typically demand research and teaching that is cross-functional, or "cross-axiomatic", this compartmentalised internal structure restricts adaptation. Bringing teams of cross-functional researchers together isn't simple. Neither is mobilising the cross-functional teaching programmes that the clients-cum-learning partners need. Achieving cross-functional fertilisation within a functionally-organised business school requires quite a large staff, and this, in turn, may imply a less than optimal use of resources.

So what is the modern business school to do? There are a number of ways to create room to move. Decreasing the number of academic departments provides more freedom to shift resources around among larger academic departments. Staffing decisions can be made on the basis of what is best for the school, and not based on departmental self-interest. Larger teams of faculty members are more readily available to work together to address the types of needs that one's customers-cum-learning partners will have. Let me give three examples I know best.

At IMD, with a faculty of 50, we have eliminated all academic departments. The school views itself as consisting of one team, where faculty members from various disciplines can team together, as teaching and research needs arise. The formal "structure" is thus built around the various teaching programmes and their faculty teams, as well as research activities. And these teams change all the time, hence, a temporary structure indeed, in which each faculty member wears several "hats" all the time. As long as the faculty is not too large, this structure is feasible: by adding a lot of flexibility to the organisation, IMD has increased its room to manoeuvre.

When I became President of the Norwegian School of Management in Oslo, Norway, I spearheaded a change of departmental structure along similar lines, reducing the number of departments from twelve to three. The benefit was to gain more flexibility in serving NSM's learning partners. The negative side? Co-ordination within each of these three mega-departments required more effort. Always there will be a tradeoff here between flexibility and co-ordination. But with faculty groups of less than 50 in a given department, the benefit from flexibility should outweigh the added co-ordination costs.

The management department at the Wharton School (of which I served as Head) initially consisted of five sub-departments: strategy, organisational behaviour, labour relations, international business and small (entrepreneurial) businesses. These departmental substructures were eliminated, and the management department worked more or less as one team, enjoying many of the benefits of added flexibility and added "room to manoeuvre".[11]

These flexible structures do not seem to be sustainable without a strong willingness to make them function right. Only leadership can make this happen. Interestingly, both the management department of the Wharton School and the Norwegian School of Management went back to a more fragmented structure later on, again creating five sub-departments within the management department of Wharton as well as recreating nine departments at the Norwegian School of Management. The benefits were less effort required for co-ordination; the disadvantages were more rigidity and the concomitant, rather more difficult adaptability challenges.

Beyond decreasing the number of departments, decreasing individual programme "ownership" can also help. This can be done by rotating the programme directorship among professors on a regular basis, or by having several professors offer a programme jointly, etc.

Most academic institutions have a hierarchical title structure, based on seniority, coupled with an "up or out" tenure-based employment structure that often adds to inflexibility. The more senior, full professors have considerable freedom to decide on their own "to do it their own way". The more junior assistant or associate professors may try to be particularly flexible, even to unnatural extremes, because they are working at getting promotion and tenure, i.e., life-long employment. The assistant professors have relatively little freedom to work out their own agendas, and often have to act more or less as glorified research associates. So this hierarchical structure also seems to add to inflexibility, diminishing the room to manoeuvre, in other words. Further, a lot of politics can be unintentionally created through a rigid promotion and tenure-granting process. A great deal of faculty time and energy will have to go to such a process, too. It follows, then, that to further increase the flexibility in how the school can best take advantage of various faculty talents, the school can take down, and do away with, the hierarchical ladder of titles — Assistant Professor, Associate Professor, Professor.

At IMD, we have no title hierarchy any more; all are simply "professors". Because teaching assignments have little to do with seniority, IMD can distribute and redistribute teaching tasks with relative ease, and without stepping on any toes. In the "opposite" (and more traditional) case, one professor offers his "own" course for several years, allowing little possibility for change. At the extreme, one might think about a tenured full professor offering his own course year after year, largely by taking out the old files, repeating the old "silver bullets" and doing at best some marginal updating here and there regarding the materials, but (unfortunately) only updating within his own functionally defined area of interest.

This individual "power" to have total freedom for one's teaching content, in total isolation from other colleagues, is perhaps accentuated by the so-called tenure structure. Again, abandoning tenure may be a solution, i.e., abandoning life-long employment, thereby further adding flexibility, more space to manoeuvre. With this "freedom to move", the school can usher ineffective faculty members out the door. IMD has no tenure system. In practice this has not led to a significantly less stable faculty pool. But the fact that anyone can be asked to leave because of inadequate performance has had the positive effect on client-based performance that was precisely the reason for dropping tenure in the first place. As this discussion shows, added room to manoeuvre not only implies having a sufficiently large resource base to allow the professors and the organisation the time to do research and more exploratory teaching, it also involves re-examining the departmental, hierarchical and work contract structure of the academic institution. A minimalist approach to structure — fewer academic departments, less formal title hierarchy, and no tenure — enhances the school's ability to adapt and create relevant value for its learning partners.

Managing Cash Flow to Serve Strategy

Moving from people to money, a considerable amount of the institution's cash flow often goes to servicing debt incurred. Constructing new buildings severely limits the flexibility of the institution. So a way to free up cash is to reduce the amount of pledged cash flows, for example, to support interest payments and down payments on brick and mortar investments. The cash flow must be freed up. Financing physical plants from cash flow, i.e., by borrowing with the intention of paying later, means "investing in the future" by taking on an additional financial burden today. This can severely constrain a school's flexibility and room to manoeuvre. The role of free cash not earmarked for debt payment is paramount. But what about the argument that the academic value-creation process may not have sufficient financial strength for such an activity? What about the further argument that the clients should be willing to pay for the research and know-how development that best serves their interests? It can be hard to argue that clients should pay for investments in brick and stone, since buildings and classrooms offer them little tangible, direct benefit (as opposed to gaining know-how). Still, the argument must be made — appealing to the learning partners to "invest" in the future.

When too much of the investment in new buildings is financed with debt, the "room to manoeuvre" will easily be severely limited. Both the Norwegian School of Management and IMD experienced the restrictions of financing expansion with debt. The "assets" of an academic institution that generate cash primarily consist of know-how that resides in the heads of the professors and support staff (in contrast, business organisations have a much heavier emphasis on the physical plant and equipment). In "non-fixed asset institutions", generating free cash flow is essential. After all, cash burns at an alarming rate when you pay salaries and other expenses that need to be covered to run a business school. The larger the difference between these two cash flow streams is, the more flexibility and "healthiness" the academic institution will have. Consider a few factors that have an impact on cash flow:

On the inflow side, it is clear that providing extensive credits, discounts, etc. will diminish the incoming cash flow stream, i.e., the free cash flow. Outstanding receivables can be a problem for academic institutions if they collect their fees too late after the learning activities have been delivered. On the cash outflow side, the danger of using too much cash for servicing debt and/or down payment of debt is clear. In addition, a strict cost management regime is particularly critical, again so that the free cash flow can be maintained.

Similarly, the institution looking for room to manoeuvre should not tie up cash flow to support professors or other staff members to undertake esoteric research projects just for the sake of it — faculty members who cannot help generate cash flow may not belong in the institution. Think of it this way: a professor must be *billable* in order to justify his presence on the academic team. If not billable, then he will inevitably become a drain on the institution's resources, thus restricting the institution's ability to adapt and to create new, relevant value for learning partners. Thus, to allow professors to stay on merely for their own benefit, without an active commitment to generating the academic value that in the end the market will pay for, is likely to be a luxury that academic institutions can ill afford in the future. In the world of tenure-based, life-long work contracts, this is of course a rather radical line of thinking. But it works in practice at IMD, and the next chapters will show you how.

Chapter 3

A Learning Partnership Model for the Dynamic Business School

Executive Summary

Corporations are increasingly reassessing the value of their learning at business schools according to its salutary effect on the bottom line. Though business schools traditionally "feed" knowledge to their "students", interactive forms of learning are gaining acceptance. Business schools can rely on the more traditional discipline-based approach to deliver their clients' learning, or they can meet executives' rising expectations for job-related relevance by forming "learning partnerships" with their executive clients. One way is through so called "tailored learning partnerships". Creating them is a straightforward four-step process, at the centre of which rests a "learning menu". Chapter 3 provides an example of such a menu, and with it a full discussion of the main difficulties in implementing it, ending on a consideration of the role of R&D in executive learning.

Learning Models

So far, I have been arguing on the assumption that the typical business school is faced with teaching individuals who belong to a firm. Firms often talk a great deal about wanting to become learning organisations, and they expect the school to help them get there. So, much of the work of the modern business school will be to provide support for organisational learning — as a learning partner to the firm.

I have further assumed, and I hope argued persuasively, that regardless of how the business school weighs teaching and research, creating value for the participants — with value measured as demonstrable effect on the bottom line — must be the *raison d'être*. For today's students, most notably practising executives and managers going back to school, the cost of time spent at the business school is higher than ever, particularly when they factor in the opportunity cost of being away from work. Understandably, among many executives and students today, there is an increasingly strong, though often tacit, conviction that time spent in business school classrooms had better add to the bottom line. Studying, particularly when it takes managers away from the office, either physically or through "online" absences, only makes sense when a clear, practical (read: applicable) take-home value is achieved. And so individuals and company-sponsored executives are insisting, with ever increasing frequency, on relevance, immediate applicability, and clearly definable pay-off potential.

At the same time, corporations need to manage their resources cost-efficiently and prudently, at least in the eyes of fellow executives and vis-à-vis the stock market. Investment in learning must be seen as a cost-effective activity, not as a luxury bonanza.

So, on the one hand, today's business school is trying to serve participants from firms interested in minimising the impact of their employee's learning and maximising the benefits; on the other hand, the business school cannot afford to ignore the needs of traditional students either: undergraduates, graduate students, and certain entirely independent executives. Much of the pedagogical innovation, particularly that which comes through applying the faculty's research to pedagogical uses, can typically be done more easily when the school has specific students in sight and mind, and works with them in open programmes. This adds additional variety and richness. Cutting edge thinking can best be safeguarded this way, working both with leading corporations *and* with leading individuals, in the latter case without the potential constraint of having to adapt to the needs of a particular corporation.

If we start with some of the key assumptions from Chapter 2, namely that the business school needs to view all of its students as "learning partners" and that it must provide relevant learning through relevant programmes, the question arises: What should the model of learning partnership be? The successful business school of the future, I believe, will be a hybrid between the two models described below. For many business schools, this hybrid is numerous steps up the ladder of evolution. This chapter will answer the key questions.

The Traditional Learning Model: Pouring Information Down Students' Throats

Individual students, undergraduate, graduate freestanding executives, etc. typically receive a set of standardised course offerings that, taken together, characterise a particular degree or programme. Individual professors, occasionally working in teams, provide it. The very best of this teaching approach are the classical academic professors we've all heard about, and maybe even seen, the ones who provide stellar, highly entertaining, even inspiring lectures. Modern-day consultant-gurus have some of this quality: they are often brilliant entertainers with sharp, memorable insights. Still, the learning goes only one way. It has precious little to do with partnerships, and nothing to do with "learning partnerships". We experience this type of learning when we listen to a speech or a presentation. Over a relatively short time, and with a limited set of key items to learn, lectures can be particularly effective. The value comes largely from whatever take-away insights such one-way communication provides.

This approach does little to tap into the particular desires of individuals to activate themselves, steer and shape their own learning. Some thirty years ago, the then Dean of the Sloan School of Management at MIT, Professor William Pounds, talked about "the art of problem finding".[1] He contrasted this so-called art with the more straightforward problem solving that students encountered in traditional university programmes and could learn with relative ease, at least compared to learning by "finding problems". Problem finding, in Pounds' mind, taught the participant to find the relevant learning, i.e., to "see" opportunities, to create new insights, to find new "space to manoeuvre", to use learning to be able to come up with business opportunities that are not obvious to everyone else yet. Thus, learning is something that calls for relevance, immediacy, and demonstrated take-home value — in other words, what many of us expect of "active learning". Winston Churchill is quoted as saying, "I love learning, but I hate being taught." If you believe, as I do, that Churchill would find a number of like students in today's business schools, then you must agree that part of forming partnerships with students is making teaching more engaging, more interesting, more interactive.

A New Learning Model: Interactive Learning

Contrary to traditional, "one-way" learning, interactive learning allows students to relate with one another other and with the professor. Typical venues are case discussions, general discussions, or group work. Thankfully, innovation in teaching approaches that increase learning through student involvement have been widespread. With it has come a stronger sense of learning partnerships among students and professors. The dusty image of the university professor declaiming "ex cathedra" and students in neat rows of pews listening attentively has become far less common. In business schools, it has pretty much disappeared. Action learning, group work, emphasis on teams, field-based projects, etc. are found in every curriculum. "Virtual" interactive learning, facilitated by information/communication technology and multimedia, has opened up even newer avenues of learning. Even the standard classroom approach has evolved — case discussions, group debates, buzz groups, and countless other forms of discussion and group learning play a part in nearly every business class.

Even the more classical cases, themselves, in many ways represent the old way of teaching, too. While students are asked to actively be involved in the classes, to discuss and take part in dialogue, listen and learn, the reality is often that the classical case approach still often represents just another form of largely one-way indoctrination of particular teaching points of view. The teachable points are merely delivered in a different way, via *seemingly* interactive classes. Needless to say, while there is clearly interaction, the question remains how much learning really goes on when the case is merely a vehicle for getting pre-determined, teachable points across.[2]

Virtual cases, in contrast, allow students to select the information they need, or want in their preparation for case discussion. They guide themselves, following their own workplace agendas, learning needs, and specific problem. This approach has done much to address the increasingly loud criticism of traditional cases. In fact, many modern cases, whether virtual or "paper" fit this description: they allow — or force — students to connect the learning points to their own work-based agendas. As examples of these newer cases, real-life virtual cases, or their paper equivalent (cases consisting, for example, of collections of figures, artefacts, interview transcripts, company reports and the like) thus might meet these demands. No successful business school can ignore either the use of such modern cases in its teaching, nor the development of cases in its research. Virtual or not, to be interactive, new cases must be problem-oriented, reflecting the latest when it comes to real-life "messy" problem realities, and allow students to come up with what are relevant "learnable" points of view rather than accepting some teachable agenda or solution the professor dictates.

What Should the Business School Teach, and How?

The Discipline-Based Approach

Whether or not the school chooses to pour new knowledge down its students' throats, or teaches, and thereby expects its students to learn, more interactively, it must still decide whether or not to follow the traditional, discipline-based approach in deciding what to teach, and how. Beyond the question of how material is delivered are the questions of *what* material to deliver to your individual students, *how* you will decide what to teach, and finally, *who* is going to make the decision. One answer is to simply follow the classical teaching model, as many business schools still do. But this they do at their own jeopardy, I believe. Let me explain why.

In the classical teaching model, each professor typically bears the responsibility for his programme. Courses are functionally based. Let me give you an example from my own teaching experience. For many years I taught the basic strategy course for MBAs, first at the Sloan School and then at the Wharton School. This course was typically broken down into a strategy content part and a strategy process part. The content part largely focused on competitive strategies and how to develop a strong competitive base. Michael Porter's thinking was paramount here.[3] The strategy process part focused more on developing strategic plans for the firm, allowing members of its various organisational units to buy into a particular strategy. Works by scholars like Richard Vancil were important here.[4] I taught the course alone. It was organised in such a way that it would be "plug-in compatible" with parallel courses in marketing (which dealt with competitive analysis of various sorts and how to serve the customers in ways that would provide value to them), operations management (which dealt with creating value chains that would ensure competitiveness), finance (which dealt with issues relating to creating shareholder value and to financing strategic initiatives), accounting and control (which dealt with issues of "balanced scorecarding" through the monitoring of strategic progress, of cash flow management, etc.) and so on. All of these courses were thus self-contained, with clear borders between them, and — as pointed out — "plug-in compatibility".

Typically, it will be relatively easy to distinguish one course from all the others, and little hands-on co-ordination is necessary. The specific disciplinary grounding and functional nature of each course thus make it easy to avoid overlaps between the courses — "what belongs to yours, what belongs to mine". Faculty members run their courses over a set of sessions in a semester, and are responsible for their own grading, feedback to the students, content, teaching decisions, etc., all in a highly self-contained manner.

Aggregating such autonomous teaching activities into an overall teaching load portfolio for a faculty member requires relatively little effort. For instance, at Wharton, my teaching load was "four courses". I taught the basic strategy course just referred to, offered in the autumn and spring terms as well as a special course on strategic control, also structured in a similar way to the basic strategy course just referred to and, finally, a doctoral seminar on strategy, which was also largely self-contained. Thus, it was easy not only to define what a normal, full-time teaching load for a faculty member such as me would be, it was equally easy to plan the overall workload assignments for the entire faculty. Wharton simply had to cover the various self-contained courses that it needed to offer, and make sure that each faculty member was "loaded up" by offering full sets of self-contained units. It follows, then, that aggregating a number of courses into an overall degree requirement was relatively simple.

This traditional "discipline-based" teaching model is consistent with the classical value system and norms in typical, research-driven business schools. The functional department is the backbone of the organisation. At the Wharton School, for example, I was a member of the "management department". Further, I was a member of the strategy group in this department. All members of this cluster followed research and teaching according more or less to the same paradigms. We had a clear, shared understanding of the basic research that had taken place so far in the field. We shared an understanding of what research methodologies were appropriate. And there was a common understanding of what research topics were relevant for further research. More simply stated, we had a singular, intense focus on going deeper within a relatively narrow functional scope. Deviations from the ruling paradigms and practices were less welcome.

In institutions run the way Wharton was, the reward schemes rest on the pillars of publishing — typically articles in refereed journals. Hence, there tend to be heavy premiums on focused research streams that are consistent with the dominating paradigms of particular functional fields. For many years in my own field, strategy, the words of Michael Porter and his associates relating to developing content-driven solutions to what consists of effective competitive strategies, represented a dominant trend of acceptable research. An underlying paradigm here was industrial economics.[5,6] For several years, much of what was published in the leading journal for strategy research, *The Strategic Management Journal*, reflected this. Of course, the leading journals in the field appreciate this fact, since the research output from such programmes is what they can publish most easily.

Not surprisingly, the actual teaching in such research-driven business schools also follows these lines. It amounts to the delivery of research, and the emphasis in teaching is often of a more satisfaction-oriented nature: so long as you did a reasonably good job of "teaching" (read: "presenting your knowledge or research"), that was enough. The key to successful value creation was to put all the institution's extra effort into research. Over-emphasis on top teaching delivery typically did not pay off in promotions and incentives. Both at the Sloan School and the Wharton, the faculty contract renewal and promotion criteria, including those that led to so-called tenure, basically emphasised research originality and a reasonable amount of output within the research field. This output had to demonstrate that we were able to come up with original research that "made a difference". It was thus not so much a matter of me sharing research volume output. I had to demonstrate that I could come up with a meaningful additional contribution to my field.

Teaching was also seen as important — in theory. It certainly did not hurt to be a good teacher; it was, however, clear that the deciding dimension was research. In practice, it was interesting to observe that if a professor was very successful at teaching, he could be "suspected" to be less successful at research. There was a more or less implicit assumption about the necessary tradeoff between teaching and research. In practice, the common wisdom just seemed to be that if you are a good researcher, you are probably not a good teacher. In order thus to safeguard your career, you had to put strong emphasis on the research side; teaching, which was seen as more of a "satisfying requirement", just didn't matter that much.

Advantages to the Discipline-Based Approach

There are distinct advantages to the discipline-based approach. Because much excellent research is still generated in academic contexts, mainly because they still attract leading scholars and benefit from the "hosting advantage" of having the best established doctoral programmes, the sheer levels of competence can be formidable in these academic settings. Consider, for instance, the Wharton School, with its more than 200 professors. The sheer depth of competence, say, in its management department or finance, with between 40 and 50 faculty members in each, provides a unique set of skills. Such an agglomeration of knowledge within specifically focused areas with this level of depth is rare anywhere else.

Further, many outstanding researchers are still also naturally strong teachers, despite the potential dysfunctionalities caused by the typical singular emphasis on research for promotion, as previously noted. It is, of course, impossible to give a numerical percentage here. Suffice it to say, however, that the clarity that comes from researching a topic and gaining superior understanding also often translates itself into clear, penetrating lectures. One of the key advantages for researchers lies in their being up to date on the discipline-based research front, including being able to directly communicate and build on their own original research findings. One example that in particular comes to mind stems from my own time as a doctoral student at Harvard Business School. There I had a chance to follow a course on game theory by Professor Howard Raffia.[7] Raffia was clearly an outstanding scholar and researcher in his field. In addition, he was also an outstanding teacher — always claiming that "if you as a student do not understand a particular aspect of the topic, then there is something wrong with my teaching, my way of explaining". He was an exceptionally clear teacher, who allowed you to learn. He was able to build on his in-depth insights from his research to make the materials alive and meaningful for the students.

Limitations to the Discipline-Based Approach

Despite the obvious advantages there are also clear disadvantages to the discipline-based approach. Granted, many business schools have made good names for themselves, produced outstanding research by leading scholars, and prepared large numbers of students for successful careers in business. Most of the leading US business schools fit into this mould. It was really started as a result of the Ford Foundation report in the early 1950s and the Clark Kerr study,[8] which emphasised the importance of disciplinary-based research and teaching as the foundation of business school value creation. The US academic context has since refined this to its extremes. Leading schools in this tradition would clearly be the Universities of Chicago and Stanford, but also more industry-oriented schools like Wharton and the Sloan School. One might argue that Harvard Business School, with its insistence on always maintaining a strong focus on "the practitioner-oriented viewpoint", has been the most successful in developing a more balanced approach to academic value creation. But even at Harvard there seems to be a sharp emphasis on discipline-based research for promotion.

As I pointed out in the previous chapters, however, business issues today tend to be complex, cross-functional, and cross-disciplinary. This simple fact alone suggests that teachers from several departments need to be co-operating. The problem for business schools, however, is that, all too often, faculties from various departments are working in the equivalent of intellectual silos, and certainly not exchanging ideas or co-ordinating their efforts. Listen to what Derek Bok has to say about his experience with this kind of departmental encapsulation (the law school example may be applied, I maintain, to any classical educational institution):

> One of my reasons for choosing to teach rather than practice law was the thought of mingling with scholars from a wild variety of fields. I have looked forward to spirited lunches at the Faculty Club with Archaeologists fresh from digging in exotic lands and Astronomers brimming with theories about life on other planets. Alas, nothing could have been further from the truth. The law school, filled as it was with friendly colleagues, seemed cut off from the rest of the University as if by a vast moat.[9]

In simple terms, to meet the needs of today's complex businesses, with their intricate and shifting management challenges, faculty need to be spending more time and effort on co-ordination than they would in a traditional academic setting. Teaching that is more responsive to the changing needs of business students simply takes more time. And since time is limited, faculty must make a choice between giving time to teaching and giving it for research.

Executive Learning Partners: Rising Expectations

The problem with the discipline-based approach for most executives — who are among the business school's most important clientele — is that it is probably too "academic". Executives need more cross-functional, multidisciplinary approaches. Their time is short, their budgets are tight, and their expectations are over the moon. Their companies are under pressure to remake themselves, manage change, and get ready for a wickedly competitive future.

So it comes as no surprise that today's successful executive programme is not discipline-based, but rather follows a modularised programme design, with more co-ordination among the various teaching faculty members; in short, it relies on faculty and administration investing more energy in designing and implementing an integrated, if you will "holistic" programme. You can see this if, for instance, you think about the preparation behind a typical business school in-company programme. After a preliminary discussion with a client/learning partner company, the business school nominates a team of faculty members in order to better understand what would be involved in developing a programme around the broadly defined client's needs. Typically, these needs reflect a particular strategic challenge the company faces, and would therefore typically be staffed by a cross-functional team of professors. The professors interview various key executives to get a better feel for what would be involved. They might also supervise the development of several cases, specifically tailored for this given in-company programme. This preparative development phase can be extensive, and, as a rule, it is becoming more and more important.

When it comes to delivering the various elements of the programme, the professors co-ordinate among themselves to ensure seamless delivery of key messages. They sit in each other's sessions so they can refer in their own teaching to the points made by their colleagues, and they may even teach various cases and organise and deliver various exercises together. All in all, in order to be able to meet the particular needs of the client company, the professors involved must co-ordinate heavily in preparation and delivery.

The faculty of such programmes will have to devote themselves, at least to a greater degree than in traditional discipline-based programmes, to co-design and co-ordination. The time and energy thus required may well grow to the point of jeopardising the research capabilities of the institution. Let us remember that meaningful programme development can also represent valuable research. And, let us not forget, lest we bemoan the loss of attention to research, that academic value creation is both discovery *and* delivery! The trick is to find just the right balance between the two.

Creating Value for Managers with Tailored Learning Partnerships

At more and more international firms, executive development is becoming a sine qua non of setting and implementing strategy. At IMD, for instance, top managers from around the world — typically more than 4,000 from more than 70 countries each year, with no country representing more than ten percent of enrolment — typically tell us that they see executive development as a quintessential part of implementing company strategy. It has almost become part of accepted management lore that a clear link exists between executive education for life-long learning and a company's ability to meet its strategic challenges by having the best people and the strongest organisation. Top managers grapple daily with knotty strategic questions like:

- How can my firm position executive development to attract the best people?
- How can we use executive development to strengthen and retain people?
- How can we share experiences and learn as teams in our company, and thereby turn individual learning into organisational learning?
- How can we make this learning ongoing?

These questions, and all the other ones around executive development and learning, add up to this: how can the company, by truly becoming a learning organisation, become so attractive that the best people are drawn to it, and stay, because of its emphasis on development? The answer? Top management has to develop its *own* vision for management education, a vision for building its human capital, consistent with and integral to the strategic vision they have for their company. How can this vision be articulated? How can it lead to a plan of action that yields effective human capital improvements relative to the efforts that are being put in? Here, beyond offering particular programmes, open and customised, the business school can help.

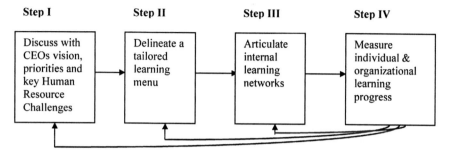

Figure 3.1: Creating tailor-made programmes in four steps.

Creating Tailor-Made Programmes

With the acute strain on corporations today, the learning partners of business schools are thus under intense pressure to adapt. Today's business school has to adapt to exactly the same pressures from its learning organisation clients as the clients — corporations and individuals — themselves face. It has to understand its clients well enough to offer them the outstretched hand of true learning partnership. To do this, the leadership of the business school, in turn, has to know which strategic issues are most critical, and who does what in the client organisation. Once it knows the key critical issues and has sorted out the players, the business school can set out to create a tailor-made programme by following a relatively simple four-step process, a model of which follows (refer to Figure 3.1 above). The four steps are: figure out the critical competencies the corporation needs; cobble together a "menu" of learning activities; figure out who, what, and when; and last, measure progress towards the learning targets.

Step 1: Figure out the critical competencies the corporation needs

A starting point for the business school might be to try to figure out, given where the corporation wants to go strategically, what critical organisational competencies it needs. More specifically, what competencies need to be strengthened *today* to reach these goals? At first glance, it may seem impossible to make such an assessment without overly extensive, in-depth analyses, almost analogous to a SWOT-type audit (strengths, weaknesses, opportunities, threats).[10] But IMD's experience has been that it is, in fact, possible to develop a relatively robust understanding of the needed competencies in a comparatively short time.

IMD typically uses four complementary analytical approaches for sensing the company's major needs for critical competencies. These approaches are, of course, carried out in the first instance on a judgemental subjective basis and then further synthesised on a judgemental basis:

- *Industry analysis*: Here the idea is to try to understand which are the main critical success factors that drive a particular industry, and how the industry evolves through consolidation and specialisation into various corporate categories, etc. An attempt is made to place the particular learning partner in one or several industries, and to understand what would make this particular firm succeed in its industry(-ies).
- *Breakpoint analysis*: Here, one tries to understand whether there are major environmental factors at work within a particular industry that might lead to major discontinuities or breakpoints. These breakpoints can be associated with technological breakthroughs, cost efficiency breakthroughs in manufacturing and distribution processes, consumer attitude breakpoints, etc. Again, we attempt to understand what particular breakpoints might apply to the industry (-ies) of this particular learning partner.
- *Organisational climate analysis*: This attempts to find the organisational pulse, and detect if possible any sense of complacency that might need remedy. Clearly this analysis is even more subjective than the two types of analytical exploration just mentioned, but it can still provide a good sense of whether the corporation has a healthy organisational climate.
- *Growth portfolio analysis*: This attempts to understand how much of the activities within the firm would fall within a "business as usual" category of these activities — we might call this "protect and extend" — and, in contrast, whether there are clear ideas for building on one's strengths by taking the basic business modus operandi into new markets, new client categories, etc., and/or by adding new technologies, new process know-hows, new product extensions to the basic business, i.e., "reposition" market-wise and/or "revitalise" business content-wise. Further to this might perhaps be activities that combine the expand/reorient focus into a more fundamental "renew" activity. Figure 3.2 provides an overview of such a business activities portfolio. The learning needs of the corporation will depend a lot on a balance of business initiatives, concerns, problems, opportunities, etc. that are associated with the relative activity balance among the four quadrants of Figure 3.2.

Needless to say, as a learning partnership with a particular firm continues, it will often be increasingly easier to determine its key learning needs. Determining them in direct dialogue with senior management, ideally including the chief executive officer, is paramount. Such dialogue gives the school an informal sense of the capabilities and the needs, as well as the gap between what the firm can do

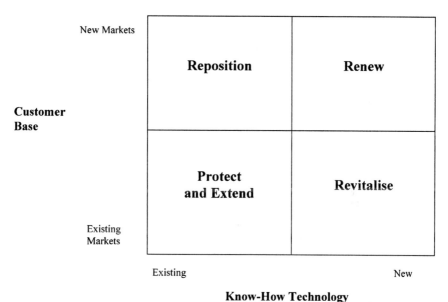

Figure 3.2: Portfolio of business growth options.[17]

now and what capabilities it needs to build. While subjective, an eclectic use of analytical frameworks like the ones above for understanding the critical competencies that will be needed must be applied. And it must lead to a synthesis, or "conclusion", albeit subjective.

Step 2: Cobble together a menu of learning activities   Once the school and the learning partner have determined which broad, overall competencies they must strengthen first, both parties have to hash out a "menu" of learning activities for the learning organisation client that will build the desired capabilities (refer to Step II in Figure 3.1). This "menu" of learning activities must be tightly tailored to the corporation's needs that the school has just determined in Step 1. It can have a variety of contents, but each element must build up the relevant competencies in a cost-beneficial way.

Typically, the learning menu activities fall into six areas:

- Open programmes;
- Tailored, in-company programmes;
- Collaborative research activities;

- Workshops for developing new business (an example of which is IMD's *Venture Booster* programme, discussed in detail later);
- Competency profiling or assessments;
- Accessing knowledge-based databases.

Step 3: Figure out the three Ws: Who, What, and When?   Step 3 exemplifies the need to determine "who" in the client organisation should participate in "what" aspects of learning, and "when". Remember that organisational learning usually means that *teams* of people will be working together to build and share competencies. They must be able to build insights in such a way that the competence is broadly shared among team members, even though one single member — or a few members — of the team might leave. Clearly, organisationally embedded competencies and organisational learning are more than the sum of the learning and competencies resting in the heads of each individual. Thus, it will be particularly important to keep in mind the actual work to be "done back home" in the firm, so that the right, representative set of executives attends.

Who should attend: Three principles   To enhance organisational learning, the school and the executive can follow three principles for determining who should participate in what.

PRINCIPLE 1: EXECUTIVES MUST REPRESENT ENTIRE WORK TEAMS   First, any executives, when asked to participate in a certain executive-development learning activity, must see themselves as representing their entire work team. The fact that one or more of them may participate alone, or only with a few members of a team, should not deter them from trying to understand the new knowledge so well that they can communicate it to, and share it with, the other team members back home. These executives need to understand major new points of learning in terms of their broader implications for the firm. Needless to say, more organisational learning takes place if several executives attend a programme together, since they can have interim discussions during the learning event, and share their insights with colleagues back at the office in a potentially more powerful way than if one person returns with a report.

PRINCIPLE 2: MAKE "LEARNING MAPS" FOR THE CORPORATION   Second, mapping the overall activities of *who* participates in *what* (at IMD, we call this a "learning map") can highlight whether all parts of an organisation are well enough represented in the formal plan for organisational learning. Certain parts of the organisation may feel that they already know enough, so they see no need to participate in a formal learning activity. Senior managers from a particular division may also feel that, since all available time should be devoted to preserving the bottom-line results, they have no time to attend. Of course, not all executives in a firm will have the same needs, and some who would benefit more than others will make excuses. If parts of the organisation are less well prepared than others, the firm's overall capabilities of pursuing certain broader strategies will be hampered.

PRINCIPLE 3: INVOLVE THE ENTIRE COMPANY   Finally, experience shows that the "learning map" often tends to be noticeably blank towards the top of the organisation. Upper management can, in principle, believe in learning, and even send their own executives to various programmes but, paradoxically, they may feel, at the same time, that they have neither the need nor the time to learn. A key part of the organisational learning approach will, therefore, be to ensure that the *entire* organisation is involved in some way or another. "Pockets of learning" in the organisation, without the overall, broad-based development of relevant competencies, will probably not get the firm where it needs to be.

Step 4: Measure progress towards the learning targets   The right-hand box in Figure 3.1, Step IV, indicates the desirability of formally measuring progress towards learning of the key target competencies in the client organisation. Developing a number of effective, useful individual measures of progress can be relatively easy. Typically, individual participants provide feedback to the business school about their satisfaction with a programme or various sessions of an event, etc. Such measures, above all, identify where the school needs to strengthen particular offerings. A potential problem with this type of feedback, however, is that it does not necessarily reflect the *organisational* learning; it says little about the relevance of the programme to an entire group of executives. On the contrary, such feedback can be biased, capturing the individual, idiosyncratic views and opinions of lone executives. Further, it can give rave reviews to the "entertainment" elements of a programme, entirely skirting the question of whether the programme provided relevant and substantive learning for an organisation. For individual participants to be happy is not enough. The critical question for both school and corporation is: How did *all* aspects of the learning help boost the competencies the firm is trying to acquire?

Another important question relating to how individuals view their own learning has to do with how well they remember. How much new knowledge is left after, say, six months or a year? In order to determine how much is actually retained, the business school and client might well want to collect feedback on individual learning some time after a particular learning activity.

As noted, the problem with measuring how much an individual learns is that it correlates poorly with how much the *organisation* benefits from the added knowledge, or whether or not any organisational learning at all has taken place. Organisational learning is much more difficult to measure. One approach would be to undertake an audit of the particular competencies among an organisation's members at certain points in time. A yearly "competence" audit could reveal whether certain competencies are getting stronger over time or not, which would provide a good measure of whether the organisation, in general, is becoming more, or less, well prepared for its major strategic challenges. One way of doing this is the so-called "balanced scorecard" approach.[11] The balanced scorecard provides an integrated review of an organisation's competencies. It should also be repeated over time, to provide a measure of whether the critical competencies are, in fact, accumulating.

The organisational learning process in a given firm will, by necessity, always be iterative. A firm's revised strategic intent must lead it not only to identify anew which key competencies to pursue, but also ensure that the strategic intent is modified to be consistent with — or at least sensitive to — those core competencies that can actually be "delivered". Furthermore, this "re-identification" calls for ongoing modifications of *who* in the organisation should participate in which aspects of the learning, to ensure that the relevant competencies get embedded in key locations. Thus, the key is internal consistency among the various dimensions of the organisational learning model portrayed in Figure 3.1.

Given the fact that learning activities *will*, one hopes, lead to the accumulation of desired new knowledge, there may be a secondary effect on the tailored learning process itself. Because of the learning taking place, the learning menu itself will probably go through modifications over time. Appropriate learning at one time might become less relevant once new organisational know-how has been built up through the learning process. Thus, it is not only because of new environmental inputs that the model needs to be seen as dynamic, or changing through successive iteration, the actual learning menu itself must reflect the firm's position at any point in time relative to its strategic needs. These needs will thus typically change over time, due to changes in the capability base of the organisation stemming from organisational learning.

Needless to say, the centrepiece of the learning partnership model of Figure 3.1 is, however, the second step, the delineation of a tailored learning menu. Getting the menu right is a large part of the task of setting up the right tailored learning partnership, so large, in fact, that it is worth further consideration. As noted, the key challenge for the business school, its faculty and staff will be to adapt meaningfully to the particular needs of a given client organisation. This adaptation will enable the school to provide a programme that sparks organisational learning. But to understand the importance of this adaptation, and the value it can create, it is essential to understand in more depth what we mean by "organisational learning". Besides, at the heart of the learning menu must be a common understanding of what after all, constitutes "organisational learning" for all concerned parties. We turn to it here in more detail.

Organisational Learning

What are the most important elements of "organisational learning"? One key element is team-based action learning, where the entire organisation finds a "solution" to a problem, i.e., an insight many can share, rather than an individual learning insight. Generally, organisational learning is more than the sum of what is being learned individually — it must also lead to *shared* insights. The organisation can develop competencies through shared patterns of learning, which is much more than an unco-ordinated accumulation of individual learning.

Careful planning is required for organisational learning to take place. In the long run, an organisation's critical strategic-capability issues should inform the "menu" of learning activities. The organisation should explicitly address more fundamental competence dimensions, beyond particular action learning problems. The organisation should select and nominate participants for various learning activities with particular care. To build clusters of common organisational understanding, persons with the right organisational jobs and responsibilities should be involved in learning. Measurement processes should emphasise and verify that organisational learning is actually taking place.

To create the right learning menu, the school has to come to grips with an ever more complex "pedagogical reality", including understanding the background of the firm and its industries, identifying the relevant learning agendas, selecting the teams to attend, and finding relevant measurement criteria. Clearly, the role of faculty members is becoming more and more demanding. No longer are they mere teachers in the classical sense, delivering research-based teaching and learning. No longer are they catalysts either, ensuring that the best joint experiences come out of the classes. Rather, they are *integrators* among key executives in the corporations, interacting extensively among them. They must be able to discern the strategic agenda from top management, so they can use it to inform the learning process. They must also interact with line managers and their team members to understand the vital business issues. They must be willing and able to do the necessary background research and development work so that the programme can be relevant and challenging. To manage all these tasks, faculty will spend relatively large amounts of time and energy on up-front programme development, research, and interaction. As the learning experience evolves, specific programme redesign through further research together with the company will take a large part of the professor's time.

The Learning Menu: An Example

Without doubt, it is critical to come up with an overall menu of learning activities that truly matches the particular needs of the learning partner firm. Figure 3.3 below divides the sample menu into four learning menu "activities", which fall broadly into two dimensions. Keep in mind that any learning menu will have to be based on the *specific* needs of particular clients, hence Learning Partner X rests at the centre of this menu.

The horizontal dimension of the menu relates to the acquisition of specific competencies within the organisation — the programme dimension. The right of the horizontal axis indicates the options for participating in open executive development programmes. A business school will typically offer a large selection of open programmes; the challenge is to find out *who* from the learning organisation should participate in *which* programme. Some programmes may be

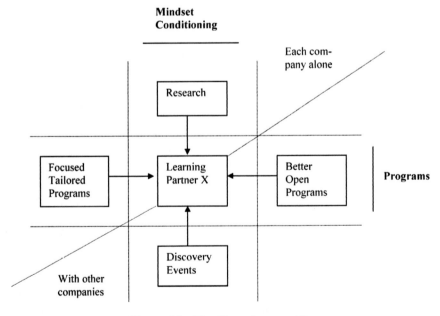

Figure 3.3: The "learning menu".

irrelevant; others might be relevant only to certain people. A company will typically achieve a better effect if more than one person participates in a given programme. This facilitates the ability to translate learning back to the organisation. Participants in any open programme should indeed see themselves as representatives for their teams back home, so they can learn on behalf of all the others who cannot attend. Of course, too, by mere power of numbers, the transfer of learning works better if more than one person attends.

A Portfolio of Programmes

In my experience, organisational learning is more effective when a client maintains a portfolio of programmes more or less intact over several years, only accounting for the adjustments in the programme menu that follow shifting priorities. When the client sticks with the portfolio, the team develops a common frame of reference — a common language — and more easily assimilates and shares key learning. Over time, internal "alumni" with a common set of references, insights, and frameworks emerge. At Nestlé, for instance, IMD's *Programme for Executive Development* (PED) has played such a role for more than a decade, with 15–30 executives attending every year. Over the years, this has had a strong impact on shaping Nestlé's performance-driven culture.

Open Programmes Versus Tailored In-Company Programmes

What are the benefits of sending employees to open programmes rather than having them all attend an in-company programme, specifically tailored for the firm? The key attraction of an open programme is working with executives from other companies. The exchange opens minds. Participants learn from what works for others, from their successes and mistakes. Arguing one's viewpoints with executives from entirely different, diverse cultures, and defending one's views in unfamiliar groups strengthens one's own position. It also breaks tendencies towards organisational near-sightedness and in-breeding. Learning from others — this is the reason to attend open programmes. It is perhaps particularly important to them that the participants come from a rich mix of settings — different companies, different countries — with no one company or country dominating. IMD's "global meeting place" concept fosters such an eclectic learning environment.

Unfortunately, the choice of open programmes is not always managed in such a way that organisational learning takes place. Members of an organisation may perceive participation in such programmes as "rewards". While individuals may well deserve recognition, I doubt the wisdom of letting them choose open programmes on their own. Individual initiatives for going to executive programmes may be evidence of motivation and determination to learn, but the organisation also needs to check its needs against the individual's choice, again, so that relevant organisational learning can take place. It is probably useful for a firm to list pre-identified and pre-evaluated programmes, say, from a set of business schools, to ensure, above all, that the programmes are compatible with the firm's needs and add to its accumulated organisational learning. Naturally, the learning partner firm should evaluate and select the open programmes and schools with a totally open mind — this would be a key function of the corporate learning officer!

Moving back to Figure 3.3, the left side of the horizontal axis features in-depth tailored programmes. The business school develops these specifically for the learning organisation. The aim is to focus more in-depth on aspects of the client firm's strategy, so that the participants can discuss and pursue the implementation of proprietary strategic issues. There is typically more action-oriented learning in this context, since participants are freer to discuss specific problems or project issues which, in a broader-based open programme, would be too "sensitive". Relative to open programmes, the benefits here will be hands-on learning: participants address their own strategic issues directly, and work with a team of colleagues who share their concerns. Corporate-specific depth and insight are the result.

Even with tailored programmes, it is just as important to assess who should participate in what. It makes sense for firms to send teams of executives to a programme to work together on strategic issues that really matter in their jobs. The resulting action-learning atmosphere ensures the take-home relevance of the lessons learned. The members of the team are more likely to develop a shared strategy and, so, they can speed up implementation, often one of the main reasons for pursuing tailored in-company programmes. The massive commitment that several firms make to such programmes undoubtedly reflects the motivation to accelerate strategy implementation.

Action-Learning in In-Company Programmes

More and more, action learning has come to be associated with tailored in-company programmes — at least, that is the case at IMD. Action learning turns out to be an excellent way to achieve certain types of learning benefits. With action learning, participants bring into the classroom the specific problems and decision-making issues they face in their businesses. These issues become the platforms for class discussion and group work. As part of the process, working with other executives facing like problems, participants figure out what actions to take and, indirectly, learn how to make the right business decisions when they return to the office.

In my experience at IMD, action learning takes place most naturally in tailored, in-company programmes, with all the executives coming from the same company. Here, the problem of confidentiality loses importance. Nevertheless, when executives from any company discuss difficult internal issues, faculty and participants alike still need to be aware of "political" sensitivities and restraints. This is why it is so important for the programme director and company to ensure that the backgrounds and competencies of the executive participants are sufficiently similar. The group needs to be able to address their company's problems "at the same level". Careful selection is paramount: deep understanding and first-hand experience are always an advantage.

Despite the clear advantages of having participants from the same company in in-company programmes, increasingly, variations of the action learning described above are coming into vogue. One example is the so-called "consortia programme", where several non-competing corporations attend with small teams. Here the objective is to present and discuss real-life problems from each participating firm in order to help participants reach decisions tempered by the experience and input of experts from other firms. This widened perspective is clearly a benefit. In my view, "consortia" programmes represent a particularly promising in-between, action-learning approach by which one can achieve both depth of the analysis by tackling a company's central strategic issues *and* breadth of solution based on diverse thinking coming from several corporate cultures.

Action Learning: The Down Side

On the down side, faculty members may find that, although this approach is stimulating, it also presents a few hurdles. Delivering the old "silver bullet" class usually works poorly in such an action-learning agenda. The reasons are clear: no "canned" material can possibly work as well as considering the "real" problems of "real" companies in a group. To succeed with action learning, the faculty member will have to have done background research that supports a detailed consideration of the company-specific problems. And a more than fleeting understanding of the industry will be indispensable. Clearly, in their role as facilitators, faculty members have to lay down their teacher/catalyst hats and put on their developmental researchers', even consultants' clothes, roll up their sleeves and help solve the problems.

Think of an effective professor working along these lines as the "orchestrator" of a "think-out". The task is to bring out learning in a multiplicity of ways, drawing on all available specific know-how in the group and applying it to the given questions, with much more emphasis on pulling everything together into emerging decisions. The professor will have to see his entire set of skills and insights — "playing on all strings" — over a longer, more intense, but sustainable period.

Another potential problem with the action-learning approach may be that the learning becomes so focused on solving the problems at hand and outlining the solutions, that more generalised insights fade into the background. This is, above all, a challenge for the professor. It not only requires specific background know-how, and deep, research-based expertise (and the homework that goes with it), but it also demands the ability to generalise about the lessons learned. Needless to say, to avoid in-breeding and gain a cross-organisational understanding, the successful business school provides open programmes that complement even their best tailored programme learning. So in Figure 3.3, although the ends of the horizontal axis reflect the acquisition of specific knowledge, they complement each other. Executives and corporate clients don't have to choose one or the other — in-company tailored programmes or open programmes — as, depending on their learning needs at any given time, they range back and forth.

Another Challenge: Keeping Managers' Minds Open with Research

A fundamental question about the efficacy of in-company programmes is, "Are executives normally 'ready' to open their minds to new knowledge?" Are they not so preoccupied in their business challenges that they spend most of their time in the programme engrossed in the problems they left on their desks at headquarters? Is there not the danger that successful executives might conclude that they already know more or less what they need to know, so why subject themselves to additional formal learning? Or, to say it even more directly, isn't it possible that a manager's success may be his own worst enemy, shuttering the windows of his mind to new ideas?

The vertical axis of Figure 3.3 models the opportunities a school has to build curiosity for new insights, in the spirit of "making good even better", and thus to "unfreeze" executives' minds. I think of it as the "conditioning" dimension because it represents the myriad ways a business school can awaken (or re-awaken!) an executive's thirst for learning, and spark the desire to find better ways for his company to do business, even if it is already a market leader.

One of the top boxes of Figure 3.3 is labelled "research". Research is one of the ways a school can try to stimulate members of a particular learning organisation to participate in certain research projects. There are several benefits:

- The research results might lead to new insights that might help the organisation to better achieve its strategic goals.
- Also, participation in a research process can heighten executives' understanding of the fact that maintaining their respect for new developments, innovations, and new thinking is the only path to success. Participation in research can remind them that they ought to appreciate new development. If they are not open to new ideas, then certainly their competitors will be!

What would be typical examples of such participative research?

- Sponsoring of, and participation in, case studies which might shed light on a particular business practice or problem in the company. The firm might also benefit from the subsequent discussion of the case in business school classes — getting a multitude of reactions and "free" advice.
- This might actually be part of the development-based research to prepare for a new in-company teaching programme. To participate in this type of research can sensitise the executive further to the nature of the key strategic issues facing his firm, and what types of capabilities his firm would need.
- Participation in clinical studies, comparative studies or broader questionnaire studies, perhaps to gain from new insights into a particular issue or from benchmarking with others, or perhaps to acquire important insights by working with co-researchers from the business school. Such insights, if gleaned before they start floating around in the public domain, can be a source of significant competitive advantage.
- Participate in presentation of the research, in the business school classroom or at conferences, typically as a joint effort with professors also involved in the research. This can further clarify what is truly critical about the given issue(s) in the executive's mind. Another important secondary benefit might be the added prestige that this type of exposure gives for the firm and for the executive.

Needless to say, some executives will find participation in such research activities difficult to justify. They cost a lot and take time. The counter argument is the fact that, properly orchestrated — with the proper internal participation — discovery activity *does* effectively open the mind to new learning. A curious, questioning mind is a key characteristic of a successful executive!

Another typical reservation about taking part in learning activities is the all too common reluctance among executives to share their latest strategic insights and thinking. This fear of giving away valuable insights to the competition is legitimate. But the faculty can always disguise the research results. Some executives — dysfunctional in my view — go so far as to try to "monopolise" new ideas. Holding the cards of new knowledge close to your chest is sadly misguided. For experience shows that the most successful firms are relatively open with cutting edge information and insight, using it as a basis to discuss and share with others. With this proactive attitude, these firms stay a few strides ahead of their competitors. While the laggards are trying to catch up, these spring ahead, sharing knowledge they internalised long before the others even heard about it. It is precisely through the process of sharing that "learning" firms hold their leads.

Research and Development: An Open Process

To think about research and development as an *open* process can thus lead to a strategic advantage. This is undoubtedly why the sharing of information more broadly, even via the Internet, is becoming more common. In a study of Hewlett-Packard's development of a new electronically-driven photographic imaging product, we saw how HP incorporated more than thirty ideas from outside sources — many identified over the Internet — which led to a dramatically faster development process.[12] To "borrow with pride" is exactly one of the positive effects from participating in research with others.

Yet another so-called "conditioning dimension" for the individual firm is taking part in a competence assessment — a thorough review of the firm's competencies on an ongoing basis. The firm, together with an outside consultant, can carry out such an assessment itself, or a specifically-trained business school staff member can do it. As we have seen, several analytical lenses might be turned to this task: industry analysis, break-point analysis, assessment of the business's organisational climate and applying the business growth portfolio. Taken together, these can yield a clear picture of the needs. The benefit is an in-depth understanding of the firm's strengths and weaknesses. A management that knows its company's "competence base" will better appreciate the need for further learning.

The first of the bottom boxes of Figure 3.3 is meant to suggest that it might be appropriate for a business school to organise knowledge-sharing events, to bring several learning organisations together and brainstorm about the implications of certain recent research findings. These events can be relatively short, say, a day or two, and give the business school faculty a chance to share their most recent research findings and their implications with a relatively broad number of interested executives from a variety of firms. At IMD, the result is often a kind of "live" benchmarking, where managers from a wide selection of companies ponder the value of new managerial practices. Thus, a vital additional benefit from such research briefings is the fact that participants assess the relevance of the findings (often with refreshing bluntness!) for various firms in various contexts. This "informal benchmarking" gives participants a strong sense of the applicability of the research generalisations to "making good even better" in the wide gambit of firms, industries and markets.

As with any programme, the business school and client companies need to choose the participants for such briefings in such a way as to make sure that they represent interest areas that need to be built up in the learning organisation and that are consistent with the already-defined competence building needs. Participants in such briefings should see themselves as "representing" the learning teams back home so that the insight can be more broadly shared.

Another possibility for learning with and from other corporations is through access to databases with general knowledge. Here, the business school works to accumulate its relevant management knowledge in a database, and then taps into that database (or allows its clients to tap into it, too) to provide the collective lessons that reside there. What type of knowledge are we talking about? The school might develop industry analyses and store them in a database; companies could then explore the data for industry and company profiles, to better understand a given industry from the composite picture. The school can also develop specific cases, which would give client firms the chance to learn by comparing a multitude of firms.

The concept of a database leads us back to Figure 3.3. Take a look at the diagonal line that slants from the bottom left to the upper right at a forty-five degree angle. It represents the fact that different types of organisational learning take place in two learning contexts: companies participating alone and companies participating with other companies. More specifically, when you participate in open research discovery events and accessing knowledge databases, you learn by interacting with executives from *other companies*. As noted, this can allow for critical mind-broadening, new perspectives, and stimulus from learning from executives from other contexts. Here, keeping the learning process "fresh" and "open" is essential, for all too often, even in the best of business schools (and even in the best corporations as well), learning can become regimented and in-bred, and fail to spark strategic renewal. The bottom right half of Figure 3.3 above all represents learning in a network context — sharing and learning with executives from other companies in the network.

The upper left half of Figure 3.3 designates the learning that takes place inside one company — or "learning organisation". The benefits of this more focused learning are clear: together with members of your own organisation, you can dive deeper, plumbing the unexplored depths of your own strategic challenges and drawing syntheses from its various parts. IMD, for example, is working with a multinational company active in the rapidly-changing telecommunications business. Consider for a moment the learning that goes on in this company. It is critically important for this firm to make sure that the learning happens ultra fast, and that its strategy evolves from an intense learning process. It is also critical that this learning be fundamentally holistic — the overall strategic direction must evolve quickly, and not be bogged down in learning more about various in-depth but increasingly irrelevant details, the co-ordination of which could slow overall learning. For this company, the learning that must take place can in many ways be compared with the "holistic" learning that goes on in a child's mind, as described by developmental psychologists like Piaget.[13] (Note: this learning contrasts starkly with the type of learning first described by Descartes, in which the learner assimilates "pieces" and then synthesises them into a whole.[14,15,16]) Focusing in-depth within the company on critical strategic issues and seeing the development of these strategic issues as a key agenda for learning is thus critical. And — analogously to the child whose brain takes on added capacity to learn as it becomes older — the firm also matures to tackle more and more demanding learning tasks related to its flexible, "fast" strategies. Only if teams of executives, from the various relevant markets and technology areas within the firm, get together and work systematically and in-depth on the firm's specific issues can this take place.

This is, thus, also a chance to assemble global teams representing the relevant parts of this telecommunication firm's global operations. While the corporate headquarters of this firm resides in a small country, it is critically important that key teams of managers who have relevant business experiences from various parts of the world work together. It is only by working together that they are likely to come up with a holistic understanding of "how to serve the customer better" by applying new integrated technologies or design earlier. It is equally important that rapid implementation for this company entails participation from its various parts. The strategy as a learning process makes little differentiation between strategy formulation and implementation. The teams involved must thus be global. The emergent technological breakthroughs must be applied globally to benefit all consumers.

To develop ties within each team might become critically important for implementation as well. The implementation challenge in this ultra-rapidly moving environment thus largely rests on the ability of each member of the various global teams to understand what they are supposed to do in their flat, cross-cultural teams. Again, the strategy as a learning process clears the ways for such an approach. Each of the members of the team can focus on their role, without being overly burdened by co-ordination, or being handicapped by excessive internal politicking. The key is to get things down, so as to implement the strategy all the time through further learning. Thus (and here we get back to Piaget), the strategic concept, implementation and further learning happen in a manner comparable to how the child gradually develops a more complex, yet complete view of a given phenomenon, as knowledge accumulates and its own brain matures. In the case of this telecom company, what is maturing is the organisational insight regarding how various strategy implementation initiatives can evolve and actually work in practice, and flexibility and speed rest at the centre of this maturation. So at IMD, in-company tailored programmes, specific research, participation in competence-assessment activities all focus in-depth on key strategic insights. We design them to help companies develop the specific working team relationships so critical for effective, speedy implementation.

Although it should now be abundantly clear that each of the six elements of the learning menu is vital in and of itself, it is even more important for the business school to remember that organisational learning is most effective when companies are involved in all, or most of these. But again, each of the six kinds of learning in the menu *must* correspond to the development and strategy needs of the client. To pursue knowledge down one avenue is a mistake. Just sending executives to open programmes, for instance, will never give sufficient penetration of particular strategic issues, to say nothing of the lack of team development. On the other hand, participation in only an in-company, tailored programme disregards the high value of cross-fertilisation from executives from other companies (and may well create a potential risk of intellectual in-breeding). In sum, the school needs to orchestrate its corporate clients' engagement in all or most of these six learning menu items.

To use an "orchestration" metaphor, we need to ask about the evolving roles of the business school faculty in this tailored learning process. The difference between their new roles as orchestrators, fully integrated members of the value-creation process for the client organisation, and their old roles as professors delivering isolated subjects is nothing less than dramatic. In the modern business school, the borderlines among all the players are blurry. What we are talking about is a team, with some players from the business school, and others from the company, and learning that takes place, more than ever before, through extensive programme design and preparation, far away from the courtly rows of seats in business school auditoriums.

Sadly, some professors will be unable to fit their own agendas to this. The evolutionary pedagogical process says to faculty, "Give up more and more of your time for up-front programme development and co-ordination with colleagues and clients." And the faculty member may think, "but what about time and energy for my research?" Worse yet, from the faculty vantage point, this may all look like an apocalyptic scenario of uncertainty and risk.

Can we, as business school leaders, somehow pull ourselves off the horns of this dilemma? We can try. We can emphasise assignment planning, so that the research agenda can benefit as much as possible from the insights and learning the faculty member gains through heavy pedagogical involvement with cutting-edge clients. For this, we must choose our clients with utmost judiciousness. Since two-way learning is essential, we absolutely must choose stimulating clients. Our faculty can only learn from firms that are riding the leading edge. Another item on our checklist of decision criteria must be "client maturity and sophistication". As it is with advertising agencies — though maybe for different reasons — an outstanding client list will be the fuel for modern business school success. Since planning and delivering the mix of sophisticated pedagogical elements is getting to be so hard, we can push our faculties to develop a strong clinical ability to observe and understand a corporate setting, to remain flexible, to stay open to experimentation and feedback and criticism. We can support our faculty: we can focus our annual performance reviews on whether a faculty member is effective in these more complicated settings of delivery, rather than merely looking at strong individual teaching programme scores under more simplistic, compartmentalised pedagogical contexts. The crux, in the end, however, is that the faculty member himself becomes convinced that there is more for him to take than to give when working adaptively with learning partners. This may mean somewhat different research outputs for him, but neither less relevant, nor less rewarding. About this, the faculty member must be convinced.

Chapter 4

Tailored Delivery for Client Firms and Individual Executives: The Examples of IMD and Wharton's Lauder Institute

Executive Summary

How can a business school provide relevant corporate learning by serving as a learning partner? How would a "real world" business school learning partner model look? IMD's four-part cross model of learning partnerships with individual clients and firms serves as a case in point, with examples of successes and failures. The chapter includes specific examples from each of the four parts of the "cross model": open programmes *(for individuals),* in-company programmes, tailored research, *and* discovery events. *Practical lessons are also drawn from the experiences of Wharton's Lauder Institute.*

If you accept that firms *must* be involved in building their own human capital, if you accept that the business school can act as a catalyst to start a "learning reaction" in a client firm, stirring it to explore, analyse and develop itself, and eventually create a long-term learning partnership; if you accept that the school can therefore deliver relevant learning programmes, built around the firms critical success factors, benchmarking research, and a variety of rich learning experiences for executives, with continual assessment, meeting both the needs of individual managers and entire organisations, then perhaps the most relevant question to ask at this point is: How can the business school manage all the requirements discussed in the previous chapters? How can the school, *in practice*, tailor its research activities and the delivery of its learning programmes to meet all its clients' needs — both the executive participant and the corporate learning partner? How can it become something akin to a learning centre and resource rather than a provider of standard solutions? In other words how can the business school put into "real world" practice all the ideas introduced so far? At the risk of repeating myself on several key points, I would interject at this point that, after all my years as a consultant, academic, and business school administrator, I remain convinced that a firm must be directly involved in building its own human capital. It cannot afford to abnegate this responsibility: it cannot outsource decisions about what is good for its people to a consultant or even to an institute of management education, say, a business school like IMD. Organisational learning is an important investment: it must have a place on the CEO's agenda. Nevertheless, the business school can support the firm by acting as a catalyst in an ongoing partnership, (though unlike in a chemical reaction, the business school will not remain unchanged and, we hope, not be discarded when it ends). The business school starts a "learning reaction". It stirs the client to think about its strategy and its needs more objectively, and launches it down a path of self-exploration, analysis and development. The school challenges un-realistic self-referencing patterns. It helps executives identify issues they might miss, if unquestioned. And it points out organisational issues that need to be redressed. The selection of the right catalyst should be based on compatible "chemistry" — mutual trust and respect, and dedication to a long-term relation-ship. A "one-off partnership" is an oxymoron — it is bound to fail.

But starting the reaction is not enough, as I have pointed out. The right busi-ness school will have the competencies to delineate specific learning programmes that meet the company's needs, link the client firm with other companies for benchmarking discussions, which of course, requires a high degree of academic professionalism. So does the delivery of unbiased research. The business school thus needs to be able to deliver bad news, and have the breadth to cover most aspects of the client's ensuing reaction which no individual professional or consultant can offer.

But even breadth isn't enough. The school must be able to generate organ-isational learning around the most likely critical success factors for each company, as suggested in the previous chapter. Progress must be continuously assessed, and where possible, measured, for both individual and organisational learning.

Clearly then, management education institutes of the future, such as business schools, can play a significant role in this learning process, but only if they meet the increasing demands of companies while also continuing to cater to the indi-vidual needs of managers. For this, business schools will have to step back into the turbulent waters of the real world of everyday business.

The best way to answer the question is first to conceive of a menu that caters to individuals, then apply that menu more widely, for the firm. As noted in the previous chapter, at IMD, we speak of creating "learning menus", and in the context of the dynamic business school, this figure of speech seems particularly appropriate.

In the next part of the book, IMD's models of learning partnerships with both firms and individuals will serve as examples of how the dynamic business can meet the vision and widely-ranging expectations of its clients. We will also look at the experiences of the Lauder Institute, the Wharton School's International MBA initiative. Various ways the school can create learning models will be considered. Understanding the models as they apply to individual participants and firms will help you make more sense of the examples of tailored delivery for firms provided later, where we give a number of examples of both successful and not-so-successful tailored delivery, both for executives and for "in-company" partners. We will also look at two highly successful "tailored delivery" models for individuals. An example of tailored research that IMD delivered to a multi-national firm brings the more theoretic discussion so far down to the level of application. For busy practitioner readers, a number of teaching innovations that have come out of IMD's efforts to deliver custom-tailored programmes to companies round out the examples.

Tailored Delivery for Learning Partners

At IMD, we apply the theory of learning partnerships outlined in the last chapter to the delivery of executive programmes and research for our corporate clients. Throughout this book, you will find references to "in-company" programmes. IMD created such programmes for more than 30 leading companies in 2001. In this chapter, you will learn more about how we ran them and why they worked.

The answer to the question of how we run our portfolio of executive programmes for a given learning partner lies in two words: "cross model", an example of which appears in Figure 4.2, later in this chapter in the Nestlé example. We also use what we call the "learning menu" as a way to think about how a company working with us should avail themselves of our various programmes. As we have seen, this cross model comprises four kinds of programmes:

1) Open programmes
2) In-company programmes
3) Tailored research
4) Discovery events.

It should be clear from the outset that our use of the cross model rests on the assumption that an "outside catalyst" — in this case, IMD, though it could be any business school — can at best help a learning partner company draw up its own "learning menu". The company needs to provide the "proactive" decision impetus for its own learning, however. A good way to understand the four main elements of our cross model is perhaps to consider examples, the focus of the next section.

By way of introduction, we shall return once more to the examples of successful open programmes: IMD's *Building on Talent* (BOT),[1] a programme for relatively young participants, and *Orchestrating Winning Performance* (OWP),[2] an extremely successful, recent innovation. Of course, not all open programmes work; some need to be scratched off the menu. It is also worth considering the fate of two such unsuccessful IMD programmes — *Doing Business in China* and *General Management for Banks and Financial Institutions*.

Tailored research offers a wealth of opportunity for company learning. One of the tasks of the dynamic business school is to create a tailored research agenda. Two powerful examples follow. Faculty at the Wurster Research Institute of the Wharton School has been doing research aimed at better understanding the international firm. And IMD's Manufacturing 2000 and CSM research projects are developing research that explores the restructuring needs of manufacturing firms. Case research completes the research agenda. IMD's case research work with Nestlé is a memorable example.

IMD's so-called discovery events bring the latest research to participating learning partner companies. They complement the other three components of our cross model. Every year, we run "research briefings" for the "Partners" and "Business Associate" members of our formal learning network. Judging by its success, the discovery event seems to be harbinger of new, successful way to disseminate research, and for members to benefit among themselves from "live" benchmarking of best managerial practice.

The challenge for IMD, for any modern business school, is to help the corporate client build each of these four types of learning — open programmes, in-company programmes, tailored research, and discovery events — into an overall menu. Working with IMD, Nestlé is perhaps the best example of an IMD corporate client that created such an effective portfolio from our "menu". How we did it is a lesson for every business school.

Open Programmes: Building on Talent

IMD's *Building on Talent* (BOT) programme targets relatively young executives, say, in their late 20s to early 30s. Typically, after an initial basic university education and two to three years of practice, they come to BOT for a general management update. BOT is for executives who are so active in business that they cannot pursue a full-time MBA. The programme has a novel structure. Students learn in class at IMD and at a distance over the Internet. They spend the first two weeks of the programme at IMD. Then, for three months, they use distance learning to work on individual projects. Finally, the participants meet for one more week at IMD. The activities at IMD also make heavy use of computer-based support.

The company that typically sends someone to BOT is growing fast, and is relying heavily on hiring relatively young executives. These young managers have little formal business experience. The company needs to create a wider, more formal understanding of general management among the younger recruits. BOT provides exactly that: a "vitamin pill", or crash course in general management. Normally, sending young recruits to BOT alone is insufficient. Companies need to send their people on other, follow-up open programmes later. IMD's ten-week *Programme for Executive Development* (PED) is one good example. Companies that are heavy users of BOT typically have in-house formal training as a follow-up, and thus create their own culture.

Open Programmes: Orchestrating Winning Performance

Orchestrating Winning Performance (OWP) programme was initiated at IMD in 1995. At the time, it was a fairly radical innovation. The entire faculty took part (and still do). Normally, smaller groups of faculty members deliver IMD's open programmes, but we wanted to offer our entire spectrum of capabilities, the collective management expertise of our entire faculty, in one intensive programme. The original aim of OWP was simple: over six days, including a working weekend, teach busy, individual executives, as well as executive teams, the latest management practice.

We wanted to heighten awareness in the market of IMD's full range of capabilities. But not only that. We believed that a real commercial need existed in the marketplace. Countless harried executives face the risk of "flattening out". We were convinced that they would invest gladly in the equivalent of a vitamin pill of the latest state-of-the-art management ideas. We assumed that these busy executives would want a lot of flexibility to tailor-make their learning to their personal needs. Experience has proved us right: since its first run with around 100 participants, each yearly OWP has drawn more and more participants, and had more than 400 paying executives in 2001.

OWP is organised in topical "streams" of learning. Participants choose from a wide palette of state-of-the-art management concerns to match their own learning needs. But this creates massive logistical challenges (Figure 4.1 gives

OWP MORNING SCHEDULE

STREAMS

	Wednesday	Thursday	Friday	Saturday	Sunday	Monday
08:30	08:00 INTRODUCTION		STRATEGIC APPROACHES & PROCESS FOR THE NEW MILLENIUM – *Jan Kubes*			
	HOW MANAGERS LEARN		"Lessons from Evolution Strategies: The Age of Temporary Advantage"			
			"Visioning, a Leadership Tool to Align Everybody Behind Strategy"			
			"Integrating Strategy and Knowledge Management = Growth and Profits"			
			"Building Intellectual and Emotional Commitment"			
09:30			"Corporate Diplomacy: a Strategy for Sustainable Growth"			
10:00			LEADING ACROSS CULTURES AND SPACE			
			BEYOND THE "E" : BACK TO BASICS			
			VENTURING FOR GROWTH			
			ASIA IN THE EARLY 21st CENTURY: OPPORTUNITIES & CHALLENGES			
			ACCELERATING INTERNAL GROWTH: GUIDING ENTREPRENEURSHIP & LEADING CHANGE			
			IMPLEMENTING ACQUISITIONS & ALLIANCES			
			MINING THE PROFIT IN YOUR PROCESSES AND SUPPLY CHAINS			
12:30	lunch	lunch	lunch	lunch	lunch	lunch

Left stream label (08:30): **Strategic Approaches & Process for the New Millenium**

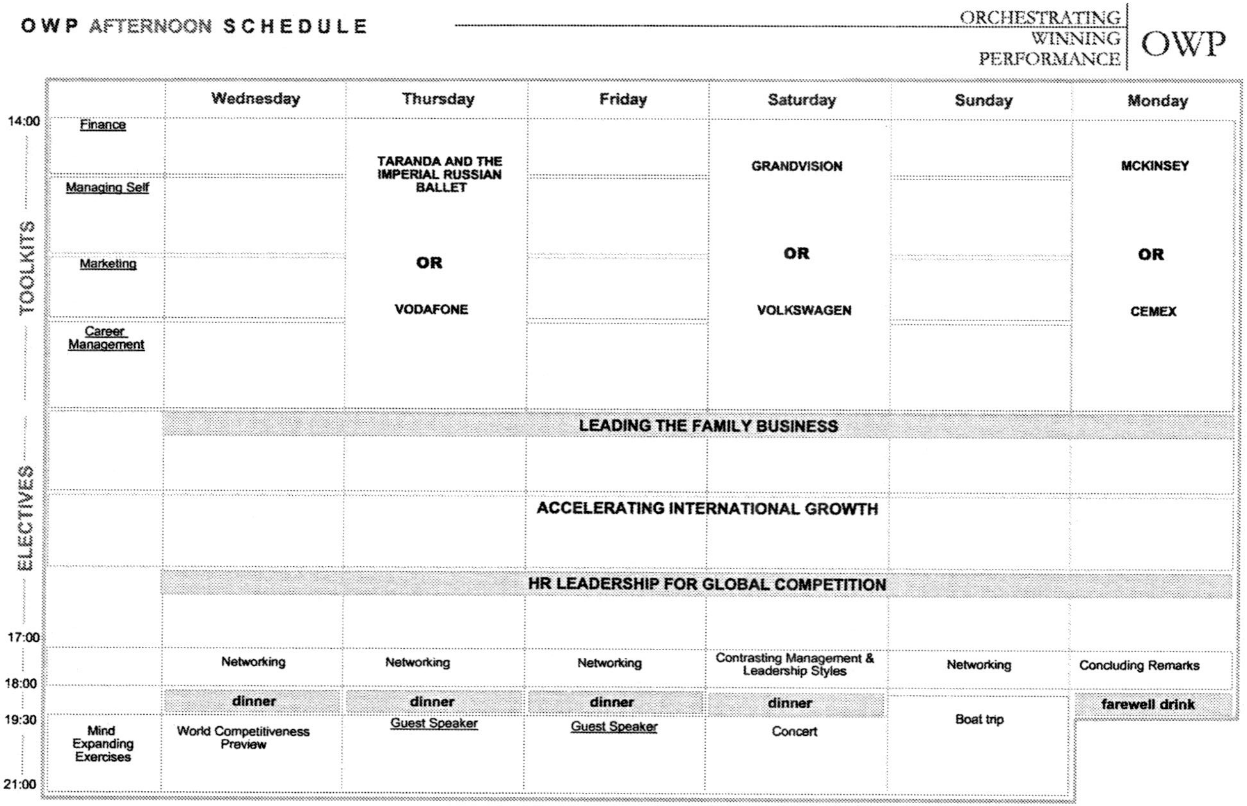

Figure 4.1: IMD's *Orchestrating Winning Performance* block diagram.

the "block diagram" for OWP).[3] To find room for the plenary events a special tent had to be erected. In addition, all of IMD's classrooms were used for parallel stream sessions, case discussions and "tool kit" sessions (to learn the latest "how to's"). Further, all of IMD's 45 study rooms were assigned to study groups.

Above and beyond the difficulty of scheduling the event is the challenge of getting the *entire* faculty to work as a team. This involves co-ordination of materials within each stream and among streams, above all. Many faculty members also sit in at classes given by colleagues, further manifesting the team-driven tone of OWP. At the same time, over the full six days, *teams* of executives from the same organisation work on common problems. This involves plenary learning, with a large, eclectic network of executives from all over the world to learn from, and learning in normal class settings and study groups.

Two Unsuccessful Open Programmes

Since our clients normally come to our campus in Lausanne, and since we work to create an image of IMD as a global meeting place, we bring large groups of students from all nationalities together with a very international faculty. Our academic value creation depends on the global network of student and faculty team all being in close proximity, which encourages open dialogue and debate. Offering programmes away from IMD comes with a high price: it takes faculty colleagues away from each other, and the opportunity for rich networking learning inherent in the internationalism of a full student body is missed.

During the 1990s, IMD ran two short residential programmes in the People's Republic of China. Despite the fact that the programmes were off campus, we were convinced that we should support management development there. And besides, IMD's faculty would learn more about business in China.

The programme did not live up to expectations. We abandoned it after three years of modifications that failed to propel it off the ground. The programme did not deliver a new enough offering to the clients, one that would have served them in a fundamentally new way. There were already many offerings in China, and in the end we did not see a unique opportunity. Thus, it was hard for participants to see why they should take IMD's programme, instead of one of the other good ones. The participants did not experience the "global meeting place effect" from the networked learning at IMD.

In another memorable disappointment, IMD's programme for general management training for the financial service sector institutions — *Performing in the New Financial Services* — ran for two years and died in 1997. We tried to offer a course that covered key general management issues for banks, insurance companies, and other financial service organisations. We made a special effort to build in action learning; we invited a number of not-directly-competing financial service institutions.

So that a nucleus of teams from each company would be present, we asked each institution to bring a minimum of participants. We put "live" management issues at the centre of discussion. The very fact that all the participants came from the same industry and could thus identify themselves with these real-life problems did, of course, make the learning far more compelling. Contributions from each participant arguably led to more relevant learning by the others, since they were all working in similar contexts. But this stressed both participants and faculty — they were dealing with issues of potential, competitive conflict.

The financial services sector programme did not work out as expected. We at IMD need to acknowledge that we do not have an established reputation and deep knowledge base in finance and banking. Perhaps the market sensed this, and therefore gave us too little response. It was, above all, hard to get corporations to send *teams* of senior executives for a relatively long period of time. And the clients found it hard to accommodate the relatively complex design of the programme, which had classes meeting over many weeks, with spaces between. Clearly, what the market needed was not what IMD thought it needed.

Open programmes need to meet real market needs. They need to fit into certain learning need niches in learning partner companies. We deliberately chose some programmes where the aims of the particular programme and the identifiable learning needs in the learning partner company were easy to match (BOT and OWP). But we also created two programmes where the aims and learning needs were too weak a match. The lesson for the business school is this: you cannot simply design and deliver open programmes; you have to find a definable niche, and fulfil specific needs in the learning partner organisation. And you must be able to come with an unquestionable competence. Often it can be tough to find and make this match in practice.

In-Company Programmes: Norsk Hydro

Norsk Hydro conceived of its in-company programme with IMD as a way to speed up decision making around projects. One of the objectives of the programme was to develop better working teams for making faster decisions in complex settings. The company wanted to focus on projects that required financial resources and that might need the involvement of a cross-functional group of executives from various parts of the Norsk Hydro global organisation.

IMD delivered eight one-week programmes. From 1994 to 1997, a total of 289 Norsk Hydro executives attended, in groups. These programmes emphasised action learning. Top management identified 44 key questions and controversial issues for the participants to work on. As a result of the action-learning programme, the company decided to pursue certain business opportunities related to 22 of the 44 issues. The company also decided to implement 12 decisions, put four projects under ongoing consideration and eventually rejected six.

To start the Norsk Hydro programme, IMD organised a two-day, pre-meeting sequence at the headquarters in Oslo. During these sessions, the company's top management listed specific problems for the participants in the programme. Keeping in mind that most participants came from different parts of Norsk Hydro, we were careful to agree on a process that would allow both parties to learn from each other. To ensure a more profitable overall learning experience, part of this learning process agreement included a commitment from all parties to look at how groups work together. Here are some examples of typical projects:

- Power and Gas opportunities in Poland;
- Recycling of aluminium;
- Market for aluminium in the road transport business in Europe;
- Plantation forestry in Latin America;
- Business opportunities in Southern Africa;
- Marketing of caustic soda;
- Strategic challenge of seafood.

The second phase was a five-day programme sequence at IMD in Lausanne. Participants attended various industry analysis lectures and worked on relevant case studies in the mornings. During the afternoons and evenings, they worked on the various specific projects under tutorial support from the faculty. On the last day, the participants gave a trial presentation of each project, and their classmates critiqued them.

A meeting in Oslo, lasting a day and a half, followed. Participants presented each of the projects to senior management, who made decisions whether to go ahead with the recommendations relatively soon thereafter. All involved viewed interaction with top management as a key feature of the programme. It should be pointed out that before and after the Lausanne gathering, participants also communicated and worked on their projects over the Internet.

The participants represented a mix of relatively senior, established executives and somewhat less experienced, high-talent candidates (who thus got visibility among top management). Top management got a better feel for the talent pool of executives that went well beyond the narrow band of executives top management normally met via the formal reporting structures.

In the case of Norsk Hydro, the action-learning process thus also entailed lower echelon executives presenting options and recommendations to top management. This was rare at the company. It represented a clear signal from top management that the projects were important; of course, top management had identified the projects. This lent the action learning a weight it otherwise would not have had.

Did the programme meet Norsk Hydro's specific needs? I think so. It strengthened the company's ability to deal with major new projects, above all, to achieve speed in conceptualisation, analysis and decision making. Executives came together in more global working teams. Participants came away with general management concepts to provide a common frame of reference. As expected, the feedback from the participants was very positive. More gratifying, however, was the fact that Norsk Hydro decided to pursue a total of 12 projects out of the 22 that had been seriously considered. The fact that the learning approach in this action-oriented tailored programme led to actual decisions, one way or another, in more than 80 percent of the cases, was in my opinion also a good indication of the programme's success.

In-Company Programmes: Norsk Hydro Once More

Norsk Hydro and IMD designed a series of annual programmes to provide a better understanding of how Norsk Hydro should bring its global top management group more closely together. Partly this was done by introducing various strategic development challenges for discussion among this large cross section of executives from various business units of this multidivisional company. At the centre was a single, vital question: who are the "customers"? The answer was the key to enhancing more profitable business growth. By grappling with the questions, Norsk Hydro was able to identify some customers, along with new ways to serve them. Other customers turned out to be more elusive, and far less clearly identifiable; the company might well have been dealing with intermediaries, not customers. Some customers were external; some came from within Norsk Hydro itself. The outcome of the work with IMD was a better understanding for Norsk Hydro of what business opportunities existed, and a sharper focus on revenue-generating strategies.

The programme looked like this: a total of around 90 executives came together for four days to deal with these issues. The group included the top 40 members of Hydro's leadership, including division heads, around 20 senior staff, and a group of 30 "young talents". The programme looked in many ways like OWP. Each day started with a common session on the various aspects of seeking business opportunities and market orientation. After that, parallel streams dealt with more specific aspects of handling this challenge, including developing a more business- and market-oriented R&D organisation, a market-oriented business outlook, focusing on key synergies, and a market-oriented R&D-driven process, focusing on cross-divisional R&D initiatives. The afternoons were given over to in-depth group discussions on how to serve various market segments better by focusing more tightly. Finally, senior executives from leading corporations within related industries gave live "benchmarking" examples.

During the last day, members of the top executive team summarised each of the morning "streams". After that, the same group of senior corporate executives recapped the various afternoon discussions. These summaries culminated in a final discussion of what the various strategic options at Norsk Hydro would mean, and the next steps the company would take.

This tailored programme had to be relatively short, given that almost all of the top membership of the company participated, including the CEO and the entire executive committee. Bringing such a core group of 90 executives together is no mean feat. It represents both strong commitment and tangible risk. But the benefits overrode the disadvantages: the broad participation developed not only a clearer strategic focus, but also a better team spirit and common understanding among the participants.

A Third Norsk Hydro In-Company Programme

The top management of Norsk Hydro continues to be concerned about strengthening the company's innovation process. Top management wanted to find ways to generate more creative thinking that would lead to clear business strategies and sound business projects with a creative edge. Consequently IMD and Norsk Hydro created the blueprint for a one-week programme for a "junior talent group" of participants, young executives who had already established themselves and been earmarked as fast trackers, but were still relatively junior. The programme focused heavily on group creative processes, brainstorming, role playing, and analysing specific case examples, etc. It turned a spotlight on creative leaders not only from the field of business, but also from other areas such as politics, global natural discovery expeditions, humanities, etc. IMD developed for the participants a specific set of "questions" that it saw as typical of the process of crafting creative business projects. Each of these questions was dealt with in group sessions, and the groups had to be satisfied that they had handled each one in sufficient depth before moving on to the next one.

Results from this in-company programme were also encouraging. Participants' feedback was strong. Again, the business divisions within Norsk Hydro adopted several of the creative projects identified by the groups, and they later served as the bases for actual business development.

Tailored Research: Manufacturing 2000 *(M2000)*

On the vertical dimension of IMD's cross model is tailored research. A good example is IMD's *Manufacturing 2000* (M2000) project. M2000 was started in 1990, with the aim of developing a better understanding of the manufacturing function in corporations. Our thought was that a more thorough appreciation might better enable manufacturing firms to re-engineer their value chains, including the challenge of outsourcing.

IMD invited 14 companies to become sponsored participants in this research. We expected them to provide specific information about the various research issues that defined the objectives of the project. According to plans, twice a year, a 1–2 day research conference would present the results from the research so far. A "governing board" of members of the M2000 companies would meet 3–4 times annually to work on the list of research questions so that the list remained up to date and relevant. Frequent field research visits to the participating companies took place.

IMD published an interim research output newsletter twice a year. Beyond this, the research output took many forms: traditional articles, several books, as well as a number of cases. This project lasted from 1990 to 1997, and was a good example of how tailored research can meet the needs of specific learning partners, particularly the manufacturing functions' revised role.

Tailored Research: Corporate Sustainability Management *(CSM)*

Our CSM programme focuses on researching the interface between environmental stakeholder issues and the modern corporation.[4] The aim is to find paths toward sustainable development. CSM emphasises the positive business development opportunities associated with compliance with environmental issues. A number of participating companies pay a fee to be part of CSM. Research workshops take place regularly, and provide the latest research results. Here too, the research output comes in the form of interim newsletters, articles, books and cases.

Membership in the network of sponsoring companies for CSM is selected from our Partner and Business Associate network. The rationale is that a business school such as IMD should have only one network for conditioning companies to learning. This single network should emphasise both the pending research initiatives, like IMD's CSM and M2000 projects, and also the dissemination of the latest management thinking. This happens more frequently through our so-called discovery events and subsequent research reports, as well as IMD's publication "Perspective for Managers", which is issued regularly.

Case-Based Research: The Nestlé Case Study Series

In 1995, Nestlé was trying to better understand how to develop a more integrated business approach in the ASEAN countries.[5] The problem was how to provide business integration in a larger region, like the one spanning the five ASEAN countries. IMD contracted to write a series of cases tackling this issue, and other managerial issues. The first case looks at how Nestlé established one designated plant for a particular product line or product family within each of the five ASEAN countries — Singapore, Malaysia, Indonesia, Thailand, and the Philippines — and, for each particular product, sourced the entire region from each of these large, modern plants.

The IMD case goes beyond describing the steps Nestlé took to develop this integrated structure. It opens discussion of some of the key implementation issues associated with the new approach. How can the country managers in each of the five countries co-ordinate their activities relative to the five designated plants? How can Nestlé calculate the bottom-line results for each country, given the fact that the various designated plants also depend on all of the other countries? How can one deal with the fact that some of the products are typically more future-oriented than others, thus perhaps "favouring" the particular host country relative to the other countries? The discussion of these and similar issues in Nestlé's own context further sensitised management to just how "good could be made even better".

Another Nestlé case, developed in 1998, concerned general strategy development in Alcon,[6] a wholly-owned subsidiary of Nestlé. Alcon was the world's market leader in medicines for the eye to support artificial lenses. The case considers how to develop a more global strategy for Alcon. As a starting point, it takes the strong US base and asks how the company can establish a fully global position, working from a strong national base. In effect, it asks: How can the successful business model of the US be transferred to the other markets?

The case provides many insights into the dilemmas of going global. It addresses questions like the following: How will the specific business approach in each market have to be modified to fit local conditions? Is there still a common global dimension? How can Alcon go global while also paying appropriate attention to the domestic business? How can the company find managerial resources to do both international and domestic business? Should Alcon establish more of its manufacturing activities abroad? The discussion around these issues led to considerable added insight into how better to handle the internationalisation strategy at Alcon. A number of executives came to new and broader insights into the more subtle issues lurking behind their strategic choices.

Another good example of tailored research is the pair of case studies dealing with internally generated growth that IMD created for Nestlé. These two case research studies illustrate some of Nestlé's key challenges in developing new business. Consider the Nespresso case.[7] It details the development of a new product for Nestlé, an ingeniously designed automatic coffee machine for the home that uses the equivalent of coffee "bags" for single cups of coffee. The vacuum-packed single portions of ground coffee, together with the specially-designed machine, produce richer coffee, with less waste. Much of Nestlé's revenue came from the sale of the consumable bags. The sale of the initial coffee machine, on the other hand, is more or less a break-even proposition.

For Nestlé this was a new opportunity in many ways. It required radical thinking, supplied by a cross team of people from technology and marketing to identify this new way of serving the customer, and also to establish that this new way would provide a much higher quality experience for the coffee drinker. It also required a lot of cross-organisational work to implement the strategy, including setting up a sales force separate from the one that normally served the coffee-drinking customer with the Nescafé brand.

In the end, the organisational set-up behind Nespresso became fully independent from the rest of Nestlé (this included physical separation); it delivered the Nespresso product from A to Z. The Nespresso case study illustrates how Nestlé perceived and implemented a radically different way of serving the customer. Perhaps the most important insight from this for IMD is how organisational momentum can create true challenges by impeding new innovations. There is simply so much built-up momentum and so many kingdoms within a large complex organisation, that it can be difficult to generate new internal growth.

The second example illustrates the case of developing a new "health oriented" set of products around Nestlé's new probiotic bacteria ingredient, called LC-1.[8] Initially LC-1 was added to yoghurt so that the bacteria could support the effective functioning of the consumer's immune system. Eating LC-1 yoghurt was supposed to strengthen immune resistance. The case illustrates again the huge practical challenges of developing business ideas that go across conventional organisational lines, in this instance involving R&D and various country market organisations. It further illustrates the importance of "buy-in" among existing organisational entities when it comes to implementing a new product, so that it receives the fundamental market support needed. The case finally illustrates the importance of internal entrepreneurs as purveyors of new ideas. Without such internal entrepreneurs as "owners" of the internally generated growth project, new projects may not take hold.

All four Nestlé case studies provide examples of links between the research agenda that IMD is pursuing and the particular strategic issues and needs of a large multinational company. Such case development is a good example of how both a large multinational *and* an academic institution can benefit from research-oriented case development.

What did Nestlé gain from this link? First, Nestlé made use of these four case studies in its own programme offerings at its "Rive-Reine" training centre. The cases represented relevant topical materials that proved very useful for Nestlé in its own internal programmes. Second, the process of developing the cases, which involved an extensive number of executives in in-depth discussions with IMD professors and case writers, led to a more profound understanding of the various key strategic issues at hand within Nestlé. Perhaps most critical were the general insights into critical motivational and career objectives of individuals as these relate to developing new strategic initiatives and implementing change processes to go with such initiatives. Third, by volunteering to provide meaningful scenarios for case studies, the four Nestlé case "stories" improved the company's reputation among companies whose executives analysed and discussed them in IMD's various programmes. Nestlé puts value on being seen as a leading progressive company. The cutting edge cases boosted this image and could arguably help Nestlé attract and retain even better managers.

What did IMD gain from these case developments? Was the considerable expense to IMD in developing these four cases, both in time and money, worth it? The answer is yes, for several reasons. First, to work on specific clinical case studies provides further insights for our professors and case researchers. Such insights are essential to more fully understanding the various topics at hand. Second, to teach complex issues requires in-depth understanding. IMD's professors gained considerable credibility vis-à-vis IMD's executive clients by standing behind these cutting-edge case developments demonstrating factual understanding. Third, state-of-the-art cases, dealing with cutting-edge current issues, are critical for the pedagogical delivery in our programmes. It is critical that the issues at hand be new. Teaching must reflect the latest research "instantly" — there can be no long time delay.

By working with a leading learning partner company on its state-of-the-art problems, management schools like IMD can ensure that their own research initiatives remain relevant. Specifically, IMD has gained invaluable insights for developing strategies in complex organisations; more generally, IMD has gained from dealing with strategy as "learning" and from helping its learning partners — like Nestlé — tackle organisational challenges that co-ordinating across established organisational units entails.

Discovery Events

The last of the four categories in the learning partnership "cross model" are IMD's so-called *discovery events*, or research-based briefings.[9] We run ten to fifteen of them each year. We need to attract a global audience so that the benchmarking among participants will be as rich as possible, so we offer roughly ten at IMD in Lausanne. However, we also run three to five events elsewhere, notably in North America and Asia. Regardless of the location, we want to make it relatively easy for members of the IMD Partner and Business Associate network (to be discussed below) to attend.

One example of such a discovery event would be "Enhancing Internally-generated Growth" (EIG). This briefs participants about ongoing research at IMD into the question of how to stimulate rapid, internally generated, profitable growth. We present various models and look at important aspects of the internally-generated growth process. A key focus is on the search for new opportunities. This also gives participants the chance to discuss the role of the internal entrepreneur and the need to modify internal management processes. Specific case examples from companies such as Nestlé, Ericsson, and Nokia provide rich, relevant illustrative material. Various professors contribute to workshops like this, often outlining complementary viewpoints. But we make a concerted effort to capture the general management implications of even the most specific, detailed research and case discussion. Perhaps most important, companies that participate in the discovery event share their own insights. This means that all participants come away with current benchmarks of effective ways to handle managerial challenges, in this case, to generate growth internally.

Events organised around a management theme are not our only topically-focused discovery events. We also run an annual "Chief Executive Officers' Roundtable". This gathering of chief executives and other senior executives zooms in on especially pertinent subjects for them. One year, for instance, the issue might be how to develop and hold a long-term focus on the strategic commitments of the firm, when stakeholders are clamouring for immediate results. Here several chief executive officers offer their insights. One could represent an established set of businesses in need of renewal, like Hoogovens (now Corus). Another might represent a set of businesses experiencing ultra-rapid growth, but which also need to stay on their ultra-fast track to survive. The Finnish mobile phone manufacturer Nokia is a good example. A third top manager might represent a family business that is free from the short-term stakeholder pressures typical of the publicly-traded firm, but that needs, nevertheless, to keep investing in growth to reach a balance between the long and the short term. Here too, the aim of the workshop would be to alert the participants to best practices. As in all our discovery events, benchmarking is essential.

Since we offer our discovery events exclusively to the members of our Partner and Business Associate network, and since discussion and the ensuing benchmarking is such an essential part of the value of such events, we have to maintain an active membership. But this active membership has a secondary benefit: it stimulates high enrolment in IMD's programmatic activities. Behind all of this is our desire — one that all modern business schools should have — to build a true learning partnership with every client company.

Such a true partnership, however, demands a commitment on both sides. Not all firms are willing to make the same level of commitment, so we recognise two types of membership in our network: "partner" and "business associate". What's the difference? A business associate gets access to the discovery events and qualifies to receive specific in-company tailored programmes. A partner company receives much more. Not only does it receive all the benefits of associate members, but it also gets IMD's assessments of the competence base profile in the company on a regular basis, and direct access to IMD's "library" of knowledge, which includes up-to-date industry analysis files and case analyses.

Putting the Cross Model to Work with Nestlé

It should not be hard to imagine that many of our learning partners use all four elements of our cross model. The trick for both parties is to figure out exactly how and how much of each element should be stitched together into an overall tailored approach. The aim in each case is to satisfy the needs of each company. Figure 4.2 provides an example of this, based on Nestlé.

Nestlé's choice of programmes was partly based on the need to develop a more in-depth general management approach. The cornerstone of Nestlé's programme portfolio at IMD has been our *Programme for Executive Development* (PED).[10] With the extensive use Nestlé has made of PED over the years, it seems fair to argue that the programme has given the company's managers a common "language" and common values. In order to build and maintain its capabilities in specific areas, Nestlé also sends people to our *Managing Corporate Resources*

- Manufacturing 2000 research project – board member
- M2000 meetings 1994
- M2000 meetings 1996
- Alcon case
- MBA project in the Czech Republic (Cokoladovny)
- Cokoladovny, A.S.: Nestlé/Danone Partnership in Czech Confectionery
- Managing Internal Growth: The Story of LC1
- Innovation and Renovation: The Nespresso Story
- Nestlé: Quality on the Boardroom Agenda

CHANGE ACCELERATION

(tailored programs)
2000
- Nestlé Norden Leadership
- Nestlé Zone AMS
- Nestlé Dairy SBU
- Nestlé SBU Ice Cream
- Nestlé SBU Ice Cream
- Nestlé SBU Food Services
2001
- 2 x Nestlé Ice Cream SBU
- Peter Lorange & SBU Innovations
- 4 teams on Venture Booster
 (35 participants)

PERSPECTIVE BROADENING

(public program participants)

1996 = 82	1999 = 83
1997 = 70	2000 = 71
1998 = 55	2001 = 92*

Learning Organization

*not counting Venture Booster program

ONGOING LEARNING DEVELOPMENT

- Nestlé is an IMD Partner
- Discovery Event participants: 1998 = 22   1999 = 45   2000 = 54   2001 = 45
- Business Advisory Council, Nestlé members
- CEO Roundtable, Nestlé participates regularly
- Special Nestlé heads of market Discovery Events = 91 participants

Figure 4.2: The overall activity pattern of the learning menu for Nestlé.

(MCR)[11] and *Breakthrough Programme for Senior Executives* (BPSE)[12] as well as functional, i.e., marketing and manufacturing, programmes.

Nestlé's involvement goes way beyond sending individuals and groups to our open programmes. Over the years they have also requested several tailored programmes. The first was for the bio-engineering division. This special division reports directly to the Chief Executive Officer and works to use Nestlé's bio-engineering capabilities in all its lines of offerings. The tailored programme for this division is meant to provide a better understanding of the major strategic challenges facing the division, and the major implementation choices. The entire senior management of the division participated.

The second tailored programme offered "young talents" from the United Kingdom a chance to develop new product ideas to enhance internally generated growth. While growth at Nestlé until recently has largely come through acquisitions (70 percent comes from acquisitions or derivatives of this), the stated overall aim of the company is to reverse this so that 70 percent of the growth in the future is expected to come from inside. So it made sense for the British Nestlé organisation to run an in-company programme specifically to look for growth opportunities in their market. All along, it has been our hope, and the company's idea, that more of these programmes would help other parts of Nestlé to search for internally generated growth.

Nestlé has another dimension of organisational structure. It has a total of eight strategic business units (SBUs) that support the global business strategies within its core business areas which, in turn, complement the execution of these strategies in three geographic zones that comprise more than 100 market organisations world wide. IMD carried out several tailored workshops for some of these SBUs. They focused on developing global growth strategies. The emphasis here was on identifying business opportunities by bringing together innovative thoughts from the various market places and new technologies and research and development results from Nestlé's R&D and central staff organisations. The focus in these workshops was on further strengthening Nestlé's growth strategies. One outcome was a set of innovation initiatives that involved the entire Nestlé organisation on a renewed basis.

On the research side (the vertical axis of the "cross model"), Nestlé has been an active member of the M2000 programme. Company executives took part in eight research briefings in 1994, seven in 1995, and eight in 1996. A senior member of Nestlé's top management is a member of the M2000 steering committee. IMD has also developed several cases with Nestlé, as noted.

Nestlé also sponsored an IMD MBA consulting project on Cokoladovny, a joint venture with Danone in Czechoslovakia. This project illustrated the challenges of going with a partner — one that is normally a major competitor — in taking over an existing company in an erstwhile Eastern European economy that is going through a transformation to the free market system. This study also illustrates the lack of long-term ability in such "co-operation" among competitors and the final breaking up of the joint venture into separate companies owned by Nestlé and Danone respectively. The MBA consulting project eventually also led to a case on Cokoladovny.[13]

Nestlé makes heavy use of our open programmes and discovery events as well. One look at the figures confirms this regular participation:

1995	1996	1997	1998	1999	2000	2001
83	106	113	77	128	125	137

It seems fair to assume that sending executives supports Nestlé's strategic activities by providing information and inspiration that is relevant "back home".

Participation may also serve as a general "reminder" to Nestlé that initiatives for general progress are in wide supply, and that there are many other companies than the traditional food company competitors Nestlé might be using as measuring sticks for its own progress.

To formulate an effective learning model, the business school needs to develop an overall understanding of the learning partner company. There is no hiding the fact that, to some extent, relatively decentralised levels in the organisational hierarchy of highly decentralised global firms, such as Nestlé, can have a significant impact on the various uses of IMD's offerings. Country managers, for instance, typically nominate their participants to the PED Programme. Nevertheless, it is the senior HR executives, working with a client manager from IMD, who plan Nestlé's total activities with IMD. Naturally, this planning de facto takes into account how effective the company's partnership with IMD has been, and how satisfied the participants are with the competence development they get on our campus in Lausanne.

The Nestlé example illustrates how an integrated, company-specific learning process can look. It shows how the learning agenda can be linked to the company's strategic human competence needs. And it supports one of the hypotheses on which our partnerships rest, namely that the value of a firm's human capital will increase if the partnership directly serves the company's *strategic* needs.

IMD's Portfolio of Executive Programmes

Partnerships with client firms are crucial to the success of any business school, but tailored programmes for individual executives — like IMD's MBA programme and Executive MBA programme, as well as the customised MBA programme at the Lauder Institute of the Wharton School — must also be part of the palette of offerings. The aim of such programmes will be similar to the aim of programmes for firms, namely, to prepare executives to meet the specific needs and challenges of competitive executives on the global scene. The question the business school needs to answer is how it can best serve these individual learners when their needs are far more specific than any generic, open programme can offer. The IMD Executive MBA programme (EMBA) and the Lauder MBA are two open programmes that students can shape to meet their unique career and management needs.

IMD's Executive MBA Programme (EMBA)

IMD has always emphasised its MBA programme for individual students. The programme requires individual students to be at IMD for one calendar year. Some highly qualified students find it difficult or impossible to be away from their work for such a long time. Should there be an MBA for working managers, or should they be "deprived" of a master's degree? At IMD, we believe in life-long learning. Our response to this manager's bind is to offer a 19-week Executive MBA programme (we call it the EMBA),[14] complemented by extensive individual distance learning, Internet-based education.

The programme starts with the participation in our *Programme for Executive Development* (PED), a ten-week general management programme that is essentially a condensed classical MBA programme. Before coming to PED, our EMBA participants must familiarise themselves with the basics of accounting, via distance learning. The rest they pick up at IMD.

After successfully completing our PED, in the year following, our EMBA candidates complete a series of modules. The majority of these modules are based on experiential learning, where the candidates are back at the office using their companies as a "laboratory". Other on-campus modules focus on further deepening general management skills learned in PED. The remaining modules are three intense one-week learning experiences in the form of discovery expeditions away from IMD and are essentially hands-on explorations of three regions. The first is in the Silicon Valley on the US west coast, where entrepreneurial, ultra-rapid growth based on high technology is the topic under discussion. Participants look at the role of start-ups and consider how hi-tech firms grow. The second learning event takes place in Shanghai. It deals with doing business in an emerging market, in this case China. Figuring out entry strategies, developing sustainable business coverage in light of the needs for realistic distribution, making sure that business can be sustained from a margin point of view — these are among the key issues in the second week. Last, the EMBA participants go to Dublin, Ireland, where they consider European entrepreneurship, the role of hi-tech in Europe, and how groups of small, networked, niche businesses have managed to succeed in high-margin, niche markets. Throughout their study trips, participants apply what they learn to the work they do in their own businesses, and look for applications to their projects, a major requirement of the EMBA.

A considerable amount of learning takes place over the Internet as the students work together on a series of major projects. For example, a student who works in a private bank might use frameworks and methodologies presented as part of the marketing project. He may spend time talking with and interviewing customers to identify service or product challenges and then, back at the office, brainstorm with colleagues to find creative solutions to those challenges. During this time, IMD supports the learning with materials (resources), direct feedback and one-on-one mentoring with faculty and research associates.

All told, this combination of learning at IMD, off-campus discovery expeditions, and learning on one's own, requires the same amount of work as a full-time MBA. But, it allows the participants to take the programme while still at their jobs. And, it allows the participants to tailor the programme to their own needs to a considerable extent, nonetheless due to the linking of learning to their job settings.

Needless to say, while the EMBA is for individuals, it assumes that each participant's company agrees to the enrolment. Employer support is critical. It ensures not only that students will have the time needed to do their studies, keeping in mind that they will still have to have enough time and energy to manage both work and school, but also that they will be allowed to use company-specific problems and issues for their EMBA assignments.

The Lauder Institute: Successful Tailoring for Individual Students

The Wharton School started to consider what later became the Lauder Institute when it realised that top-notch candidates for *international* management positions could not be trained in a traditional MBA programme. At the time, Wharton's MBA programme appeared to be too domestic, too American to be a suitable vehicle for educating young executives to become truly effective in an international context. From this awareness came the Lauder Institute. To prepare to be better international managers, students took not only an MBA with a specific international focus, but also an MA degree in a particular language, offered through the School of Arts and Sciences at the University of Pennsylvania.

From a top-down institutional strategic viewpoint, the presence of the Institute highlighted a dilemma: should innovation take place as part of the established structure, or should it borrow relevant elements from the established structure and put them together in a more free-standing way? More specifically, could Wharton find or make "the space" for a different type of academic value creation? Russell Palmer, then Wharton's Dean, who himself had broad international managerial experience, saw the Lauder Institute as a top priority for Wharton. Palmer wanted to internationalise Wharton as a whole. The problem was, how could Wharton avoid having the Lauder Institute become just another diversion? Would the establishment of Lauder lead to a slow-down of the agenda to internationalise Wharton itself? Or, could the innovations pioneered at Lauder somehow become forerunners of the more broad-based internationalisation?

The outcome was a memorable example of cross-fertilisation: Wharton eventually adopted many of the innovations Lauder had initially established, and incorporated them into its own mainstream MBA programme. Prime examples were the international components of the various functional programmes, first developed at Lauder. A number of new Wharton courses had their trial runs at Lauder, and Lauder initiatives attracted new faculty. Simply put, Lauder spearheaded innovation, and Wharton co-opted it. Innovation at Lauder boosted Wharton's continuing internationalisation.

This, however, created a stressful situation inside the Lauder Institute, since its initial "competitive edge" gradually eroded. Why take Lauder's MBA programme when — after some time — you could get more or less the same from Wharton's main MBA programme? The upshot was this: Lauder's mission would be based on continuing innovation. To stay ahead, it would work to spearhead novel academic value-creating activities. Gradually, the Wharton community began to better understand the benefits of Lauder's teaching-based, cross-disciplinary approach. New programmes could easily be run in Lauder's small, flexible, cross-disciplinary structure, and then, if successful, adopted more largely at Wharton, and elsewhere at the University of Pennsylvania.

It is thus interesting to see that academic programme innovation is often easier to carry out in small organisational entities, where there is much less cross-personal co-ordination involved than would be the case between large organisational units. The Lauder programme, consisting of one cohort unit, would be excellent for such innovation, with a designated faculty team committed to it. When the benefits of given innovations are then seen by the larger organisational entity, i.e., Wharton's MBA programme in this case, innovation is also easier to carry out. A successful example, "in the small", makes it easier to innovate "in the large". Still the very co-ordination among a larger number of faculty members, offering several parallel streams of each given course along several cohort groups does, of course, represent a formidable challenge to innovation.

It should be noticed that this smallness of an MBA programme in general might be a critical prerequisite to aggressive innovation. Such is the case of IMD's MBA programme, where we have only one cohort with 80 students. It would be much harder to innovate if the MBA programme were larger, with several cohorts taking courses in parallel. While such outstanding MBA schools as the Harvard Business School, Wharton and Insead are well known for their innovation activities, major programmatic overhauls are typically much harder to undertake there because of the heavy burden of co-ordination between the many parallel sections and their professors. Typically, major overhauls take place at these large schools at certain intervals, with task forces leading the way. The ongoing innovation, setting innovative stone upon innovative stone, on the other hand, can more easily take place in small MBA programme contexts, such as IMD, the Tuck School, Dartmouth College and other small, elite programmes.

Lauder Lessons: Institutional Energy Needed for Innovation

What is the important lesson in the Lauder experience for the modern business school? To create innovation in well-established, successful academic pro-grammes, those responsible should perhaps start with small, "experimental" innovations before undertaking mainstream revisions across the board. Sweeping innovation typically takes so much energy and so many resources that it at times represents too considerable a risk.

Indeed, the biggest challenge with the Lauder Institute experience was its massive drain on the institute's energy. Individual faculty members from across a large sprawling university had to be brought together. The time required for planning and co-ordination was extensive. This was made even more difficult by the fact that faculty members belonged formally to different schools and academic departments from all over the university. Lauder needs the equivalent of "volunteers". If a particular faculty member did not want to participate after a while, so be it — the consequences were mild. Thus, fluidity in the composi-tion of the faculty team became a problem, for which the only solution was considerable energy and resources devoted to finding new faculty. There was a positive side, however. New faculty infused the programme with new ideas, and the faculty who stayed were deeply committed.

Clearly, then, establishing cross-functional matrix initiatives, whether in a teaching programme, as in the case of the Lauder Institute, or in research insti-tutes, such as the Wurster Centre for International Research, implies a substantial infusion of the institution's energy. The school can justify the energy drain only if the new initiatives support major, institution-wide portfolio-based agenda priorities. The risk always exists that such initiatives might weaken the traditional academic programmes — faculty may be distracted, their energy deflected from the ongoing upgrading of core programmes. But it is a fact that organisational fluidity — even bordering on chaos — goes together with innovation. And energy must be infused to manage it. It is exactly in such situations that a top-down strategic vision needs to inform cross-disciplinary innovation on a small scale, in such a way that it does not disrupt, but rather bolsters the institution's overall academic value creation.

Lauder Lessons: Impact on Faculty

Let us shift our lens from the impact of such innovation in the design of programmes for individuals to its impact on faculty. The Lauder Institute represented an interesting vehicle to teaching innovation by adding new international dimensions to extant programmes. The Institute devoted resources — time and money — to develop new teaching materials with an international focus. It recruited a number of very interesting students from all over the world. This created a stimulating teaching atmosphere for the faculty. As such, the faculty's individual academic value-creation agendas got tangible reinforcement.

At the same time, there were difficulties. Faculty incentives put on the excellence of teaching at the University of Pennsylvania were relatively minor. The major emphasis of incentives at this university, including the Wharton School, was demonstrated academic research excellence, primarily judged through the publishing of refereed articles. As such, the "risk" of participating in teaching activities outside of the classical functional departmental structure in which one would be judged, was indeed real.

The Lauder Institute brought together a diverse group of interested faculty members from all over the university, each committed to teaching international management. For instance, a dialogue ensued between strategy professors, whose base was the Wharton School, and professional colleagues from the rest of the university, such as specialists in cultural and social science of particular geographic areas, economists with regional expertise, and members of the language faculty, who brought expertise for the same geographic regions. For Wharton, this was a unique mix. The various teachers found their work with colleagues from other academic disciplines and their teaching assignments highly stimulating.

A basic hurdle here was to ensure a degree of practical pedagogical compatibility among the various team members. In some instances, compatibility was not feasible. Some of the language professors from the School of Arts and Sciences, while being specialists in literature analysis, language structure analysis, and grammatical structure research, were not as interested in, nor particularly useful in the actual teaching of effective oral business communication. Being part of this teaching initiative made them uncomfortable. So Lauder recruited additional freelance language instructors who could teach foreign languages more effectively to practitioners. In this case it was possible to adjust the composition of the faculty team to improve teaching compatibility. But this adjustment isn't always so easy. Discipline-based biases may hamper efforts to put together effective cross-functional teams.

Lauder Lessons: A Sub-Optimal Steering Model

The Lauder Institute had, for want of a better term, a "formal steering model" that had potentially serious negative impacts. The Institute had its own board, partly from business, partly from the University of Pennsylvania's academic cadres, including the Deans of Wharton and the School of Arts and Sciences. The director reported directly to the University of Pennsylvania's provost. At times, conflicts erupted between the various groupings in the university over who provided what resources and who got what back. At the heart of these conflicts was the implicit — and at times explicit — competitive friction between Lauder and Wharton. This disharmony again took a lot of energy; all too often, the university's top leadership needed to give a considerable amount of attention to resolve it.

Lauder Lessons: Link with the Marketplace

The link with the marketplace was also an issue. Here, Lauder provided a very attractive forum for a number of executives. But this came as no surprise, since the Lauder pedagogical innovations had grown out of the needs expressed by the environment to create a vehicle to train top-notch executive talents to enhance the competitiveness of their organisations globally. Leonard Lauder stated this objective from the outset: train executives who could make their companies world winners. His hope was that many US corporations would take advantage of Lauder and thus that this donation would indirectly strengthen US competitiveness in general.

Lauder Institute's success demonstrates that, with enough resources, sufficient energy, and top leadership vision and support, "radical innovations" in academia are possible. It shows that innovative academic value creation, regardless of rapidity or size, must strengthen the entire academic institution, not just benefit individual faculty members. The danger of innovative initiatives deflecting resources and draining energy from mainstream academic value creation always exists. Designated research centres and teaching programmes are no exception.

The people at the top will have to judge how many and what kind of innovative activities to go for. They will have to ask: How can we reintegrate the results from these pioneering activities into the main part of the academic institution? They will have to pick the appropriate agenda items for innovation centres like Lauder with a particularly critical eye. No matter how many individual students they attract, and no matter how well they prepare those students for the hurdles they will have to clear as global managers, they must be truly central to the mission of the larger institution.

Major innovations in academic institutions can, thus, perhaps best take place when key initiatives are allowed to develop outside the mainstream. Later on, to reap the full, broader benefits from the innovation, one must, however, integrate the "outside" innovations into the larger organisational entity. Considerable energy is needed during both of these innovation phases. Energy is first needed to steer the isolated innovative initiatives clear of the established academic structure and routines. And then, to modify the main organisation's established structures and routines in order to incorporate the innovative thrust, even more energy is needed later on.

Chapter 5

Developing Relevant Competencies

Executive Summary

A business school must be a learning organisation, just like its learning partners. This chapter proposes two models for organisational learning within the business school. These two models influence each other positively, creating a strengthened sense of organisational learning within the dynamic business school. The first model, mapping the learning menu *for each of one's key learning partners, can be extended into looking at how the totality of learning partner inputs might impact the school's learning. The business school can and should learn, partly by being led by the market, and partly by leading the market. The second model involves the school "seeing" new research opportunities on its own, before others, and developing its own resource commitments to actually mine these opportunities. The chapter also looks at several modes of research:* renew, reposition, revitalise, *and* protect and extend. *The chapter shows the critical interplay between the two learning models. It further explores how the school can create a constructive internal dialogue around the tension between the competencies it needs to meet its clients' needs (i.e., the market) and its current competence base, i.e., where it is. The key challenge is to create a constructive internal dialogue between how the school's competence map might look when seen from two sets of lenses, one stemming from the clients (the market), the other stemming from the school's competence base (where it is coming from and where it thus might go).*

To set strategy effectively, which as I have argued entails providing relevant corporate learning — becoming a true learning partner by following the four-step approach outlined in Chapter 3 and illustrated in Chapter 4 — the dynamic business school will have to build its own competencies. It will, like its corporate learning partner, have to build its own intellectual capital. It, too, will have to be a learning organisation. Academic institutions, in order to be market driven, must probably be much more network-oriented vis-à-vis their external stakeholders, much more of what we might call learning organisations. As Rowley *et al.* state:

> the academy now finds itself in the position of not being the generator of a good deal of the knowledge spawned by the information age ... emerging events and activities, which the scholarship of the academy has not created and about which it may be unaware. The challenge is to merge the academy's abilities for knowledge generation and knowledge transfer with what emerges from the technology and tempo of the information age and to accomplish this, in part, by considering the genuine educational needs of new learners. The academy must become a learning organisation, not an organisation of learners. The academy must become a learning organisation, not an organisation of learners. It must also be a knowledge-generating organisation. A learning organisation transforms as it scans, evaluates, and uses information.[1]

For this pursuit, the school needs to follow two models concurrently. In the first, the school maps its own learning by looking at the totality of inputs from its learning partners. This means looking at the totality of requests for open and in-company programmes. It means being led by the market. This perspective will require the school to adapt to emerging patterns in the demands from the market, but also to pick up "weak signals" from the market about what programmes might be needed in the way of research and discovery events. This, of course, amounts to leading the market.

The second model has the school spotting research opportunities on its own, mobilising its resources to mine them, before the competition does. To do this effectively the school can choose among several models of research. I call them renew, reposition, revitalise, and protect and extend. All these research activities are important. It is incumbent on the school, should it truly wish to enhance its intellectual capital, to understand its research challenges and the learning organisation challenges that go with them.

The challenge for the business school as it grapples with the problems that stem from using both models — i.e., looking through two sets of lenses — is to maximise the benefits in their interplay, worry about ensuring that it has the intellectual capabilities to improve its own intellectual capital consistently. And the main challenge, as Chapter 5 shows, will be to create a constructive internal dialogue between how the school's competence map might look when seen through each set of lenses, one that focuses on clients (the market) and the other focusing on the school's competence base (where it is coming from and where it might go).

This dialogue, which can engender constructive friction and recognising delivery gaps, will, in all likelihood, further boost the building-up of relevant, dynamic intellectual capital and, most importantly, school-based organisational learning.

If a business school wants to work with its clients as a learning partner, with relevant open programmes and tailored programmes of all kinds, it, too, has to put learning at the centre of its agenda. A school such as IMD, or any institution that offers its clients open programmes, tailored in-company arrangements, and discovery events, depends on a rich stream of research. That stream will only be as rich as the knowledge, theory and data that flow into it. Seeking, finding and presenting new management material in a variety of forms is often called the "research process", and it rests on the school's firm commitment to discovery. It rests on the commitment of each faculty member, trained through a doctoral programme and on the job, to pursue new ideas, discover new truths, test untried hypotheses, to learn new things.

While trying to manage all this seems laudable, the business school faces two dilemmas. First, it is close to impossible to figure out whether or not "purposeful learning" is going on. What is *purposeful* learning after all? Whether the learning helps develop competencies that will meet the needs of the school's clients is, at best, hard to say, at worst, akin to figuring out the precise effect of the flutter of a butterfly's wings in Sapporo, Japan on the weather in New York. Second, beyond the sum of learning taking place inside each individual, I challenge anyone to argue a priori that purposeful *organisational* learning is going on in any business school. It cannot be easily done.

One way out of the predicament is to ask if the institution can somehow encourage complementary learning processes. By this, I mean asking if the school can find ways both to respect the needs of individual professors to pursue their own learning through their own research, and also to allow, even encourage, purposeful and team learning in various forms. This two-pronged pursuit of knowledge would amount to *organisational learning*. So in the end, the business school faces exactly the same challenges as its major learning partner clients: mastering organisational learning. This is more easily said than done, which may be why so many scholars of school administration claim that academic institutions cannot be managed and throw up their hands. Nevertheless, I believe the business school can manage its own organisational learning.

Managing the Organisation's Learning

Even at typical business schools, ways do exist to encourage shared learning in the various discipline-based academic departments. Colleagues who have backgrounds in the same disciplines and who use the same paradigms and research methodologies work together, sharing insights through discussions, presentations, and working papers. In the best of cases, this leads to joint research projects, which further accelerate discipline-based learning. In many instances, specific teaching programmes flow out of this co-operation, with the various members of a department bringing their latest insights into new functional programmes.

Two brief examples from my own research career serve my point. The first is from my co-operation with Professor Michael Scott-Morton at the Sloan School, MIT, and Sumantra Ghoshal, now at London Business School (then also at Sloan). We were interested in strategic control, i.e., understanding how control could become a vehicle for not only monitoring but even for improving the quality of a particular extant strategy. After considerable research, both conceptual and clinical, and much discussion, our materials eventually became part of the Management Control Processes course at the Sloan School. After further research, teaching and discussion, we produced a small book, *Strategic Control.*[2] Our output flowed out of teamwork centred around a joint disciplinary base. At the Wharton School, I worked with Professor Bala Chakravarthy. We were both interested in strategic planning processes, and did a lot of joint research, stimulated by joint teaching. The basic strategy course at the Wharton School gave us fertile ground for bringing in new results from our joint research and discussions. Together, we wrote *Managing the Strategy Process: A Framework for a Multibusiness Firm,*[3] a book on how to tailor management processes to various settings, both at the corporate and business unit levels. Again, sharing an axiomatic base and belonging to the same academic department facilitated our research collaboration.

This axiomatic, departmental collaboration is not without risk, however; a potential weakness is that it can lead to segmented value creation, particularly from the point of view of students and learning partner firms. Each academic department explores only particular aspects of the business creation process, but no one sees the whole. This segmented perspective is further accentuated by the fact that conflicts between the various disciplinary-based departments — rivalry, disagreement on strategic direction of the school, and so on — may flare up. Go back to the two previous examples, but this time hypothetically. With strategic control work, it is intriguing to think about co-operating with colleagues from other disciplinary areas, such as finance people, when it comes to control at the corporate portfolio level, say, by introducing options theory. Similarly, so far as monitoring control goes, the balanced scorecard research might have been relevant for the logic of our two books. Interestingly, both of these research trends were developed independently of what we were doing, and would probably have led to more relevant findings if integrated into our research. My point is that it is important to have *actual* groups of scholars working together in a cross-disciplinary way to ensure cross-fertilisation *at the act of creation*, not post facto.

In retrospect, it also seems to me that our work on strategic processes might have benefited from a closer co-operation with organisational behaviour scholars, both macro and micro. Macro organisational behaviour research might have added relevant insights about meaningful organisational designs, such as matrices, teams, temporary organisational forms, etc., and thus added a more flexible view of tailoring the process design to the organisational structure, the book's main message. At the micro level, one might have added behavioural implications from incentive schemes. Again, we came up with tailored incentive scheme designs that assume various behavioural reactions. But was this fully representative? It is clear that thicker (more detailed) cross-fertilisation during the period when researchers are conceptualising, rather than merely adding mental appendices later on, is critical for getting improved research results.

Given the fact that the business school may be little more than a collection of loosely autonomous academic departments, it must somehow find a formula for giving its corporate learning partners a meaningful, holistic tailored approach. Each academic department can develop into an independent "fortress" or "kingdom", making it exceedingly difficult for the school as a unified organisation to tailor its efforts to a particular student group or learning partner. It must find a way to break out of the silo world.

Emphasise Curricular Integration

One way of drawing a discipline-based faculty into a working team might be to organise a teaching curriculum with more relative emphasis on integration. The Wharton School did this. It redesigned its entire MBA programme during 1995–96. A high-level cross-departmental task force appointed by the Dean shepherded the redesign, which emphasised a more integrated scheme. It worked to integrate international leadership and business development viewpoints. Teaching happened in modules, and the old autonomous course structure was broken up. After an initial trial period on a small scale, the curriculum for the entire MBA programme was changed as of 1997. Note that the renewing efforts to foster integration carried out by the Lauder Institute might, at least indirectly, have had an impact on this process at the Wharton School. The result of the redesign was not only a better programme from the students' view, but also more complete integration among the faculty members involved. Perhaps this shouldn't surprise, since integration can bring participants from various academic disciplines together in a particular teaching context. Sometimes such integration follows naturally, say, from a request from a learning partner company; sometimes it stems from the need to develop a more integrated programme for individual students, say, in an MBA course.

To get a better grasp on the idea of integration, try thinking about ongoing learning as a *hierarchy* or pyramid of learning activities. Its base would be the fundamental needs for the individual academicians to learn from their own research. This learning would, one hopes, have to be generally relevant to the school's students or clients, too. One layer above the faculty would be the discipline-based organisational learning *among* academicians from the same or closely related departments with shared disciplinary interests. Significant subgroups of students would find output from this second layer relevant. At the top would be the cross-disciplinary learning among faculty from *unrelated* disciplinary departments, who share their knowledge and learning in a particular cross-disciplinary programme. Here the main motivation would likely be to serve customer needs. In a business school, the learning is typically a mix, an *accumulation* of all these kinds of integration, so the more variety in learning contexts, probably the better, since it would ensure that every student or client would be able to find the learning inputs they seek.

Systematic Learning with Partner Companies

The problem with an effort at integration as I have described it is that it is, perhaps, rather haphazard, leaving a great deal to chance, and to the vagaries of shifting individual interests and whims. For instance, there is the risk that inputs from the past would largely shape the competence offerings of the school. And it could then well be the case that the school overlooks, in particular, new, emerging needs. A potentially more powerful type of organisational learning, especially for an executive development-oriented business school, is the systematic learning a business school can gain from mapping the total set of its activities with a learning partner firm. Take a look at Figure 5.1. You will remember it from our previous discussion of the learning menu.

Recall that the school can work with each client firm to determine which of the four types of offerings — open programmes, tailored programmes, research, and/or discovery events — are most appropriate, and in what relative proportions. By considering the various combinations and permutations of all the

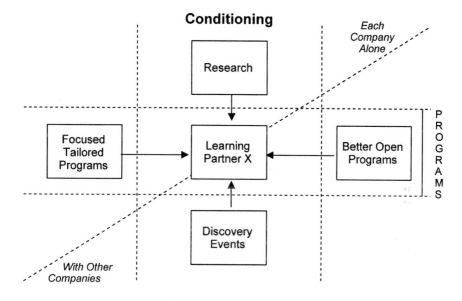

Figure 5.1: The learning menu of an individual firm.

learning activities of all of the partner firms, the business school can learn, over time, more systematically. Let's take a look at how this might work.

As previously stated, the learning partner (here learning partner X) can learn in myriad ways from the school's activities. From the horizontal dimension the school can deliver learning by offering various types of tailored and/or open programmes — and the faculty members involved can also learn! Open or tailored programmes should be selected so that they satisfy the particular needs of the learning partner. By having a good match of topical coverage to the specific needs of the given learning partner's firm, the school increases the likelihood of more engaged, turned-on participants who are willing to bring their specific experiences and challenges to the table. The learning for the faculty member in this case derives from this agenda. On the vertical dimension, the school works to condition the partner organisation to actually learn in complementary ways. Rather than feeding the client specific content, the school helps the client *learn how to learn*. This conditioning can take place by involving the learning partner in specific research (exemplified at the top of the vertical axis), or by engaging the learning partner in sharing experiences through specific benchmarking (the bottom part). The faculty will learn through activities, too, particularly if they deal with strong firms that are tackling relevant issues. Another way to put this is in to say that, in general, a faculty learns by being market driven.

Learning from the research side offers faculty a particular opportunity to be market driving, i.e., to a much larger extent to *lead* the development of new thinking, and proactively bring in the viewpoints of the school's learning partners. Much of the research on internally generated growth, for instance, stems from a proactive view of how to develop further value creation, a view that complements the typical growth — via acquisitions — that we saw prominently driving the bulk of the growth at several leading corporations in the 1980s and 1990s. Several professors at IMD, including me, felt that to lay continued heavy emphasis on acquisition-driven growth, which was so common for many leading multinationals, might in the long run be unsustainable. It seemed to us that the number of acquisition candidates could dwindle and become more and more expensive. This, in our view, would have made acquisition-driven growth less attractive. Further, from a social standpoint, the fundamental creation of new jobs in society, new opportunities for the youth, etc., might be linked to a stronger internally generated growth process in leading firms. The upshot was that IMD developed an extensive research programme on growth, again working with leading learning partners, but not driven by them. The co-operation with the firms kept the research anchored in "reality" and led to a lot of cross-fertilisation of excellent ideas for internally generated growth, thus far existing as depository knowledge here and there inside the various learning partner firms.

Close faculty–client relationships usually lead to the school "learning" as much as the client. This might be particularly the case when the research — and learning — can also be moved forward through participation in a number of discovery events (the box at the bottom of the vertical axis in Figure 5.1). This would not only allow the learning partner to gauge his own position vis-à-vis other leading firms, but also allow the business school to gauge its own knowledge of current practices, and to learn from the participants. The initial insights from research would thus undergo a broader testing and, hence, generate further learning. The internal growth example illustrates this point. The research led to a fruitful two-day discovery event with several presentations and case studies on how to stimulate internally generated growth, which allowed a large, cross-section of 50 executives from some 35 firms to share their views on internally generated growth. Not only did an action-oriented learning process take place for the participants as well as for the faculty members testing out new materials, a valuable real-life benchmarking also took place among various leading executive-practitioners. No doubt, the IMD faculty learned at least as much as the participants. All felt it was a "fair deal".

Learning by Meeting Clients' Needs in Four Complementary Ways

For the business school, there is thus an opportunity to learn from the total pattern of learning activities pursued by (or "with") a given learning partner. Getting the maximum learning out of it will be key, to ensure that the specific needs of a given firm are being addressed, and, of course, that the school is working with a strong firm.

- How then can the school and the client pick a set of programmes that best satisfies the company's needs?
- What, for instance, are the links between companies' needs and open programme design and selection?
- Or, how can the school choose those research programmes that directly meet the needs of the given client?
- How can the school develop research that directly stimulates the learning partner firm to be more open-minded in its approach to meeting its own needs?
- How can the school help the client choose discovery events that will stimulate the learning partner to be open to its own needs?
- How can the school select discovery events in a way that meets the needs of its learning partner as well as possible?
- How can a school actually come up with tailored programmes that provide valuable learning inputs to meet the needs of a given, specific learning partner? (This might thus include a number of issues, such as creating a link between the identified needs of a company and actually designing a programme to meet those needs.)

Answering such questions involves listening to the learning partners' needs as well as providing one's own school-driven vision regarding what the learning partner might need. We can perhaps reduce these many questions to a general one: How can the business school develop its own integrated learning in a way that will address the *total* of the learning needs of a particular client? At the risk of belabouring the obvious, merely posing the questions isn't enough. Any business school worth its salt can learn to ask the right questions. The challenge is to figure out the best possible answers for the client. If you want to serve the client's needs, you've got to look at the four complementary ways already fleshed out: research, discovery events, tailored programmes and open programmes. By learning in these four ways, the school gets itself into a loop of learning: it learns in order to meet client X's needs, applies that learning to ask what client Y needs,

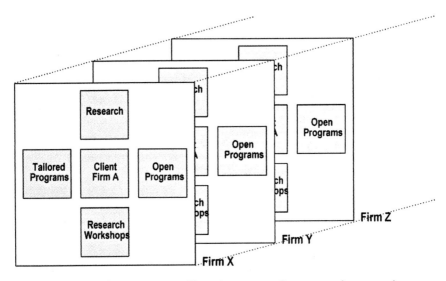

Figure 5.2: The aggregate of learning menus from several corporations.

meets those needs, and applies the new learning to figure out what client Z needs. And so on, back to continuous, organisational learning. Interestingly, the horizontal axis in Figure 5.1 will have a relatively heavier emphasis on adapting to one's learning partner's needs (market driven). In contrast, the vertical axis will have more of an emphasis on how the school should lead the development, ("market driving").

What does this add up to for the business school leadership? It can put together the individual "menus" from all of the major clients, then analyse them for patterns. Figure 5.2 presents this idea graphically.[4] Holding all the menus in its hands, the business school leadership can thus get a more general feel for which key issues leading firms are grappling with, which ones they would like, in particular, to deal with in open programmes, in-company programmes, research initiatives and discovery events/briefings. The trick is to find these more general patterns, much the way you do when you take an IQ test. Though here, the school's "client issues' IQ is being tested". Taking the discussion down one level of specificity — and addressing more practical issues — the question is, how, *specifically*, does the school "look" at the four complementary ways to create learning? How does it actually use the four areas to enhance its own continuous organisational learning? What questions must it ask and what approaches must it take?

Open Programmes

For open programme choices, the school might perhaps look for particular strategic agenda shifts. For instance, is the firm chasing one or two particular aspects of strategy implementation, mobilising people, or competing strategically with information and technology? Are there particular shifts in topics of interest, say, from managing supply chain to attempting to manage demand? Recently, we've seen a growing emphasis on building capabilities to work in teams, even in most of our open programmes. Similarly, the interest in focusing on leadership is rising. What type of teaching methodologies seems to work the best, on-campus or distance learning, case studies or simulation? More specifically, there appear to be five significant differences between the open programmes of the past and today's. These differences have had a profound impact on the types of capabilities the school needs in order to serve its clients' needs.

- In the past, one was primarily focusing on learning on campus; now the demand is more for hybrid learning, partly on campus, partly on the job scene, supported by the now readily available virtual technologies.
- In the past, open programmes were typically somewhat longer; now the emphasis is more on modularised programmes that allow the learners to incorporate more of what they learn on an ongoing basis, back at their own job places, and also allowing them to be more action oriented by drawing on specific job-related projects in their learning.
- In the past, business schools may well have principally emphasised the various functional points of view; now the learning seems to be much more action-driven, more cross-functional, more integrative.
- Previously the emphasis was perhaps more on providing knowledge for the individual-cum-manager; now the emphasis is more on providing knowledge for the team and to the individual-cum-member of a team of managers.
- Some years ago executive programmes tended to emphasise the nuts and bolts of running a business, becoming a highly efficient administrator/manager; now the emphasis is more on how to develop a business, i.e., how to become a better, more inspiring leader.

In-Company Programmes

To design in-company programmes the school has to root out topics of shared interest or insights that more than one client company will value. It may find, for example, a shift in the client companies' interest in leadership processes, as these relate to groups. For example, examining the demands from several of its learning partners, IMD found that all of them were asking how to develop a better capability to implement new growth initiatives. Analysing this further, IMD noted that one of the keys might have to do with developing a more effective capability for having cross-functional, cross-cultural, cross-disciplinary teams implementing new business ideas. These were often virtual teams, with members located around the world. IMD found, for instance, that a number of single companies sought ways to develop more open, change-oriented, "fast culture" so that they could embrace change more proactively.

IMD developed a series of tailored programmes to meet these specific needs of individual learning partners. All had strong common knowledge features along team-based leadership lines. All supported internal cultural change, to allow for a more proactive, "fast" culture. Thus, while each of these programmes was tailored to each individual learning partner, a common knowledge was developed at IMD, focusing on proactive cultural change issues.

Of course, change issues are not the only concerns of learning partners. All companies would probably have an interest in such global management themes, like effective strategies in times of austerity or managing across borders with a more flexible, change-oriented culture. IMD discovered that virtually all its partner firms wanted to develop better synergies among operating units. Many felt that their geographic structure might lead to too little cross-fertilisation across geography, with slow, expensive new product introduction as a result. Others felt that there would be too little cross-fertilisation among business areas, again leading to expensive and slow new business development. IMD thus developed a capability to provide tailored programmes that would, on the one hand, maintain operating effectiveness along geographic or business unit lines, and on the other hand, have a capability to develop more flexible business initiatives through co-ordinated research, experimenting through pilot marketing, and scale-ups, typically across the operating organisational units for more effective synergies. The challenge for IMD is to develop capabilities that might allow us to better meet these demand trends.

Research and Research Discovery Events/Workshops

The business school should also take a close look at its accumulated learning from its research interventions with various client partners.

● Are there some underlying tendencies in their demands? Is there, for instance, a relatively stronger emphasis on industry analysis as the basis for development of specific business strategies? Are companies looking to develop specific research on comparative best practices? This search for patterns applies equally to research briefings. For instance, is there a particular interest in discovery events that emphasise the international dimension? What about discovery events that deal with various aspects of cross-cultural management issues?

- By analysing the cross-section patterns of "signals" from learning partners about their interest in research issues as well as discovery events, it may be possible for the school to pick up "weak signals" that allow the school to more proactively shape its own agenda for knowledge build-up, with the purpose of *leading* the development within one's learning partners, rather than *being led*.[5] Still, a careful link between such a proactive view and the reality is necessary. For this reason, the cross section of overall pattern of inputs from a large number of learning partners is invaluable. "Weak signal" analysis can lead to particularly inspiring guidelines for fleshing out an agenda of knowledge build-up intended to lead future development.

- A business school that analyses the aggregate patterns of its learning partners should be particularly well suited to pick up and adapt to the overall learning activity trends of leading firms. The analysis can thus lead to a much more deliberate understanding of what types of capabilities the school itself must be able to mobilise. The broad sweep indicates to the school which competencies it needs to develop to meet the needs of its clients in a more aggregate way — both today and in an anticipated future. To accomplish this, at least in part, the school should make every effort to develop the faculty to be both adaptive and proactive. For effective action, the faculty itself must see — and accept — the aggregate patterns of, often faint, signals. Faculty self-belief, not dictation from the school's administration or Dean's office, must drive the process. To further enhance the capabilities in relatively weak areas — present and/or anticipated — the school can also recruit new faculty. Thus the faculty recruiting process may take its direction from this type of analysis.

This approach is valid only if the school analyses each learning partner's needs and patterns in a systematic way that allows comparison. This provides another rationale for adapting the learning menu approach. It allows easy mapping of the learning activities of each learning partner in a compatible way per firm, and it thus provides the basis for cross-firm comparisons and the analysis of aggregate patterns of learning. In other words, it allows accumulation of learning by the school to be able to deliver relevant programmes as a function of its adapting to market needs, and the development of competencies by the school to be able to lead the development of management practices through research and research discovery events.

By choosing to work with truly state-of-the-art firms, the business school can better develop an overall picture of state-of-the-art trends, enhance its learning and stretch its capabilities. Why? Because leading companies will typically provide a more reliable picture of state-of-the-art trends. This robust picture, learned from analysing the various insights from individual learning partners, can provide unique insights and thus be a competitive advantage.

The various approaches the business school uses to adapt to the needs of its client firms in the short run largely determine the school's economic results. Effective adaptation in both the short and long run, however, is likely to generate ample resources for attracting and keeping faculty; both to provide competitive salaries as well as to develop research and infrastructure. The business school's available resources will be closely connected with the outcome of its efforts to adapt to its learning partners. Still, is this enough, or is there a risk that a very close market focus might lead to too much short-term emphasis? Are there, for instance, new trends emerging that the firms themselves might still not be aware of? Do business schools need to develop capabilities that go *beyond* those stemming from the adaptive pressures? We shall claim — absolutely!

Long-Run Innovation

It may thus not be enough to believe that a school can lead the development in management thinking by "adapting to weak signals" from its clients. This may still be too much of a "me too" approach, too much "thinking in the small" rather than innovating "in the large". Think about a large corporation. A critical obstacle to the innovative strategic development of entirely new businesses in large firms is the fact that developing of a particular strategy tends to be incremental, marked by extrapolative thinking. Businesses normally innovate in the short run, building on the current momentum. The budgetary process, with its need to demonstrate relatively immediate bottom-line results, typically supports short-term innovation. You extend on the business activities where you know what already works. The problem with this approach is that such thinking rarely yields major breakthrough innovation. It insufficiently meets the need for the firm's long-term growth and success. How can firms — and with them dynamic business schools — better understand this pernicious problem? And what can they do to circumvent it? To understand the challenge of what I call "leapfrog-oriented thinking" and new knowledge development in the progressive business school, consider again what such thinking means for business organisations.[6]

The first critical question is: Do we see opportunities that are not obvious to everyone else? In an academic setting, this means that professors should search for opportunities that their colleagues might not have seen: new research or pedagogical ideas, geographical extensions of what one is already doing elsewhere, and so on. Faculty should push to articulate ideas that might be promising, but that remain hidden to everyone else. Important here are cross-disciplinary thinking and interacting with a number of entities inside or outside one's own business school, including scholars and executives from other contexts, people on the Internet. And so on.

The aim of such activities would be to come up with tentative research ideas, pilot research results that offer interesting opportunities for one's learning partners to alter their practices in ways that they don't even initially consider or comprehend. It is, thus, truly a matter of stretching development, based on the researcher's own viewpoints on how to "see" new opportunities. The competence of the researcher is particularly critical in this respect, in the sense that it requires a lot of hands-on experience to be able to pull off "realistic seeing of the non-obvious". This amounts to being able to develop what might typically be enhanced via cross-disciplinary teams to further pursue such exploratory, tentatively promising, research leads. Here, of course, the lead researcher would need to be able to "convince" a group of colleagues that this more outlying research might be worthwhile. With success, the colleagues would then gradually and more easily follow the lead researcher's arguments because of his track record, reputation, enthusiasm for the new project, and ability to visualise for fellow researchers exactly what might be in it for them. Having such leading researchers, who have seen new non-obvious opportunities early, is key. Their insights can lead to the need for further research and build a research momentum for pursuing these ideas. One might call these direction-setting researchers "internal research entrepreneurs". They represent a critical resource within the broader faculty team for pulling off path-breaking research activities, and the school needs enough of them.

The second question is: Do we have the organisational capabilities in place to pursue this particular set of path-breaking opportunities. The answer reveals whether the necessary competencies are available or missing in the school, and thus need to be built up, or whether it can actually realign and apply the existing competencies to this bold new idea. Again, resources might be found, both inside and outside the school. Today there is no excuse for not seeking out virtual resources as well.

Figure 5.3 combines these two questions and provides a simple model the business school can use to think about, analyse, and make decisions about its current and future value-creating activities.[7] It provides an overall portfolio view of the school's strategic value-creating activities (one might also see them in business).

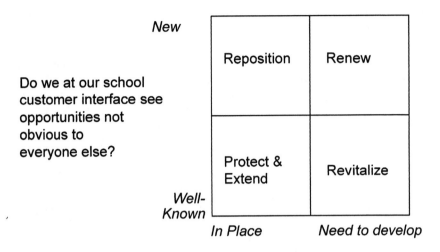

Figure 5.3: An overall portfolio picture of the school's strategic research initiatives.

As the graphic makes clear, there would be four strategic contexts for value-creating activities within the business school's portfolio of research activities:

1) **Protect and Extend** Consolidate, build on the established resources, and defend one's position, both by developing existing businesses further within the firm and, analogously, by building on what we know within the business school.
2) **Reposition** Focus on driving the proven idea rapidly forward, by extending workable business propositions into new markets, new customer interfaces in the business world; or, analogously for the academic world, by extending developed theories or applications into broader settings and new applications.
3) **Revitalise** Realign parts of the business that are under-performing, become competitive through re-engineering to add new computers, introduce new technologies, etc.; similarly, for academics to add new theoretical constructs to an already working body of knowledge, to add our insights, thus making the concept richer.

4) **Renew** Heavy focus on experimentation, based on entirely new market forces *and* new technology in business, not necessarily building on established strengths per se; the analogue in academia may be entirely new theory building, with clear breaks from established theories and fields of application.

Value Creation with Protect and Extend

In the protect and extend phase, a school would typically build on much of the established, successful academic value-creating activities. It would build on the existing learning partner base as much as possible. Michael Porter's work on competitive strategies can serve as an example here. After the outstanding reception that Professor Porter's models for developing effective competitive strategies got, he went on to consider the development of sustainable advantage. To further exploit his new ideas, he extended his thinking to include national strategies, the building of clusters of competencies in national economic contexts to enhance the intellectual competence dimension by focusing within such national contexts. Thus, a string of intellectual developments, one building on another, extends the initial idea in a highly productive and useful way. The business school can and should do the same.

This phase is not characterised by leapfrogging, but rather by incremental learning and the evolution of value creation. The research around IMD's *World Competitiveness Yearbook* is a good case in point.[8] The research tries to develop a better understanding of productivity and competitiveness within 49 country economies and to compare how nations score, along 300 variables, grouped into four indices, each illustrating a certain aspect of a nation's competitiveness. Finally, and perhaps more to satisfy curiosity than anything else, these four indices are then combined into an overall ranking of nations' competitiveness. In order to further exploit the strong position that IMD's research team has developed for world competitiveness, in the future it will perhaps be particularly important to increasingly focus on the intellectual capital side behind competitiveness. What are the various factors that characterise intellectual capital, and how do they affect the competitiveness of nations? Which intellectual capital dimensions are critical? These are probably important questions to pursue for further exploiting the position developed at IMD regarding world competitiveness, i.e., new variables will have to be added to maintain a sustainable research lead here — to protect and extend.

Value Creation with Reposition Activities

Reposition, a second model of strategy, is what a business school does when it takes old theories and insights and modifies them, so as to find new applications — the analogy of new markets for new business! It basically repositions them in light of the latest academic insights. An example of this might be the research at IMD and elsewhere on value chain configurations for linking a firm's diverse business activities to yield more effectiveness and efficiency. Classical research on cost efficiency and rationalisation is long-established, yielding a well-defined body of knowledge of how to approach these challenges. It turns out, however, that research on value chains has come up with dramatically new insights into what it takes to be effective and efficient. This is an excellent example of reposition-driven research. Needless to say, one should not equate the label reposition with something less valuable than the other research labels we have, i.e., renew, revitalise, and protect and extend. The originality of the research might be equally strong in each of the four categories; the difference is simply the nature of the output from the research, whether it builds on established strengths and insights "in the small" (protect and extend), whether it takes the established into new applications (reposition), whether it adds new know-how, new theories to the established (revitalise) or whether it comes up with entirely new insights (renew).

All four research agendas are, of course, perfectly legitimate. IMD's *Manufacturing 2000* research project illustrates the fine line between reposition and renew research activities. The concepts for looking at the value chain in radically new ways can perhaps better be classified as a new wave of renew, rather than the more incremental repositioning based on past knowledge. Significantly, however, the research would have to go through a repositioning phase before being able to focus on renewal. Perhaps we are talking about a circle of discovery phases here that eventually leads to renewal type research, but, initially, is based on repositioning (or revitalisation in other cases). This new base might then again be followed by a new wave of repositioning (or in other cases revitalisation) research, then leading to renew again, and so on. It may be exactly this ability to develop long-term viability and continuous renewal along certain research trajectories that characterises the truly successful academic entities and their ongoing development of their intellectual competencies.

In essence, the school builds on capabilities it already possesses, to try to create a new opportunity through repackaging. As we have just seen, this typically involves building incrementally, in order for them to get to some form of leapfrogging. Indeed, successful reposition can lead to a new renew thrust.

Value Creation with Revitalise Activities

Revitalisation is a third possible path to academic value creation. Here the school would be in a position to add new theory, or a new insight, a unique idea to its own proprietary established know-how. The school sees clear ways to add new dimensions to established strengths, and to mobilise its capabilities to bring the idea to fruition. Let's go back to the case of the LC-1 yoghurt innovation to further illustrate this. We recall that this was based on bacteria added to yoghurt in order to strengthen the immune system, as renewed by Nestlé and as alluded to briefly earlier. Its conventional yoghurt business was thereby revitalised. Interestingly, one can now ask what it would take to expand on this idea by also taking it into several new markets, in order to create global pre-eminence. Research might involve looking at how to introduce the LC-1 yoghurt into all major markets around the world. This research would then try to analyse what it would take, say, to conquer markets that are already well "occupied" by the major competitor Danone, which already features the health characteristics of its own yoghurts' properties, most notably in the European and Latin countries. What would the brand-switching characteristics be in such a market to enhance a rapid expansion? Partly, too, it might involve learning how to break into large domestic markets that tend to "know it best themselves" and reject the "not invented here", such as large US yoghurt markets. Perhaps the development of a suitable distribution system might be part of the equation to be researched here. By first doing revitalisation (adding new know-how) and then doing repositioning (extending the concept to new markets) one would indirectly reach a renew focus.

Even more far reaching would be to ask what it would take to add the LC-1 bacteria into other parts of products in order to use the LC-1 brand as a vehicle for growth in related products. What would it take to "load" the brand successfully without overloading it? How different can such add-on products be, without creating a sense of meaninglessness on behalf of the customer? How can promotional and advertising campaigns be launched which feature the brand rather than the specific product? These are all important research questions that could be part of a second-phase revitalise and/or reposition strategy leading to another renew strategy leading to another renew strategy, and so on. Needless to say, the research agenda must be dynamic here, in order to understand how to indirectly get to several stages of renew, as this example underscores.

The difficulty is to use the idea in teaching and research somehow — to "scale up" as quickly and as broadly as possible. Several key members of the faculty should share in the new ideas, so that they find a place in teaching programmes and research briefings. Given the individualistic bent of faculty members, but also reckoning for the fact that new discoveries in the head of a given faculty member may be difficult to immediately share with others, perhaps due to a more or less conscious fear that colleagues may "steal" one's ideas, it may be hard for academic institutions to get to their own renew situations. It is simply hard to get more faculty members behind a valuable new intellectual concept in order to have a renew benefit for the school.

Value Creation with Renew Activities

Start with a situation where the business school sees a truly unique opportunity for research, teaching and/or other academic value creation, but recognises that it does not have the right organisational resources to exploit it. Consider the question of organisational learning in rapidly-growing, highly dynamic business organisations. How can such organisations learn faster, so that they can use the learning process to effectively and rapidly evolve and modify their strategies as they grow? Can they leapfrog to new strategic renew positions, or does one have to build on established strengths, i.e., go via reposition or revitalise? As we have already answered, the latter is normally the case. An interesting research question here will be whether the "classical Cartesian learning approach" — learning all about each element and then synthesising the parts into a whole *can* allow for fast enough learning. The likely answer is: almost certainly no. Perhaps a better way to think about the kind of learning needed to spearhead renewing activities is to consider the parallels with a child's learning. Children learn incredibly fast. Piaget showed us how this rapid learning happens. It depends, above all, on the learner keeping a "holistic" view, and merely revising it with experience. An interesting renew research project would try to understand the nature of learning in ultra-rapidly growing organisations, as opposed to the learning in more classical organisations.

With any opportunity to experiment, to "renew" — the school has a shot at creating entirely new types of academic value. The school tests out whether it really has a worthwhile idea. Preliminary checking with other colleagues might be especially appropriate here: Has this idea been pursued by others elsewhere? Keep in mind that the academic ocean is wide and deep. The risk of reinventing the wheel is high. It is best to test out the potential of an idea vis-à-vis leading learning partners. They are its prospective adapters. Of course, the school would have to work with learning partners who have an ultra-rapid fast growth trajectory in order to gain insights regarding these issues. Perhaps such companies do this type of holistic learning intuitively already. Perhaps they have a relatively clear view of why their own learning for fast adaptation is different, in which case they might be unwilling to share their insight. Still, it is these types of leading companies relative to the phenomenon one is studying that would be critical to involve in research. Remember, however, that the learning partner/ customer may be yet unaware that he even needs this new idea.

Sufficient resources have to fund such a broader, portfolio-based discovery scenario so that larger-scale research and knowledge accumulation can take place. The school's leadership can thus support particularly promising research activities in order to make the revitalise–renew (or reposition–renew) process more robust. Still, as alluded to, there may be attitudinal impediments among the faculty, slowing down renewal. Perhaps another equally, or more, critical issue for the school's leadership therefore would be to attempt to foster more of a culture of sharing and of supporting each other among the faculty members, to attempt to orchestrate that renew-based research breakthroughs actually come through. All ideas are proprietary only for a relatively short time; it is essential to utilise one's time advantage. Still within the faculty team, within the school, sharing must take place to ensure renew strategies.

Revitalisation leading to renewal is an example of leapfrogging in academia. The school identifies these strategic contexts specifically and articulates them to provide a "breeding ground" for fresh new ideas. This will perhaps represent a school's best approach to staying in the race, and remaining an interesting place to come to for really stimulating new ideas. To make such revitalisation (or repositioning), leading to renewal of new ideas and research breakthroughs, happen, at least three important characteristics need to characterise the school's faculty:

- A willingness to look for truly new thoughts, i.e. not being afraid of the potential failure of thinking new; i.e., not stigmatising if dead ends are being encountered, rather than having a culture that encourages such extreme curiosity.
- Strong "academic" entrepreneurs who are able to not only be robust enough and self confident enough to pursue the "seeing" of radically new research topics, but also have the ability to inspire and mobilise their colleagues to get involved in such projects.
- A culture of sharing and support among the school's faculty members, rather than keeping ideas under wraps. Needless to say, all of these three characteristics tend to conflict with classical academic values and thinking.

Implications of the Portfolio View

Reposition and/or revitalise activities, if successful, lead to opportunities for renew. The question is, when do you go from reposition (or revitalise) to renew?

And how? When is reposition (revitalise) experimentation sufficiently promising to justify moving ahead? Here is my advice: when you feel that the reposition (or revitalise) idea has been adequately debated and tested out, you must be willing to take some risk and try to scale up. Go or no go! It is that simple. In this respect, faculty will have to remain open to one another, not isolating or hoarding their ideas. Sadly, all too often, this never happens in academia. Many renewing activities go under-utilised. Others later "re-discover" them and get the credit. To succeed, the business school — and I repeat myself, I know — must have the organisational chutzpah to open itself up, to encourage and reward openness, new ideas for research projects or teaching initiatives.

But what about renew? The critical aspect of renew is to be able to scale up without waiting endlessly for the train of resources to come in. Quick, even ad hoc, access to resources is key. Endless hassles for resources should not be necessary. Quick access to seed money may be critical, including quick access to research associates. The key is to capture the almost immediate inspiration associated with new research discovery, in contrast to the bureaucratic, lengthy delivery of research proposals for funding, so typical for funding from many schools' research budgets (and perhaps even more typically characterising the research programmes of the European community, various national research organisations, etc.). The very requirement of lengthy bureaucratic funding documentation and process will in itself lead to less emphasis on proactive reposition/revitalise leading to renew research. Rather, this type of resource allocation will tend to lead to less risk-prone research — it is easier to document the research steps involved here, the potential payoffs, etc. Unfortunately, one of the unintended side effects from large governmental and/or trans-governmental research funding has been this shift from "fresh thinking" to more "developmental" research. A school's administration can thus do a lot by having easily accessible seed money for reposition/revitalise and renew research projects. Needless to say, however, this is likely to be the smallest barrier; what has already been discussed regarding the cultural ability to share and support each other among faculty members remains the major hurdle to this type of research. A hope for this is the added momentum from radical "unbureaucratising" of the resource allocation process. Perhaps only in this way will the school be able to ensure that energy and enthusiasm are not lost in the transition from reposition/revitalise to renew.

Once you've managed renew, how do you move on to domination? This step is primarily about recognising when other researchers and schools have internalised the same idea. Look again at IMD's world competitiveness research. Several other respected institutions are publishing similar research, notably the World Economic Forum and *The Economist*. The challenge for IMD's research team, therefore, is to not only recognise what the others are doing, but to continue to innovate, say, by adding more of the intellectual property dimensions into the equation that might explain a nation's competitiveness. The challenge is to innovate relative to the other players in this particular research tradition.

You've got to take safeguarding measures so that resources are not being used on the same large scale after the research is no longer of high relevance. Too often, over-abundant resources are sunk into a mature strategic context in order to replicate research already done and programme developments already achieved. Again, IMD's world competitiveness research springs to mind. Rather than replicate what has already been done for more than a decade, and is now also being more or less done by other research teams, it seems important for our competitiveness research to shift more resources to adding new *variables* for research, so as to constantly develop a better picture of what world competitiveness means. Thus, the resource shift towards new aspects of research must be dynamic in order to ensure a continuing build-up of new intellectual know-how by the research team and for the school. Such dynamism prevents the wasting of resources and of having faculty spending time on relatively less interesting, long-established ideas and approaches to avoiding reinventing the wheel.

The school must pursue leapfrog activities without being bound by the immediate adaptive pressures from each learning partnership company. A business school can stay at the cutting edge, having enough ideas to attract truly outstanding client firms, *only* by having leapfrogging activities complementing incremental learning. Without leapfrogging ideas, a school all too easily becomes what I call a "me too" business, which in turn, can lead to sub-optimal adaptive learning. This may be particularly critical if top firms may no longer be willing to sign on as partners, if they no longer see the leapfrogging.

Working with second-tier clients will lead to second-tier cases, and secondary learning. And this, in turn, will fail to attract the top firms. Lack of innovation easily takes a school into a downward, negative spiral. The upward, positive spiral is leapfrog learning. It attracts top-notch learning partners, leads to top notch incremental adaptive learning from them and, in turn, generates even more leapfrog learning.

Academic Leadership Challenges

Above and beyond using the specific application of the two models introduced so far — mapping the learning menus of clients and "seeing" new research opportunities by taking a portfolio view — the business school leadership must find ways to strengthen the school's ability to mobilise its resources so that it can chase and catch such opportunities. What a great chance for opportunity-driven hands-on discovery and implementation! To reiterate the key points made thus far, the academic leadership can do at least four things to make the most of this chance:

- It can encourage academic entrepreneurs by supporting them during periods of (hopefully) temporary setbacks by providing incentives for renew research initiatives, and also by allowing for what may turn out to be less-than-excellent results, rather than judging them as failures.
- It can encourage the creation of an organisational climate, that can "see" new opportunities:
  - By encouraging its members to make use of things that are already discovered, by putting them together in new ways, by avoiding the "not invented here" trap.
  - By encouraging its organisational members to not be afraid of taking radical views on new phenomena, particularly by judging the new idea against known theories and approaches.
  - By encouraging its members to, in effect, experiment by trying things — new ideas, new approaches, new theories — and then adjusting and developing further. With this experimentation will, in all likelihood, come higher speed in developing new approaches.
  - By helping to create "meeting places" between various ideas, between various forces of ideas, such as brown bag luncheons, discussion groups, brainstorming sessions, research seminars, etc.
- It can provide seed money in a non-bureaucratic way so that funding can be made immediately available for renewing and rapid expansion research initiatives, when the minds of the researchers are fresh and enthusiastic. This also involves providing research associate support quickly and efficiently. In effect, this implies a sense of experimentation to clarify the extent to which the new idea has merit. By assuring that enough resources are allocated one would expect an answer relatively soon — "yes" or "no go". This clarifies what to continue to work on, and preserves the organisation's capacity to focus on issues of strong potential.
- Above all, the key is to create a culture of sharing among the faculty members, emphasising the need to work together to mobilise one's energies further, rather than isolating oneself and being overly protective of one's thoughts. This sharing is perhaps the most critical element for preparing the ground for renewing and rapid expansion research. Perhaps one way of measuring it would be to monitor the number of co-authored research outputs a particular faculty member is involved in. More co-authored research

might be a good indication of openness towards working with others. One of the leading renewing business schools to launch the modern wave of academically-driven business schools was the Carnegie Institute of Technology in the 1960s. One of Carnegie's key characteristics was the extensive sharing in publications among its world-renowned professors.

However, much of this process should and must go on at the individual faculty level. Faculty must always be driven to see new things in their research. They need to be hungry for discovery, and dismiss mere replication of what has been done before. Faculty members must have the discipline — and also be given the resources — today to carry out activities with a potential payoff tomorrow, or ten pages farther down the calendar. The faculty will have to manage their discovery activities while they are teaching day-to-day and meeting their institutional obligations. The leadership can support this process in at least three ways:

- It can help the individual faculty members plan their agendas in such a way that they are not too "chopped up". This is relatively easy in classical business school settings, where individual faculty members have their own courses to teach. The challenge is to make sure that these courses are batched to create free time during parts of the academic year. Even when a faculty member is involved in a lot of co-teaching, or being heavily involved in typically shorter executive development programmes that inevitably lead to more fragmentation in the agenda, it is still possible to do a fair amount of planning at least to keep fragmentation to an absolute minimum. It is an important responsibility of the leadership of the school to assist proactively in this.
- When a faculty member needs time for particularly critical phases of a given research activity, like an intensive field research intervention, or to develop a full-fledged first draft of a new manuscript, then the academic leadership should provide "mini sabbaticals". The key is to be able to plan such breaks relatively ad hoc — not follow the classical concept of an automatic sabbatical, say, once every seven years.
- The academic leadership can also insist on reviewing the research outputs from the faculty member more or less regularly. Experience shows that research productivity has to do with getting things down and out on a regular basis. It is much easier to do this as a set of working papers and articles, and then perhaps later reposition the material into a book, than going the other way. Academic leadership can help plan for this, and provide incentives for such strings of relatively limited output. Regular face-to-face interaction among all is key.

A clear sign of organisational weakness of a business school is too few members spending sufficient time and energy on the discovery process — all must do some research! One can ask what is too few? The answer: all faculty members must be involved in the discovery process. After all, as we have argued, the only true asset of an academic institution is the quality of its intellectual capital, essentially the faculty (or rather, the quality of their know-how). All the members of the team must keep this know-how up to date. The school cannot afford to have only a few people active in renewing their know-how, with the rest drifting along complacently. The entire team must renew itself. The "blood circulation" of the team must not pool in the extremities. One of my former colleagues at Wharton said that he often thought about an academic team as one-third burned out, in essence dead wood; one-third "cautious" — academicians who did research on their own, but were not in effective contact with executives and students; and one-third doing active research for active benefits to all the students and learning partner corporations. Needless to say, this equation is unacceptable in today's brain-driven academic reality. All the faculty members must be involved in systematic renewal of their competencies. This does not mean, of course, that all the faculty members must be involved in the same type of research. There are many ways of renewing oneself, via more fundamental research versus applied research, large sample statistical research versus in-depth clinical research, publishing in refereed academic journals versus publishing in more practitioner-oriented synthesis-focused journals, publishing articles versus more synthesis-oriented books, etc. In my opinion, it matters little or not at all what type of research and what type of publishing a particular faculty member is undertaking, as long as he/she actively pursues new knowledge. Knowledge renewal and development are the critical justifications for research, not the pretence that the benefits to society from new discoveries in themselves will be so earth-shaking that they can justify the commitment of resources. Lack of time, support, and energy, but also lack of talent, may all lead to a grossly inadequate value creation — de facto, ad hoc, crisis-driven, day-to-day. This is no way to sustain a quality institution. The faculty tenure phenomenon may also have a dampening effect here, in that some tenured professors may feel that they no longer need to do research.

Some of the most powerful examples of strong academic value creation can take place when teams of faculty members carry out research projects together, an argument I have made repeatedly. They try to "see" new things together, through multiple lenses, and explore implementation by drawing on their cumulative research experiences. The dilemma remains the same, however: how to discipline oneself to set aside energy today on research tasks with only a potential, often a highly uncertain potential, for payoff in the future, when you are already burdened with fighting today's academic fires.

Keep in mind that we are not talking only about innovative research or management concepts. A part of academic value creation is what happens among the participants and faculty in an auditorium after the doors are closed and discussion, or lecture, or group work begins. Such innovative "leaps" are clear signals that the vital signs of an academic institution are in order, that the faculty is creating academic value in a healthy, "innovative" way. The very fact that faculty see a new programme opportunity others have missed, and that the organisation can mobilise itself to take advantage of the opportunity, suggests that the school stands a good chance of being able to deliver the programme in a useful way as time goes on. Thus, an opportunity-seeking initiative might end up leading to a broader understanding among a number of faculty members regarding their comparative strengths. Hence, we see how important an opportunity-motivated initiative can be, not only for creating more innovation but also for recognising how to bolster effective implementation.

Key Success Factors for Seeing New Opportunities

Institutions are rampant with new ideas and suggestions. But only a handful are captured and exploited. Nothing works unless someone steps forward and says, "I will." Any new programme initiative needs a clear champion or "owner" who waves the banner. Without this commitment of time and energy, and the willingness to be exposed to the potential risks and discomfort of failure, the school will never see such opportunities pursued and transformed into real research or teaching programme progress. Every new initiative has to have an internal champion — an internal academic entrepreneur.

The faculty, as owners and as partners, are the intellectual proprietors of a school. It is they who should be concerned with innovations. As part of a healthy portfolio strategy, the faculty must be renewing *and* rapidly expanding. As owners, the faculty should be concerned with the overall activity mix of the school. They should support innovations on this basis. Arguably, owners or top administrators are perhaps better able to see the need for development of new activities, as they must take a long-term view in order to safeguard their value. An owner-inspired culture might thus create the possibility for stronger innovation. It has been argued that family-owned corporations, because they are not subject to the day-to-day pressures of the stock exchange, can take a longer-term view regarding the commitment they can give to their business. We can say the same about academic institutions: an owner mentality may free them to develop themselves. Thus, the school's leadership must create such an owner mentality.

Everyone should feel a pressure, a positive stimulus, to consider opportunity seeking as appropriate and urgent. The spotting of new opportunities can come out of dialogue among faculty members and with leading clients, who can help each other see them. Such exploratory discussions are indispensable. They also help set the tone of the school culture, contributing to the school's ability to innovate. Return for a moment to the example of IMD's research to find new ways to stimulate internally generated growth.

IMD's renewing came, to some extent, out of the fact that the school looked at various fields that might support renewing in the area of ultra-rapid internally generated growth, or as Baghai, Coley, and White of McKinsey would say it, by looking at a number of technologies together.[10] In part, this involved entrepreneurship: we needed to understand the role of the internal entrepreneur in this process. It also involved organisational behaviour: to understand the importance of autonomous and semi-autonomous groups standing more or less free from the conventional organisation in order to stimulate growth. It clearly also involved marketing research: to understand how to "test" the tentative business model one was pursuing for the renewing, etc. Adding a multitude of disciplinary approaches might thus lead to a new, more holistic concept for renewing.

Having dialogues with colleagues was absolutely critical. I benefited a lot from conversations with colleagues and, I hope, vice versa. And in this case, sharing the different perspectives seemed a good, fundamental way to stimulate renewing.

The link with a small group of learning partner companies, or the "link to the marketplace", as McKinsey would call it, was a source of inspiration to me as well. By understanding aspects of their internally generated growth challenges, as illustrated by specific examples, I gained further insights, particularly when it came to understanding which variables might be particularly worthwhile to pursue. While it is hard to generalise from clinical cases, it is perhaps particularly useful to think about them in a "pre-paradigmatic" context, such as the one we frequently have when doing renewing research. Variable indication and relationships indication might thus be critically stimulated by looking at specific cases.

Interestingly, all this dialogue around internally generated growth eventually led to a highly innovative new teaching programme, the *Venture Booster* (VB).[11] The market-based rationale for this programme was founded on three pillars.

First, speed is of the essence for the modern corporation when it comes to testing new business out further, to verify whether the new business concept has any meaning or not.

Second, in practice, there are many internal silos, one might even say king-doms, well-ingrained management processes, etc., that can truly slow down the development of new business ideas, simply by fragmenting the process, bureau-cratising it, and making it more cumbersome. Third, eclectic teams from a corporation would typically have to be mobilised to stand behind a new business idea, to take it forward. In practice, it can be difficult for corporations to bring such teams together for longer periods of time. IMD could provide such a meeting place for the creative minds of broad-based teams.

The VB programme invited teams of executives from leading learning part-nership corporations of IMD to come to the school for one week. They would bring with them an initial business idea that, however, would be tentative, i.e., still in need of refinement. Each team was supported by so-called "process coaches" during the week at IMD; two faculty members were assigned, to be with each team all the time to help move group processes ahead. Each team was also assigned a research associate, who would explore background data sources, relating to competition, consumers, etc. Further, for each team, "expert coaches" from IMD's faculty were available upon demand for each team to provide specific knowledge input relating to various aspects of the new venture development process.

As Figure 5.4 shows, during the mornings of each day, there were three lectures on the various aspects of developing internally generated growth projects. In the afternoons there was group work. During some of the evenings there were open sessions, comparing notes on some of the insights of this process. Needless to say, the content of what each team worked on would be confidential and the strictest measures were taken at IMD to preserve this confi-dentiality. Still, various general insights regarding how the internally generated growth process would take place, i.e., discussions of dos and don'ts, could be beneficially shared among the teams.

According to the feedback from the participating companies, this programme was a great success, above all because it helped create more focus, more clear unified direction for the particular new business ideas from each team, and, in essence, gained speed.

Here again, we come back to one of this book's main points: the culture is key! The school leadership needs to be able to answer these specific questions about stimulating renew: Do the relevant faculty members get a chance to do it, without going through endless committees and formal procedures? And do they get the recognition? Equally, what happens in terms of learning if an innovation fails? Here it is key to "do it" — and learn as you go, develop the concept further as you live through the delivery process. Do faculty members get stigmatised by their failures, thereby potentially discouraging others from such experimentation

The Venture Booster Program
"Accelerating New Businesses"

	Monday	Tuesday	Wednesday	Thursday	Friday	Saturday
08:30		Effective Business Planning	Building Team Culture	Information Capabilities for Start Ups	Ramping up Supply Chain	Presentation Preparation
	Breakthrough Customer Value					Process Coaches
09:45						
10:00		Industry Analysis	Decision Making in New Environments	Managing Internal Entrepreneurs	Using Architectures for Growth	Presentation
11:15						Process Coaches
11:30	Jumpstarting Teams	Reengineering the Idea Flow	Presentation Skills	Financial analysis for New Ventures	Exploiting Industry Breakpoints	Debriefing
12:45						
14:00	BUFFET LUNCH	BUFFET LUNCH	BUFFET LUNCH	BUFFET LUNCH	BUFFET LUNCH	CLOSING BUFFET LUNCH

Team Work

Faculty Coaches

Knowledge Network Sharing — 17:45

Ideo Video Conference — 18:30

SNACK — 19:00 (Monday)
SNACK — 19:30 (Wednesday)
SNACK — 19:00 (Thursday)

DINNER — 19:00 (Thursday)

18:00 Opening Session

19:15 DINNER & POSTER SESSION

19:30 Opening DINNER

Figure 5.4: A block diagram of this innovative programme.

in the future? The answer must be no. Tolerance from colleagues in case of failure is a must. Discreditation for failure makes further experimentation and risk-taking less likely. Faculty members who get lower than the expected "normal" ratings for the delivery of new academic materials, for instance, should not feel that they have failed. Institutional stigmatisation along these lines will choke off innovation — positive institutional back-up is needed.

So what is the institution to do about creating a climate culture that accepts failure as part of innovation? Give faculty members "space" to innovate. Give them the freedom and independence to experiment. They should be strongly encouraged to try it out. Give them resources and encouragement. They must feel that they have autonomy, but also that the school will back them up. They must not be bogged down by school-imposed bureaucracy, committees and routines.

A final condition relates to providing incentives for faculty members to innovate. IMD believes, for example, that faculty members who see opportunities and/or who are able to mobilise their resources to deliver on them should have special incentives. A fundamental incentive is the financial recognition that a faculty member receives by successfully developing an innovative research project and/or teaching programme. At IMD, money is the major reward for the faculty champion of a concrete, successful innovation. Financial incentives above and beyond fixed salary represent a sizeable fraction of the total faculty financial package. Incentives fall in two parts, and support the fixed faculty salary that IMD sees mainly as a "safety net". The two types of incentives are:

- A group incentive, to be given equally to each faculty member, as recognition for what the team has done to create the school's success. The team dimension of innovation and success is thereby underscored. For year 2000 this team incentive was 18 percent of each faculty member's fixed salary.
- An individual incentive to reflect the specific innovative efforts of a given faculty member. Thirty percent is based on strong pedagogical innovations, and 20 percent is based on innovative ways of serving IMD's learning partners. The individual bonus can be rather significant for some faculty members, but of course much less for others. In total the individual bonus pool also represented 18 percent of the fixed salary pool at IMD for the year 2000.

Thus, strong financial recognition underscores the school's belief that innovation does matter, and it provides each faculty member with a financial reward for contributing, quite analogous to what you would expect in a partnership organisation.

The matter of rewarding innovation leads to the question of how the business school can combine and weave two modes of academic value creation into a symbiosis. How can the incremental value creation and the leapfrog learning take place together? Given the fact that it is typically the *same* academic resources — above all faculty members' time and energy — that provide for incremental and leapfrog learning, how can a business school reconcile the two sets of demands?

The nature of the learning probably differs. Take, for instance, the aforementioned task of developing an embryonic renew activity at IMD. On the one hand, developing ideas around renewing seemed to fit well into a free-standing process of discovery by seeing opportunities that were not obvious to everyone else, and then gradually mobilising internal organisational resources to pursue these opportunities. Typically there will be a few leading learning partners, with their implicit learning menus, and their focus on research and discovery event dimensions in particular, that will be willing to encourage this type of research. On the other hand, the "try it out" dimension, to learn as you go, i.e., experiment, is large. One can thus say that the renew research input comes partly as a consequence of our free-standing ability to create an atmosphere to "see", of the desire to "lead the market" with proactive research and research briefings, and partly through incremental learning as you do it, by getting one's feet wet.

To try to generalise, to develop a prescription for internally generated knowledge enhancement, it would seem appropriate to start by reiterating that the learning here seems to be quite similar to the holistic learning that goes on in the child, as described by Piaget and others.[12] Developing a theory for internally generated growth, for instance, would involve a multitude of inputs, based on several disciplinary-based cases, as indicated. Rather than testing out the relevance of rapidly internally generated growth vis-à-vis each of these disciplinary fields, it seemed more useful, at least at IMD, to think about it as holistic learning, i.e., to think about how holistic learning regarding growth might be advanced, based on progress when it comes to the role of the internal entrepreneur, together with the role of marketing research for testing of the business model, the role of organisational design for autonomy of the growth initiative, etc. The key seems to be to keep the learning on all of these elements together, rather than to break it down to specific sub-segments. Such holistic learning not only adds to a better understanding of the renew type phenomenon, but also adds to the speed of learning about it. A more classical, Cartesian learning, focusing on how each disciplinary element will be adapted to the internally generated growth challenge, might be too slow or even confusing. This formal learning emphasises the creation of increasingly clear holistic pictures of the phenomenon, without getting bogged down in specific details. Also, as pointed out by Piaget, the developmental stage of an individual will determine how much he/she can comprehend, i.e., the level of ability to deal with complex holistic phenomena. A small child can obviously handle less holistic complexity than an adult. Similarly, the same is true when it comes to the development of new theories and concepts within an academic institution. One would typically start out with rather simple, in retrospect even premature, ideas before making the gradual transition to richer and more realistic ideas, as the academic team becomes more insightful, more mature. Piaget emphasised the importance of trial and error for this holistic learning. The same is, of course, true within an academic team working on developing a particular body of knowledge, as we have seen.

The classical, Cartesian form of learning, which focuses on the individual parts — learning everything about each before putting them together into a new, holistic picture — might apply to the learning that goes on in well-established, more mature business settings.[13] This may also be true for learning associated with research within more well-established academic fields or pedagogical advances when it comes to classical teaching agendas. Here, the overall direction of the phenomenon, such as for instance the overall understanding of what it involves to develop research for world competitiveness, often by largely repeating the same type of research inquiry year after year, calls for an incremental approach towards learning for the researchers involved. For a group of executives, this type of learning may be associated with incremental improvements in established business agendas — running the "business as usual", in a better way. This Cartesian approach, however, may not be so effective for renew teams. Why? Because here, the basic direction for the research may be open to question. To break the phenomenon down into its various elements, and then put it together, might at best slow down the research process; at worst, it will derail it. To follow the example of my own research on rapidly internally generated growth, it would probably be less meaningful to study entrepreneurship, market research/business model testing and organisational issues as separate phenomena relative to the research question. Rather, they need to be seen together, interacting with each other for portraying a holistic picture. This probably will lead to more rapid research progress and probably also more relevant research.

During a rapid expansion of the business, the quest may be for a pathfinder type of learning, to make sure that the most effective implementation effort takes place through constantly experimenting with finding the right path to carry out the task, i.e., a pathfinder form of learning as described by Levitt.[14] The issue might thus be one of not seeing a failure as something finite, i.e., not to give up, but rather to see a failure as something of a stimulus to try to find another path in the forest. For example, one of the hypotheses of our growth research there was that, in the case of renew growth, one would need a high, separate project-based budget for the renew growth. According to our hypothesis, this would contrast with the more established reposition and revitalise, where one would need less earmarked development budget. The research did not corroborate this. What seemed to be the case was that, in most instances, it would not be important to have an independent organisation with a designated development budget. There seemed to be little difference between the renew versus the reposition/revitalise versus the protect and extend phases. Under all circumstances, new business growth was part of the main organisational team's responsibility — indeed its *raison d'être*. The organisation cannot abdicate delivering on the growth challenge to special dedicated task forces.

However, there might be more to this — one might thus also look for another "path through the forest" as a way to further explain some critical phenomena around this which would highlight differences among the four modes of growth. It turns out that when it comes to pursuing a "dual" strategy,[15] this seems to be different when it comes to renew versus protect and extend. In the former case, we are talking much more about an earmarked task force structure, it seems, which fundamentally is rather free to focus on the developmental dimension only. Definitely, members of these free-standing tasks might also wear other hats, from operations, but they would still be relatively clear in terms of their responsibility for the renew development. In contrast to this, on the other hand, one would find that for the protect and extend developmental activities, this should be seen much more as a mainstream part of the operating tasks that the various executives would already have. Nevertheless, it is *one* organisation, and thus, developing a dual strategy with different priorities, only a matter of *degree* in determining who will be doing what in the balance of strategic development and operations. Thus, by looking at the issue of how these resources are focused as delineational tasks, one might be able to find a clear "path in the forest" with initial explanations around the notion of separate organisations, not leading to meaningful insights, but with added insights, introducing the "dual" structure within the same organisation.

Chapter 6

Improving Learning and Delivery
with Information Technology

Executive Summary

The modern business school must make every effort to use the full range of information technologies to improve its pedagogical and delivery capabilities. Many business schools, including IMD, are using IT as a pivotal learning vehicle, especially for what has come to be called distance learning. It has already taken root in, shaped, and enhanced, typical business school strategy. Among the more common applications are multimedia formats for research delivery and teaching tools, Web technology, including virtual classroom and setting up and leveraging Web-based learning and sharing networks. For the business school leader, IT therefore has important implications: decisions must be made about the proportion of traditional in-class learning versus virtual learning, the degree to which the leadership should be involved in the details of IT (platforms, software, etc.), the use and value of Web-based networks. IT uses at IMD and other leading business schools provide examples and point the way for business school Deans who need to make tough choices about the place of IT in their evolving strategies.

James Duderstadt points out that "the most dramatic impact on our world today from information technology is not in the continuing increase in computer power. It is in a dramatic increase in band width, the rate at which we can transmit digital information. . . . As a consequence, the nature of human interaction with the digital world — and with other humans through computer-mediated interactions — is evolving rapidly. We have moved beyond the simple text interactions of electronic conferencing to graphical mail and electronic user interfaces . . . to voice to video. With the rapid development of sensors and robotic actuators, touch and action at a distance will soon be available."[1]

Clearly then, information technology can enhance both the school's pedagogical and its delivery capabilities. I would argue *must*. Examples include audiovisual developments, uses of the Internet, Intranet, and Web, as well as dissemination of learning materials via CD-ROM. These information technologies represent unique opportunities for making quantum leaps in effective delivery of executive education, perhaps above all in enhancing possibilities to learn on the job. Significantly, also, the new technology opens up new opportunities for the faculty to try new approaches, which means enhanced learning for them.

Information technology has become a learning vehicle in the classrooms of today's business school. Virtual learning is rapidly becoming a part of almost every programme. Networks and network-based learning are at the centre of vast numbers of business school programmes. Rowley *et al.*, for instance, report on several: Western Governors University, Virtual Online University, Open University of Catalonia, IBM Global Campus, Global Network Academy, World Space, Inc.[2] The tendency toward more virtual and networked universities and other higher learning institutions will clearly increase.

Distance learning has become a reality. Students are on their own, using laptops, studying various topics, some of them leading to degrees. Perhaps spearheaded by the pioneering work of the Open University, this activity has grown extensively. Nevertheless, to a greater or lesser degree, students still also participate in actual classroom sessions, say, over weekends. These face-to-face sessions enhance motivation, and establish trust-bonding among the participants.

IMD sees distance learning (learning by using Internet and other digital technologies) essentially as a complement to the learning that happens when students meet at IMD. Our Executive MBA programme is a prime example.[3] Virtual learning enhances the 19-week programme (we think of the "virtual" part as providing roughly the equivalent of the 19 weeks on campus). This individual learning falls into four areas:

- Learning the basics, including distance testing;
- Working on projects, often together with fellow students, and getting feedback via the Internet;
- Developing solutions to problems, in essence mini-cases, and again receiving feedback via the Internet;
- Using the Internet to gather background materials needed for the activities mentioned above, and also background materials to prepare the participants for several weeks of field trips that are part of the programme and deal with far away regions, for example Shanghai, Ireland, Silicon Valley, etc.

Another successful IMD programme that incorporates large amounts of individual virtual learning is our programme *Building on Talent*.[4] Here, participants do a fair amount of individual technical work before they come to their first two weeks at IMD, and they learn virtually by working on an extensive project together with fellow students between their first session at IMD and their last week-long session. The virtual learning component amounts to about three weeks' work, again, more or less equal to the amount of work done at IMD.

The benefits of these examples are clear. First, students can work on basic topics at home rather than using the expensive IMD-based learning time for it. Second, students can work on projects while they are still on the job. And third, students can pace their learning according to their agendas and abilities.

Virtual learning does not have to stop with the individual student. IMD sponsors in-company-based virtual learning, again, a "hybrid" of distance learning and learning at IMD and/or at the learning partner's corporate setting with IMD professors. Both for a leading automotive manufacturing corporation with truly global operations, and for a leading telecommunications corporation operating around the globe, IMD has developed a series of virtual cases. Accessible on the Web, these cases allow IMD faculty to formulate problems around a theme for students to consider before they arrive at IMD, before they take part in regular classroom sessions. One advantage of the virtual case study is that it gives students immediate access to enough background information — competitive facts and market demand data, for example — to undertake what could be seen as an "industry analysis well before the classroom discussion". The online case also gives students immediate access to an extremely wide variety of additional backup materials, including technical notes on approaches to analysis, factual analysis regarding attractiveness of various countries, based on IMD's *World Competitiveness Yearbook*,[5] etc. It can further provide video-clips of testimonials from actual executives on aspects of the problem at hand. Students work on these materials on their own, and then share the case analysis with the IMD professor — also online. The whole exercise might finally culminate with a final "live" case discussion.

The benefits are obvious: a large number of students can quickly learn a lot about the topic. They can study at their own work places. They can get a much fuller set of real-life data from which to choose, thus having to make critical judgements regarding what is more or less relevant. This, of course, is nearer to real-life management experience than the traditional paper case that internally selects and spoon-feeds the relevant industry, competitive, and other background research to students. They can interact with other colleagues, again, according to need. All in all, the learning is flexible enough to fit the individual students' pace and needs, more so than they would find in a typical class discussion. With this sort of learning, the final case discussion in class is only a small part of the learning take-home value.

Information technology may have already affected IMD's delivery of programmes, but how has it affected corporate universities? How has it affected the workings of the so-called "corporate university", the co-operation between business schools like IMD and a select number of corporate universities? Typically, a corporate university builds itself around programme elements, which, together, lead to full blown programmes. These programmes, likewise, are typically modules that fit into a "meta-plan" for the scope and content of the corporate university's offerings. Classically, corporate universities have given their own classroom-based courses, but this is changing. More and more, corporate universities are becoming largely virtual, with distance learning at their centres (or at least forming an increasingly big part of their curricula). Leading schools like IMD see themselves more and more as "partners" with such corporate universities, not so much "subcontracting" programmes, or parts of them, but taking responsibility for entire programmes, and/or even the planning of groups of them. Again, it is information technology that provides the basic vehicle for these partnerships. Further, business schools themselves are becoming members of networks, and major clients are becoming members of the schools' Web-based networks. At IMD, members come from our partners and business associates. Here, too, information technology already enhances — or will soon reshape — the basic strategy of the leading business school in the future.

IT as a Learning Vehicle

At every business school today, students must have simple access to PC databases they can use in their analyses. Access provides them with background industry notes, corporate reports, case studies, and financials. Multimedia cases give them access to background information in a multitude of new forms which help in their analysis and problem-solving. Electronic spreadsheets for working with financial data are common. Increasingly, individual students will have access to special tutorial programmes to facilitate the learning of business fundamentals or to enhance the review of materials learned. All of these uses of information technology bolster learning by enabling students to learn, review, test themselves, and even communicate with their professors at their own pace and on their own time. Since the use of information technology is generally well known, it has no place in our further discussion here. Multimedia case studies, however, are still in their infancy, yet already appear to offer tremendous possibilities to combine audio, visual, and Web-based data exchange and communication to appeal to a wide variety of teaching and learning styles. In their power to stimulate "real world, real business" situations, they represent a teaching tool that no programme can afford to ignore.

Multimedia Applications

As already alluded to, IMD has completed comprehensive multimedia cases for several large corporations, including the "automotive company" and the "telecommunications company". It represents a large amount of data, complementing what you normally find in paper-bound research on a particular firm or industry — clippings and articles relating to one industry, for example, automobiles, pharmaceuticals, banking, or hotel and tourism. Traditionally, students go to the "industry box" in a library and pick out annual reports, various press clippings, articles about the background of the industry, its growth potential, major competitors, trends, etc. To prepare for a class discussion on the particular firm in its industry, drawing on the relevant materials, the student sorts it all out, often by hours of painstaking paper shuffling.

These multimedia cases do essentially the same thing, except that the data is available in various media: video streams of interviews with senior executives, customers and competitors; exhibits with data that the student can manipulate on screen, press clippings, often direct from the publication's home page, access to industry information on the Web, links to further information, etc. The combination of picture, text, and sound provides multiple stimuli for learning. To access the various pieces of data, the student merely clicks on the appropriate icons and follows the cybertrail. Among the benefits are more exciting presentation of materials, "fresher" interviews and information, which can be up-dated regularly. Students may also have the possibility to link up with their own company over the Internet. In in-company programmes, students may actually have access to vital, real-life company information.

The countless advantages for the business school and its students of this new technology have fuelled its popularity. For one, it is new. And like all things new, it has attracted legions of followers, particularly those tired of traditional book- and desk-bound learning. It appeals to different learning styles, providing for all sorts of learners, from listeners to readers, from those who remember words to those who remember images, from those who need guidance to those who like to sniffle around on their own. CD-ROMs are small, wafer-thin discs that can hold awesome volumes of data about companies or cases. A telecommunications company CD-ROM would need half a room to keep its information on traditional storage media, like paper, celluloid, and magnetic tapes. The link to

Internet sites is a feature offered by no other case media, and offers students a unique, direct path to the real world of business, in real time, as they pursue the issues of the case. CD-ROM technology brings professors and students one step nearer to having the company located across the street. If it wishes to keep up with the latest in teaching and learning technology, the dynamic business school will have to ramp itself up to be able to produce high-quality research on CD-ROMs.

Web Technology

World Wide Web-based information systems are increasingly having profound impacts on the way universities and business schools work. With Internet/ Intranet/Web technology, students and teacher can interact in real time, regardless of location. The student may, for instance, discuss a problem with the development of a real project report for a real job at a real firm. Consider for instance how a modern learning network approach, based on virtual technologies, can facilitate such discussion:

- It may have interactive features, a built-in business simulator module for example, so that the participants can "play" and thus get a better feel for the consequences of their "make-believe" decisions.
- It can provide just-in-time information and "support" for addressing certain challenges and problems that tend to come up in management classes. Students access important information without getting bogged down in overly technical issues.
- It can provide feedback to the learner: learners can test their comprehension of various concepts and lessons.
- Learner mentors can provide individual feedback to the learner online. Similarly networks make "learning forums" possible, so learners can discuss the problems they are working on.

All in all, the term "learning network" seems indeed justified for this type of an approach to learning. Learning network-based support can help the student do a more powerful analysis, drawing on a broader set of relevant data as well as online comments and feedback from the professor, and thus speed up and enrich learning. First of all, a comprehensive set of underlying data will be readily available so that students can do their "industry analysis" with immediate information. They thus have an overabundance of possibly relevant data. Circumventing the process of gathering the information, they can go directly to figuring out which data is relevant, selecting it, and then framing their responses to the management problem at hand.

But this is not all: consider the interactive nature of this form of learning itself. Here, the students can provide their inputs and thus allow the professor/mentor and/or fellow students to give feedback when they are ready for it. This means that the interactive and iterative processes are being sped up, not slowed down. It is much harder to assemble people on a face-to-face basis, than by using multimedia. Now interaction can be done when the participants find it most useful and convenient. Students also have direct access to tutorials as needed, and interact with others as part of a group of learners through interactive/communicative features. Information technology allows the participant to take extensive advantage of "connectivity", whether via Internet, Intranet, or the Web. In groups, or classes, students can share experiences with each other and with the professors (who act more as coaches) through the online community. This sharing, of course, puts a heavier emphasis on learning by interaction, and in several steps, arguably one of the richest ways to learn.

The Implications for the Business School Leader

Distance learning today is a highly sophisticated approach to working with real-time, state-of-the-art insights and problems. This is quite naturally the result of a confluence of several factors: above all, the capabilities and know-how to develop distance-learning inputs have increased. Also, the interactive features of the information technology-based support are much stronger. They allow for comfortable interaction and relatively instant feedback, not only between the student and the teacher, but also among students themselves. Finally, the pedagogical insights into how best to incorporate virtual learning into a broader, hybrid learning agenda are increasing; however, there is still a lot of work to be done to yield the full potential of the technology.

Considering all the changes that have already occurred and the massive work yet to be done, what strategy should the business school follow for IT? Simply, what should the leadership of a business school do? Should, for instance, this leadership be concerned with various technical aspects of the technology, such as choice of platforms, standards, etc.? The answer is no. The overall aim must be to maintain as much flexibility as possible, so that the school is not welded to a particular technological solution that quickly might become obsolete. Still, the leadership may well have to get involved with pedagogical issues that are inextricably bound to technological questions. Considering the state of the art of the all-critical learning platform, for instance, it is easy to argue that existing, available platforms, such as the "learning space" and others, have basically been developed with high school students and undergraduate students in mind. Such platforms are not likely to be well-suited to building learning programmes for senior executives. The school's leadership may have to develop its own learning platform to meet the needs of one's rather atypical more senior, experienced learning clientele. This is IMD's approach.

Regarding the business side, there are, however, several clear agenda items for the leadership of the school. One obvious one would be to stimulate the incorporation of these types of virtual uses in the various courses, to ensure that as much as possible of the basic work can be done at home, to ensure more in-between modules work, etc. The net effect of this is that one can cover more material, and save classroom time for more advanced discussions.

Another item is developing a closer relationship with select companies, say, to support their corporate universities. This is, obviously, a critical business decision for the school. If the leadership believes that corporate universities are a threat to the business school, they will choose not to co-operate. However, the counter-argument says that strong synergies could come out of what the business school can offer, including pedagogical support (substantive input offerings) and, perhaps the most critical, what I like to call "catalytic professorial support" for the learning processes. The corporate university, on the other hand, can provide important revenue, including the possible upside of offering the business school to be paid "per click", i.e., whenever a user makes use of a case or other teaching material developed by the business school for this corporate university. The corporate university can definitely provide access to an interesting clientele of learners, particularly if a company is a leading one.

The intellectual challenge to a business school's faculty, including the ability to learn on behalf of the business school team, might also therefore be a true attraction. My feeling is that choosing which corporate universities to co-operate with is natural, so long as the school focuses on those with whom it has already had a long relationship (co-operating, for example) on in-company programmes. Such companies already know the business school and have a much better springboard from which to make the new technology-based learning a reality. Supporting the corporate university then becomes nothing more than extending, if you will, the in-company learning initiatives that already exist. In this way, the new type of learning will be seen as a natural evolution, not something new or radical.

One final comment. The school leadership must attend to the possibility of developing strategic alliances with other institutions, using the new technology. For each of the cells in a school's activity "matrix", one can discuss what type of relationship one wishes to establish with select outside organisations, such as other business schools, other specialised providers, etc. One can thereby develop a rich set of offerings, but of course guided by the school's own "meta-plan" of how this set might look. With the absence of such a meta-plan a school can all too easily — and inadvertently — become a "subcontractor" in someone else's meta-plan, which is not a viable long-term solution for a leading business school. But once a business school has decided in which programmes it wants to use distance learning — whether open programmes, in-company programmes, or as part of corporate university support — the leadership will have to figure out how, exactly, it wishes to put the powerful tools to use. One example follows.

Virtual Learning

As already noted, IMD's programme *Building on Talent* (BOT) is one of the programmes that uses IT extensively for virtual learning.[6] Participants come initially for two weeks, followed by a third week sometime later. Before they come, as well as between the first two weeks and the third week at IMD, students work heavily on the Internet on special projects and on background studies. The IMD faculty has prepared a number of Internet-based background learning modules. These modules provide learning support when it comes to comprehending more basic management approaches and techniques, i.e., how to analytically deal with common business challenges in the areas of finance, accounting and operations management. The modules help the student to use analytical tools to arrive at specific solutions, and the professors support them by explaining what the typical problem areas might be. These allow the student to prepare on their own, learning what they can master well alone, rather than using expensive time for it at IMD. Basic accounting and finance, for instance, are covered this way. Self-tests allow students to check their own mastery.

During the time at IMD, extensive individual modules for learning are available on the Net. Typically, these modules provide background notes on cases, industry notes, etc., in a multimedia format. Partly, these modules are the same as the ones mentioned above, providing support for analysing particular business problems, drawing on basic finance, basic accounting, basic operations management, etc. Partly, however, background access is provided via the modern technology to industry analysis information, which is useful for the development of given cases. Thus, by preparing a case, the student not only reads and discusses this, but he/she also accesses the Web for background data. In many instances, this also involves direct access to the Web pages of the companies involved.

Needless to say, this is a "for free" source of learning input, but increasingly a critical one, as it adds liveliness and life-like realism via this broader Web-based industry analysis context.

Between the two modules at IMD, students work extensively on their own projects. In teams, they interact via the Internet about the project's specific key issues. They also interact with the tutor/professor. During this time in between, students develop a presentation on the Net, for submission to IMD via the Net, to be critiqued face-to-face when they return to IMD. A significant part of the BOT learning is therefore based on team-based project work via the Internet.

Advantages and Disadvantages of Virtual Learning

Imagine virtual learning approaches that would be based 100 percent on the students acquiring their education virtually, via the Internet. Today this idea is not far-fetched. Such a distance-learning approach would have distinct advantages. Above all, students can combine their studies with normal jobs and career-enhancing activities. They can take the learning to the job — indeed to learn better on the job. Still, the top quality learning cannot be fully duplicated by 100 percent virtual, distance learning. Face-to-face interaction between the student and the professors, coupled with similar interaction among the students themselves, will always have an important role in learning. A study done by *Training Magazine*, for instance, underscores the fact that training by computer consisted of 19 percent of all training options, versus 70 percent for classroom training and 11 percent "other". Focusing on the computer-delivered training, this breaks down as follows: CD-ROM 28 percent, Intranet 26 percent, other means 21 percent, diskette 17 percent and Internet eight percent.[7]

Learning, after all, is to a large degree a matter of socialisation, based on developing a multitude of perceptions among a group of professors and students who learn together. Thus, learning is an extremely complex process. Piaget, for example, claimed that children learn primarily due to two factors, each of which is a direct consequence of the physiological development of the child's brain. First, they learn, according to the Swiss psychologist, by being stimulated to learn via interactions with adults, factoring these stimuli into holistic frames of increasingly more complete learning around a phenomenon. Second, they learn in the context of harmony and trust between the child and the "teacher".

While the first item is largely outside the control of human beings, we can certainly do something about the second, i.e., the interaction between the student and the professor, as well as the development of an atmosphere of trust as part of this learning, assuming that we want to borrow the critical aspects of learning from Piaget, wanting to replicate the fast learning going on in children. Face-to-face interaction is thus not only inevitable but highly desirable.[8]

If Piaget is correct, it would be impossible to duplicate the complex processes he describes by virtual learning alone. Consider for instance the nature of interaction. Clearly only some of the more likely avenues of interaction can be pre-programmed or pre-anticipated, thus allowing them to be built into information technology-based simulation vehicles. This clearly limits the richness of interaction between student and the "learning body". Admittedly, much more richness in the interaction can take place between the student and a real-life professor tutor, even though they are interacting in a virtual way. Still, eye contact is missing, which has to limit the richness of the interaction, and hence limit the learning. Even more importantly, however, is the question of build-up of trust between teacher and student. Trust is, after all, very much an interpersonal matter. Learning over a virtual network is less likely to form the same bonds of trust between student and professor as can be formed when the two meet in person. Thus, one cannot expect to replicate the rich learning process by virtual means alone. I believe, however, that virtual learning can go a considerable way toward effective learning — it can add significantly to the effectiveness of the learning process, by above all improving the learning of more basic material, and project-based group work.

It is easy to say that virtual learning is an important, even indispensable learning tool for the future, but what are the specific benefits/costs of virtual group learning? What about personal motivation in the virtual classroom? How can one be sure that the student is challenged? Is there a way to check for active participation? No doubt, individual, virtual learning always will have a major handicap associated with it, namely a sense of loneliness, and the individual having to rely on exceptional self-discipline on the lonesome marathon of distance learning. Still, enough students can do it. Perhaps this discipline can even be built up over time. Needless to say, the quality of the current technology and the interactive learning is much higher than before. To counterbalance the "loneliness effect" with some sort of "excitement" stemming from the high quality of input that the virtual interactive process now can offer, an active sense of learning via participation, with feedback and additional stimuli, is critical. The higher the quality of this dimension, supported by the improved technological feasibility context, the better. Still, if the personal self-discipline is not there, and the student depends on the social discipline typical of classroom learning, it might be difficult to achieve the necessary self-motivation via distance-based learning.

What about learning in groups? Distance learning offers none of the richness or rewards of, for example, the Socratic method in small or large groups, learning by questioning, challenging one's assumptions, etc. Distance learning at this point offers few of the benefits of examining the counterbalancing viewpoints of colleagues in a classroom, where, as the arguments go forward, participants re-examine, revise, or even change their views. It may be difficult to replicate this type of group learning via the virtual technology. With distance learning, one can work in groups, say, on projects, by splitting up the work, holding online discussions of the particular approaches taken in the group project, etc. But it is hard to see how a true Socratic dialogue can unfold. Group learning in cyber-space still seems a poor substitute for the rough and tumble of the auditorium. Nevertheless, over the Net, people thousands of miles apart can share best prac-tice — any time, any place. As such, virtual group processes provide accessi-bility, convenience, and realism in group learning — something which is often missed if students physically have to be together.

In general, then, the debate about the benefits of face-to-face teaching and virtual learning seems to come down to a tradeoff between quality and efficiency. The benefits of being together in the face-to-face classroom seem greater, both when it comes to the nature of the interactive learning process as well as when it comes to the development of the necessary trust to facilitate learning. In a group learning sense, the Socratic process is more likely to take place in the face-to-face context. On the other side is the argument that distance learning allows the participant to learn on the job, and even to apply the learning to the job and to immediately report the results. Even better, you can learn what you need, efficiently tailor your learning agenda, both familial and professional.

I believe, though, that this balance will change. What now still looks like a tradeoff will soon look like complementarity. Why? Because, keeping in mind the time and resource constraint of today's busy individuals, some elements of learning work better on a virtual basis. Further, keeping in mind the rapid evolu-tion of learning technology and the pedagogy that goes with virtual teaching/learning, one can expect that the challenge in the future will not be for the busi-ness school leadership to decide which way to go, but how to create the best hybrid for its purposes. It is difficult to predict what the ideal mix between the two pedagogical modes might be. It seems clear, however, that, for more senior executive education, one would expect relatively more emphasis on the actual classroom. For more junior executives, with a higher fraction of the teaching/learning aimed at acquiring actual facts and relatively straightforward know-ledge, virtual learning pedagogy will get the nod. Needless to say, pressures towards day-to-day, on-the-job work focus can be expected to tilt the emphasis toward the virtual learning dimension for all categories of executives.

In the near future, we should expect academic value creation from other kinds of virtual learning, too, not just one-on-one exchange and conversations over groupware. We have, for some time, seen the uses of powerful simulation exercises, negotiations, etc., involving participants in various locations interacting via the Web. Fine examples come from two essays in the "Learning Network" of the Ninth House Network, one of the leading US-based corporations that offer virtual learning to executives. The first is "Interactive Adventures: Learn by Doing", which focuses on the network as the "ultimate business simulator". Here, "learners test their new-found knowledge and acumen in a series of [. . .] interactive movies. The outcome of this adventure is a direct result of the good — or bad — decisions they make." What this means is that the simulation represents "a unique opportunity to rehearse real-world business skills in a safe environment and to achieve a depth of understanding and retention not otherwise available".[9] The other example is "Games and Activities: Testing your Knowledge", where "each learning module has related interactive games and activities. These fast-paced fun exercises instantly reinforce each learning experience and help learners better assimilate the content over all."[10] These two examples illustrate the dynamism of development, and the variety in approaches to virtual learning that are now flourishing.

Other Web-Based Learning Vehicles

Business school leaders should prepare themselves for the advent of even more powerful Web-based learning vehicles. They may face the problem of easily becoming rather reactive, responding to any offer and suggestion to adapt any one of these new learning vehicles. The result could be that their school's approach to virtual learning becomes an ad hoc portfolio of activities that neither make sense overall, have the pedagogical features associated with them when taken in total, nor necessarily serve the overall needs of their key clients. What is needed, therefore, is a plan, worked out by the school itself. It is important that the school's leadership articulate what it sees as a meta-structure of its own virtual learning network, thus allowing various elements of the network to be developed on an ad hoc basis, but with an overall portfolio fit in mind. This will also allow for a clear cost benefit assessment of any distance-learning initiative which must thus focus on *both* the cost benefits of a project in its own right *and* the value of the project as part of the overall, portfolio-based meta-plan.

The technological assessments relating to obsolescence and the need to update and renew the various learning tools will also be more easily assessed when a learning activity is part of an overall portfolio. Here, the overall meta-logic should allow for a compatibility of approaches, seen from *both* a user's point of view *and* a school's delivery point of view. Some form of stability over time will be essential. At the same time, users and the school's delivery must have some sort of efficiency in the use of the various elements within an overall virtual learning network, above all regarding the stability in choices of technological options. After all, the expense side can be formidable if the technology is allowed to drive the school in too many directions — in this field, the difficult dictum of "strategy means choice" certainly applies. All in all, while the various choices of virtual learning initiatives, both pedagogical and technological, may be difficult, my experience is that, with a clear meta-structure in place for your portfolio of virtual learning activities, it will be easier to make the necessary decisions.

Web-Based Networks

World Wide Web-based information systems can have a profound impact on the way the university or the business school works. Consider, to begin with, one of the first examples of a Web-based network in action, namely America Online (AOL). This Web-based network approach brings content from a variety of sources, internal and external, to a single location. It is based on a friendly community of like-minded Internet enthusiasts communicating over the Web. It has become a continually growing resource that its members can use to find exactly the information they need. This information ranges from work-related to leisure-related, from disciplinary problem solving, to answering day-to-day, life-related questions, from shopping on the Web, to looking around for the best deal. Consider further that "the personal computer dates back to a mere 25 years, email only to 1987, and the World Wide Web to 1993". E-commerce, which is already transforming the face of business, is relatively new-born. Clearly, technology plays a pivotal role in an organisation's ability to compete effectively in a new economy. Consider finally that 2.2 billion email messages are sent per day versus 293 million pieces of first-class mail in the United States.[11] Needless to say, all of this can lead to profound changes at the business school, regarding the way a business school — or, for that matter, a university — works regarding communication with its constituents — from marketing to research discrimination, from applications to alumni, now to be discussed. Web-based systems can also have an especially profound effect on the communication links associated with the internationalisation of a particular school.

Above all, these developments will add to people's accessibility to each other in networks. This accessibility will not only lead to potentially profound changes in the relationship between the researcher/teacher/catalyst and the student/learner, with a potentially dramatic increase in the possibility for instant interaction and in iterative possibilities. It will also lead to an increase in exchanges of perspectives, and an increase in exposure of ideas that one person may have. Research perspectives will be more widely shared and debated, with no geographical boundaries. The Web truly embraces one world. The "virtual dimension" of the business school will thus become truly global.

Are there limitations to knowledge exchange and learning over the Web? I see at least two. We cannot get around the fact that the world is round and divided into a number of time zones. Interaction can thus not effectively be carried out simultaneously or in real time worldwide. For conversations over the Net in real time, people would have to be up around the clock (until someone invents a way to store and edit information so that everybody gets it at the same time, still a seeming impossibility). Also, the sheer ease of interaction may lead to an over-abundance of interaction, without enough attention paid to the content of the interaction. In recent years, email has flourished. Emails addressed to "all" are flooding our computer screens. Clearly, this may lead to degradation in quality of interaction, and thus end up in jeopardising true Web-based knowledge exchange and learning, due to the fact that it may be hard for the individual to differentiate between meaningful elements for serious thought and useless junk. Perhaps a heightening of the sense of "interaction culture" is needed here; perhaps learners in a virtual learning network need to develop an effective culture of electronic exchange that focuses on promoting "true, valuable" substance, while filtering out the senseless, or worse yet, pornographic. For many, an element of communication fatigue can set in.

Web-based information systems link up many schools from various countries, co-operating on various teaching and/or research topics. The Consortium of European Management Schools (CEMS), an association of leading business schools in European countries, has developed one such Web-based campus infor-mation system. CEMS has one leading business school member per country. In this regard, perhaps one particularly important use of such a World Wide Web network would be for specialised research, where researchers interact more directly via the Web, including searching for new information very efficiently, having a dialogue with other researchers to find answers to their questions, faster and perhaps better.

Consider another example: a European group of researchers working on pedagogical advances in business schools. This group consists of approximately 30 participants, from ten countries. They meet once a year, face-to-face, for a three-day conference. In between, however, they interact over the Web, sharing drafts of each other's papers, sharing comments and feedback, posting ques-tions, references, etc., and sharing all the members' particular points of dialogue between individual members. This group is a highly cost-effective network for sharing ideas, and for each member of the network to be reached by this inter-active process.

Or consider further a research network that stems from the Wharton School and focuses on the health care management research field. This global network is more open, in that there seems to be no limitation to people joining (or leaving) the network. Its main thrust is to share research ideas — again, to share among all members the essence of comments between various members of the network, dates regarding communication of relevant new articles, books, conferences, and so on. In other words, this is a community of practice. Even with such a network, the fundamental research process is not necessarily dramatically different, whether one is part of such a network or not. What *is* different is the ability to quickly mobilise fellow researchers in various capacities to make for a more time-effective research process. The facts that time and speed are becoming more critical in more aspects of life will probably also therefore increase the quality of the research via this type of networking. Today these research-based networks have become truly abundant. Faculty members can be part of several networks at a time, interacting with colleagues with similar research interests, from all over the world. Physical proximity on campus is less of an issue.

And this will have an impact on business schools, in all academic settings, the leaders of which will have to consider them when they are making the "meta-plans" I mentioned above. Perhaps the faculty members' reality will need to be thought of in a different way, emphasising the development of collegiality on campus too — not only "virtual network collegiality". Particular attention must be given to holding a school together in the network age.

A network-based research approach does not, of course, necessarily have to be strictly applied to academic settings, but to business as well. The leadership of the business school must keep this in mind because many of the school's part-ners and clients will come from companies where networking is part-and-parcel of new product development. If the school, therefore, does not offer network interface enhanced by various information technology tools, it will appear to be falling behind. It will lose credibility. Let us illustrate how one such company, Hewlett-Packard, used networking for its product development. This example helps us to understand how universities and business schools become part of this development process. Hewlett-Packard (HP) developed a new line of commer-cial products for electronic photographic imaging, largely based on effective use of the Web. The development team saw their role as interacting with others, with complementary knowledge, within Hewlett-Packard as well as within free-standing universities, business schools, independent research organisations, and even with other companies in related fields. More than 30 critical ideas and knowledge contributions were acquired via the Web, allowing the development team to significantly reduce the time and cost of development. This information was generally made available for free.

The HP team put this all together in a systems-integration fashion to create a new line of products.[12] Using the Web, the team got things done much faster. This transformed the role of the team into integrating knowledge from others, rather than developing its own knowledge. The team had a broad vision of what it was trying to create. This "leitbild" allowed it to integrate a diverse set of knowledge inputs, all taken from the Net. Three aspects of this process may have general implications for how discovery can take place in a network:

- The role of the "internal entrepreneur" was critical, in the sense that he was pulling various ideas together, based on his own "model" for what he was looking for, what to try, what was missing, etc. It was thus a purposeful search for additional information, based on someone's clear mental math regarding what he was attempting to do, and where the gaps were. In general, one would think that such a purposeful search is critical for most Web-based discovery applications. An integrative point-of-view seems to be a precondition for effective networking.
- The search was carried out in an open-ended way through a truly open-ended network. Some of the ideas came from sister organisations within HP; some came from public sources including universities; some came from competitors, but with clear up-front statements from HP of what they were trying to do, with HP seeing how this information could be valuable, while the competitor probably saw it more as a piece of information in a narrow, non-contextual sense; and from various university sources, again with clear up-front statements from HP regarding what they were trying to do, but with the university sources probably seeing this in a "narrower" sense. Clearly, in such a case, networks need to be broadly framed, much more widely than can be defined by the formal organisational limits of the organisation one is in. And clearly, universities need to prepare themselves to be part of this if they want to fulfil their roles of knowledge-providers in the new discovery network age.
- The Hewlett-Packard international entrepreneur and his team were not afraid of borrowing ideas from others, as long as they fitted into their vision. Rather than rediscover everything from scratch, they asked the question: "Where can we find it?" "Steal with pride", as they say at ABB (Asea Brown Boveri).[13] The general implication here is, of course, not one of ethics, but that the "not invented here" syndrome must not be allowed to slow down the network-based discovery process. Furthermore, it would be necessary to share with the various sources from which one "borrows", the overall context for which one

is looking for input. This attitudinal approach will also have implications for many academic settings, in that they will have to fight their own oft-inspired "not invented here" attitudes.

Look at how this might work for a business school. As part of IMD's discovery event of the Spring of 1999 on "Internally Generated Growth", led by Professor Bala Chakravarthy and me, we distributed preliminary reading materials to a large number of interested parties via the Web. This allowed busy executives to more accurately judge whether or not they should actually come in person to the discovery event. During the event, we taped the various presentations, and edited them into a manageable length. We also had interviews with several participants who raised questions and comments, which were further commented upon by the professors involved. All of this was shared by *all* member companies in our Partner and Business Associate Learning Network, who thereby had access to a synthesis of what went on during the two days, not only as a summary, but — more importantly — a flavour of the critical issues that were debated and the tentative answers. Finally, each recipient of the ensuing CD-ROM was asked to provide comments and raise further questions afterwards — i.e., network-based dialoguing within an ad hoc common community to understand internally generated growth.

We can expect a lot of specialised research to flourish out of interaction on the World Wide Web in a similar vein to the above examples. A critical dimension of a particular researcher's or research team's capabilities will increasingly be to have an overall vision to integrate knowledge from others. In this sense, ability to think holistically, to synthesise a systems-integration approach will be needed. The researchers will, to a large extent, "borrow with pride" from others, and synthesise it, rather than themselves undertaking the specific discovery of each piece of knowledge needed for a new breakthrough. Random browsing on the Web, without overall direction, is unlikely to yield such promising research results.

Setting Up Useful Web-Based Networks

Web-based approaches can support a network of, say, partner and business associate firms. Recall that this network supports the activities of firms that work with IMD on life-long learning. A major part of the value creation comes from exposing executives from these firms to the results of our "discovery events" on a regular basis. These discovery events present the results of IMD's latest research, with an emphasis on the particular implications and new benchmarks for the members of our learning network.

Using technology to disseminate the research findings and learning rapidly around the world, IMD can now invite executives to participate in the discovery events in a much more flexible way. Wherever they happen to be, executives can "attend" the meetings on a virtual basis, gaining access to the knowledge shared at the events. Admittedly, most of the recipients of this knowledge play a passive role at these virtual meetings. They miss out on the chance to talk with others. While Web-based networks clearly allow for two-way communication, no one expects to be able to communicate with the other participants as intimately as if they were at IMD. Still, options for virtual interaction and participation are better than not coming at all.

Another advantage: we can edit and tighten up the syntheses of the discovery events on the Web, offering concentrated versions for quicker, more focused consumption. Such précis no longer has to be in real time, which allows the participating executives more flexibility in use. Executives far away can review the materials from the discovery event at any time. Of course, these boiled down versions are backed up by the possibility to interact with specific professors on particular questions and comments. Returning to the example of the "Internally Generated Growth" discovery event, one could easily see how a "question and answer" session could have been organised from a distance. This would involve various executives sending in their questions and comments over the phone, via email and telefax, which would then be edited, grouped together into clusters of related issues, which would then allow for more systematic responses from the professors. Of course, therefore, the interaction within such a discovery event-based network would need some "editing", rather than being totally open-ended (to allow for safeguarding a thematic focus through the interchange, avoiding "random rambling").

In effect, the Web also makes it possible for IMD to create a "library" of discovery event syntheses for the learning partner. Thus, these can be seen as specific inputs to a "library" of relevant briefing events that would be part of the overall meta-logic for a school's Web-based approach to virtual knowledge development and learning. It is important that the school aims to focus the discovery process in such a way that it can lead to the accumulation of relevant "library pieces" for such a learning network.

In a related development, members of our learning network can increasingly develop direct links among themselves in order to discuss specific management issues. Some might want, for example, to share best practices or particularly successful approaches. During a recent discovery event on how to develop effective corporate universities, a number of direct links among participating companies formed. Specifically, one company, which was in the process of establishing its own corporate university, sought a way to develop consistent action plans, made specific contacts with a number of other companies that were present, and exchanged ideas with them regarding how to proceed. Thus, the Web-based network led to further purposeful interaction on a small scale.

Another network is the alumni. Traditionally, alumni are organised in clubs that bring them together to learn about specific topics of interest, and strengthen their social ties. Developing alumni who are more oriented toward life-long learning is facilitated by Web-based technology. Schools can spread the word about discovery events, share research results, pose management questions, even hold virtual forums, all in the name of making learning part of the members' regular trips on the electronic highway. Alternatively, the school can create specific learning modules accessible only to its alumni. Parts of major public programme offerings, such as the *Orchestrating Winning Performance* programme, can be found only a few clicks and a password away.

This all sounds fine and good, but the question of how to get paid for the knowledge you put on the Web is a thorny one. Typically, many alumni take the existence of their business school for granted, and they are not necessarily prepared to pay additional fees for life-long learning. While the tradition of generous gifts to the business school is well developed in the United States, gift giving is not so common in Europe or the rest of the world. Many alumni of European business schools consider the payment of their initial tuition as leading to a "right" to receive subsequent benefits for free, via the alumni network, for the rest of their lives. This attitude makes it doubly hard to instil the habit and provide the content for life-long learning.

Successful approaches do exist, however. The school can ensure that information and learning it has developed for one purpose finds its way into the hands — and minds — of its alumni. Every year, IMD issues ten to 15 volumes of its *Perspectives for Managers*, a four-page document mailed to more than 5,000 executives. Summaries on the Web would offer many more executives this regular overview of IMD's latest management thinking. After reading an electronic issue, the executive-readers could request more information direct from the faculty author. Offering materials on a Web home page — calendars, summaries of events, news on faculty and alumni — is not only good marketing; it is also a good opportunity for executives to zoom in on their particular management interests, thus stimulating life-long learning. Above all, by having these "Perspectives" on the Web, one would again develop a "library" of substantive knowledge which would find its useful place as part of the overall meta-structure of the learning network of a business school. Thus, knowledge is accumulated rather effectively, while knowledge affixed to pieces of paper easily gets lost and is typically harder to retrieve from one's files.

How does the Web Change Business School Strategy?

A major thrust of IMD's strategy has been to become the most international business school. To lend a true meaning to the phrase "most international", we have "insisted" that all participants come to IMD, so that our Lausanne campus can be a global meeting place. Participants from all over the world come to the shores of Lake Léman to learn, not least by exchanging ideas among themselves. The Web can help a school turn itself into a virtual, and of course global, meeting place. This clearly requires a lot of thought: you cannot simply link people up more or less randomly over a Web site. A school has to think about which learners will have access. Carefully developed, however, a virtual campus does give the school the possibility of linking people in far-flung reaches of the world, which can enhance its image as a global meeting place, albeit on a cyber-campus. Think of how successful Geocities has been in building such a virtual community — no bricks and mortar, but an active, electronic fellowship of people with like interests and needs.

Perhaps this could lead to a different configuration of IMD's campus in Lausanne. A new and integral part of the campus would now be a "world communications centre", with studio-like auditoriums, equipped with the necessary cameras and other transmission equipment, backed up by editing facilities. Imagine screens in the auditorium that would allow people to see each other while interacting. Relatively small groups of students could physically participate in the new auditoriums, but they would be linked with executives from all over the world via modern communication networks. The physical campus might get smaller, given that classical auditoriums and study rooms might be substituted with network-based, virtual classes, and virtual group work.

Take this line of reasoning one step further. Why should the professors physically be together in one place? Would it not be feasible for the professors to be located wherever they want, and to interact among themselves and with the students via communication networks from wherever they are? Would this option not allow professors to physically locate wherever they are happiest, from a quality of life point of view, while still being able to play an entirely effective role as a member of the faculty, but now via network-based interaction? This of course calls for a revaluation of the role of the professor. School leadership would have to worry anew about building and maintaining school cohesion and creating a widely shared school philosophy. Further, the question of whether faculty could belong to more than one school would arise.

Of course, we are not at this stage yet. And besides, face-to-face interaction will probably always be a part of effective networks. Electronic interaction cannot substitute fully for the social dimension of developing trust and compatibility face-to-face among network members. Further, one can actually ask whether the academic value-creation process can take place in such a virtual networked context, at least when it comes to the core of this value creation. While we have discussed how research can benefit from a Web-based approach, there are probably aspects of the research process that might not lend themselves to such an approach, such as face-to-face dialoguing during the formative, often "pre-paradigmatic" stage of research. It is hard to see how creative brainstorming can effectively take place over the Net, as the researchers must share compatibility, trust, and common respect. Such research colloquia cannot be recreated on the Web. Compatibility and trust again come to bear when the school develops teams for its teaching and its preparation. This involves faculty members sitting in on each others' classes, discussing methods, etc. — again a matter of trust, mutual respect, and willingness to "give and take", dimensions hard to envision over the Web. One must not forget that discovery and learning is also a *social* process, with constituents of people physically building social and professional ties — hence, the role of the campus.

Still, an important strategic dimension for the emerging network-based busi-ness school will be how to mix the "glue" to hold the participants together in the network, keeping the "common sense issue" aside. Why should professors work together in *our* particular network, for instance? Why should students enrol in our virtual, network-based school and not in another? What would be the nature of such "glue" to make our network preferred, and stable?

First, a network is not for free. Faculty members would receive salaries, for instance. Research to create knowledge for dissemination in the network also requires funds. All of this does allow for some "policing" of the professionals in a network — i.e., that they would be required to deliver their services to the network. Any contractual arrangement thus creates some sort of stability in the network. Similarly, the students pay tuition to the network-based school, and if the school's network is good enough, students will pay to play.

Second, common values — indeed, a common virtual culture — among the participants in the network will probably be a key ingredient in our glue. These common values would probably be built around common pedagogical approaches to learning, common viewpoints on research, and common substantive interests regarding what types of phenomena would be important to study. These values would include a sense of ethics regarding how to interact in a network, including respect for the ownership of information and ideas coming from the various participants.

A third compound in the virtual glue would be select, but increasingly important, physical get-togethers by the members of the network indeed to re-instate a "campus effect"! These get-togethers would primarily emphasise the building of common understanding, the development of mutual respect, and the enhancement of a sense of trust among the participants. Such physical gatherings would have to be designed specifically to make the glue "stickier". The gatherings could include group work, plenary discussions, small break-out discussions — any number of face-to-face interactions, both in the long and the short run.

No one can say what the impact of the Web will be on the strategy of the business school of the future. There will clearly be significant new opportunities for new knowledge generation, for border-breaking pedagogy, for better communication, etc., all within a virtual context. But there will also be clear threats of disintegration of the classical campus, with its emphasis on the face-to-face, social dimension of discovery and learning. We can only guess about the net effects the Web will have on the configuration of business school activities. We can say, however, that the Web will have some impact. It is not absurd to claim that the Web will be a key factor in business school strategy: it will generate strategic uncertainty, but with it, untold opportunity. It is up to the school's leadership to push for the latter, while attempting to ameliorate the former.

Chapter 7

The Value of Vision and Mission in Strategic Focus

Executive Summary

The modern business school will be more effective if it has a clear vision than if it doesn't. A vision helps the organisation focus on a general direction. But the business school, like many of its clients, must translate its vision into a more detailed mission that mirrors a sharp strategic focus. Vision sets overall direction; mission highlights the details. Without a vision statement, the business school will likely lose focus, having no basis on which to make the key strategic choices on which its success will depend. Further, following a particular strategic direction demands resources, and a clear vision (mission, etc.) will help the school allocate them most effectively. The faculty-cum-entrepreneurs will also play a central role in defining, redefining or extending the mission, and hence adjusting the strategy.

Though management gurus, academics and pundits often scoff at corporate vision and mission statements, I am convinced that the modern business will be less effective than it could be without a clear vision. The reason for this is that a vision helps establish a clear, though general *focus* for the organisation. Consider, for instance, IMD's vision, which provides a general direction for the school. Three elements are particularly salient:

- The major focus for the school will be to provide executive education for managers, primarily from the larger, international firm. Research will have to be key to meet this vision, i.e., to focus on the latest.
- The school should communicate its value concept so as to be "the most practical" business school. A strong teaching pedagogy is thus a sine qua non.
- The school should be the most international business school.

But such a vision has to be translated into a somewhat more detailed *mission*, that reflects a clear *strategic focus* for the school. Vision sets general direction; mission sets out the details. The mission is therefore more focused on *how* to do it, *how* to bring the vision to life, which is often expressed in more quantitative terms than the vision. IMD's mission consists of a number of elements. First is a certain balance between the mix of value-creating activities in the form of open programmes, in-company programmes, and learning-network activities, presently representing approximately 40 percent, 40 percent, and 20 percent respectively of the revenue.

The open programmes will have as their backbone a sequence of general programmes that provide a progression for the learning executive so that he/she can attend a sequence of programmes over his/her career — i.e., IMD will provided life-long learning support. This would start with the programme *Building on Talent*, followed by the *Programme for Executive Development*, *Management of Corporate Resources*, the *Seminar for Senior Executives*, and culminating in the *Senior Executive Forum*.[1]

One would expect that a growing part of the programme delivery would be to *teams* of executives, working on specific projects related to their own work experience. For instance, these projects could be focused on developing new growth opportunities, such as in IMD's *New Venture Booster* programme. In several of IMD's programmes, such as also in *Orchestrating Winning Performance* programme and *PRISM* (for high impact project teams), we have adopted a design that makes team-based, action-oriented learning more prominent.[2]

One would further expect that each programme offered would be given in such a way that the time spent at IMD would be as short as possible, given the pedagogical intent of the programme, and that the rest of the learning experience would be virtual. The programme *Building on Talent* represents a good example of such a hybrid.

While it is difficult to delineate the research activities that would be part of IMD's mission, it would be safe to expect that its faculty would be actively working on issues that are relevant for the management of the large multinational firm. Rather than having a clear research policy, IMD has followed the belief that individual initiative is key here. IMD has actively supported all research initiatives that can have relevance ultimately in enhancing the knowledge of how to manage the international firm. Thus, within this broad focal point, all initiatives are strongly encouraged. In general, I strongly believe that research missions must be bottom-up driven.

It should be evident, even after this brief overview (the subject of visions and missions has been extensively covered in the literature elsewhere), that the mission therefore implies an important articulation of the more general vision, much — but not all — of it along more quantitative lines.

The Role of the Mission in Setting Strategy

Whether vision or mission, general statements of direction like the ones above help provide focus: without a vision statement, IMD would not go heavily into MBA delivery, or heavily into functional delivery of executive programmes, above ones for junior executives. The now-familiar adage "strategy means choice" is arguably even more relevant in brain-driven service sector organisations such as a leading business school than anywhere else. The key to a brain-driven corporation would, in fact, be the collection of talent and brains that is part of the organisation. And since time is critical for the use of brains and talent, time is de facto the strategic asset. It is therefore important that the time-spending patterns of the individuals be focused and purposeful. Lack of focus leads to the scattering of activities, i.e., a misuse of brains and time or, in other words, a misallocation of the most important strategic resources. Time cannot be stored; it is expended as one goes. Focus is, therefore, particularly essential. This is why a vision and mission are essential.

To illustrate this need for focus, consider Figure 7.1. At the top part of the figure, one sees a picture with centrifugal forces — a collection of diverse activities, which could typically take place within a business school. The "problem" is that these activities are not anchored to a core direction of the school; thus, the various activities end up taking the school in several directions, actually serving as centrifugal factors.

Consider instead the bottom part of Figure 7.1. Here the core activity of the business school is clearly laid out (it actually portrays IMD). The core aim is to serve the large multi-national corporation with relevant knowledge and pedagogy. The various additional activities are no longer preferential, but undertaken to further support and add the strength to the core. Thus, to put it somewhat simplistically, it is the relation that pulls various activities of the school together.

Following a given strategic direction requires resources. The business school needs to designate these resources. We are of course talking about designated faculty. To illustrate, remember IMD's mission. More specifically, ask yourself what faculty resources would be needed to make IMD's mission come alive. Consider the following three points:

A. <u>Are we over-spending our faculty resources?</u>

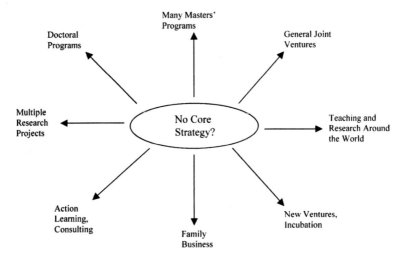

B. <u>The faculty resources must yield comparable return for all activities</u>

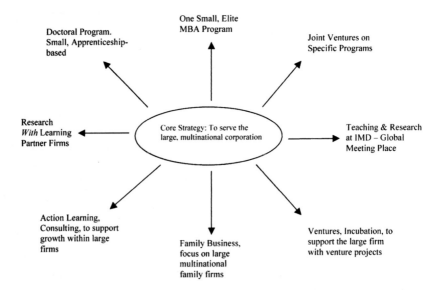

Figure 7.1: Where are we going strategically: centrifugal or centripetal?

1) The necessary faculty would have to be able to carry out relevant research that interested executives would find appealing.
2) They would further have to be able to teach this type of executive segment — i.e., interact with them, serve as catalysts, and play a role in a learning partnership with leading senior executives.
3) The faculty members would also have to be able to work together in teams, so that a particular corporation as a learning partner can be served by the relevant competencies embedded in a given team.

Thus, IMD needs specific resources to chart a given strategic direction. Simply adding faculty and thereby developing the illusion that this would mean an increase in strategic resources is not necessarily a meaningful strategy. The resources must be of such a high calibre that they can be relevant in terms of the know-how they represent relative to the given mission that a school pursues. If a school is, however, following an unfocused strategy, with activities going in all directions like scatter-shot, then simply adding on faculty without concern for their know-how might perhaps be all right. A faculty member at IMD must, however, be able to contribute with strong teaching excellence relevant for executives — more often in the form of discussion leadership than in classical "teaching". And he/she must be able to work effectively in teams.

Typically, the resources I am describing are difficult to replenish, at least in the shorter run. Given the fact that the school needs particular brain-driven resource characteristics — say, expertise in international joint ventures and alliances, or internal growth — it may be extremely difficult to replace the expertise of departing faculty. Implementation of the strategy will be a matter of having the designated resources in place, and this will, obviously, be a function largely of the extent to which the school can replace designated resources as needed. For brain-driven organisations like business schools, the challenge of making strategy "real" is the challenge of having enough faculty resources of the right kind. An acid test is that the faculty members must be "billable", i.e., in demand by the client firms and executives.

Since strategic success hinges on how well the school matches the demands for services with relevant resources, it follows that a broad strategy, with a number of focal points, creates vast, even dramatic, needs for resources. We are now talking about having several clusters of designated faculty resources, each cluster having the requisite capabilities to implement its part of the school's widening mission. It goes without saying that to add diversity of mission and strategy thus requires a very pragmatic understanding of what the faculty resource implications indeed would be. Often, in the real world of business school administration, schools tend to develop diverse strategies with no clear link to the strategy and with a lack of a realistic acknowledgement of the constraints of a limited strategy resource. In my experience, a general, unfocused strategy, matched by a general, non-designated faculty resource, is the sure scenario for non-excellence!

What does having a clear focus mean specifically? At IMD, for example, the focus is squarely on executive development types of academic delivery, and not on a broad delivery of, say, mainstream MBA teaching, nor a focus on a Ph.D. programme (IMD does, however, have a critically important elite MBA programme for promising younger executives — with strong practical experience). The necessary, designated resources are clearly defined. Strategic focus and faculty-resource focus go together. This means that, with a broadening of IMD's strategic focus, from perhaps one or two foci to many, the designated faculty focus broadens in parallel. Such a burgeoning, multi-focus development within one's faculty team will greatly add to the complexity of managing the school. Obviously, as resources allow, the school can contemplate broadening its vision and mission. Consider the faculty resource implications of the somewhat broader strategy of one of IMD's major competitors: INSEAD.

- INSEAD has a large MBA programme, with 700 students per year, as opposed to IMD's 85 students. This calls for additional MBA teachers, additional co-ordination among teachers involved in parallel sections, additional emphasis on developing compatible quality standards across the programme, i.e., faculty resource requirements that are much more demanding than a small, one-section programme such as IMD's.

- INSEAD has developed a full-fledged Ph.D. programme. This requires having the ability to deliver a series of Ph.D.-type courses, as well as having an extensive faculty capacity for thesis supervision. IMD does not have a Ph.D. programme, but rather is pursuing co-operative arrangements with other universities instead, most notably with the University of Lausanne and the Swiss Federal Institute of Technology. This frees IMD's faculty to teach only a limited number of Ph.D. students. IMD's faculty can concentrate on thesis supervision, however, where this fits with the research interests of the faculty members. Again, the demand on designated faculty capabilities would be much less at IMD than at INSEAD for Ph.D. programme delivery.

- INSEAD has built a second campus in Singapore, thus once more dramatically signalling its strong commitment to internationalisation. In contrast, IMD sees its campus at Lausanne as "the global meeting place", with emphasis on bringing students together from all over the world to learn at one location. INSEAD will have a much more demanding faculty requirement, running two campuses, with parallel activities, as well as with a need to be specifically relevant in two geographic settings: Singapore and Fontainebleau.

Overall, one can say that INSEAD follows a more ambitious, multi-focused strategy, but that this also has clear faculty resource implications. One cannot expect to realistically implement a more multidimensional strategy without a designated multi-capability faculty to back it up. IMD's strategy is perhaps less ambitious, but it allows the school to be managed with a simpler focus.

Sadly, one look around the world of management education confirms that all too many business schools have missed this lesson: they suffer from trying to do too many things, relative to what they can expect to deliver, given their faculty resources. And here I am not alluding to INSEAD, which has an outstanding faculty, and should be fully able to deliver on its ambitious — and laudable — strategy. I do not feel that I should mention names of schools here, but rather describe them in general terms. A major European business school has a plethora of MBA programmes, backed up by a plethora of functional executive programmes, as well as a broad, sprawling Ph.D. programme. Each faculty member has his/her own opinions regarding which elements of this broad, sprawling programme activity portfolio is the most important. The result is a lack of general focus on priorities; rather, the effect is a sprawl of activities that do not lead to a strategy that hangs together. Similar examples abound. In our terms: they have "unrealistic" visions and missions. The fuzzy focus is practically a guarantee of lower quality and less-than-desirable success.

But if the lesson is really so obvious, why do so many business schools lack focus? For one, business schools are what I call "highly-talented organisations". Initiatives veritably sprout in the halls. Suggestions for various directional initiatives pop up in emails, in the cafeteria, in the halls, by the coffee machine and at faculty meetings. It is as if a number of centrifugal forces are pulling the business school in every direction of the strategic "compass". The best antidote to this "pull" is a strategic focus. It serves as a counterbalance, a "centripetal force" to keep all the players on track, or in equilibrium, if you will. Again, I refer to Figure 7.1.

The visioning and "missioning" process should of course fully involve the faculty — indeed, it is the faculty's process. This process is ongoing, and lends itself well to being a key topic during an annual or semi-annual faculty retreat. Perhaps such discussions end up merely reconfirming the vision/mission statements of the past; perhaps others lead to some evolutionary changes or to major shifts in vision/mission. The key is that the faculty must be able to distance themselves from the discussion enough to ask whether their proposals go well with the school's stated vision/mission. With this distance, when individual proposals come up, it will then be relatively easy, and non-controversial, to ask how these proposals would fit within the overall vision and mission. Very often, a proposal is not necessarily "good" or "bad" per se; further, it makes little sense to assess an initiative only in its own, narrow, free-standing sense. What matters is to see any initiative in terms of its fit with the overall vision and mission. Is this good for the school? What may be right for one school might thus be wrong for another. A nice effect of having a well-articulated vision/mission is that it tempers political forces. To turn down ideas proposed by individual faculty members because the ideas don't further the school's strategy is not controversial. So, in such cases, the strategic focus helps the school's management to make the choices that are so much an inherent part of strategy. And, above all, by focusing on "what is right for the school" these decisions can be kept objective, not personalised, not win/lose!

Effective Business School Visions: Examples

A few years ago, Wharton's mission was dramatically expanded to include a heavy emphasis on executive development. A new centre, the Aresty Institute, was built under the leadership of the Dean at the time, Russell Palmer. The succeeding Dean, Thomas Garrity, further expanded the mission of strengthening executive development. This extension of Wharton's mission ran into some snags, however. The faculty, being primarily committed to academic research along functional departments, did not necessarily have an overtly great interest at large in doing executive development. Not only was the research perhaps often too specialised and perhaps too overly academically focused to have a direct relevance for the practising executive, the teaching preferences would often be along the lines of working with Ph.D. and advanced masters students, again in areas of interest of the faculty members, rather than within the general management field. To staff the executive development efforts, Wharton offered faculty members extra pay, and the normal teaching load did not include these types of executive development services. Consequently, executive development teaching was soon perceived as "slightly second rate", often offered by adjunct faculty members, and therefore considered less prestigious. Wharton's new mission was thus not easily matched by faculty capabilities relevant for this mission extension.

The Norwegian School of Management extended its mission differently. The school evolved primarily an undergraduate school, even a night school offering programmes on the side for working executives. Gradually, this undergraduate focus was strengthened, leading to accreditation for offering a bachelor's degree in business. The mission was then further extended, with a build-up of a master's programme capability, which led to a considerable increase in demand for faculty, and at times severe scrambling to be able to staff the master's courses with qualified faculty members. The difference between being a good teacher for the undergraduates and master's students became a factor to be reckoned with. The school's mission was extended even further: the school decided to offer its own Ph.D. programme. Initially, co-operation was launched with the University of Oslo and with Copenhagen School of Management, so that the students could take some of their doctoral courses there, while being supervised by a mixed team of Danish and Norwegian faculty members. Over time, the school built up a full offering of its own doctoral programme, and granted its own doctoral degrees. This led to further stress, given the need to *stretch* the faculty capabilities to cope with one more distinctive teaching and research requirement. As the mission was extended, the demands on the faculty as a resource thus also increased dramatically, leading at times to discontinuity between what would be required to fulfil the ever increasingly complex mission and the availability of relevant, designated faculty resources. A key message here is that it takes time to build up a requisite resource to meet a changed mission.

Now let us take the example of IMD. As noted, our vision is simple. We want to focus on executive development for the international firm and be recognised as a world leader in executive development. IMD's mission, thus, is stated another way: to be the preferred learning partner for the *best* global companies, current and potential. Another way to capture IMD's mission is the fact that we want to significantly support our learning partners in attracting, keeping, and developing the best managerial talents. The customer thus defines our mission. Sketched out further, this mission highlights the basic strengths that IMD must develop and follow. We have already looked at a few general statements from IMD's mission; consider now the following two implications:

- IMD aims to truly be the most international business school in all respects: participant mix; faculty mix; teaching materials; research. This also implies providing a global meeting place with no home country dominating in clients, programmes, or participants. There must therefore also be a clear commitment to *deliver* on this — say, in faculty recruiting and worldwide marketing.
- IMD is dedicated to creating learning partnerships with executives, not focusing on the classical undergraduate market, the mass MBA, or doctoral studies. IMD does, however, have a small, elite MBA programme, which — in terms of participants, curriculum, and teaching mode — can be seen as a long executive development programme. It is, however, vital that we thus stick to this "customer segment".

Such a clearly articulated vision and mission for the school must also provide guidelines for the search for new opportunities — it must *not* be confining! This vision might, for instance, be inspiring and broad enough to allow the organisation to rally around certain areas of interest. For the business school to develop, faculty members must feel that they can do new things, *as long as they fit broadly in with the vision and mission*. This dynamic, "can do" attitude is essential to the dynamism, and hence the success of the school.

The Role of Faculty Initiative in Extending the Mission

The addition of the *Senior Executive Forum* programme at IMD was an initiative, spearheaded by a faculty member and a small team, to bring the latest in general management strategic research to leading senior executives.[3] The programme content changes from year to year, depending on a confluence between the evolving research interests of the faculty and the current practical interests of senior executive, according to the ad hoc pressures they face at any time. *Internally generated growth* was the first topic pursued. This was followed by the issue of integrating acquisitions and mergers as a vehicle for strengthening growth. Both topics reflected ongoing, vibrant research within the IMD faculty, and the "can do" attitude, well captured by the phrases, "no limits" and "no confining vision and mission".

The *Orchestrating Winning Performance* programme at IMD is another example of how carefully we tailor our programmes to our mission.[4] Every year the programme's contents are updated, the aim being to renew the contents by between 75 percent and 100 percent from year to year, and the reality falling not too short of this. The teaching is typically channelled into a number of "streams". This past year, the streams were: "Growth Through Mergers and Acquisitions", "The Technology Dimension as an Impetus for Business Growth", "Developing More Effective International Strategies", "Developing Organisational Designs for the Next Millennium", and "Stakeholder Management Challenges, With Special Focus on Environmental Research" (see Figure 4.1 for a block diagram of this programme). Again, it was up to the faculty to be inspired, to demonstrate for themselves and their colleagues — as well as for the participants — that they *"can do it"*. The vision/mission was inspiring, not confining.

A third example was research spearheaded by Professor Don Marchand at IMD into the managerial uses of information technology as a strategic tool. This research, co-sponsored by (then) Andersen Consulting (now Accenture) led to a large amount of empirical data gathering, which then led to two books and two research monographs, as well as to a new executive programme. Professor Marchand's initiative dovetailed neatly with the vision and mission of the school in the sense that he focused on the information technology needs facing the large, complex organisation.[5]

In general, it is thus critically important that faculty members feel that they can do what they are interested in, what they are inspired by, what they wish — based on their own perception rather than having to force-fit their interests into programmes designed by others. This is perfectly natural and feasible within a broad-based, yet focused, vision and mission. In fact, it has only been possible for the IMD faculty to develop its capabilities because the vision/mission is sufficiently broad and at the same time so clearly defined. For instance, because a key element of IMD's mission is executive development, the faculty at IMD has a strongly developed capability for case-based research. They typically need little time from the moment of conception of the case to the signing-off of the finalised case by a leading corporation, and the subsequently rapid introduction of this case research into the classroom. This ability to orchestrate case-based research specifically, and perhaps clinical research in more general terms, is thus a major asset of the IMD faculty that fits with the mission — among other aims, to "deliver faster, and on time" from research to the classroom.

IMD's faculty is also very adept at quickly designing new in-company programmes, based on a rapid perception of what a learning partner needs, drawn on built-up experience in listening and generalising from this. This up-front development work can, in fact, represent valuable research, leading to considerable cutting-edge knowledge. This again helps the school fulfil part of its stated mission — developing fast responses to the client. The same goes for the development of new open programmes. In the past, it typically took several years to develop a new open programme, but this development cycle has now been dramatically reduced. In line with our mission, we have built a generalised body of knowledge of how to design, test, and market new programmes. Even our marketing team has got involved in this process. The key is to execute an effective transformation from general programme ideas to specific classroom implementation.

Problems with Vision and Mission Statements

Despite my claims of the power of missions to focus an organisation, there can be problems with such vision or mission statements. As noted, they can be so broad, so general that they fail to inspire. They can be expressed in such vacuous terms that nobody in the organisation can tell you what they mean, or relate them to what they do day-in and day-out. Think about the many mission statements you have probably read over the years. The ones that claim that the organisation "wants to be the world leader, the very best!". Logically, only one — or a handful — of organisations can make these claims. For a good, but demonstrably second-rate organisation, such expansive claims can be too ambitious, even leading to cynical behaviour among its members, and this can be the case for business school faculty, too. The vision/mission statements wind up sounding rather meaningless, fail to guide or inspire the faculty, provide little direction for administrators. Such unrealistic statements will not have a meaningful purpose; they will not lead to meaningful focus within the business school.

As the former head of London Business School, George Bain, pointed out in oral communication, it is important that a vision/mission can be told as a "story". Organisational members can truly relate to stories, and are more likely to be able to use them to make effective choices. A good example of this can also be found in comments made to me by the former President of Nestlé, Helmut Maucher. He had continuously backed IMD, both financially and concretely, sending senior executives to IMD's programmes over many years. Nestlé was, in fact, the founder of IMEDE, one of the schools that merged to form what is IMD today. When I asked him why he supported IMD, he answered very directly:

> This is easy. There are three reasons why IMD is highly relevant to us here at Nestlé. First, it is the most practical business school in the world. Second, it is the world's most international school. And, third, it receives no government support and is therefore independent of government influence. These are the reasons why we subscribe to IMD.

This "story" beautifully sums up IMD's vision/mission. In many ways, Maucher's story gives a much livelier picture of what IMD is all about by adding meat and blood to it. To be able to tell one's vision/mission as a compelling story may just be a good acid test for whether one's vision/mission hangs together.

Consider how you might "tell" the story. Your vision may be to empower and enable your employees (faculty and staff) to deliver the best executive development experience for your learning partners (executives from corporations and individual executives). This means providing superior value to your participants and their sponsors. Your first "story line" could have to do with the international side of the activities, emphasising that not only the faculty, but the student body, would be highly international, and with no home country dominance. This internationalisation issue could — and should — be brought out as part of the "story" when you describe the teaching and the research, so that the participants (students and faculty alike) are reminded of the positive power of this.

Second, the issue of best practice can be "told" all the time. By referring to what is working among the participants in one's classes, one can easily develop a strong "story". Consider, for instance, the 450 participants in the *Orchestrating*

Winning Performance programme. If you assume that they have an average 30 years' experience, that would make a total of 13,500 years' of experience in the programme. Another good "story" would be to refer to this on an ongoing basis, drawing on what would be best practices. For instance, how can one tell the "story" about action-learning teams actually accelerating the development of new strategic initiatives, such as what took place in the creation of IMD's *Venture Booster* programme?

In general, it is important to be sure that one's context reflects the vision/mission one is committed to. If not, there will clearly be an inconsistency and a lack of logic. The context must, however, be used on an active basis to illustrate what the vision/mission is all about — a "live" story. In IMD's case, this also means creating satisfactory economic returns for IMD's stakeholders (faculty, staff, foundation board, clients in general), and enhancing the well-being of the IMD community. The fact that IMD's academic value creation also leads to economic success is a strong "story". And this will involve always being open to adjusting the vision so that it includes adapting to the marketplace, the subject of the next chapter.

Chapter 8

Adapting to the Marketplace

Executive Summary

The dynamic business school of the future can — indeed, should — do without government support. Too much government support can harm the school. Rather, the dynamic business school can — indeed, must — be directly responsive to the market. Only when it generates resources by providing the value that the marketplace most desires will it be able to maximise those resources it needs to create the valuable offerings its clients demand. However, the school must take a responsible stance, tightly linked with, but not just blindly adapting to the market. The school needs to keep the balance in its funds-flow: what it creates should cost less than or equal to what its clients will pay (resource spending must be less than resource generation). Since tuition income will normally not balance this equation, the school must find other sources of revenue. These will most likely come from the school basing its strategy on being a comprehensive learning partner in all the ways outlined so far. These include generating market-based and relevant research, faculty ownership to increase market relevance, keeping the "long view" in value creation, and adapting by envisioning clients' future needs.

An issue under much debate in institutes of higher education is whether the leading academic institution — we are, of course, especially interested in the dynamic business school — *can* be more directly responsive to the marketplace, reaping rewards from the market if it succeeds in creating value that the market is willing to pay for. Or, should governments finance the leading business school (which amounts to societal support)? This second position seems to rest on the belief that building up and maintaining a state-of-the-art faculty with its know-how base can *only* take place with government support. Belief or not, the fact is that government as an automatic source for funding is rapidly drying up.

The market will increasingly be called on for sourcing teaching and/or research activities of the academic institution. According to Barry Munitz, this can only work if one begins with a clear and uncomplicated assessment of the external environment. One must "begin with a clear and uncomplicated assessment of the external environment, isolate the opportunities and threats found in that environment, and build a set of responses based on strengths and areas of distinction".[1] According to Rowley *et al.*, Munitz "argues that the old consensus is gone and for the first time in American experience, we will have to create educational change without significant new resources".[2] They further state,

> When you do not have enough resources and are faced with events of catastrophic magnitude, you devise a sequence in which help or resolution will be provided. In a world of global change, *triage* means to take the healing strategies for change that will shape the future and use them to transform higher education through some reasonable sequence into a better and more responsive contributor to quality and to competent solutions for humanity's pressing problems. This requires linking knowledge to real-world needs. He (i.e., Munitz) believes funding must be tied to societal needs and the need for 1990 and beyond is the polytechnic model of applied research, technology transfer and faculty involvement with undergraduates, skills for the work place. . . . Moving from ivory tower to polytechnic will require a new consensus about the University and its environment.[3,4,5]

But whether with government support or by following the market, the question remains: How can we create what Burton R. Clark calls "entrepreneurial universities"?[6] I believe that too much government support harms more than it helps: rather than motivating the school to adapt, it provides a "sleeping pillow". After years of business school management, I believe that strong market pressure is the key to delivering high quality — with a few caveats. Above all, as we shall see, the school needs to take a stance for *responsible* market adaptation, i.e., with some balance, not "blindly" adapting to the market.

Tighter Links to the Market

It is easy to imagine why society, in general, might be happy with well-adapted business schools that take care of their own needs. After all, such institutions then take care of themselves. And if they can't generate enough resources from their own activities as well-adapted learning partners to a rich stream of business firms, the obvious diagnosis for their lack of resources might well be: the business school isn't providing enough market value. If that happens, market mechanisms will accelerate the school's demise or even extinction. Looked at from the more positive perspective of market motivation, however, we could also say that the market will provide strong rewards for a business school that is well adapted and truly provides recognisable value for each of its learning partners. Further, with many competing demands for funds in modern society, governments are more and more likely to restrict their resource pay-outs. To cope with these shrinking grants and rising expectations, the academic institution needs to create a stronger link with the market. Only with this tighter link can the academic institution adapt more closely to the emerging needs of the "customers", and thereby better justify the price of their resources.

Regardless of where the money comes from, with the rapidly developing field of management theory trying to keep up with an equally rapid development of the practice of global management, a business school needs significant resources to create relevant academic value. Staying on top of the rapid knowledge evolution means massive research and regular renewal of the teaching programmes. Both are resource-intensive activities. These resources must be paid for — someone must provide.

Further, it is important to have a realistic view of the resource balance — sources and uses in the business school. Up to now, we have been discussing the faculty as a resource, making the point that we must have enough faculty input to meet demand — teaching and research, but also governance tasks, administration, etc. Here, therefore, we shall discuss the funds-flow side, the resulting equation of flow-in versus flow-out, which results, of course, from academic value creation.

Funds-Flow: The Balance of Resources

What the school creates in teaching programme offerings and other academic output should be less than or equal in value to what participants pay to indulge in them. The resource spending side — salaries and other expenses, like research, administration, maintenance, as well as interest and debt repayment if the school's facilities have been in part or totally financed by loan — must be less than or equal to the resource-generating side. It should be pointed out that the business school may have to deal with rather tricky periodisation problems, particularly when it comes to pre-paid tuition, say, typically for the longer programmes such as the MBA, or outstanding tuition, which might be more typical for shorter programmes, where you "pay as you attend". Needless to say, however, few first-rate academic institutions can normally generate enough resources by charging tuition only. Other sources include fees from businesses working with the business school, donations from alumni and others, and also significantly in many cases, support from the government sector. The problem with any sources of funds that are not directly earned is that there will typically be restrictions or strings attached to their use. Clearly, careful planning of the flow of funds is therefore necessary; a budgeting and monitoring procedure must be in place. A process which pre-empts surprises is a critical foundation for managing any academic institution. Paradoxically, in many academic institutions this obvious cornerstone is often weak. For this lack, of course, there is no excuse.

The market will probably reward those schools only where the long-term business plan or budget is fundamentally based on a comprehensive learning-partnership picture, i.e., an explicit willingness to serve the business sector in ways valuable to them. Only then, in all likelihood, can a sustainable budgetary balance be maintained. Financing academic value-creating activities through loans to support operations is clearly not viable; even for short-term, exceptional crises, the school should avoid debt financing to create value from operations. Even financing buildings and grounds expansion through debt is also probably questionable. Resources the school generates must thus cover the basic "going concern" of academic value creation. But since the key customers of the future will increasingly be corporations and executives (less and less the classical undergraduate and/or graduate students), if a school adapts well to its learning partners, it should be able to build a budgetary base that will allow it to continue doing well, even without borrowing to run its programmes. By pushing the school to make "good even better" by building on what it has already achieved (with both incremental improvements and pioneering breakthroughs), the adaptive pressures of the market are the strongest, most reliable motor for the school's momentum.

In all instances, therefore, the members of the academic institution must remember that someone will have to pay for their efforts to create value. Too often, this isn't the case; faculty members may have access to their own resources through the budget process, and worry little about the source — so long as the support remains. In addition to a fixed salary, the faculty member may have his own research grants, a designated research associate he feels he "owns", and at times a rather lackadaisical attitude towards incurring research expenses that goes with this, even though these may even exceed his budget. He simply does not see the need for stringent fund-flow planning as a high priority for him. Somehow, additional resources will become available. While a faculty member must feel that his institution is flexible enough to support unexpected financing needs, the critical problem might thus be that he lacks financial discipline. This may further manifest itself in the professor's attempt to "grab" resources wherever he can. Resources come from "them" and are therefore not seen as something the faculty member also "owns", or is therefore in any way responsible for. In order to develop more of the "owner's attitude" toward resource spending among faculty, I recommend that a business school install a profit-sharing bonus system. With such a system, faculty stick to their budgets, and spending resources wisely — as if they were their own, in fact — and then, at the end of the year, the school can distribute excess funds as bonuses (after some funds have been put aside for a rainy day, of course).

Research: Market-Based and Relevant

The key is a sense of market-based relevance-seeking. A member of the academic institution cannot expect his school or society to support academic value creation that comes without relevant research, advancements in teaching or contributions to the greater business community. If a faculty member is neither renewing him/herself pedagogically, nor pursuing research actively, the school can easily explain that no further funds will be available. Stopping support will be much harder to justify if the demands for resources are affiliated with research activities that might be seen as marginal relative to a school's vision/mission, or even falling entirely outside the activities of the school.

Let me give two examples, both from the Norwegian School of Management. A professor was studying the Brazilian indigenous population, as an extension of his initial degree in social anthropology. This research, though of presumably very high quality, was felt to fall outside the mission of the school. After considerable discussion, funding (both time and money) was declined. Even though the quality of the research may well have been beyond dispute, perhaps even indisputably excellent, it was simply too far away from the interests of the market. Another professor was working on a research project on the development of democratic processes in pre-World War I France. Though here, too, the research was of a very high quality, it clearly fell outside the mission of the business school, and was thus not automatically funded by the school's resources. The point here is simple: generally, the school must scrutinise all funding. Such scrutiny is most important when the funded research and more fundamental pedagogical developments may have a possible pay-off only sometime in the more distant future. It is essential that funding be so disciplined that it is akin to each faculty member asking, "Would I fund this if it had to come out of my own pocket?" Good judgement decisions are thus called for when it comes to research funding decisions. It seems key to have a stringent, but balanced and responsible approach, keeping in mind that one's research must "lead the market, not only be led by the market".[7]

The growing demand for relevance may take many forms, among them, resistance to paying extraordinarily high tuition fees, for example, unless true management value counterbalances the steep bill. Even with the louder call for "management relevance", participants are typically ready to pay for quality. At IMD, for instance, tuition is rather high, but this reflects what the market is ready to pay, and seems to equate quality with these high prices in our clients' minds. In general, there seems to be relatively little price elasticity within the segment of the market where IMD is most active. When it comes to the annual fee paid for membership in our Partnership Network, this elasticity may, however, more easily change with different economic times. The fee for a "Partner" membership is Sfr. 100,000 per year; for a "Business Associate", it is Sfr. 50,000. There are instances, relatively frequent, especially during periods of relatively tough economic conditions, where corporations might question these annual fees. This typically happens when the corporation has never been an active member of the Learning Network, has not sent participants to the discovery events, has, in effect, not taken advantage of what membership in our networks offers. In such cases of non-use, it is not surprising that perceived benefits do not match expenses. Of course, it is not only the responsibility of the corporate member to look for full advantage in membership; IMD's own organisation must do its utmost to activate the member firms to facilitate the use of the network so that such value gaps do not develop.

Increasing Market Relevance: Faculty "Ownership"

The faculty members of a business school can be seen in many respects to "own" their school, even though in strict legal terms this is not the case. In order to protect their "ownership", to secure the resource base, the school must forge as many strong, dynamic links with the customer as possible. I have already recommended that a bonus system should be created allowing the faculty members to share in any surplus cash flow generated as a consequence of superior academic value creation at the school, where income might exceed expenses. I also indicated that the faculty members be encouraged to think about all expenses as if they were their own. But, it should also be stressed that one can probably not "save oneself to richness". There are clearly limits to what can be gained by tight expense control (even though it must take place, as a necessary condition). More fundamental, therefore, would be an added focus on the revenue side. Here, too, the faculty members must think actively, almost as if they were independent entrepreneurs or even business people in their own right. Whatever a faculty member can do to help secure new revenue from the market will be critical. All members of an academic institution — administration, faculty, and staff — need to feel this responsibility. This is why "freeloaders" (faculty members who only use resources, but neither contribute to serving the customer nor generate resources) have no place in the modern business school.

Faculty members must do their share to secure the resources for the most relevant value creation. Faculty members may develop special relationships with particular client companies, say, when they deliver in-company programmes. A faculty member may in fact work on such a relationship to the extent that he can be seen as an informal custodian of a "key account relationship". Such a faculty member will be responsible for quick responses when the client raises concerns, for being a "gatekeeper" vis-à-vis his/her colleagues in modifying the team-based programme at the request of the client, resolving various practical problems relating to scheduling, perhaps some marginal changes in the faculty staffing, some adjustments of the programme content, etc. All in all, an "active" attitude by a faculty member vis-à-vis a client can mean a lot in strengthening the school-to-business relationship and thus creating a more secure revenue stream.

Regardless of all of the above exhortations, the school must adapt with care. It must be market-driven within the framework of an overall notion of what is *reasonable*, as the school's formal policies and informal norms establish or define. Balanced judgement is vital here, to strive for a responsible market adaptation approach. Also, however, the school must take a fair, balanced approach to all client demands. For instance, excessive demands for cases that merely "sugarcoat" various problematic administrative issues at a given company, excessive scheduling demands, and excessive demands for faculty members to duplicate each other in co-teaching and, thus, in listening presence, might call for sanctions. Often such demands are made in an unco-ordinated way by different members of the learning partner organisation. Though they can make good sense on a small scale, they can be excessive when aggregated. To avoid such cases, the school must ensure that it can serve all the clients in its portfolio fairly.

Keeping the Long View in Academic Value Creation

Academic value creation does not mean taking short cuts and caving in to unreasonable, even whimsical demands, from various practitioners, whether they might be able to pay or not. Perhaps the most difficult of such requests is when a client insists on having only certain faculty members delivering his/her in-company programme. It goes without saying that the school's strategic resources will easily become significantly diminished if it tries to meet such limiting requests. This means that the school would have to be staffed with competent faculty members in much higher numbers, assuming of course that they can be found. It should be a prerogative of the school, not the client, to control major staffing decisions. The short view may only lead to responding to sudden, but short-lived shifts in the job demands market, or following the next flavour-of-the-month management fad.

Consider the following example from IMD. One of our major clients assigned their own, but relatively junior relationship-officer to take the lead from their side in developing a large in-company programme for several hundred top managers from their organisations all over the world. This young manager, perhaps eager to be "tough", or at least eager to show that he was in charge, demanded the right to make a number of pedagogical and staffing decisions. It turned out that the substantive basis for his making these judgements was rather limited, which is perhaps not surprising, given the lack of his actual experience. As a result, new requests, at times quite contrary to the preceding ones, came up, and the development process became difficult. In retrospect, it seems safe to say that the quality of the actual programme delivered did not live up to the high aspirations that should have been set, and would have been met, had the young man not impeded delivery with his insistence on making important programme decisions. In another instance, we encountered a large multinational corporation where an increasing number of staff executives became involved in designing the programme over time, which created great difficulty in responding to all of them, particularly since the requests were, at times, contradictory. IMD then called for a "time out", insisting on a classification of and commitment to, a few funda-mental principles that should guide the development of the programme. Perhaps this calls for clarification of what can be expected relatively early in the process of developing tailored in-company cases. The more up-front clarity, and the more up-front "anchorage" of this process in the learning partner's own organisation, the better. A holistic perspective based on true insights about what management deliveries are needed, but also what new knowledge must be developed is more critical today than ever before. A leading business school must thus act and clearly believe that it is a professional organisation, that it knows how to design and deliver its programmes. It *must* speak out on these issues, bringing its own experience and competencies forward with its learning partner clients with authority, so that the latter can benefit from this repository of insights on programme design and implementation. Thus, adaptation does not primarily mean following, but above all anticipating — envisioning what business will need in the years to come.

Adapting by Envisioning Clients' Future Business Needs

To be able to anticipate what business will need, the business school needs to be exposed to the pressures of the marketplace. The pressure will essentially force the business school to come up with a *relevant* research agenda that actually stimulates high levels of excellence. Over the years, many academic institutions have been free of this pressure. Ample financing has rained down on them routinely — from government sources in most cases. They have also benefited from huge endowment funds, built up by previous generations of academic value creators. I believe that these fat, soft resource cushions are likely to have a deleterious effect in the long term on academic value creation. I had a chance to discuss my position with the former Dean of a leading US business school. He felt that large endowments might have discouraged market-oriented value creation. He had found it particularly important to recruit faculty members with a strong academic commitment, not only to facilitate good academic work, but also to set expectations and standards for the others. He further felt that it was necessary to have strong progress assessment of each faculty member, so that faculty members could get some sense of expectations, and some feedback on their progress. He was, however, surprised that much of this academic focus became rather esoteric, driven by the researcher's own narrow interests — and funded by the school's endowment! One might say that, with a strong resource base, it is certainly more difficult to instil a sense of immediate adaptive pressure on the faculty. Clearly, the faculty of such a well-funded institution will operate under a clear assumption that there are indeed resources available "for a rainy day", a luxury other business schools may perhaps not have.

What do you do when you do not have such a resource base, but are faced with trying to build up stability in case of difficult market situations, despite this? As I have already argued, "partnerships" between the best groups of practitioners and a realistic, real world-oriented academic focus are the most direct line to the marketplace. They provide the best basis for strong academic value creation, and therefore for securing the necessary resource base.

Most business schools are part of a larger university structure. This will typically have resource implications, with net resources flowing to — or coming from — the business school. For the business schools that manage to respond to the market and create relevant academic value, it may be particularly hard to be part of larger university structures. They may easily be "subsidising" other parts of the university. Such schools foot the bill for expensive overheads or contribute to "weaker" departments. At the Wharton School, for example, the University of Pennsylvania exacted a considerable tax on the school, significantly diminishing the discretionary cash flows that the school might have enjoyed. Similar situations can be found in many universities where a successful business school flourishes, but where other departments of the university are in financial trouble. It should be kept in mind that, when top university officials take the step of taxing a successful business school, the tax in fact puts an extra burden on their *clients*, or learning partners. In the long run, this situation is untenable. The environmental stakeholders who pay for the academic value creation of the business school cannot be expected to contribute (or be willing to contribute), even indirectly, more than they get back. Not only should they not be expected to pay, but sooner or later, they will simply stop paying. Take the example of a wealthy Wharton business school graduate who showed his interest in donating a building to the Wharton School. In the university planning process, this came back to the donor as a proposal for an undergraduate student welfare centre, for the entire student body at the University of Pennsylvania. The donor subsequently withdrew from the project, largely due to the fact that he felt that he would end up "subsidising" a number of student activities which had little to do with his own understanding of value creation at the Wharton School. As resources get scarce, a business partner is unlikely to be pleased about his funding going to pay for a new pool or a tenured chair in, say, Ancient Greek Civilisations.

It is interesting that, at outstanding universities such as Harvard, each academic school is expected to stand on its own, with a relatively small common overhead structure and little joint infrastructure. This maintains the pressure to adapt and be relevant. A similar approach has worked well at Oxford and Cambridge, where each of the colleges within these universities is a free-standing economic institution that has to generate its own funds to pay for the academic value creation they support. At more centralised universities, such as the University of Pennsylvania and MIT, for instance, the business schools — Wharton and Sloan — have to pay considerable "taxes" to the central university. It becomes an obvious priority for a Dean of such a business school to fight such taxation trends.

Interestingly, at one such school, the Dean was able to reduce the taxation burden, even down to the point where the school was left neutral vis-à-vis the "big" university. The Dean argued that, in order to "invest" in the build-up of the necessary intellectual capital to be a world-class institution for the future, his school needed to be free of paying a heavy tax to the university. Interestingly, therefore, the tax burden may go up and down. Again, in the long term, it is hard to imagine this being an effective way to organise academic value creation. Nevertheless, parts of universities are still thriving as a result of such subsidisation — why? Universities are typically quite complex examples of stakeholder-managed organisations, with a multitude of varied viewpoints, tradeoffs, and power bases. It may be relatively easy for a large university to therefore join focus on a smaller unit such as a successful business school to ameliorate what might initially be seen as short-term financial problems at the university level. My feeling is that these types of taxation schemes often come about as "simply happening" and also are often "quite incremental", i.e., implying that it may be more convenient for a university's leadership to solve its restructuring problems this way, rather than "bite the bullet" and close down certain non-performing, problematic units with little future, rather than allowing them to keep on.

Adapting to Market Pressures: The Example of IMD

Among the business schools of my experience and knowledge, IMD is unique in the degree to which it responds to market pressures, and it is relatively successful. IMD receives no government money. The institute has relatively small financial reserves. No one client represents more than four percent of the school's revenue. So far, the results have been generally very good, with a turnover per faculty member of more than SFr 1.6 million, or a turnover per employee in general of more than SFr 310,000. These figures compare well with turnover-per-professional in high-performing service organisations such as McKinsey (with a turnover per professional of approximately SFr 2 million, the consulting industry leader). It should be pointed out that the relatively heavier emphasis on executive education — rather than on MBA programmes — tends to bring the numbers up for IMD.

IMD is probably more market-focused than many other business schools. Its well-defined vision and mission tie it strongly to the global market. And the result is that it aims to be the most international of all leading business schools. This is manifested by the fact that in 1998, for instance, executives from more than 60 nations attended the school. Fifty-four percent of these came from various European countries, 20 percent from Asia, 20 percent from the Americas, and the rest came from other parts of the world. The school's home country, Switzerland, did not play a dominant role in any way, with Swiss participants numbering less than ten percent. IMD's faculty of 50 members similarly comes from 19 nations. IMD's location in a minority language part of, already small, Switzerland is also significant — it does not have to grapple with a home country influence that one would typically find in schools in large countries, such as those in the USA or any of the major European countries. IMD thus has a home-country neutral location, giving all participants an interesting equal vantage point regarding being heard and being "right"!

In trying to be finely tuned to the needs of its market, IMD aims to be highly relevant for executives. This is the sole focus — there is no Ph.D. programme and no large MBA programme (the small MBA programme aims at somewhat older students with an average of six years of management experience, executives in their own right). A strong, practical, up-to-date orientation to serve leading international executives is therefore part of the *raison d'être* of IMD's teaching, research, and academic staffing. This reason for being comes directly from the school's strong market orientation.

An important innovation within IMD — to create explicit service to the school's learning partners, a stronger value proposition — is the establishment of a so-called "field force" of senior associates. They work full time on supporting IMD's learning partners throughout the world and thus work to keep IMD "close to the market". There are a total of nine field force members, splitting up the world geographically among themselves. The task of these field force members is to support the marketing of IMD on a global basis, i.e., going significantly beyond the more "passive" marketing via brochures, word-of-mouth referrals, and advertising.

A key message to bring across for the field force is to explore how IMD might complement other executive development offerings, not substitute them — not disrupt what the firms are already doing! IMD offers a global learning value proposition, thus complementing the typically already established local/regional offerings available to most clients in their home markets or nearby markets. It is not a matter of either/or but of utilising both IMD and the local offering. This strong value proposition requires a real life service organisation to come alive!

An active field force has thus been an important innovation for the development of IMD's globally-based value proposition. Above all, it can be seen as a service to our learning partner clients, both when it comes to discussing how to make use of our open programmes, how to suggest in-company programme alternatives, and how to make better use of IMD's learning network activities. Experience so far indicates that our learning partners truly appreciate this unique value proposition and, in the end, are willing to pay for it!

In the delivery of academic value, IMD emphasises pedagogical relevance for its executive participants. The key is excellence in, and efficiency with, executive development, both in the classroom and in other aspects of managing the school. The professors are more facilitators of learning than teachers — more catalysts than lecturers. Perhaps this is best illustrated by two examples of IMD learning partnerships with corporations headquartered far away from IMD's campus in Lausanne, Switzerland, one in the US and one in Japan. Why would these two corporations choose to work with a school so far away from their home ground? The US corporation considers that the basic qualities of IMD's programme deliveries are similar to those of leading US business schools. According to this source, any differences in technical competence are insignificant. What the US-based multinational appreciates is the fact that IMD is on neutral ground, not located in a large home-country market setting. By operating in this context, IMD can be more neutral, taking an implicitly, even explicitly, less biased view of management issues than they could find in a school in their home market. This client company feels that true internationalisation, with no home-country bias, is a major advantage. For the US firm, the issue is to make use both of its strong business schools at home and of IMD. The two complement each other, they do not compete.

A Japanese multinational was considering how to internationalise its management talents further, and felt that the company's operating style was perhaps too confined due to its Japanese roots. It was felt that making use of an institution such as IMD could better benefit the development of a more multicultural corporate base. The Japanese executives could also more effectively participate in the class activities, given the international flavour of the IMD classes, including a small English mother-tongue contingent, making it easier for anyone to participate than might have been the case in a UK or US business school. It was felt that IMD's professors-cum-catalysts made participant learning easier for them — not an easy challenge for Japanese executives who are normally not as comfortable with this type of learning.

Market Driving or Market Driven?

Still, even if the business school manages to be finely responsive to its customer's needs, a number of questions remain: Is this type of academic value creation, based on such a strong adaptation to the customers' basic needs, enough? Is the business firm — the market — willing to pay for and support more fundamental research with a more uncertain long-term payoff? Would short-term market pressure, for instance, lead to relatively too much adaptation to day-to-day issues in the small, based on incremental improvements and incremental insights, and stemming from responses to the specific needs of the leading client firms? Would this not be too reactive? Would not, indeed, the lead thinking of the learning partner firms themselves dominate, even drive this type of incremental learning process? If the answer to many of these questions is "yes", then the business school runs the risk of becoming little more than the sum of best practice among its leading learning partners. And this sum would not likely result in longer-term academic leadership and direction and, consequently, would lead to little long-lasting value creation.

Well, there probably *is* a danger, with strong competitive pressures, that serving leading clients can go so far as to limit fresh thinking of a more fundamental nature. Developing and maintaining a balance between "market driven versus driving the market"[8] or leading versus being led may be tricky. Perhaps the most robust side of this equation will be the market driven/being led dimension, where there will be clear, immediate input from one's learning partner stakeholders for maintenance and articulation of this focus. The more long-term, typically less tangible, dimension of driving the market/leading will thus easily be less robust. It will be an important leadership function of the school's management to make sure that this balance is deliberate, therefore, and not the result of excessive short-term pressures, leading to an untenable (im)balance. So we need to ask how the business school can pursue a train of more fundamental, "leapfrog" learning and innovation activities, complementing the incremental adaptive academic value creation stemming from the learning partnership approach. We need to ensure that the learning partners get "fresh" new thoughts from their business school intellectual learning partner. In my experience, the only way the business school will take its responsibilities seriously of being a lead purveyor of major thoughts and ideas, in addition to incrementally perfecting existing knowledge in the small, is by having a clear market focus combined with proactive leadership from those in charge.

This point leads to one of the most critical difficulties of being market driven: How can you do this while still being proactive? How can you exert leadership to develop an appropriate balance between market driven/adaptive to the market and driving the market/proactive vis-à-vis the market? How can the leadership of a school such as IMD have the power act on this balance? To tackle these questions, think about the similarity between business institutions that frequently find themselves under pressure from stockholders, to deliver quarterly stable or increasing dividends. Ask yourself how such organisations can add an element of longer-term thinking and investing to complement their activities. For such institutions, as well as for business schools, the balance should probably be one of incorporating a number of stakeholders, not only the stockholders, or — for the business school — not only the relationship, human resource, or training manager of the learning partner. A broader stakeholder interface will help to gradually establish a more balanced approach with a longer-term dimension. Over time, a clear balance will be equated with success. In the corporate example, this means that the stock market appreciates that a firm is positioned for the future. For the business school, it means that the client base appreciates that the school's know-how base must also be developed with the future in mind. One can say that a tenable balance between the long and short term, between market driving and market driven, between leading and being led, can be maintained as long as the school is successful. The problem occurs primarily when there is a crisis, and short-term cuts need to be made, which may make re-establishing a meaningful balance difficult. For academic leadership, however, this view may offer little consolation. What happens if you actually have no other option but to respond to short-term crises? Any such short-term decisions must clearly lead to temporary "imbalances" that must, in turn, lead quickly to a re-building of the relationship. For an academic leader — a Dean, or a President — letting the drive for short-term gains become the status quo, on the other hand, is typically not very responsible.

Is there a more stable lever that the school's leadership can apply to maintain a healthy balance between the short- and long-term pressures? Yes, there is: emphasis on research. As just indicated, research emphasis represents the key to a proper value-creation balance. Research is the "medicine" that faculty members will have to take on a regular basis, to maintain the value of their intellectual capital. And although the school's leadership plays an important role in ensuring that the school is emphasising research enough and that the long-term/short-term balance is thus being maintained, it goes without saying that the leadership cannot dictate research. Research is related to faculty motivation and commitment — a faculty member has to believe in research; he or she cannot be ordered to do research. Thus, the true basis for a long-term/short-term balance and pro-active market responsiveness is therefore the presence of professors who are committed to research, to the development of their own intellectual capital, to the scientific discovery process. The professors themselves have an ability to "see", to drive the market, to be proactive — for each professor a research vision is called for.

Of course, research also develops the school's intellectual capital, not only in terms of the aggregation of the intellectual capital of each individual faculty member, but also, one hopes, in terms of capitalising on synergies among the various research initiatives of individual faculty members. Such a strong belief in research, a willingness to support research, is the most critical part of maintaining long-term commitment, i.e., of strengthening the otherwise "weaker" side of the long-term/short-term equation. Thus, I strongly believe that being proactive involves heavy commitment to research, but that research also represents the key to being responsive to the market. Proactiveness and market response go hand-in-hand. If it is not "proactively responsive", the business school ends up being unable to sustain a market-adaptive relationship. Market adaptation must be based on balance and strength, not on overly short-term focus. The basic academic values of the school must support this balance. It is, however, a critical managerial challenge for the leadership of the school to make sure that the institution is taking a balanced approach. Anything else, namely to cave in to short-term pressures in an unreflective manner, would be leadership vacation.

Still, regardless of all I have said about the responsibilities of the business school's administrators, and no matter how proactive the leadership, no matter how well the school listens to the market, long-term sustainability will have much to do with the abilities and the values of the faculty. That is the topic explored in the next chapter.

Chapter 9

The Heart of Value Creation:
Faculty Motivation and Values

Executive Summary

Faculty commitment to academic value creation is the driver of the business school's strategic process. At the top of the faculty member's agenda, economic gain must come after academic value creation. The school can compensate for this sacrifice by offering other, perhaps less tangible, rewards. The school must clearly define the place of outside consulting. It must also try to minimise constitutional politicking that, if not reined in, can severely diminish the energy necessary for individual and group or team value creation. Here, a sense of ownership (bolstered by financial rewards) can help the school keep rules and regulations to a minimum, to give the faculty space (freedom) and not drain their energy by asking them to don straitjackets of tight guidelines and cumbersome procedures. This stepping back will help unleash faculty energy and help create a constructive atmosphere characterised by meaningful debates and rich academic interchange. And it will give the individual faculty members enough "room" to handle the typically high short-term pressures of their work. Lastly, the school can help unleash faculty energy to respond to the market by regulatory teaching plans — with assessment and by serving as an "accelerator" — and actually regulating teaching activities.

Most strategic direction setting in an academic institution, including in the business driven one must, in the end, be focused around the individual faculty member. Duderstadt puts it this way:

> Probably the most important internal constituency of a university is its faculty, since the quality and achievements of this body, more than any other factor, determine the quality of the institution. From the perspective of the academy any great University

should be 'run by the faculty for the faculty' (an objective that would be contested by students or elements of broader society, of course). The involvement of faculty in the governance of the modern university in a meaningful and effective fashion is both an important goal and a major challenge. While the faculty plays a key role in the academic matters of most Universities, its ability to become directly involved in the detailed management of the institution has long since disappeared as issues have become more complex and the time scale of the decision process has shortened. Little wonder that the faculty frequently feels powerless, buffeted by forces only dimly understood, and thwarted by bureaucracy at every turn.[1]

Despite the accepted importance of faculty in university governance, notes F. H. Rhodes in "The New University", his contribution to *Challenges Facing Higher Education at the Millennium*,

faculty loyalty has tended to drift from the university to external professional guilds, funding agencies, corporate sponsors, and private patrons, so that institutional engagement of faculty members has often declined, or is sometimes used to promote special interests or abstract proposal reforms.[2]

Regardless of Rhodes' concerns, it seems clear that, even with diminishing faculty loyalty, faculty commitment to academic value creation is the backbone for *any* strategic progress. Faculty motivation matters. Every faculty member must have the drive and energy to commit to excellence. But above all, it is the faculty's individual interests and motivation for academic work that matter: commitment to the discovery process, transformation of research into terms that can be shared with others, dissemination of the results through writing and teaching, discussions with colleagues and supervision of students — in short, the whole integrated academic value-creation process. To attract and keep such dedicated faculty, an academic institution has to be an eminently attractive and interesting place. Thus, the "fit" or "commonality" between the individual's style and the school's environment or "context" is critical. To excel, the faculty members need to feel comfortable, and be able to say they feel good about the institution.

Faculty Motives

Intrinsic Academic Value Creation

Some faculty members may have other motives than strict academic value creation. They may be attracted to outside consulting work, for example. This may be understandable, particularly in light of the fact that faculty members will want to care for themselves and their families in reasonable economic conditions. Still, maximisation of economic returns is not the prime mover of an effective academic value-creation career. Most business school faculty members will have the option to join a business organisation, perhaps a management consulting firm, or another type of profit maximisation organisation. The market value of the intellectual capital that resides in each faculty member will typically be higher than what the business school can pay. Thus, most faculty members do have the option to change careers to maximise their salaries. Whether it is realistic for faculty members to consider taking jobs outside, whether the labour market for highly-specialised academic intellectual capital allows them to go back into practice is another question. My feeling is that, at least when it comes to younger faculty members adapting to and entering into practice, it may be a realistic alternative, but for older faculty members this is probably less the case. It should also be pointed out that re-entry into an academic career after time in practice, especially if the length of time is considerable, may be difficult, if not impossible. Either way, if economic gain sits at the top of the personal agenda, other places will probably be a better match than the modern business school.

At a business school, the willingness to sublimate financial gain to academic value creation is a key commitment. This "voluntary sacrifice" is, in my opinion, part of academic value creation. But the school has to ensure that the individual "pain" of creating academic value leads to other rewards that more than outweigh the sacrifice of high economic returns. Among the key motivators would be, for example, the excitement of discovering new ideas and the joy of teaching, helping managers to do their jobs better, and to create more value for the community. The excitement of working with the real-life business sector on *their* problems through consulting will also be an inducement. The financial side of consulting will, of course, also attract many.

Consulting

The leadership of the business school needs to be clear about the weight of other motives and how to manage them. These other motives — whether they be fame or fortune — must not come in the way of the basic academic value-creating premise. More specifically, an individual faculty member's consulting activities can of course be legitimate and useful, particularly when it helps the faculty member to learn more by applying his knowledge in practical settings. It is, however, important to realise that there can be a fine line between such legitimate consulting and merely utilising the "franchise" that the school provides for each of its members through its institutional prestige. Excessive teaching assignments on the outside, for instance, that merely mean repetitions of what is taught inside the academic institution, can represent weighty diversions from academic value creation. Unfortunately, however, individual academicians can easily lose their balance, preferring relatively easy, short-term profit maximisation to on-going commitment to the academic value-creating process. At the extreme — and I have seen this more than once — such an approach can lead to a faculty member actually competing with his own institution for teaching assignments. And the extreme result can be a lack of loyalty to the very institution that is providing the essential context for the academic value creation in the first place.

Some years ago, a professor was negotiating an in-company programme with a learning partner. He designed the programme, together with the partner, and, when it came to the question of pricing, he stated that "you can have this program offered by my school at price X, but, if you wish, you can have the same program, with the same faculty, at half the price offered privately at a location across the lake". This attitude is unacceptable. The school must undertake at least three measures to counterbalance such misuse of the consulting privilege that the individual faculty will have. First, it is a long-standing norm in management education that a faculty member will be allowed to consult on average one day per week. It is typically also specified that this consulting must go along with the institution's own strategies. Let us briefly review the three critical measures that prevent this conflict from happening:

● It is important to have a clear set of faculty guidelines and approval processes for individual faculty members' outside work. At IMD, these guidelines are broadly shared by all faculty members, and they emphasise that longer programmes, involving a team of IMD faculty members (in contrast to short, individual interventions) fall in IMD's ken. This is further underscored by the fact that, with a learning partner who is a member of IMD's learning network, the school works to keep the integrity of its programmes by preventing faculty from undertaking unco-ordinated, individualistic, independent "business deals". To ensure this integrity, the faculty member is expected to keep the school's leadership informed semi-annually about the type of consulting they are doing, and also to ask for permission when in doubt.

- All negotiations of in-company programme activities go through a central source at the school itself. This ensures standard prices and terms. It also adds pressure on the organisation to deal with all learning partnership relationships as though the school "owns" them. It is much harder for a faculty member to "forget" school policy when he has to go via this official administrative channel.
- Most importantly are the underlying issues of norms and ethics. A school must be run as a team that can pride itself on being open and transparent, where individual faculty members understand that, as "owners", they also have a sense of responsibility, a need to maintain a set of standards shared by all in the team, to behave professionally and ethically. This is one of the most critical aspects of academic value creation, namely that it can go on in a professional, transparent, and ethical context.

Politics

Other motives can drive faculty members. A propensity for organisational power, and a preference for playing institutional politics, are among the most common. Granted, it is essential that any academic institution be managed with strong participation by the individual faculty members to ensure that the context is the best one for individual academic value creation. Still, institutional politics and power struggles can easily escalate and lead to dysfunctionality of at least some of the parties concerned. This excessive use of energy on politics may diminish the energy balance necessary to achieve strong individual academic value creation. A sense of individual maturity is thus called for — to safeguard the spending of energy on what is critical for one's school, as opposed to wasting individual energy on "win/lose" politicking and myopic debates.

How can the school keep a lid on the politicking dimension? Where does the leadership of the school come in? I have three recommendations:

- It is fundamental that the faculty and staff have clearly delineated forums which call for active participation. These forums should be made to function so that crucial decisions are discussed, thus allowing for a broad team-based understanding of the critical sentiments within school when it comes to strategic issues. Perhaps most important in this context would be an active faculty meeting. At IMD, we have such meetings once a month, for discussion of many pertinent issues, perhaps not so much for decision, but more for debate, so that viewpoints can be shared and maturity "built". In addition, we have a "Co-ordinating Committee" consisting of a small group of faculty members who are much more involved in decisions relating to policy direction, and articulation of the school's vision and mission. The insights of these individuals are important in setting the fundamental direction of the school with the faculty. Further, there is a faculty committee dealing with appointment of new faculty members, which further ensures that new members of the team fit in with the rest of the culture, seen from a faculty point of view. Finally, there is a committee made up of the senior administrative staff, the "Operating Committee", that allows the senior staff to air their views, perhaps not so much for decision, but to highlight how to approach major administrative and implementation issues. It is therefore critical to have forums and meeting places which allow people to participate in an orderly fashion.

- It is also important for the school's leadership to tackle problems as they come up, in a straightforward manner. Concerning any problem that might arise, I tend to ask myself, "What is best for the school?" Most people feel uncomfortable about conflict resolution and problem solving with colleagues with different points of view. Relating such issues back to the simple question of what would be best for the school often makes arriving at a solution easier, and limits some of the politicking.
- Finally we have the issue of faculty "ownership". A strong faculty incentive system that allows faculty to share in the profits of the school encourages faculty members to accept that politicking is likely to lead to value destruction, in the end handicapping each faculty member's possibility to make an even healthier salary and take-home pay. This factor induces faculty members to be pragmatic and avoid politicking and, as I see it, enhance their "maturity".

It is thus critical for the members of an academic staff to develop a realistic ("honest") picture of why they want to be committed to and involved in their academic work. The individual must continuously test the validity of his or her motivations. Plans, ambitions, desires and dreams — all the elements of "personal" politics — must harmonise so that the output amounts to valuable research, publications and teaching. This self-assessment may reveal, for instance, that too little true individual academic value creation is being achieved — an indication that other priorities may have taken over, or that some sort of "imbalance" has developed. Such an imbalance, for example, may show itself in the faculty member's teaching agenda becoming so complex that it leaves too little time for publication.

Again the leadership will have to ask what it can do to help "manage" the agenda-balancing, including the political side, so that it does not become dysfunctional. It is, of course, very difficult to bring a politically "degenerated" faculty team back into productive balance. In my experience, however, business school leadership should keep the four following guidelines in mind (I will get back to the question of turning around politically degenerated situations later):

- The academic leadership must adopt a consistent decision-making style, an even-handed, transparent one. Secret, side deals are devastating. In any case, anyone who has worked in academia knows that any and all decisions quickly become known throughout the organisation — transparency prevails! I know of no other organisational context more transparent than academia. In fact, this is one of the major strengths of academic organisations; nevertheless, one must manage accordingly.
- The faculty review process, though primarily meant to deal with a particular professor's research or pedagogical progress, can also address the faculty member's working relationship within the team in general. Regular reviews allow the school's leadership to give advice and suggestions to the faculty member about actions and attitudes that might, if not addressed, lead to dysfunctional, political behaviour. It goes without saying that, even though not deviously political, a faculty member may still be dysfunctional if he requires too much time from colleagues on senseless interaction and myopic co-ordination.
- A third recommendation concerns the tenure process, or perhaps in more general terms, the so-called "work contract" of the faculty member. I have already indicated that tenure can be dysfunctional, in the sense that, if a faculty member is no longer able to contribute productively to his academic institution, he/she should suffer the consequences and leave. Without tenure, the leadership can ask particularly disruptive faculty members to leave the institution. This would of course be highly exceptional, but the very fact that such action *can* be taken is important. At IMD, we had such a situation, and the faculty member's departure led to a clearing of the air and significantly less political dysfunction.
- What about situations where you do not have the freedom of asking a faculty member to leave because of tenure? The only way to handle this is through strong team norms. Commitment to pragmatic value creation, a joint commitment to focusing on what really matters, discouraging anyone from corridor talk — these are the fundamental solutions. Such norms, as long as they are actively practised, will help freeze out faculty members who are distracting the team with unnecessary politics. The school's leadership must do whatever it can to establish such pragmatic, value-creating norms. Leading by example and "walking around" are valuable approaches.

A sense of realism and discipline is thus paramount. Faculty members must understand that they have a responsibility to safeguard the working climate of the academic institution. They must understand that engaging in politics does not support the school. They must have the discipline to understand that membership in an outstanding academic institution also requires realistic behaviour. Again, perhaps a sense of "ownership" is required, to manage the academic institution according to this type of value, appealing to its members to feel responsible, to understand that they must think about their own acts as "owners". The academic value creation requires sensible maturity. Faculty members must commit energy today to an academic climate. Only then can a true academic value-creation process, grounded in an individual's true motivation, be achieved. Without a cadre of faculty members with such mature qualities, there will not be a realistic basis for sustainable high quality academic value creation, nor for a deliberate strategic direction setting. If the individual is not willing to show the commitment to set aside enough time and energy today for the future, but instead wishes to spend today's energy for the more immediate tasks, such as excessive politicking and/or excessive outside consulting, then there will not be a realistic basis for academic value creation.

One approach towards establishing this positive focus that I have used both in my capacity as President of the Norwegian School of Management, and as President of IMD, is the following: simply to ask each faculty member to submit a short memorandum with:

1) the three most critical issues he/she sees as paramount for the leadership to focus on in its agenda qua leader of the organisation;
2) the three issues that the faculty members see as the *least* critical for me to focus on.

Such a delineation provides surprisingly good mapping out of the sentiments of the faculty members, providing a way for the leadership to establish action plans that establish a better political climate immediately, and allow faculty members a "say" in the political context of the institution. Perhaps this approach is particularly effective when a new Dean/President steps in. It can also be used at regular intervals after the new Dean/President has been on the job for a while, especially to rectify politically degenerated situations.

"Energy-Based" Faculty Management

Once you've got committed faculty members as the corner-stones of your academic value creation, you need to give them a "context" to excel — a "space". A school's leadership must not provide too many specific rules, too many specific guidelines, bombarding the faculty members with memoranda on what to do and what not to do. This easily creates a tone of confinement and a lack of space and runs contrary to the very essence of the management of academic institutions. Faculty members, on the contrary, must feel that they are working on their own, that they have a considerable amount of freedom to do what they want. I recommend two procedures to stimulate this sense:

- Guidelines should be made very general, giving broad directions only, and appealing to a faculty member's common sense. They should be backed up by a strong guideline to "when in doubt, ask for clarification". Needless to say, one should hope that the guidelines might be self-reinforcing, so that, as Norman Schwarzkopf says, "When in doubt, do the right thing".[3] No unnecessary guidelines should exist. Faculty work best when they have a sense of "freedom — with accountability". They typically dislike being "controlled".
- Resource allocations can, to a considerable extent, be made as lump sums or "envelopes". This allows the faculty member to spend the funds *à discretion*, within the overall allocation granted. Research budgets, for instance, should largely be set on this basis, giving the faculty member freedom and expecting him to be responsible for executing his/her own research activities within the overall budget. Travel money, for instance, should be dealt with on this basis, as well as money for conferences. Book, software, and various hardware purchases can also be dealt with in this manner; so long as the faculty member stays within the amount in the "envelope", he/she is fine. It seems fair to assume that the faculty member will grow from having the responsibility to spend up to the limit in his/her envelope, but nothing more.

Only by finding ways to enhance faculty "maturity" will energies be unleashed to create strong academic progress. Although a critical strategic resource is the know-how of the faculty member, represented by his/her competencies, capabilities, and values, it is his/her *energy* that plays the most vital role. Thus, the scarce strategic resource is the *mobilised* know-how of the faculty member. Availability of academic energy can thus be seen as the real strategic asset.

Such academic energy can be unleashed — in the form of individual and academic team achievements — when a stimulating and constructive atmosphere prevails at the institution. How can such a constructive atmosphere be created?

In fact, we have touched upon this several times already — a constructive atmosphere is the exact opposite of what I previously called a "political organisation". Here again, following a few simple guidelines can help.

- Allow the faculty to feel that they have the opportunity to do their own thing. Nothing satisfies faculty members more than feeling that they can follow their inspiration, have sufficient flexibility in their teaching schedules and the resources to match. Of course, this is fundamentally an individualistic process. The leadership can only hope that team-based research and team-based pedagogical developments will also take place, but business school leaders must probably accept the fact that the fundamental building block in developing high-energy academic organisations is individual drive.
- The leadership can do more than provide a time schedule and financial support; it can also provide positive reinforcement through feedback and coaching. The thinking to follow here is: "good can always be done better", and "adopt a healthy scepticism of the status quo". The key is to give positive reinforcement, encouragement, and praise rather than no feedback at all, or even negative feedback. Perhaps one of the greatest challenges in brain-driven, human resource management-based organisations is the intrinsic problem people often have with giving positive feedback. Somehow, criticism and negativity seem to be rather more natural than constructive feedback and being positive in such organisational settings. All members of the organisation, stimulated in particular by the leadership, must work to create a high-energy, positive outlook.
- The leadership can avoid demanding of the faculty unnecessarily time- and energy-consuming activities that do not directly support the vision and the mission of the institution. It is up to the leadership to be very careful here. Many "good things" should thus not be requested of faculty members. The taxing of their time and energy is a much larger and graver problem that all too many academic leaders recognise. One of the least attractive sides of academia is the tendency to establish committees to address all kinds of issues. Such excessive committee focus can easily burn faculty time — and create a dysfunctional feeling of "slowness" rather than "speed".
- Last, but not least, meaningless controls, unnecessary bureaucracy, and excessive guidelines should be avoided. Faculty members simply detest excessive control. Active assessment of internal procedures on a regular basis — to keep them minimalist and streamlined — is key.

The "size" of the energy pool is to a large extent a function of whether a constructive and stimulating atmosphere exists. To create and conserve institutional energy, the school's leadership must create a constructive atmosphere. We have already discussed several aspects of what this entails, but I would now like to give an example that highlights two aspects. First, a positive feeling often comes from being close to the learning partners, receiving positive reinforcement about how much the learning partners appreciate the co-operation and value the contribution of the faculty. Such feedback from the marketplace tends to have a strong — even a sensational — power to boost the energy of the organisation. Second, the leadership must make sure that faculty members *share* positive feedback. Faculty members working together, in teams, need positive feedback and reinforcement for their work as members of the team. A learning partner who praises the programme faculty team, stressing how much they appreciate the team-based benefits will, knowingly or not, reinforce positive energy.

IMD's unique teaching programme *Orchestrating Winning Performance* excels in both these dimensions, and is therefore a positive reinforcement of the high-energy atmosphere of IMD.[4] As I noted earlier, the entire IMD faculty takes part in this programme, all working together, co-ordinating their efforts overall and in small teams formed around the various option streams participants enrol in. A total of 400 participants makes for an exceptionally large amount of feedback, typically quite enthusiastic. This is not only a result of the learning between faculty and participants, but also of the interchange among faculty members themselves. A huge, eclectic learning network is created. Each individual — participant or faculty member — is likely to find strong interpersonal learning links within it.

"Energy based" academic management is also a matter of using an individual faculty member's energy in a wise, considered way. Unfortunately, energy can be senselessly misused by inessential activities, as stated, like endless committee meetings, the only purpose of which, often, is to comply with bureaucratic procedures. Beyond the guidelines mentioned earlier, we can add that co-ordination among faculty members, especially in teaching, is necessary, but can also eat up excessive amounts of time and energy. Too much co-ordination can be counterproductive. Faculty members must therefore develop a professional attitude towards working with each other, perhaps getting to know each other over time and thus interacting without much specific co-ordination — more "intuitively", if you will. From the point of view of the learning partner, the faculty will often appear to be as co-ordinated as if they devoted far more time to co-ordination than they actually do. A relatively small faculty, with some degree of stability in its membership, can perhaps most easily lead to such "natural co-ordination" because so many faculty members know one another, at least better than they would in a large faculty. This is, of course, the ideal situation.

I vividly remember participating in a large-programme co-ordination group for one of IMD's keynote executive open programmes, when I was a visiting faculty member at the predecessor school, IMEDE, some 20 years ago. The programme director spent excessive amounts of time painstakingly running co-ordination meetings among faculty members, going through the items to be covered class by class. This excessive co-ordination created not only a lot of stress, but probably led to an undesirable weakening of the pressure and alertness that a faculty member must always have about linking up with the other members of the teaching team. It is thus important that bureaucracy in the form of excessive co-ordination meetings should not take place.

Academic debates, critical as they are, must be run with the utmost of sensitivity to the fact that energy is limited. Endless faculty meetings, without constructive results, are a real drain on a school's energy. Meaningful debates and academic interchange are the essence of healthy academic value creation. However, to be meaningful, debates must have a purpose, an intended pay-off in the academic value creation. A healthy academic atmosphere encompasses this understanding of energy efficiency when it comes to interchanges and debates.

What are some "recipes" for successful debates and intellectual exchange? Which practices energise faculty, and which eat up time and energy? Some of the following ideas are more of a cultural nature, which cannot easily be managed as such, but can perhaps be encouraged, while others, in contrast, are more possible to influence.

- Each faculty member must understand that time is money. It is particularly important that a faculty member be able to self-start, particularly in light of the often rather chaotic work schedules, with team-based involvement in teaching, often in a relatively large number of programmes. Thus, the discipline to "get going again fast" is critical. Some faculty members cannot manage this. The good old days, when one would have a semester or more totally free, at one's disposal for research and writing, are probably gone forever. If a faculty member needs this context to work, then he/she will have a hard time excelling in the modern, high-pressure business school.
- About the nature of the academic debate itself, two critical cultural observations can be made. First, it is important that all members of the faculty work to move the debate forward, toward a conclusion, rather than allow themselves to be sidelined into blind-alley arguments. Further, faculty members must respect the rest of the team by not monopolising one or more narrow points of self-interest in debates; they must be able to restrain themselves to maintain balance and dynamics of academic discussions. Perhaps this, too, is a matter of encouraging security and collegiality in the academic team. It is

usually the less secure members of the team who feel they need to show their brilliance by excessive or disruptive participation.

- The leadership can of course have an impact on all of this, in part by acting as an example of mature academic debate. Further, the school's leadership can reinforce focused, constructive academic debate through the incentive system. Since quality output, especially in research, but also in pedagogy, would be the primary way to receive individual incentives, a heavy emphasis on *output* "forces" or at least "encourages" faculty to be parsimonious with their time by taking part constructively — through a kind of self-policing — in academic debate. The key is not to work with one's own — or others' — time.

It is primarily an individual responsibility to be energy efficient. From a leadership point of view, this statement could be seen as a cop-out. The question is, what can the leadership do to stimulate faculty energy efficiency? I have already made several suggestions regarding this, but they can be summarised into three recommendations.

- Facilitate better faculty planning. In frequent review meetings go over faculty plans and progress. This allows the academic leadership to help shape the institutional agenda, and allows the faculty member to draw on the experiences of the academic leadership. Also, the leadership has the opportunity to give praise as well as, if necessary, critical and constructive feedback.
- Second, the academic leadership needs to provide guidelines, regulations, and rules that are as minimalist, as open-ended and as non-bureaucratic as possible. They should allow the faculty members to "do the right thing" within a sense of "space". The faculty should never see guidelines as bureaucratic impositions.
- Third, an incentive system can create a sense of "ownership" in faculty members. The incentives can be partly team-based, such as overall profit-sharing at the end of the year from surplus cash that has been generated as a result of good faculty teamwork. They can also be individual, based on exceptional *output*, signifying the efficiency of an individual faculty member's research "production" and exceptional teaching innovations.

Thus, energy-based management means a few clear steps, therefore, by the school's leadership. To work, it of course also needs to be complemented by a clear sense of maturity on the part of the individual faculty members. One must safeguard one's own energy, and channel it into constructive academic value creation as much as possible. Individual faculty members must create "space" to do the things they want. Colleagues must similarly attempt to enhance the

"space" for themselves and respect the needs of others. The school has the oblig-
ation to safeguard the space of members by keeping to a minimum unnecessary
meetings, requests, and committees. The administrative leadership of the school
must also be committed to preserving the individual faculty member's "space",
dismantling unessential administrative routines. One example from business
comes to mind here. During the heyday of ITT some decades ago, when Harold
Geneen was at the helm, the chief financial officer, Herbert Knortz, championed
the principle that "whenever we add one more administrative routine, we take
one of the old ones out". He kept the bureaucracy more or less under control by
following this heuristic, which it seems to me, can probably serve the academic
institution very well.[5]

Faculty Evaluation of Colleagues

A critical use of faculty energy I have not yet touched on is the set of activities
directed towards the evaluation of colleagues, for contract renewal, promotion
and/or granting tenure. While, in the end, such evaluations ought to be kept to a
minimum, anyone who has worked at a business school will tell you that, at
times, the process can go too far, taking too much "space" away from the individual faculty members, needlessly diminishing their capacity for work. Some
faculty members may actually feel that it is difficult for them to come to work
at the office, because colleagues and corridor discussions distract them. They
may be further distracted by the flood of emails, especially when they are sent
in a cultural context that may not fully respect the capacity implications on the
organisation by sending them to "all". The dilemma is, of course, that it is desirable that faculty members come to work at the office, and interact. This type of
intellectual cross-fertilisation should be encouraged. I remember vividly that we
used to say that "the office lights were on" at the Wharton School, since we all
came to work — for dialogue — in contrast to many of the business schools,
where people tended to work at home instead. There might have been natural
reasons for this in some cases, due to the fact that the faculty was spread out
over a large geographic area, but cultural forces may also have been in play.

Can the leadership, in fact, do anything to preserve faculty "space" while still
urging faculty to interact? I have three recommendations:

- Get broad agreement on an efficient paper culture: minimal emails, memoranda, less copying others on correspondence. Needless to say, it is good
to include many people on the information trail; still, good judgement is
needed.

- Group meetings on certain days of the week and month, so as not to clutter the individual faculty member's agenda more than necessary. At IMD, for instance, we have all committee meetings, including faculty meetings on the last Friday of each month. This makes it easier for people to plan effectively.
- Set aside quiet time for the faculty members, when they can work alone — say, during the morning of each day — and group telephoning, meetings, and informal dialogue toward the latter part of the day. It is during the morning hours when the mind is at its freshest and best disposed toward creative research.

It is, of course, not only the energies of the academic members of the business school that matter; it is the combined energy of the entire team, academic and administrative that must be managed and safeguarded. If the overall energy pool is enhanced through a positive atmosphere, a school can go a very long way. Unfortunately, many academic institutions do not understand the value of preserving individual and group energy as a critical strategic resource. Managing "space" to preserve energy will be key! Paradoxically, it almost seems that the less the institutional leadership does in "managing", the better. This does not mean that abdication and "laissez-faire" should be the rule. On the contrary, the leadership must take a minimalist approach, focus on developing rules and guidelines that allow people to figure out by themselves what makes sense, planning processes that allow people to grow, and incentives that allow people to understand why certain behaviours associated with the more effective academic value-creation aspects are desirable.

Short-Term Pressure

The individual faculty members at schools like IMD typically have a very intense exposure to business. They are involved in a large number of executive development programmes taking place almost continuously throughout the year. These activities are typically rather short, lasting one to three weeks. The longer programmes last up to ten weeks, in addition to the one-year MBA programme. The part-time Executive MBA typically lasts one year and a half. In addition, every year they run the many "discovery events" that report on their research progress. The workload and fragmentation facing a faculty member can be formidable, or so it seems at first glance. Short-term pressure prevails.

Consider Professor X. He will want to build up the normal teaching load of the school, which consists of participating in a number of programmes, serve as a programme director of other programmes, and even participate in some background development work for particular programmes. The problem with Professor X is that he may not be, for a number of reasons, much sought after as a programme director. This may be because the professor's capabilities are rather specialised and/or he is relatively new to the team. The net effect is that, to fill his "billable" teaching load, he must teach in a large number of programmes, often with relatively short-term, self-contained involvement in each programme. Consequently, Professor X's days, weeks, months, and year can be excessively chopped up into independent, free-standing — but still highly demanding — teaching interventions.

Professor Y, on the contrary, can start by planning his/her teaching load around a few programmes in which he/she is programme director. He/she is not only getting workload credit for this, but for specific teaching within this programme, specific development efforts to support this programme, etc. — i.e., a much more concentrated focus on his/her agenda. The result will be a much more manageable, less chopped-up workload picture. It is this latter workload scenario that the school's leadership tries to plan for as much as possible.

Pressure can be further exacerbated by needs for heavy interaction among the teaching teams of professors as well as contact with the learning partner client. This context can present a dilemma. On the one hand, it is a dynamic environment with many opportunities for faculty members to learn from leading executives attending programmes as well as from working together with colleagues. However, the intensity of this short-term pressure can make it difficult for faculty members to follow deliberate plans for expending energy. Specifically, they may struggle to find the *balance* between the amount of energy they can spend today for today's teaching delivery activities and how much time and energy they can spend today for activities with a more long-term pay-off, like research. The risk therefore is that a particular faculty member might end up "flat" or, more dramatically, "burned out" due to lack of sufficient systematic efforts on new research and self-development activities.

What can the school leadership do? As already alluded to, it can oversee, for one, faculty workload planning. This planning must allow each faculty member to play a certain role in programme management, to build up both his/her classroom teaching around it and also the programme development side around this. Needless to say, such an "internal point of view" cannot be taken too far to the extreme. After all, it is the learning partner who must be satisfied; the learning partner's ideas about who should be programme director and who should teach must be heard. In any successful business school, all concerned must see workload planning as a top-down, holistic portfolio-driven process, not one that is "managed in the corridors" by each more-or-less self-appointed programme director (as an extreme example), independently signing up the faculty teams he/she prefers to work with. Such an extreme, bottom-up approach to faculty workload planning leads to excessive inequities. The distribution of "pleasure and pain" in teaching loads should follow the principles of equity and fairness.

It is important that the teaching activities of individual faculty members be linked as much as possible to their research interests and their intellectual capital focus. As such, the teaching can be seen as a learning process, allowing the professor to further develop his/her materials. There can then be relatively little distinction between pure research and teaching.

At the annual review meetings between the leadership and the faculty members, the issue of "fatigue" should be addressed. Those faculty members that are most tired are often those who do significant outside consulting. It is clearly not acceptable for the academic institution that the faculty member see his work for the school as residual, an activity done after all consulting is finished. Rather, outside activities such as consulting must be managed not only according to what is contractually permissible, but — much more importantly — also according to what the faculty member can sustain *after* meeting his responsibilities at the school. One way to handle such consulting–teaching conflicts of interest is to state, by policy, that any outside teaching intervention more than two days long is, by definition, the school's work. In this way, the faculty member will be "protected" against the temptation to take on too much outside work.

Contact with, and exposure to, executives naturally sharpen the appetite of most faculty members for doing outside consulting. In the context of the learning partnership concept, it is natural for an executive to continue to draw on a particular faculty member's resources that he finds particularly effective and stimulating. While such consulting can clearly be beneficial, and should indeed be encouraged, it can lead to further fragmentation of the little time and energy the faculty member has left. When this happens, individual research and self-development agendas are the casualties. The challenge of managing for today in balance with managing for the future can become a complicated task for the involved faculty member.

The Research Imperative

Research is defined rather broadly, at least in contrast to some of the classical academic research that leads solely to publications in refereed journals. Most important is that research activities *are* undertaken, with the main purpose being to safeguard each faculty member's self-development/self-renewal process. The diversity of research output can, however, be broader than classic academic research, and can include books to more practitioner-oriented readers, executive briefings of various sorts, and case research leading to the development of new materials — case studies, teaching notes, group exercises, videos, chat room presentations, etc. — many of these outputs primarily for teaching purposes, but with research implications.

The question of finding the balance between the faculty's service to the school and individual research, even consulting, raised the question of the rights of the individual versus the rights of the school. Specifically, are faculty members allowed to compete with their own school? At IMD the answer is "no". Faculty can only spend one day per week on outside consulting, as already alluded to, and can only work with a maximum of one colleague, and on relatively short outside teaching assignments. Faculty members cannot prioritise their own research trips or academic conferences at the expense of teaching assignments that need to be covered at IMD. In general, faculty members who find such basic guidelines and regulations too restrictive for their agendas should probably elect to leave for other institutions. After all, if faculty can solely focus on their own research as well as take the most interesting learning partner engagements, the entire economic foundation of the school would be in jeopardy. The norms for outside work must be such that the faculty members consider themselves as "owners", as mentioned before. Thus, they must see it as natural and meaningful to subjugate their own research or business pursuits to the school's overall strategy and interests. If unwilling to do this, the faculty member will, of course, have the option to leave the school to go freelance. When these faculty work-load guidelines were clarified and articulated at IMD a few years ago, a small number of faculty members indeed chose to leave IMD to work on their own, finding that the consulting guidelines had become too restrictive for them. Similarly, new faculty members should be aware of these basic expectations, rules, regulations, and values governing faculty member behaviour.

In more concrete terms, what does IMD do to clarify these contractual obligations vis-à-vis new faculty members? First of all, and most effective, there are strong informal norms among the faculty members themselves. The institute has an atmosphere of self-policing, for new as well as old faculty members, regarding the extent to which they are involved in outside consulting. Again, even though such consulting can perhaps be kept secret for a while, it is surprising how openly known such consulting activities tend to be in the school. After a while, one can expect that everyone will know about it. There is nothing better than this system of self-discipline.

Increasingly, IMD allocates senior leadership resources to extensive coaching of new faculty members. This coaching focuses primarily on teaching and research, but also touches the expectations for individual faculty members' behaviour vis-à-vis the norms of consulting and workload ethics, so as to create/safeguard "space", management style, etc., to avoid corridor politics.

Last, but not least, the faculty guidelines are written up so that they can be easily referred to. While this author is not a big believer in extensive written guidelines and faculty rules, it should not be denied that it is useful to have a set of such unambiguous rules as a basis.

The Faculty Plan

It follows that it is not only faculty members who must be self-disciplined and deliberate in developing themselves and setting their own research agendas. The institute will have to create a context that supports the faculty member's development, too. The development of an individual faculty member's plan for academic development is the cornerstone in the planning challenge. The plan must be based on and firmly developed according to perceived needs and preferences — and thus reconciled with the school's needs.

The individual plan should contain the research agenda, with some deadlines and expected outputs and a realistic estimate of resources needed, particularly time. The objective is not to hold the faculty to the letter of the plan, but to try to develop a stronger sense of self-commitment and focus. In other words, the plan's primary function is to help the faculty member to strengthen the "today for the future" dimension.

Perhaps a good way to see such a plan would be as an expression of a vision and a mission for an individual faculty member, both in terms of the area for research and teaching, and also some specific action steps to make this happen, including some specification of expected output. Thus, the individual plan should help the faculty member to maintain focus in a creative academic environment, such as the one we have at IMD. Of course, temptation and even distraction will always exist, perhaps pulling the faculty member toward other (at the moment) interesting research opportunities and pedagogical approaches. This is why it is so important for the individual faculty member to be disciplined, to remember our oft-repeated adage that "strategy means choice". Sticking to the plan is essential. To revise the plan mid-stream normally requires — should require — considerable soul-searching and clarification.

As I have already suggested, the development plan must indicate expected output. All too often it is much easier to start a number of activities, to let all flowers bloom, than to bring research and pedagogical exploration to fruitful closure. This is why the plan must address closure. I recommend focusing on shorter, relatively self-contained outputs, including a number of working papers leading to articles, which in turn may evolve into a book, rather than outlining some over-ambitious project that may take many years and may — or often may not — eventually result in a book. Book writing can come later, after the basic output has been secured in a more sequential manner, with working papers, reports, and articles.

Of course, the school cannot impose a strict planning requirement on a faculty member. Such an imposition can only lead to an artificial plan with little commitment. This means that the planning process must be bottom-up. It is not feasible, and certainly would not be appropriate, for the business school's leadership to dictate what the research topic should be. As long as this general requirement for a faculty member to put together his/her play is satisfied, there will be no need — nor right — for the leadership to impose any further direction on faculty. All the school can and should do, practically speaking, is work with faculty to implement the individual plan by reviewing it and encouraging or guiding its execution and improvement. Above all, the school must back this up by offering significant funds and time.

At IMD such faculty planning reviews are mandatory. Although plans are reviewed every six months, the review does not include an entire re-drafting. Rather, such frequent reviews allow the faculty member, together with the school's leadership, to assess progress and discuss occasional adjustments of the individual faculty member's direction, vision, and mission. The frequency itself exerts pressure on the faculty members to progress, to feel committed to deliver according to plan.

The extreme bottom-up nature of the faculty planning process will of course lead to plans that reflect individual faculty needs. But what about all-important team research? Developing team-based research, that is, synergy among the faculty members in their research is, as a norm, typically both challenging and difficult. In practice, such team synergies can come out of co-ordinated efforts by individual faculty members that flow from the understanding that the give-and-take of working together can produce more benefits than costs, that pooling complementary talents of several faculty members often leads to greater excellence. Again, creating such research teams is normally not a top-down process; it cannot be legislated. What the school's leadership *can* do is to provide ample reward for team-based research, so that individuals are, at least, not handicapped by following this path.

The benefits of this loose, individual and team-oriented planning process are at least threefold. First, such discussions can lead to a better plan, through feedback from colleagues, as well as a stronger commitment by the faculty member. At best, such a planning process establishes a *contract* between the faculty member and the institution. In ongoing reviews, the continuing practicality of the plan in terms of the school's needs to commit financial resources and available time can be assessed. The President/Dean can encourage progress, or raise a red flag. When plans are assessed annually, self-imposed self-assessment of progress takes place almost automatically. It is, of course, important that the faculty member see the planning process as a vehicle for self-help, and not as a "negative" control device.

Second, progress toward fulfilling the plan should also be a criterion in performance assessments and in the granting of bonuses. The key here is *fulfilling* the plan — *completing* research. Should work-in-progress count towards a bonus? The answer is no. To put pressure on the faculty member to bring a project to closure is vital. To avoid potential double counting of particular pieces of work over several years, it is best not to count work-in-progress.

Third, the plan allows the school's leadership to act as an accelerator — to push for more academic value creation. This it can do by offering its inputs and suggestions about the specific plans, backed up by allocating funds and time to speed up the actual implementation of the plan, and by offering strong rewards for research results. It is amazing how much a school's leadership can do to speed up academic value creation in these three ways.

Above and beyond establishing the right climate, "making space for faculty", hiring and keeping committed, mature faculty, and working with them to set out workable plans, the leaders of business schools need to clarify two further matters in order to unleash faculty energy as we have alluded to already: regulating teaching loads and faculty consulting activities. Let us now consider these issues in some more detail.

Teaching assignments and loads don't just need to be reasonable (to accommodate research), they also need to be transparent. Matching faculty members' research interests — and, in a broader sense, self-motivating interests — with their teaching loads and agendas is a big challenge. A reasonable teaching load — both content and schedule — will be seen by faculty as one that is meaningful and fair, relative to colleagues. Often, faculty may view teaching as a burden, or distraction, a *condition* for staying in academia. Ideally, teaching should be an integral part of the individual faculty member's academic value creation.

At IMD, a carefully developed process of teaching assignments is particularly important. It is managed by one of the senior faculty members, the Senior Associate Dean for Academic Affairs. The starting point is to ask for input and preferences from each faculty member. These requests typically follow a pattern of teaching activities developed over a number of years. Faculty members who find it useful and stimulating to teach in particular programmes will tend to request a continuation. But there will always be suggestions for new teaching activities as well. New teaching requests will also come from the faculty programme directors of open or in-company programmes and from the Senior Associate Dean, who administers the teaching allocation process. He will typically also suggest specific assignments both for developing each faculty member and for ensuring that all of the school's teaching needs are ultimately covered. The purpose of the process is to reconcile the requests, and interact both with programme faculty directors and faculty members to ensure that teaching assignments meet both individual and organisational needs. This iterative process thus allows for flexibility, innovation and self-renewal.

One particularly useful way to assemble the teaching assignment puzzle is to re-group faculty members' assignments so they have more time uninterrupted by shorter teaching activities. These free blocks give more time for research, and the peace of mind for it. This process will, of course, never be perfect; still, some "batching" of teaching time provides faculty with research time. But it only works with a modicum of self-discipline: a successful faculty member will always have to carry out much of his research around a very busy school agenda. The ability to say "no" to ad hoc, last-minute teaching requests is, however, part and parcel of this. Further, the individual faculty-planning review meetings should highlight the extent to which a faculty member is being overly distracted by ad hoc institutional requests on an ongoing basis. Lack of progress in plans may indicate this. It is then up to the school's leadership to intervene to eliminate such last minute workload assignment problems.

The teaching load is not only a matter of delivering classes, but also consists of programme management, which involves programme design, the development of new teaching materials, pedagogical innovations, co-ordination with colleagues, and execution. A certain amount of marketing is also part of the programme responsibility, in that some interface with prospective students will be needed. The active support of developing brochures for marketing is also part of this. The faculty member in charge must also feel that he has a commercial responsibility.

At IMD, we also count the delivery of major research briefings as part of the "teaching load". Such "discovery events" typically require substantial preparation. Since practising executives attend them, the demands on faculty to "deliver" pedagogically are also great here. Executives paying high fees are not likely to sit quietly during a lacklustre teaching abstract or overly theoretical research briefing. Although it could be debated whether the dissemination of research should be "counted" as part of the teaching load, I would suggest that it brings research and teaching more closely together. Indeed, there should perhaps be many more discovery events, in order to create meeting places where participants can spark the discussion of research and development as a process of interaction between academe and business.

The aggregate workload statistics provide a picture of how equitably the work is spread among the faculty members. This "snapshot" should be made public, for full transparency. Debate will perhaps ensue. Some faculty members are simply better pedagogically than others and can thus often be seen as "safer" members of a teaching team. Certain faculty members are seen as more attractive because of their topical strengths. Some faculty members are more willing to take a heavier share of the teaching than their counterparts. For all of these reasons, the leadership needs to ensure overall fairness by setting some parameters that define acceptable upper and lower workload limits. The process must be credible and transparent.

Additional compensation, in the form of buy-back of time by the school of capacity initially set aside for consulting, is often a good recompense for faculty with excessive workloads. The great danger of buying back time, however, is that some faculty members may work so hard that they burn themselves out. In the end, this may hurt the entire institution! The people with the greatest load must guard themselves against such burn-out. The school must also forbid excessive overload. Even though the individual may want to work so hard because of the generous buy-back compensation, this trend must be managed.

Despite having a clear process for assigning teaching loads, and people to oversee it, the question of workload relates to each faculty member's *feelings* about teaching. Some faculty members see the teaching activities as a natural extension of their academic value creation. In their view, teaching stimulates and develops them, and provides them with "real world" examples of the ideas they are exploring in their research. Others see teaching as a free-standing activity that takes time from research. These "others" easily get tired of teaching.

A certain amount of self-selection is important. Enough flexibility should exist in the planning of faculty members' agendas so that they can, to some extent, do more teaching, or put more emphasis on research. The best way to work out the balance of the two activities, and to make sure that they help realise the faculty member's plan is, as previously noted, to strive as much as possible for a natural link between a faculty member's teaching and research activity. An advantage of having a relatively small MBA-level programme with only candidates of exceptional quality, for instance, as at IMD, is that linking research and teaching is relatively easy.

At the level of individual faculty, putting these ideas to work in reality is, of course, always a challenge. It is always difficult to fully link preferred research activities with teaching activities so that the result is research-based teaching that best serves the institution. How can the school make the assignments to programmes and the choices of company learning partners so that they enhance the preferred overall personal plan of the faculty member? In some instances, we may reluctantly accept that an integrated plan for a faculty member simply does not exist. The faculty member's de facto plan becomes the sum of more or less incidental, independent focal points, with research seen on its own, teaching seen on its own, and programme assignments seen on their own. The totality of all of this often makes much less sense than it might have if more effort had gone into developing a meta-logic for the faculty member's individual overall value creation.

In practice, IMD has significant challenges with this. Individual programme directors may, for instance, "attack" faculty members with requests to teach in "their" programmes. These aggressive requests may well have little to do with an individual faculty member's strategy. While very well intended, this sort of intense recruiting can have the unforeseen — and even severely disabling — effect of pulling an individual faculty member in too many directions, making it close to impossible to strive for an overall meta-logic.

The major challenge is thus to come up with a credible planning process that encourages faculty members to develop mature plans informed by a meta-logic for their own value creation — along lines such as the ones discussed above. As an institution, IMD faces the great challenge of making sure that consistency in due process must prevail. Faculty must, for instance, get institutional support consistent with both the collective individual as well as the overall, institutional meta-logic. In other words, decisions must be logical, fair and transparent to be credible. They must consequently be consistent with the plans of each faculty member. They must also be taken in the context of the overall strategy of IMD.

Even if the institution has an effective process for assigning teaching loads, it still has to wrestle with the thorny problem I mentioned earlier: regulating outside individual faculty consulting. Recall that at IMD — as seems to be the case in most leading business schools — a faculty member is free to do consulting one day per week, so long as this does not conflict with the school's strategy and planning. Individual consulting can indeed be highly beneficial, particularly when it complements what the faculty members experience through their normal research and teaching activities. For instance, problem-oriented consulting can lead to insights about how to apply a faculty member's competencies in real business. This, in turn, can lead to better research and teaching. Hopefully "win-win" can become the reality.

My own work with Ericsson Telecommunications is a good example. I was involved from the very beginning in Ericsson's efforts in mobile telephones, working with the then general manager of the unit, Mr Åke Lundqvist, to develop a planning process approach for this rapidly growing, rapidly changing, advanced technology-based business. The approach attempted to quantify how to see business opportunities that were truly unique, not obvious to everyone else, particularly not to Ericsson's target customers. The emphasis was also on how to mobilise the scarce resources within Ericsson to be able to implement the most critical aspects of the strategy, and to monitor how this implementation took place. A flexible process approach was developed and implemented, and a large number of executives participated in hands-on mini-sessions to discuss how the implementation challenges could be understood at the individual manager's level. I gained invaluable inputs about how to develop ultra-rapid growth strategies based on key human talents and how to stimulate internal entrepreneurs to be active in this process. The effective roles of top management in such contexts also became clearer to me as a result of this consulting project.

In a second instance from my own consulting work, the Norwegian multinational metals firm, Elkem, was developing a new planning approach. This approach consisted of identifying a number of strategic business units for Elkem, thus exposing the company's leadership and management at large to the fact that the company was indeed active in a large number of business areas, perhaps too large, it turned out. The high diversity of Elkem was in part due to a series of acquisitions that had been made earlier on, and that had led to a rather blurry picture of the company's businesses. A planning process was therefore institutionalised to help each business unit come up with competitive strategies. An additional planning process was put together to help the corporate management assess the overall portfolio of the company. As indicated, this led to shedding a number of businesses, in order to instil a more effective portfolio within Elkem. Thanks to this consulting project I gained inestimable insights into how to segment a company into strong business units that can each become truly competitive, and also learnt a lot about creating shareholder value in a conglomerate setting. These insights helped me later in my teaching and research.

Finally, I was heavily involved over a number of years with the Philippine multinational, the San Miguel Corporation, again in implementing a planning approach consisting of developing effective planning around their various business units. Here various groups — or clusters — of businesses were combined into larger divisions, with more emphasis on developing a synergy as part of the plans. Thus, the planning process consisted partly of focused business unit strategies, and partly of a delineation of synergies among such business units. The key insight I gained was how to make people work together more effectively to create synergies — again, insights that I have been able to draw on extensively later in my research and teaching.[6]

All of these examples illustrate consulting interventions that required a day or two of work here and there, but ongoing, over longer spans of time. I thus ended up gaining the confidence of senior management in each of the three companies, was therefore able to play perhaps an important role in the shaping of the strategies in each of the firms. This was highly complementary to my own research. I was — and am — interested in the processes that stimulate internally generated growth. The consulting represented three huge live laboratory cases for me to better understand these processes. Significant pre-paradigmatic thinking was thus done, leading to subsequent framing of the research questions in a "grounded theory sense"[7] which I believe would not have been possible had I not had this rich and deep involvement over a number of years at the senior levels in these firms.

A contrast to this is so-called "consulting" which, in fact, is nothing more than the delivery of established, institutional teaching activities to outside clients — corporations as well as other academic institutions — nothing more than what faculty members do at their own institution day-to-day. This is unlikely to invigorate faculty members or contribute to their development.

For many schools, heavy dependency on executive development and programmes for business organisations can potentially be worrisome in one respect — because it means that faculty members might be able to deliver exactly the same services on their own. At lower cost! Faculty members have no overheads to charge. They have, however, already benefited from the institution's financing their research and development; now they may feel that they can turn around and deliver it to an outside client at a lower fee! No need to worry about regenerating their knowledge base — it is financially supported by the institution anyway! Needless to say, such a "diversion" of faculty energy is not commensurate with the long-term interest, not to mention survival, of the academic institution. This diversion jeopardises the institution's long-term economic viability, since its most intense competition would now come from its own faculty. Corporate clients should not have low-cost access to the faculty through cherry-picking, benefiting from know-how the institution is funding. Over time, such freeloading can lead only to the demise of high-quality, research-based executive development — a situation probably of little benefit for anyone.

At IMD, the regulations for consulting, as I have explained, attempt to safeguard the competitive interests of the institution. This is done partly by limiting the number of faculty members who are allowed to consult on the outside *as a team* to two. This limitation stops firms from cherry-picking the best people and ideas from our internally developed programmes. The guidelines call for transparency: faculty must report consulting activities. And if they are in any doubt about possible conflicts of interest, they must approach the President or academic Dean before any consulting occurs. The school's leadership, in turn, may decide that individual faculty consulting activities to certain firms may be put on hold, or even discontinued, if a particular firm should want to try to change to a self-organised programme delivered in a "cherry-picking" mode.

Ultimately, of course, all the guidelines and rules in the world will be ineffective if the faculty see them as meaningless. If a faculty member does not see the long-term intellectual and economic well-being of his institution as real and central, but assumes that its know-how will somehow be replenished through other means, then the guidelines will not work. Faculty members must realise that they are responsible to their colleagues and the school, as well as to themselves, for securing the long-term know-how and economic solidity of their institution. The next chapter will look at the importance of shared faculty values in that endeavour.

Chapter 10

Groups and Team Values

Executive Summary

The dynamic business school models proposed in this book put a great deal of pressure on faculty, more perhaps than in a traditional business school. Faculty in the modern business school are no longer kings of their own fiefdoms, but rather members of highly variegated groups and heterogeneous teams. Although the burden of promoting open, collegial processes and values that support team and group work will fall most heavily on the faculty (hence the utmost importance of effective recruiting), the leadership must also work to encourage the right values and behaviours. This will include encouraging faculty to work in teams of colleagues from different disciplines and with different views, encouraging them to work with large numbers of executives as partners, not as mere purveyors of content, trying to encourage active dialogue, co-operation, and sharing. This mode of working will require the leadership to promote, specifically, discussion and listening, feedback, give and take, faculty presence on campus, and an effort by all as much as possible to be constructive, honest, and respectful of the intellectual property of colleagues.

The culture of the business school must be fostered by faculty members who are able to work with a relatively large number of colleagues to create multi-perspective, holistic approaches that are tailored to the needs of the client firm. Faculty members have to know *their* core competencies, how these can be articulated for executives, and how they can be made as "compatible" as possible with complementary "modules" of colleagues. The working style of the faculty needs to shift from the classical provision of "their" courses to being members of several programme teams that work with a relatively large number of learning-partner clients. Faculty members will have to relinquish "ownership" of particular programmes for particular clients. The *ability* to serve on teams with faculty colleagues will, thus, become more important. In this new model of faculty responsibility, each faculty member contributes as a member of a symphony orchestra rather than as a soloist — and this means teamwork *and* interchangeability.

Although the pressures to adapt to the client are very real for each member of the business school's faculty and staff, the potential rewards for the business school can be significant, particularly if it is fortunate enough to work with truly outstanding corporations with interesting learning agendas. Teamwork among faculty trying to meet the high demands of learning partners is vital, since no one faculty member (or group) working each in isolation will suffice.

One internationally renowned firm in the speciality chemicals business asked IMD to work with them to develop the capability to foster internally generated growth more effectively. This programme had one sequence for the top management the company expected to act as prime catalysts for internally generated growth. Another sequence dealt directly with the growth-instigating executives. These two programmes are now staffed by an eclectic team of faculty with backgrounds in strategy, culture and values, and finance and accounting. They must be able to work together. All faculty members are directly interested in the research question of how to stimulate internally generated growth by trying to identify business opportunities early — before they might become obvious to competitors. Although the team of faculty members come to our work with the chemical firm with differing points of view, their divergent views are based on a shared body of knowledge, which we then co-ordinate with the chemical firm, our learning partner, to create the "holistic" tailored approach mentioned above.

A second example is IMD's programme for developing internal strategy for a leading telecommunications equipment maker, helping it see its strategy as a learning process. This programme is spearheaded by a team of three professors, representing the diverse disciplines of strategy, finance and accounting, and human resource management. As a result of this programme intervention, delivered to and focused on a large group of executives, yet in relatively small action-learning groups, the concept of strategy as learning is shared by a large number of executives, and by the three professors, too. To make it a success, the team members needed to work effectively with one another, and with a large *group* of executives. And they needed to be comfortable working with many divergent views. For strong academic value creation to take place, a multitude of viewpoints will also be desirable. Even though single committed faculty members can achieve a lot on their own, colleagues working together — and learning together — can inspire each other to accomplish even more. This co-operation can be particularly fruitful among colleagues from different disciplines, as IMD's open programme, the *Programme for Executive Development* (PED) further illustrates.[1] Nine professors comprise this general management programme, which means that the professional group is characterised by exceptional diversity, but joined together by a common commitment to strengthening general management practices and abilities in up-and-coming executives in their mid-30s to mid-40s, who will soon take on general management responsibilities. In PED, the faculty wrestle with the question of how the school can, in essence, provide a "mini-MBA" over a short period of ten weeks. The eclecticism and diversity are real, but the purpose of teaching bonds the points of view.

This programme, marked as it is by both "pockets" of discipline-based depth, and diversity, seems to help faculty members stay out of the trap of thinking too narrowly. The mix of professors extends and enriches ideas, and forges deeper understanding from the insights of others. The depth and efficiency of interaction among faculty members may, to some extent, be enhanced by sharing a similar paradigm or a similar research tradition, including compatible research tools, but unless faculty members whose work is based on different paradigms take part, intellectual myopia may result.

Active Dialogue

Faculty members must be willing to engage in active dialogue. They must be comfortable with intellectual "give and take". Granted, it is often painfully difficult to give feedback to colleagues and receive it from them. And faculty members are notorious for their professional defensiveness. Accustomed to being the kings of their own fiefdoms, they often have to struggle to listen with open minds to the ideas of others. Schedules are busy, time short, and taking the time to reflect on a colleague's viewpoints and to give meaningful commentary is just plain hard. Most of us like to believe we know best. It is, however, a matter of duty and responsibility to oneself and to one's colleagues to take as open an approach as possible here, including a willingness to work in teams.

In practice, this will, of course, never be fully achieved. One can ask what the school's leadership can provide in the way of impetus for such an open, collegial process. Shared debriefing feedback is one step. Every programme provides for written feedback, giving the participants a chance to voice their opinions on the content and process of the programme. Problem areas are singled out, and the leadership of the school can sit down with the professor to support and assist him/her in making improvements. To be effective this must, of course, be done in the spirit captured by the phrase "good can always be done better", and not in the spirit of control. If highly critical and justifiable feedback persists, the school leadership might, however, consider more drastic measures.

Most effective, of course, is for faculty members to do such debriefings themselves. The director of each of IMD's programmes will typically go over feedback and suggestions for future runs of a programme with the teaching team. This process is not equally effective throughout, but it nevertheless represents an important step towards enhancing the quality of a programme, and the practice of quality improvement for "making good even better". Clear norms for positive improvement thus need to be developed, so that any type of programme can be envisioned as a learning *process*, rather than a finite end process on its own.

Intellectual pressure is always part of a give and take team-orientation. Bearing up under pressure may well require degrees of intellectual robustness that are typically scarce, even among the brightest faculty stars. But the pay-off for making sure that the school has faculty with this sort of rigour will be a more supportive, creative, and progressive approach to academic value creation. The alternative — faculty members toiling away in isolation — may lead to faculty burn-out, or entrapment in idiosyncratic thinking. And so, the leadership of the business school must encourage faculty members with similar interests to work with each other on research and in teaching teams. The reward for this "investment" will be increasing returns of value creation.

Consider, for instance, the development of our tailored programme for a large toy manufacturer. This was run by two faculty members, one being predominantly interested in strategy and the latter in behavioural processes. Through joint efforts, this programme ended up focusing on developing strategy as "serious play" — or, practising how individual executives, working alone and in teams, could conceive of more creative strategies when freed from the organisational contexts and constraints they were faced with day-to-day. In the programme, the toy company executives worked with IMD faculty in the equivalent of a "learning laboratory", which allowed them to carry out the "serious play". For the IMD professors, this also meant an inspiring cross-fertilisation among faculty members with entirely different backgrounds; it led to an entire new research stream focused on developing creative strategies.[2] One can say that the up-front investment from the faculty members to create an effective bridge across disciplinary diversity more than paid off.

Team Activities: Multiple Dimensions

If you consider the possible team activities in a business school under a more powerful lens, you will see that faculty team activities can have several dimensions.

Faculty members who have common research interests, and who therefore pursue the same management phenomenon or business topic, whether they have similar or varying backgrounds or methods, can work together in many different ways to reap the benefits of their unique chemistry. Although I have prescribed eclecticism, one must also be open to the fact that colleagues with similar backgrounds may find ways to collaborate effectively. I have, for example, enjoyed regular collaboration with Professor Bala Chakravarthy over many years. Dr Chakravarthy was trained at the Harvard Business School, as was I, in management processes and strategic administrative systems. As such, we are relatively close in our methodological and research focus, and share a body of literature from which we tend to draw. We also undertake some similar research primarily based on in-depth clinical work with one or two dozen sites, and frequently written up in a format that can benefit not only fellow academicians, but also enlightened practitioners. Why, then, are we co-operating, given the fact that we have, in a sense, such similar outlooks?

We recognise that positive value creation can take place through discussion and interaction, by working on joint articles and books, by "pushing" one another's understanding of particular phenomena. Clearly, it seems as if we get more out of this by reasoning around the issues together rather than seeing these as totally independent discovery processes. The discovery process by combining forces will thus be stronger. I am convinced that it will increasingly be key for faculty members to fine-tune their abilities to gain from co-operation.

Such research-based co-operation may rest on the pillars of broad, eclectic value creation, or on common methodological approaches and a shared underlying paradigm. On the research topic at hand — whether it be, say, strategy making, demand chain management, or managing currency risk — academic value-creation activities may focus narrowly or broadly. Even the methods may differ. But the value of the co-operation flows from intellectual synergy.

The degree of co-operation in a team of faculty members may also differ widely — from relatively infrequent, general discussions to in-depth co-operation on specific projects, where even the ownership of the research output may be jointly shared. For example, a large number of IMD faculty members are interested in the research subject of internally generated growth. Several professors deliver programmes on this subject. One such programme is called the *Senior Executive Forum*. This was structured so as to open up a relatively broad exchange of ideas on the topic. Growth through acquisitions and mergers was seen as highly related, and the programme thus focused on how to carry out both of these growth models in parallel. Similarly, a special stream was developed around internally generated growth as part of the *Orchestrating Winning Performance* programme. Finally, three books of essays from several faculty members were written, edited by Professors P. Strebel, D. Marchand, and P. Rosenzweig *et al.*, which focused on internal growth, growth via acquisitions, the role of IT in growth and the international dimension in growth.[3, 4, 5] Truly diverse aspects relating to understanding the growth challenge thus came out of these multi-faculty efforts, allowing many to work on the agenda, but in their own ways. Co-operation took place — subordination did not!

Given this wide palette of team options, a faculty member may thus play on several teams, heavily involved in some, superficially with others. For instance, I work in-depth on internally generated growth with my colleague, Dr Chakravarthy, but I also work with a number of my other colleagues who are interested in growth. In the first instance we are deeply co-ordinated; in the second, I work more with a somewhat looser link. My point is that this wide variety of involvement with a topic, from individual research to a collaborative partnership to membership of a larger group, must lead to a richer academic value-creation process that can benefit the school and its faculty in countless ways.

Business schools thus have everything to gain and nothing to lose by "insisting" on a variety of types of co-operation not only in research, but also in teaching. The same considerations apply: How can the quality of a teaching or research programme be further enhanced by co-teaching or co-researching the programme based on working in depth, irrespective of particular disciplinary foci? How can a set of complementary skills be brought to bear on a programme in order to enhance eclecticism and scope?

All too many established business schools may be wed to the old models of academic value creation: faculty members, each in their own bubbles, run their classes in virtual isolation from colleagues — and they prefer to work alone on their research. Faculty in such traditional settings may feel they have little to gain from opening the doors of their classrooms and offices to share their insights and see what their colleagues are up to. The successful business school will more and more insist that they do so. But there can be institutional constraints — perceived or not. Both at the Sloan School and at the Wharton school, for instance, it was common knowledge among non-tenured faculty members that it was important to have a relatively sizeable number of *solely authored* articles in top-refereed journals in order to have a realistic shot at receiving tenure. Co-authored articles were (are) not sufficient. Of course, one could have a few of these also, but there would be no substitute for individually authored articles. Thus, one could say that the norms behind the academic value-creation process gave premium to individualistic, "me-alone" type of academic work.

We can see this also at IMD, even though there is no tenure process to lend bias to the academic value creation. Some professors may tend to be overly concerned that their colleagues will "steal" their ideas. They may well see it as a must to keep things to themselves, rather than sharing. My own view on this is that this type of concern normally has little merit. What is important is that the development of knowledge moves forward at such a rate that there is little need today to hold back and safeguard one's own thoughts. One gains more by interacting with others on how to push the thoughts further, than by isolation. This has probably always been true, but is more important today than ever. The discovery process these days is therefore a much more open network process than it ever has been.

For the individual faculty members, this call to sharing means choice. An individual faculty member can end up with a large number of opportunities to participate in open network sharing processes with colleagues. So each will have to be disciplined, and thus also say "no" to some options, even though they may be interesting in themselves. Again, the individual plan of the faculty member, his/her individual vision/mission, is critical here. It should guide the faculty members in deciding which teams, collegial contacts, and open networks to engage in, as well as showing where to follow individual interests or where to be involved more on the periphery. There is no doubt that the number of exciting opportunities for a faculty member is higher than ever. I have seen examples of faculty members getting so excited about almost everything that they end up actually losing focus. Co-operation and "strategy means choice" go together more than ever!

Co-operation should only take place where they feel the vibration of true synergy. Co-operation is a matter of give and take, so there has to be enough additional value to counterbalance the transaction-cost energy. But now, one more time, how does "co-operation" — I will also call it "teamwork" — look? And how will it work? For one thing, team-based academic value creation can only come out of a practicable working process. This way of creating value will have several characteristics: discussion, listening, feedback, give and take, and presence. Making sure they are all present is tough work. Scheduling sufficient time together is critical. Although this point about scheduling should be obvious — almost trivial — it is, in practice, hard to set aside the time needed for research-related interaction and reasoning. Planning around sufficient segments of quality time, with all the key researchers involved, is thus crucial, and requires proactive discipline. It is often no more than wishful thinking. But it must be done, and done right, since problems with, or absence of, one or more parts of the process will lower the value created. Above all, an open mind, and a true belief in eclecticism and the benefits of working together is key — the antithesis of "me, me, me"! Let us now move on to a somewhat more detailed discussion of some of the implications from this mode of working.

Discussions and Listening

The presence of discussion is the first characteristic: discussing research and/or teaching issues, exchanging viewpoints, trying to see things from different ways. Of course, to discuss you have to listen. Without an open ear, interchanges of viewpoints lead nowhere. Sending without receiving is not enough. An open mind, sure enough of itself to accept different views, the willingness to consider what others say, an active passion not to be entrapped in one's own viewpoints — these are key preconditions for team-based academic value creation.

Researchers are inherently very committed to their work. This may lead to a strong feeling that "my own agenda is the most important". It is no surprise, therefore, that researchers often struggle to listen to others, or do not like to think about ideas not their own. Reacting to others' ideas with fairness and an open mind does not come easily. When such a strong bias is reinforced by immaturity, dialogue among faculty may turn into little more than one professor trying to tell another that he's right, the other manifestly wrong. Accepting that as a given, what can a school's leadership do to enhance effective interactive/iterative research style? Very little, really — one can only try to encourage people to work together. This is perhaps easier with those who have different capabilities and thus can complement each other rather than those with similar capabilities who, as a result, compete with each other. For instance, in research seminars, the school's leadership can encourage that, say, three positive contributions from a given research paper are first highlighted and discussed before one starts dissecting with mordant, exceedingly negative criticism. The leadership can perhaps add an element of positive thinking here.

I vividly remember being a guest professor at the Stockholm School of Economics, responsible for the doctoral seminar in International Business. We had a number of articles that we all were assigned to read and discuss. The typical line of discussion was on weaknesses in methodology, in research questions, in execution, etc. — with all present demonstrating a highly sophisticated ability to see weaknesses in the research. I needed to insist that we focus on a handful of positive contributions by any type of research before going into a discussion of weaknesses, and only then based on the spirit of the question, "how can good be done even better?" This more positive approach led to a much more difficult process of looking for positive contributions and avenues of improvement, rather than focusing on rather narrow, static negativism.

Feedback

Listening is only half the equation; the other half is giving feedback. Often we fail to provide feedback. Personally, I find that it often is futile to give feedback for two reasons. First, it may not be worth giving feedback to individuals who, in essence, do not want to hear it, assuming that they know better. Why provide feedback to people who have a rather set, dogmatic mind regarding what is right and what is wrong? Second, academics often take feedback as "criticism". How can the business school leader provide feedback positively, if you will, as a healthy dissatisfaction with the status quo, a good-can-be-done-better attitude? The leadership must work to create an atmosphere in which faculty see feedback as a privilege, as what it is — as constructive criticism. Admittedly, because we are often uncomfortable with it, feedback is frequently unwelcome.

Regardless of the reasons, we often don't take the time and energy to review a team colleague's working papers or materials. Perhaps we avoid giving feedback out of a false sense of kindness. In many circles, things may be packed so heavily in cotton that the substance of the message essentially gets lost. In this case, giving clear and honest feedback just isn't "comme il faut". Faculty find it unnecessarily upsetting; after all, who wants to break the fragile china of social etiquette? In academia, implicit and/or explicit seniority issues may make it particularly difficult for junior faculty members to tell an older colleague exactly what they think.

This may be particularly so where the so-called tenure system is in place. The junior faculty member comes to depend on the senior faculty member to take care of giving feedback, if it's given at all. Such an abnegation will colour the interaction among the senior and junior colleagues. Even where a position based on tenure is not a factor, the perceived power of seniority can lead to such asymmetry of interaction.

Give and Take

When the faculty are willing to listen to each other and provide feedback, "give and take" becomes more than just an empty phrase. Faculty should see it, not as a mere duty, but as an institutional right. To join an academic institution thus means being granted the right to open dialogue, and the requirement to take part in it. Working at an academic institution is thus not reconcilable with intellectual isolation. But the question for us is: How can this be encouraged, or even enforced? How can an institution develop a culture which is conducive to this open dialogue? What can the Dean/President do to have an impact on such development? I know of three ways the President can do this — two are relatively concrete, and the third is perhaps more indirect.

First, the school needs to institutionalise various faculty tasks in such a way that the faculty can — or must — be present regularly. This will discourage them from seeing their offices as mere mailboxes. What might this involve? Faculty members can serve on committees and task forces, for example. Of course, strong faculty input is essential when the school is making strategic decisions, for example, when it is staking out key strategic direction or hiring new faculty members. Here faculty committees are essential. Such involvement is desirable in itself, and brings the team together. Naturally, any such requirement must be reconcilable with an individual faculty member's workload plan. What the school must avoid is planning faculty absences to allow them months off for individual scholarly activities in isolation. The school can also provide incentives for citizenship. At IMD, this includes incentives for active participation on committees, in marketing meetings, for recognition for coaching of new colleagues, etc. It is important, however, to resist involving the faculty in non-essential tasks. Some academic milieus are characterised by an over-abundance of committees and meetings *ad absurdum*. This can only be dysfunctional, even unproductive. The faculty must be involved when it matters — otherwise not.

Second, research workshops are essential, and — in most business schools — they are institutionalised. These provide potentially fantastic forums for open discussions of research in progress. Some of these research workshops must be reserved for outside scholars — to increase the cross-fertilisation from a broader set of scholarly stimuli — and for presentations by prospective new faculty members. But there should also be room for one's own faculty to lead such presentations. Regardless, all such workshops provide a "community" of open exchange. The school's leadership can arrange such seminars.

The less tangible action for the school's leadership will be to try to positively create — or at least encourage — an atmosphere of open debate and presence in the institution, by setting an example, "walking the talk", say, by encouraging ad hoc meetings to discuss research substance. For most academic administrators — Deans and Presidents — the day can be so filled with administrative, "myopic" tasks, that they may not feel they have the time for ad hoc, intellectual exchanges. Clearly, not finding the time is unfortunate. The head of the school must lead the way by example toward an open, intellectual, exchange-based atmosphere.

Presence

One way to keep the faculty out of the darkened corners of intellectual isolation is to expect them to be present. Specifically, this means being in the office, available for critical meetings, and present for spontaneous team get-togethers. They must "be around"! Without face-to-face interaction, which often happens extemporaneously, academic value creation will easily stagnate. Every member of the faculty should be able to count on their colleagues being accessible, and email exchange cannot substitute. I have already mentioned faculty presence on committees, task forces, and attendance in research seminars, all of which can be reinforced by an incentive process that puts weight on "citizenship". But what if the faculty members are still not inclined to participate? What if they actually prefer isolation? And what if this isolation is in conflict with the team-building, collegial spirit of the school? In my experience, group pressure, or peer influence, is perhaps the only effective way to create a better team attitude. At IMD, we have seen that faculty members who do not appreciate the more participative attitude, but rather come in or out randomly and follow an approach of involving themselves selectively and irregularly, tend to have less influence among their peers. In extreme cases, this can lead to such isolation that the faculty contract renewal process may be in jeopardy.

So, it seems to me that faculty members must be physically present a minimum amount of time. It is of course difficult to provide concrete guidelines. At a minimum, committee meeting schedules must be set well ahead of time, half a year or even a year, so that faculty members can plan their agendas around them. Dates should only be rescheduled in the most exceptional circumstances, since, as I've argued, a robust, proactively planned meeting schedule is crucial to participation. Beyond this, it will be up to the team to implicitly set the guidelines for what is good participation. My own feeling is that "the more, the better". But physical presence means more than bringing your body to work!

Members of the team have to be present mentally as well. By "mental presence", I mean a willingness to be truly engaged in intellectual exchange, discussions with colleagues, faculty debates, etc. The team culture must be "open", in the sense that all must feel that they are welcome in the team. The antithesis of this would be an aloof, elitist attitude, where one would simply "speak to the rest of the group" or withdraw onto one's own pedestal. In my opinion, a school's team needs to manage this dimension carefully, again with much of the responsibility falling on the school's leadership, particularly in the school's striving for an "open" team spirit. For instance, some schools are heavily committed to hiring "academic stars". Such people, if they are unwilling/unable to integrate with the rest of the team, might not necessarily play a positive value-creation role in the school. In today's academic environment, with heavy emphasis on being able to adapt, readjust, and create different team contexts, it may be difficult, even impossible, to integrate the old "academic superstars".

Over-commitment to consulting can lead, metaphorically speaking, to an empty brain. That's why, as I stated earlier, the faculty must understand that their work for the school comes first; they must manage their extra teaching and outside consulting to reinforce and complement the school's activities, not take the leading role in the theatre of their egos. Doing too much consulting can lead to the faculty member being burned out and unfocused. Take the case of one professor on the IMD team having a strong interest in developing his writings and pursuing his research. This is, of course, desirable and good — things that the entire IMD faculty team should indirectly support. He has a relatively small, highly focused collegial group, mainly focused on the outside, with whom he exchanges viewpoints. This is also fine, in principle. The "problem" has to do with the way he practises all of this. He does not proactively share with other in-house colleagues, but rather — perhaps thoughtlessly — nurses an attitude that leads others to feel unwelcome. He locks the door to his office, rather than participating in formal or ad hoc group discussions, etc. While following focused research plans is excellent, things must not be taken to the extreme of isolation from colleagues. If the research implementation commitment leads to intellectual isolation, from the rest of the team's point of view, things have gone too far.

Another example concerns a professor who was becoming increasingly popular as an outside facilitator. He was greatly in demand in companies looking for someone to stimulate change processes in executive teams. As such, his research was also largely conducted on his own, and often through the frequent interventions with a client. Thus, the professor could naturally build up a large consulting practice on his own, without being in jeopardy by breaking the formal requirements to individual consulting versus IMD assignments. As such, he did reach the top limit of what is permissible at IMD, namely 50 days per year of outside consulting. Given the strong emotional commitment the professor had to put into these team-driven change processes, he then ended up too exhausted to do a proper job at IMD. Needless to say, such priorities are unacceptable.

Leaders of business schools can think about the "necessary conditions of team-based academic value creation" in terms of a couple of simple exhortations — principles, if you will. Each is based on the values the school wants its faculty to follow. The school can encourage and develop these values. If the faculty can somehow be made to adopt them, the leadership can assume it is well on the way to creating the right culture for organisational learning and effective value creation. Thus, the school can assess the work, or the likelihood of success, of academic teams by asking to what degree the members are abiding by these values. In my experience, success rests on three essential values: a constructive attitude, honesty, and its corollary, not "stealing".

Be Constructive

First, team members have to be constructive. Though this exhortation runs dangerously close to the dicta of pop-psychology, it is serious. And it is absolutely necessary. Members of academic teams must strive not to embarrass or diminish their colleagues. I am sad to report that years of experience have shown me that large egos and prodigiously self-centred tendencies can be rampant in academia. When massive egos and self-absorption set the tone for teamwork, winning and losing count most. And this kills constructive interaction, and dooms all efforts to create academic value.

By "being constructive" I mean resolving issues so that they fit a broader purpose, in line with what's best for the school, rather than what's best for the individual. It also means "making good even better", rather than resolving issues in terms of winners and losers. By making any and all issues to be resolved in a dynamic sense, with a potential for future positive pay-off, one can avoid such statically-driven, win/lose outcomes. The school's leadership can play an important role in this by setting examples. After all, much decision making and problem solving will involve the school's leadership in various ways, often quite directly. How? To reiterate: by setting a constructive tone.

While the necessity and benefits of the faculty having a positive attitude and all that it implies would seem pretty clear, the school's leadership still needs to know what to do when faculty members just aren't being constructive, despite every policy, example, and exhortation. For such difficult cases — experience tells me they happen often — I have two recommendations. The leadership must accept that there are times when the only recourse is direct intervention. The Dean may have to bring the parties together, and try to convince them that a positive solution is best. More often than not, such conflict resolution is a matter of having a good catalyst map out a win/win solution and mediate. By thinking in terms of what is best in the long run, taking into account positive value-creating developments that might stem from resolving the conflict, the conflicting parties are more likely to spot the proactive, positive solutions. This is an important role of a school's leadership, but one that it may not have to play too often. And, when keeping in mind that the key to all of this is to find solutions that are *best for the school* — not to enter into compromises that jeopardise this — the task for the leadership may become quite manageable.

Beyond this, the leadership must recognise that some people are simply less positive than others. Some people see issues more as a problem than an opportunity. If a faculty member has a rather more extreme, perhaps confrontational bent, then he/she may be best left alone. There is perhaps nothing much wrong with letting faculty members "count themselves out" relative to the rest of the team, if they are too set on confrontation. They will have to recognise that if they want to play a continuing, meaningful role; however, they will have to get into more of a give-and-take spirit. The school's leadership can thus — perhaps indirectly — play a constructive role by "letting people isolate themselves", up to a point. Given the fact that we have argued so strongly for a participative team culture as the *raison d'être* for strong academic value creation, one can of course not accept that too many faculty members isolate themselves. A few such cases, however, may be worth it, if the prize is less dysfunctional conflict and discussion.

Be Honest

Team members have to be honest, real, and genuine. They have to say what they think, and base it on what they experience and see. Consider the example of faculty member X. He is a fantastic colleague: he gives honest, to-the-point feedback. Faculty member Y, in contrast, is unable to give straightforward feedback. X proactively gives feedback to all, using face-to-face dialogue, email and small written notes, always trying to pinpoint things that could be done differently and better. He is very positive, but also able to indicate, by strong implication, the weak points in what a given colleague was doing. Professor X is a master at giving positive reinforcement, and can point out realistically what can be done. In contrast, Professor Y is inclined to pinpoint "errors" in his colleagues' work. While technically he may even be correct, his comments are not balanced. As such, even though the feedback is "honest", it lacks temperance. Clearly, it is X who reinforces the positive climate at the school.

Honest feedback may well be one of the most precious features of good academic value creation. Honesty means both focusing on the substantive arguments *and* giving feedback in a balanced way. Faculty have to be honest with themselves about their ability to contribute to the team efforts. Neither false humility nor overweening pride will bode well for the team. Often team members avoid the introspection necessary to be honest about their own contributions. Let us again focus on Professor Y. He has, through his rather negative style, developed a way to shelter himself — he takes feedback but dismisses it as "wrong" and continues with what he is doing, more or less without recognising other faculty members' points of view. Further, Professor Y is highly unpredictable —

at times quite reasonable, at times totally the opposite. Such an oscillating style can only make things more difficult.

While such robustness will be necessary to some extent in academia, it is also important to have a sensitive willingness to think about one's own work in a broader context. The ability to see feedback as a privilege is probably more a matter of maturity, of not being overly insecure, than anything else. And this, of course, the leadership cannot control, or nurture. But with faculty who lack this maturity, who ignore or refuse to admit that they do not understand a particular management phenomenon as well as a colleague, and thus make shallow, or worse, irrelevant contributions, the leadership must fall back on the power of an effective, individual planning process.

It is in regular review meetings that the Dean can discuss such issues openly with faculty members. Open discussion of course implies giving honest, constructive feedback, but also discussing with a faculty member the effectiveness of his own style within the team. Needless to say, such discussions can, at times, be difficult. They require a high level of interpersonal skill and understanding of the value-creation process. They require a sense of respect and security. I vividly remember such a meeting when I was head of the Norwegian School of Management. The professor, falling squarely into the category of rather isolated, insensitive, "me-alone" academicians, took the feedback very poorly and indeed stormed out of the review meeting. Several follow-up meetings were necessary in order to "sugarcoat" the message. In such situations, it is particularly important that honesty is not being buried, but that the true message gets conveyed, even if in a watered-down version. Patience is key in such situations, accepting that it is a long-term, step-by-step process to turn such a faculty member in a more positive direction.

Do Not Steal

To sound rather biblical, no team member should "steal" from the others on the team. As is so often the case with such commandments, this may appear simple at first sight, but in practice, plagiarism can happen, and this can have an extremely deleterious effect on the atmosphere of the school. Some examples from my experience spring to mind.

In the first, a professor was copying verbatim large excerpts from a colleague's working paper in one of his books. The fact that the professor who was abused had not yet published the material was, of course, no excuse at all. Even though this is a clear case at the extreme, it can still represent a potential dilemma if it is taken in another context. We do want, as we recall, to encourage co-operation among faculty members, to exchange and to build on each other's ideas. How, then, is the line drawn between this, and actually stealing ideas? My own feeling, as already stated several times, is that a dynamic view on sharing is most constructive. One should simply not be afraid of sharing ideas, debating and letting one's colleagues benefit from these, as long as this is part of a true give-and-take process. One typically ends up getting more back that one gives by engaging in such mind-expanding dialogue. Still, one should perhaps use the notion "borrow with pride" rather than the more abrasive "steal with pride", which is attributed to some senior executives at ABB.[6] It goes without saying that proper acknowledgement for incorporating another colleague's work is a must. This process should be entirely above board vis-à-vis the colleagues in question, so that they are not presented with any "surprises".

More generally speaking, there can be little give and take unless every member is secure in the knowledge that his colleagues will not lift his intellectual property. Attribution must be given where it belongs. This is a very important issue, and it is unfortunately sometimes underplayed. It demands sensitivity and care to be stringent here. Clearly, this is an issue for each faculty member fundamentally. This is part of one's basic value norms for being in the academic business. Still, the school's leadership must play an important role in reinforcing this. As an extreme example, I was involved in asking a faculty colleague to leave IMD when he had committed a significant amount of plagiarism. Even though this was clear from a page-by-page comparison of the work that was done by another colleague with what ended up in this faculty member's book, it was puzzling to observe the types of defence mechanisms the culprit used. He tried to rationalise away what had taken place. Unfortunately, in instances like this, the leadership has no choice but to be entirely uncompromising. There may also be instances which are perhaps less serious, involving a seemingly occasional omission of an attribution to a colleague. However, this, too, must be brought up by the school's leadership in a forceful manner — it is a serious matter. This is therefore an instance where the school's leadership is indeed critical. Plagiarism is simply not on.

Dialogue and exchange of ideas can only thrive on the premise that everyone has the right to build on what comes out of the dialogue. The institution must ensure that its members play by the following precept: the "owner" of an idea can work in the firm conviction that these ideas are protected. Here, long-term trust is perhaps paramount. It typically takes time for a good working relationship among researchers to get established. Typically these relationships evolve over time — and can ultimately become so strong from a trust-base point of view that back-and-forth exchange of ideas is seen as completely natural.

A breakdown here usually means the end of academic value creation. Some years ago, when a professor at IMD was confronted about borrowing from colleagues' presentations, he excused himself with the defence that he was under pressure to perform, having too little time to prepare, etc. He appealed to the school's overall needs for outstanding delivery of its academic values as an excuse for such behaviour. Interestingly, as he initially got away with these excuses, his abuse started to increase, and became rampant. Thus, lack of clear enforcement of this uncompromising norm led to a breakdown of his own judgement and an acceleration of friction with colleagues. In the end, all trust had been destroyed. There was no other way than to ask this faculty member to leave.

Another example from the business side is also telling. A few years ago, a number of faculty members were given licence by the school's leadership itself to take various programmes privately. The school was at the time not interested in undertaking these activities institutionally, and it was also felt that perhaps this was a good, indirect way to boost faculty members' salaries. Interestingly, those faculty members who were involved seemed to become more and more aggressive, to increasingly interpret the norms in light of what would fit their own agenda. They became less constructive team players. Their colleagues gradually lost trust in them. In the end, these faculty members were also asked to leave IMD. They had ended up in a self-generated value-destructive process.

Business schools facing such cases, whether it is plagiarism or taking "business" from the school, would do well to heed, even practise and enforce, General Schwarzkopf's now famous admonishment, "when in doubt, do the right thing".[7] What is the "right thing"? Behave so as to allow others to maintain strong trust in you. Give generous credit to others, be sensitive, fair and honest before typing only one's own name on a piece of work. Assume that outside "business" comes because of the school's reputation — and ask for permission to do such work when in doubt. More specifically, the school's leadership must play a clear, uncompromising role in the prevention of, or dealing with, intellectual theft, whether it relates to academic materials from colleagues, or to stealing business from one's own institution.

As the above examples underscore, unacceptable practices must be stopped right away. If not, they may lend credence to a "redefinition" by individuals of where the borders might go — these may now be changed based on retroactive rationalisation. Faculty members must be confronted with plagiarism when it happens. If it is an especially serious or recurring case, the faculty member must leave the institution. It should be made clear to every faculty member in an uncompromising way, that this is a norm that will be fully enforced. At Wharton, we had an example similar to the one above, involving a full professor with tenure. Here, the process was especially difficult, given that tenure protected the faculty member. He ended up being given an extended leave of absence. Once he returned, he was never again able to play a central role in Wharton's academic value creation because he was stigmatised in the team. He had lost trust.

The school's leadership also needs to be forceful in its stand on "commercial theft". Clear guidelines on consulting must exist, and must be enforced. Openness and consultation when in doubt are essential. If a faculty member abuses these guidelines, this, again, is time for clear confrontation and, with serious or recurring violation, dismissal. The school has to take a stand. There is no room for compromise. Borders cannot be moved based on an individual's discretion.

Although it is clear that the school must be uncompromising in cases of plagiarism, what about situations that may involve only relatively minor abuses, or "grey" areas? First, it is crucial to create a context to keep one's faculty busy with central academic value creation. If faculty members are occupied with actual research, they typically may experience that they are fulfilling their own private vision/mission, and this leads to a constructive climate! Similarly, if busy with meaningful teaching involvement, then the faculty will feel positive. Thus, emphasising the creation of a favourable value-creating context for each faculty member to be productive is essential. By doing good work there is little time or room left for temptations to be dishonest. As discussed in the previous chapter, the many specific approaches are all contained in a good strategic plan for a faculty member:

- Stimulate the faculty member's planning and support this with constructive planning meetings;
- Help the faculty member with realising a well-planned teaching schedule;
- Make research support readily available without bureaucratic routines;
- Provide for other types of support — for travel and miscellaneous expenses — to "make things easier" for the faculty member;
- Perhaps most important: provide positive intellectual support, encouragement, feedback. The leadership must take the time to be with the faculty members — to work with them.

In the context of the present discussion the key is that a proper plan be in place, and properly lived up to, to provide a faculty member with a strong platform of interface with his/her colleagues. The academic value creation thus also builds up inter-collegiate trust. An honest, ethical atmosphere is the result.

The Dean must be entirely consistent in practising the norms of presence, positivism, and honesty. By setting a positive example, the Dean can significantly cultivate such a positive culture. We have already commented on the Dean/President's roles as a "can do", "good must be done even better" catalyst! Some aspects of this can perhaps at times be hard — keeping in mind, for instance, that "presence" is what is *perceived* as presence by the other faculty members. There will be clear outside demands on the Dean's time for learning partners, financial supporters, political authorities, and alumni. It will be difficult to strike a good balance. Too many, as well as too little, outside activities are undesirable. My own rule of thumb is 50 percent of the time inside, and 50 percent outside. Any private part of the outside activities must be entirely non-controversial, with no possibility for conflict of interest. Rather than undertaking problem-oriented consulting for instance — which might be *perceived* as conflicting with the school's interests, I recommend that the private agenda be taken up primarily with board memberships. Again, this assumes that it can be fitted into the overall agenda without jeopardising the school's demands.

Chapter 11

The Job of the Dean: Top-Down Leadership

Executive Summary

The Dean has a role in the "top-down" value creation. Inside the school, Deans serve as symbiotic counterpoints to the bottom-up value creation of individual faculty members and teams. The Dean needs to stimulate creative synergy among faculty members. As such, the Dean must be a "catalyst" for bringing out the best in the individual faculty and teams. Deans are energy preserving stewards who resolve conflicts, insist on best practices and norms that allow the faculty to use their energy productively, even make tough decisions about promotion and termination, work to allocate tasks fairly, encourage renewal and new thinking and experimentation, all the while keeping a dynamic, flexible view of the school's vision and mission (which they must *safeguard). As a "businessman", the Dean needs to orchestrate the school's overall pattern of activities, keeping a keen eye on the mix of activities, and watching closely the pattern of resource generation and use, and risk exposure. Externally, the Dean must communicate the school's vision and spearhead the school's desire to spread visionary business practices. The Dean is also concerned with external stakeholder issues, including public relations. Overall, then, the Dean's critical work is about process: serving as a leader of individual faculty members, the team's catalyst, and creator of a positive atmosphere. Nevertheless, all Deans will have to find ways to balance countless internal and external needs at the same time, which entails delegation, "walking the talk", and, ultimately, "good management".*

Recent scholarship seems to suggest that professional management and control in the university are, at best, limited. Barry, Chandler, and Clark, reporting on a study of the introduction of new managerial practices in two UK universities, conclude that the level of professional managerial practices and of more sophisticated control procedures is still relatively low. "We have attempted to introduce evidence to suggest the existence of forms of managerial control in universities, which it has been argued are associated with significant changes in working conditions. At the same time the evidence presented has pointed to a range of individual responses and an uncertain link between what happens at senior levels and first-line management. Certainly at the point at which our respondents came into face-to-face contact with managers we found limited evidence of direct managerial control of daily routines. This suggests that any claim that managerialism has somehow colonised, or is otherwise embedded in, university life is, at best, exaggerated. Nor did we find too much evidence of overly directive or autocratic managerial style."[1]

Despite these apparent trends, there have been significant shifts toward Barry, Chandler, and Clark's "managerialism" in academic institutions. For example, H. de Boer points out that "it is clear that in many countries profound changes have taken place or will take place in the near future, [and] all these institutional reforms somehow point into the same direction — a more corporate manage-ment-like style of governance — the tendency towards more managerialism is evident".[2]

Perhaps reflecting this trend toward managerialism, in recent years leading thinkers on the subject of higher education have pondered just how much the President can actually *do*. Derek Bok from his seminal work, *Higher Learning*:

> I quickly set about accumulating a list of what I thought were splendid ideas, great and small, to improve education at Harvard ... At the end of two years none of these ideas had taken root. ... At this point I felt disheartened. I could accept disagreement, even outright rejection, but silence followed by inaction seemed peculiarly frustrating. ... Several years later, reflecting on the state of the University, I suddenly realised that almost all my early suggestions had now more or less come into being. I wondered: Whose ideas *were* these now that they had undergone this process of hibernation and reawakening? Perhaps it was wiser not to ask.[3]

Cohen and March see the President's role as rather confined: "The college President is an executive who does not know exactly what he should be doing and does not have much confidence that he can do anything important anyway."[4] Clark Kerr states:

> [The Dean] wins few clear cut victories, he must aim more at avoid-ing the worst than at seizing the best. He must find satisfaction

in being *equally* distasteful to each of his constituencies: he must reconcile himself to the harsh reality that successes are shrouded in silence while failures are spotlighted in notoriety. The President of the Multiversity must be content to hold its constituent elements loosely together and to move the whole enterprise another foot ahead in what often seems an equal race with history ... Innovations sometimes succeed best when they have no obvious author.

F. M. Cornford offers advice to younger academic colleagues. "You think (do you not?) that you have only to state a reasonable case, and people must listen to reason and act upon it at once. It is just this conviction that makes you so unpleasant."[6] And, I might add, so difficult for the leadership to meld into a team. This difficulty surely puts limits on the Dean's ability to effect change.

Rhodes sees the role of the President as diminishing:

The President — once an influential public figure and a considerable external voice — is now seen by external observers as less and less desirable and less and less effective, so that the average incumbency has declined to less than five years in public institutions and less than seven in all institutions.[7]

On this subject of Presidential power, Leslie and Fretwell observe:

Making hard, authoritative decisions at the "top" of the organization is counter to the culture and traditions of higher education. In effect, the greater the need for hard and clear decisions, the greater the resistance to the central administration acting alone. Uncertainty and conflict therefore make it difficult for presidents, vice-presidents, decision-making committees, and trustees — to move freely in any direction.[8]

I have mentioned in the previous discussion the responsibilities of the President (or Dean), and provided suggestions for how the leader might deal with some of the management problems covered so far, despite the eloquent misgivings above. So it ought to be clear by now that I believe the Dean has at least a modicum of power and, if he uses it right, has the potential to create value. The business school can be likened to a football team: it needs a coach! A top-flight academic team needs *both* the excellent players *and* a leader to enhance their ability to work as *one* team! This chapter takes a deeper look at the need for this "top-down" orchestration of the business school and some of the ways the need can be best met.

Value creation in the business school has a "top-down" element: the Dean.* Duderstadt outlines the more general top-down leadership roles:

> First there is substantive leadership. A President is expected to develop, articulate, and implement visions of the University that sustain and enhance the quality of the institution. This includes bold and creative long-range thinking about a broad area of intellectual, social, financial, human, and physical resources, and political issues that envelop the University.
>
> There is a broad range of important responsibilities that might be termed symbolic leadership. In the role as head of the University, the President has a responsibility for the complex area of relationship with both internal and external constituencies. This includes students, faculty, and staff on the campus ... So too, there are significant management responsibilities, since in the end the buck does indeed stop on the President's desk.
>
> A final leadership role of the President might best be termed pastoral care. In a very real sense, the President frequently becomes a key source of guidance, energy, and emotional support for the institution. Not only must this critical role be kept in mind when working directly with University colleagues, but also when working in broader University venues, such as ceremonial events and communications.
>
> Here, there is an important and obvious fact of life. No President can possibly fulfil all these dimensions of his role. One must first determine which aspects of the role best utilise his or her talents. Then a team of executive officers and senior staff must be assembled that can extend and complement the activities of the President to deal with the full spectrum of the University leadership role.[9]

* As stated in Chapter 1, the normal label used for the person heading a business school would be the "Dean". Other labels are Principal (as in the case of the London Business School), or the Director General (INSEAD). When, however, the business school is a free-standing institution, not part of a larger university, I prefer to use "President", as is the case at the Norwegian School of Management and at IMD. This signifies that the senior officer of the institution is indeed the "top of the pyramid", in that he does not have the President of a university above him. When the connotation "Dean" is used, we shall assume that there will be a President appointed for the university as a whole, to whom the Dean would report.

Despite the apparent difficulties, I believe the Dean *can* successfully fill the roles and meet the challenges Duderstadt highlights, and in so doing significantly add an overall context for value creation from the top down. As Derek Bok notes:

> the reforms most needed in higher education are unlikely to occur automatically from the effects of competition, or from the initiatives of foundations and government agencies, or from the spontaneous efforts of professors. While few important changes can occur without faculty support, something more is required in the form of entrepreneurial skills in order to bring about major educational reforms. Deans, provosts and ultimately, presidents are the obvious candidates to supply this added impetus.[10]

Mittlehurst identifies five roles for the President (he uses the term Vice Chancellor, which is the common notion for this title in the UK): clarifying and determining direction, positioning the institution, improving the climate through communication, decision taking and adjudication, and institutional representation. In many ways this checklist captures much of the essence of the academic leader's role as I see it — partly strategic, partly behavioural, partly decision oriented, and partly institutional.[11]

The effective business school leader can serve as a symbiotic counterpoint to the bottom-up academic value creation. This top-down counterpoint to the bottom-up academic value creation of individual faculty members and teams thereof is critical. Bok outlines the many ways he thinks Deans can lead change from the top:

> The authority retained by Presidents and Deans enables them not only to shape the academic agenda but to create an environment that promotes innovation and develops support for new ideas, [to wield their] power to allocate resources [and] create incentives to support experimentation, encourage greater attention to teaching and education, offer funds, make available expensive equipment, persuade influential faculty members to try out promising initiatives, find ways of rewarding and recognising, mobilise information to promote reform, create a committee of outside experts, have special capabilities to implement new initiatives.[12]

To accomplish all this, and more, the Dean must create what I think of as a "complementary symbiosis". This symbiosis involves the Dean playing a "counterpoint" to the bottom-up input from the various faculty members. He interacts with them regarding their thoughts on research and teaching. Although faculty, in part, lead the interaction, the good Dean can be decidedly more pro-active in trying to argue his/her view about teaching or research issues with the faculty. This "Dean-driven" interaction can help promote academic value creation by guiding, steering, and tempering the back-and-forth arguments. The Dean can help the faculty "stretch" themselves, encourage thought leadership, in short, be the true supportive catalyst I mentioned previously.

Another important part of the Dean's top-down value creation is safeguarding the overall vision and mission of the school, from a point of view of portfolio fit. Faculty members will propose many interesting ideas, and the Dean may have interesting issues that he might like to pursue on his own. But the key question from the Dean's point of view is how well these ideas fit with the school's vision and mission, so as to ensure that the various research and teaching activities really do fall into an overall portfolio pattern in a meaningful way. This "strategy means choice"-cum-"strategy means choosing activities that fit" represents a crit-ical additional value-creation proposition on the part of the Dean.

Stimulating the development of creative synergy among various faculty members is another task. Typically, there is nothing better than the spontaneous synergy of various bottom-up forces working in parallel and the ensuing bene-fits of the initiatives fitting together. In practice, however, a Dean's top-down viewpoint can often be very helpful in bringing the right types of faculty members together for a given teaching programme and/or research project.

The Dean can encourage a break with the not-invented-here attitude, so typical among many academicians in universities and business schools, pushing for a willingness to be more open-minded, to share more, to discuss more, to incor-porate inputs among colleagues to a larger extent! In this respect, it is interesting to go back in history and look at the pioneering activities at the then Carnegie Institute of Technology's business school in the 1960s. This school housed such classical faculty giants as J. March, D. C. Cyert, H. Simon, T. Ansoff, Y. Ijiri, and others. Carnegie Tech emphasised co-authored articles and books, stressing that a pillar of academic value creation should be based on a broader sharing. As such, Carnegie Tech set a tradition, which broke with the classical "me-alone" sole-authored publishing, which was then — and is still today — very strongly embedded within academia. As of today, joint articles, books, etc. should be more strongly "incentivated" and encouraged by the academic leadership — a clear "top-down" priority!

The Dean should also encourage the faculty to "experiment" more. Key is getting working papers out, based on tentative findings, completing works without revising, revising, revising (often for years) only to achieve small additional gains in quality. The Dean needs to motivate the faculty to state their research outputs — not as the final words but as contributions to an ongoing discovery process — to be bold and take risks. Such an atmosphere of experimentation is critical in academia today. Too often, academic faculty tend to be overly conservative, overly worried about exposing their ideas due to fear of criticism from colleagues. Many are too much preoccupied by going for the last one percent of quality improvement, but with a dramatic loss in speed of delivery as a consequence. The institutional leadership clearly has a challenge here — to impact outputs via aggressive incentives.

Further, the Dean needs to make sure that classical thinking about specific problems, theories, paradigms, etc. gets deliberately contrasted with radically different ideas. Such radical juxtapositioning is critical. Unconventional thinking — brainstorming across axiomatic traditions — is key here. IMD's approach — to abandon all academic departments, in order to think around the customers-cum-learning partners' needs — is an important step in the direction of more proactively radical thinking. The academic leadership can do a lot here, by bringing faculty members together on specific teaching programmes, or research projects based on heterogeneous axiomatic background. Cultural differences are also good to enhance eclecticism here!

The Dean and other leaders need to work to create internal "meeting places" where faculty members can present "problems" they are working on, meeting "solutions" that other faculty members might have. Workshops are critical here. Often, such workshops, say, "brown bag luncheons", research seminars, etc., tend to be characterised by predominantly negative thinking, i.e., criticising a given academic working paper that a particular faculty member is presenting. Instead, such "meetings" should look at positive contributions of a given paper, to highlight positive extensions of a given research effort, to see how a given set of propositions in a paper can be augmented by other insights, be a source of inspiration to other faculty members. Thus, it is important that research seminars get recast into "positive meeting places" rather than negative "killing" sessions. Here the leadership can play an important top-down role — perhaps, above all by setting example. For instance, I often insist that each faculty member brings three positive contributions from a given paper in a faculty workshop before "earning the right" to come with critical remarks.

Last, but not least, it is vital for the Dean to have a dynamic and flexible view of the portfolio of vision and mission for the school. This, so that he can contribute to the faculty trying out new things, even though the new initiative might at first fit only marginally in the school's portfolio, as well as stimulating new thinking. As such, static concepts of what the portfolio is would not hinder a dynamic value-creating process.

Essentially then, the Dean provides a sort of "glue" that holds it all together. In a way he/she orchestrates the overall pattern of activities — but in a catalytic way, not via heavy-handed top-down dictum. This orchestration includes keeping an eye on the overall mix of portfolio activities, asking how the overall pattern of resource generation and resource uses might be balanced, and trying to minimise the school's risk exposure. Top-down leadership is, thus, essential for effective strategic management in a business school. But the Dean can function effectively only when the school already meets the many other conditions we have previously discussed: strong, committed faculty members; teams or "families" of faculty members working together; a clear recognition of the need for "energy conservation"; and a broadly shared sense of the need to adapt and evolve in order to secure a solid resource base for the benefit of all.

So, Deans clearly play a multitude of roles. First and foremost, they are catalysts for bringing out the best in individual faculty members and their teams. They are also energy-preserving stewards, working to resolve conflicts and insisting on work practices and norms that allow the faculty to spend their energies productively; Deans must also take decisions, even when they can be difficult and unpopular, such as faculty promotion or termination decisions; Deans work with external stakeholders in a variety of capacities — they communicate the school's vision and spearhead the school's drive to forge visionary, ideal business practices. Vis-à-vis this role, the outside business constituency is perhaps particularly critical — the Dean must lead the school's thrust to create value that can also ensure commercial success of the organisation. The Dean must also be a businessman.

The role of the Dean can thus partly be defined in terms of a number of internal activities. Involvement in a number of internal committees and in decision making within the academic organisation is one. The Dean's role, however, can also be defined in terms of concern with a number of external stakeholder-related issues. Not only must the Dean be the link between these two sets of forces — external and internal — he has to translate the positive pressures from the external environment to the internal organisation. This way, he encourages valuable adaptation.

The Dean's Internal Tasks

Faculty Reviews

The Dean stimulates individual faculty members and groups of faculty members in their academic value creation. The Dean counsels, advises, reviews individual plans, and follows up with feedback. For individual renewal it is critical to have a hands-on understanding of what each member of his faculty team is contributing. One way to gain this understanding — and, one hopes, apply it — is through positive and constructive involvement with each faculty member. As I have pointed out repeatedly, the Dean must be involved in the faculty members' academic planning process. This should probably involve regular (yearly or more often) meetings to review a faculty member's activities. Typically, such a review involves going over the individual faculty member's research plan with a critical eye toward the direction he wishes to pursue, and the various steps he contemplates to get there. The Dean helps measure progress toward the stated goals, stressing demonstrated output, rather than promises and wishes for the future. This combination of review of output and reassessment of the faculty member's basic direction is a constructive way to reinforce the faculty member's research thrust.

In the yearly review, the Dean will also re-examine the faculty member's workload, the teaching load, and their mix. This, of course, is then tied uniquely to the faculty member's resource needs, such as for research associates or funding. Typically, these discussions tend to be rather easy, in light of the general research plan and the teaching load discussion, which provide content and time availability for the research. The rest of the resource issues are then usually straightforward.

As discussed, one of the key objectives at a school such as IMD will be to provide individual faculty incentives that encourage them to consider themselves "owners" of the institution. It is important to discuss the general notion of incentive criteria at the review meeting, to help the faculty member link the incentive process to his own research (I prefer to emphasise demonstrated research output), teaching (I prefer to emphasise teaching innovation), and citizenship (I prefer to emphasise market contributions for enhanced revenue, cross-organisational contributions, etc.).

Looking at outside consulting activities should be another straightforward part of the review. It is a matter of ensuring that the faculty member understands that the school is monitoring outside work, so that self-policing can take place. Fundamentally, the faculty members must themselves abide by the ethics and group norms to make sure that everyone stays within the guidelines; the Dean can, however, enforce these norms.

Of course, style issues may come up. The key issue here is to strive for a trust-building style. The Dean may himself point out to the individual faculty member that his style vis-à-vis colleagues is "dysfunctional", i.e., not leading to collegial trust-building. Conversely, the faculty member could mention how he sees himself fit in with the collegial group. Again, meaningful mentoring can take place, to help the faculty member to be more effective, to build a platform of trust within the team.

All of this may sound relatively easy, but anyone who has carried the banner of administration at a business school will tell you that the task is actually fraught with pitfalls. Interestingly, there are parallels between what can go wrong with the Dean's involvement in the faculty review processes in a narrow sense, and his ability to perform in a broader sense. In both senses, the Dean must maintain strong credibility. He cannot expect to be effective if not respected by each faculty colleague, and also seen as a credible representative of the entire faculty as their preferred leader. The faculty must, in essence, give the Dean the mandate, for the ability to manage flows out of the faculty's confidence. Managing without this trust is impossible.

Faculty members may find the review process awkward; for some it is even threatening, particularly if issues are being addressed that could lead to some contention over the faculty member's research, teaching, and/or consulting direction. Only if the Dean is seen as "doing his job", trying to muster arguments related to what's best for the school as a whole, will he have a fair chance of being credible in the eyes of the individual faculty member. If, on the other hand, the faculty member considers the Dean an adversary, the faculty review process easily becomes futile.

Key Principles for Completing Internal Tasks

In recent years, Deans have come and gone at some of the world's leading business schools as though they were winners and losers in a game of musical Deanships. To survive, to say nothing of succeeding, the Dean as "conductor" would be well advised to follow certain principles when carrying out the rest of the key internal tasks.

For the school as a whole, the Dean simply has to establish himself as a figure of trust and credibility. The Dean will simply not be able to continue if he does not have the broad trust of the faculty. Perhaps this trust can more easily be maintained if the Dean points out that he considers himself as "in the job" only as long as he can be an effective custodian of the faculty's trust. If seen clinging to the job, the Dean may lose credibility. Consider the ill-fated Dean of one of the leading US business schools. He had, previous to his appointment, been an effective associate Dean under a highly successful, charismatic Dean at another school. He was seen as very traditional, but also risk averse and cautious. He was not *perceived* as inspiring. He was not *perceived* as a particularly effective fundraiser nor as an internal leader inside the school. Without a strong, superior profile, externally or internally, he could not, over time, maintain his credibility vis-à-vis the faculty. After four years, he was therefore asked to leave by a broad faculty-sponsored petition. A good number two man in one successful institution does not necessarily make or become a good Dean.

Another Dean of one of the Eastern US private business schools who has a good academic reputation and a loyal MBA alumni following came to his job from an outstanding position as an executive in business. As Dean, he did a very good job working on external issues, especially fundraising, but was perceived as highly inefficient internally, with almost no impact on the intellectual direction in the school to inspire the various faculty members in their research or teaching. His practitioner-oriented background neither automatically gave him academic credibility, nor provided him with insight for being a catalyst for individual faculty members. Time came to renew the Dean's contract after three years. There was a general consensus among the faculty members that it would be undesirable to seek a contract renewal for him, since without a greater ability to influence the internal academic value creation, he would simply not be suitable. His track record, though good on certain items on his agenda, was not enough: balance was lacking.

Let me give a third example, this time involving a long-serving Dean of another US business school who got entangled in a legal dispute over his handling of a female faculty candidate. The issue of sex discrimination and equal opportunity is a critical one; it can be easy to agree on certain points in theory, but it can have its controversial side in practice. For instance, can the standards for hiring faculty be different for women than for men? Even though no school would admit to different standards, in practice, they give various attributes different weight when hiring women. It is perhaps not so much a matter of what is right or wrong, but of trying to look for attributes that will get the right eclectic mix of women and men, in a mixed-gender, positive, and creative professional group. The Dean of this school mishandled the recruitment of a woman candidate for a faculty position. He was subsequently questioned whether he was sufficiently open to her candidacy, or if he was trying to "hide" what might be considered "mistakes" or weaknesses. His objectivity was called into question, his credibility eroded, and ultimately a general call for his departure rang through the halls. Having served for such a long time, the Dean would have been smart to assume that a number of points of contention had built up with a large segment of the faculty, some concerning one issue and some concerning others. When the recruiting controversy broke, the Dean had few friends to back him up.

In all three examples, we see a breakdown in the faculty's trust in the Dean, the first primarily relating to lack of external effectiveness, the second to lack of internal effectiveness, and the third to lack of credibility and honesty in a difficult decision. And all three sooner or later precipitated the Dean's departure.

Allocate Tasks to Each Faculty Member Fairly

The Dean must make sure that teaching loads and other duties are being distributed evenly. As already noted, the basis for assigning faculty workloads must be clear. This is one of the few tasks that must be unambiguous, centrally run with the school's overall portfolio interests clear. No one faculty member should be unfairly treated. Of course, workload distribution is no mathematical exercise; we must accept that some faculty members will at times get a somewhat higher workload than others, due to special circumstances. Still, everyone should feel that the workload planning is fair and that, over time, everyone is treated equally.

IMD had no overall centralised process for faculty allocation until some years ago. The previous ad hoc situation had led to unsustainable situations. Professor X, who was by nature a very conscientious member of the team, said yes to every request that came his way, and ended up with what was close to a double teaching load, year after year. The fact that he is an excellent teacher, with great positive feedback from the participants, further exacerbated the situation. The professor *wanted* to teach a lot. He thrived on accumulating good feedback as well as feeling that he was productive and appreciated this way. Professor Y, on the other hand, systematically avoided all teaching. Whenever a suggestion was made, he simply said that his schedule was already full on that day, and he was not able to pick up more. Whether that was true or not is a different matter. If his schedule *was* full, it was perhaps full of consulting engagements! Again, it is clear that the consulting agenda should not override the teaching that the professor is actually paid for. This goes without saying, but it was not obvious to Professor Y. Year after year he ended up with an exceptionally light teaching load as a result. But there was no transparency: the faculty team had no concrete data for understanding these facts.

This example illustrates several things. First, even distribution of teaching loads is a question of fairness, which requires transparency. Clearly, we cannot allow some people to get away with doing little, and others to be overloaded. Factual data must document workloads, and it must be accessible to all. Second, therefore, it must not be accepted that some faculty members consistently teach too much, year after year. It is also a matter of protecting the health of these faculty members. Third, an ethical and sound morale within the team must be developed. Clearly, Professor Y getting away with no teaching is not building team spirit.

The Dean must strive to manage this in such a way that individual faculty members see their assignments as a part of their natural agenda. The faculty member, given his particular research interests, may for instance be attracted by being deeply involved in a particular in-company programme, and/or a specific open programme. It is important that the teaching mix matches his "natural agenda" when it comes to his research. Clearly, the school should not be asking faculty members to take on tasks that have little or no apparent link to their own value-creating agendas.

Even if task allocation is fair, the Dean needs to be sure that it is linked to rewards, such as merit-based salary increases, bonuses, additional time off for research, additional pay for work more than the norm, and sabbaticals on a need basis. A pre-requisite to this allocation is a clear understanding of the overall value-creating efforts of each individual. Most business schools put great emphasis on research *output* as a basis for faculty incentives. Professor Q was heavily committed to research and spent a lot of his "free energy" on this, focusing on how to better understand the way organisations can restructure and adapt, and to come out of such processes as more vigorous, technology-embracing organisations, rather than ending up as "restructured shells". He put all of his effort into a book manuscript that was ultimately published by a leading university press, which confirmed the high quality of his research. However, when the time came to grant bonuses, he was ineligible one year because his manuscript was still in progress. He did not get a bonus and did not understand it, because of his feeling that he was so committed to research. The following year, when the book was out, he did of course receive his full bonus. Accountants will call this a periodisation issue. By separating rewards from actual time when the value was created we may generate a demotivator. At a minimum, this issue of time to take into consideration needs to be kept transparent so that everyone understands.

Assess the Portfolio for the School's Overall Direction

The Dean has to assess the school's portfolio for overall direction, by aggregating the effects of the bottom-up inputs from each faculty member. The Dean can also have an impact on the evolution of the school's portfolio, however, by bringing his own vision into play, rather than merely reacting to the bottom-up input. Still, setting direction is fundamentally a process where the Dean is the custodian of all the input from the faculty members, more or less tempered by his own vision. This is precisely the direction-setting job of the Dean at IMD.

As noted, IMD is primarily committed to executive development, but with a small MBA programme. The small MBA programme, however, is vital for the IMD faculty, since it gives them a chance, through their interactions with especially bright students, to research innovative pedagogical ideas and thereby find new teaching approaches. With around 1,000 applicants for 85 seats, the IMD MBA programme adds significantly to IMD's prestige as a programme for the best, most "elite" students. At one time, a proposal came on the table to scale the IMD MBA up to 160 — or even more than 200 — participants. After all, the applicants were there, it was argued, so why not take advantage of this easy cash flow? But the proposal was rejected, largely because it did not fit with IMD's portfolio strategy. IMD did not want to significantly expand its MBA teaching, which might have led to an overly heavy commitment in what could have been seen as a rather mature segment of the school's business. More significantly, it could have led to a need for more faculty members, possibly viewed or branded as "MBA specialists" and not as bona fide members of the general management teaching team who normally work in all IMD executive teaching assignments. Even though the relatively small MBA programme teaching is a responsibility of the entire IMD faculty, it is viewed as a major strength. And expanding it might not merely have altered the strategic direction of the school, but actually added excessive costs of co-ordination among several sections. This example shows clearly the necessity of the Dean's involvement: he needed to remind all concerned that an expanded MBA simply did not fit well with the school's portfolio.

A similar question of IMD portfolio strategy came up when we were considering our new Executive MBA (EMBA) programme. The EMBA was to be built on the already existing and successful ten-week *Programme for Executive Development* (PED). Essentially, it would admit the most qualified PED students and added an additional — and roughly the same — time requirement as the PED demanded (on new subjects, of course), with one-third of the curriculum devoted to "travel studies" or off-site learning experiences. Virtual learning would be a significant part of the programme, between the modular visits to IMD. On close examination, it was clear that the EMBA programme fitted very well in IMD's portfolio; it represented an important addition to the executive offerings. Likely it would see an increasing demand from practising executives who wished to work on an MBA while on the job — a growth segment indeed. IMD's major clients, the large multi-national corporations, would find this offering of good value.

Regardless of these two examples, the Dean must not follow some vague, or unguided intent to steer the overall direction of the school. The school must have some overall logic for its value creation. This, too, is the Dean's job — to outline and pursue this guiding logic. It is relatively easy to come up with examples of schools with portfolios of activities that may be nothing more than a mere collection of free-standing elements, and thus easily become too complex and in their complexity lose synergy. Consider an institution we'll call School A. School A has been built around taking and presenting a managerial, practitioner's point of view. It has always been committed, for instance, to educating international students for a general management MBA degree. Over time, its portfolio has naturally expanded into executive development, with both open and tailored programmes. At some point, a new question comes up: Should a doctoral programme be added to School A's portfolio? A Ph.D. programme seems necessary to heighten A's research profile and strengthen faculty recruitment. Given the considerable resource commitment required it is hard to see how this could actually fit into the school's portfolio in a neat, clear way.

First of all, running a Ph.D. programme does not necessarily reinforce research among the faculty members. A Ph.D. programme *uses* a lot of resources, normally involving a few faculty members who are more heavily involved in research-oriented activities. It easily *takes* more resources than it *adds* to the school's portfolio of teaching activities. Ironically, it also takes away slack that could have been used by faculty members for research. Now School A's faculty members must commit time and energy to Ph.D. student feedback and supervision. Also, since it is probably not a good idea to hire the School's own Ph.D. candidates as new faculty members, there would be no sizeable advantage for attracting new faculty (although the potential benefits of an improved general academic reputation must be acknowledged). All in all, it was thus difficult to understand how School A's decision to start a new Ph.D. programme fitted into the portfolio of its managerial orientation.

Another example, from School B, is about the expansion of campuses around the world as a kind of geographic expansion of the teaching portfolio. School B was very committed to being international, and thus wanted to build a second MBA campus on another continent. The problem with this was, while the regional recruiting of students grew stronger, the overall programme did not necessarily become global. Students typically went to the campus most convenient to them, thus not necessarily enhancing the global-meeting-place effect of having only one campus. Non-academic factors such as the state of the local weather played a role for some students, for instance, when they were selecting their campus of residence. It further turned out to be difficult to bring faculty permanently to the new campus; instead, many faculty members had to be flown in for shorter stints. Managing the increased faculty complexity with two campuses became a big challenge. Again, one can ask whether School B's approach was consistent with a *realistic* vision of becoming totally global. The physical spread of a school into many campuses around the world certainly creates regionalism, but not "globalism". And it creates much more complexity! What is needed at School B, therefore, was a clear vision for the school's value creation, to determine if the decision fitted in with the overall portfolio. Here is where the Dean comes in, helping to make sure that the direction — and any decisions relating to it — is backed up by consistent, concrete mission statements, as well as an assessment of the risks taken and added resources needed with this added complexity. All to guide the choice of direction, to safeguard the decision-making process within the context of the vision and the mission.

Arbitrate and Resolve Conflicts

From time to time, the Dean is called upon to be the arbitrator in conflict resolution, of which two common examples follow. They will not be of the pure interpersonal conflict sort, although the Dean has to deal with those as well, usually in relatively small number. Most of the time, the Dean's arbitration will be a question of potential friction due to unexpected shifts in purely job-related events. For instance, consider Professor A, who has developed a carefully thought-out research plan, involving not only himself, but also a number of research associates; another professor is also involved to some extent. Now, an unexpected in-company programme comes up. The school's Dean can choose between several "natural choice" professors to be the programme director. He goes to Professor A, who then feels that there is a conflict between the school's demands on him and the maintenance of the integrity of his research plan. He feels that it would therefore be much more natural that another professor be asked to be the new in-company programme's director. It is likely that no persuasive arguments can be found for who *should be* the new programme director, at least not ones that everyone involved will buy into — after all, all professors have legitimate agenda plans! No matter how you look at it, therefore, the Dean must help to resolve the conflict in terms of *what is best for the school*! This means that customer focus should prevail — how to serve this client firm in the best way. The faculty staffing decision thus becomes impersonal, more objective!

Another conflict may arise when a faculty member highly sought after by several programme directors simply cannot say yes to all of them. It would dilute the concentration of his individual research plan, and lower his quality of life with an unacceptably high workload. How can the Dean help resolve this? By trying to keep the school's overall interests in mind, and appealing to all concerned for some flexibility and give and take. Again client needs should guide the decisions here. Everyone may, however, come out worse in the short run. The

Dean may, therefore, have to promise lesser teaching loads later, to allow the involved faculty members to catch up on their research.

In general, such ad hoc problems come up because of last-minute changes in a school's overall teaching agenda. Their consequences for the individual teaching loads are difficult to handle and potentially disruptive. Resolving such problems is especially hard since at least one individual faculty member's research plan typically suffers.

Regardless of the details of the particular conflict, the Dean must find ways to resolve and arbitrate such conflicts. No matter what view he takes, he must guarantee due process. By letting the clients needs guide him, he will come a long way in the right direction. Normally, this will involve looking at the negative consequence of any decision on each faculty member's plan, and holding the "competing" negative consequences up against each other, relative to the benefits for the school in taking on an additional programme. Thus, there must be a due process in assessing added teaching, added benefits to the client, with its accompanying added revenue, against the disruption of research. This point is relevant here because this "holding up for inspection" is a kind of "mini-portfolio" assessment, similar to the portfolio assessment discussed above. It involves all the relevant faculty members, so that the disruptions on the research plans can be shared, spread among several people, and thus minimised. The Dean's work must be fair, with no favouritism, and driven by what is best for the school as a whole. The Dean must conclude, at times, as he did on the question of the expanded IMD MBA programme, that an additional teaching programme should simply not be pursued, particularly if there is nothing much of unique value that might be added, say, if this is a rather standard programme design, in light of excessive negative consequences for faculty members' research plans.

In resolving conflicts, the Dean must further ensure that the organisation tolerates what might be seen as repeated "abuses" in the short run. What I mean is, so long as a faculty member understands that changes may have to be made in the best interest of the school, he may then be more easily amenable to such ad hoc add-ons in his working plan. If, on the other hand, these last-minute changes are dealt with in a vacuum, as ad hoc crises and not within an overall portfolio point of view, the faculty are less likely to tolerate them. Conflicts around teaching loads and research can turn nasty if they are not well handled. A resistance to such essential flexibility may then build up over time, and start to hurt the school.

In effect, all these tasks for the Dean may be seen to add up to bolstering organisational pride in delivering customer value — and also shoring up integrity and creating a stronger organisational climate by pushing for transparency. By helping set portfolio direction and effectively resolving teaching and research agenda conflicts, the Dean can help create a "can do" attitude, with the faculty members experiencing the power of flexibility and of being able to respond quickly to new and interesting teaching assignments. This type of highly professional execution, in the light of short deadlines and need for high flexibility, can justifiably lead to a lot of pride among the faculty team members. To experiment with speed, dynamism, and flexibility can be highly rewarding! Again, it is critical that due process prevail, so that the call for flexibility does not end up becoming a call for a few to suffer with their research plans going up in flames and the others getting a free ride. Transparency is critical here; workload adjustments are indeed portfolio issues based on how to serve the clients in the best possible way. With transparency, the Dean can ensure that the institution not only conserves energy, but builds a stronger organisational climate.

The Dean's External Tasks

Relationship Manager

The Dean has critical external tasks, the most important of which may well be helping to establish a multiplicity of relationships and links with environmental stakeholders. This helps the school translate the external inputs (external feedback) into suggestions for improvement, and inspiration for adaptation from the environment, etc. — and such inputs are *critical*! IMD's "Business Advisory Council" (BAC) provides a good example. The BAC consists of representatives from IMD's major learning partners — members of our Partner and Business Associate network. Each company usually has one member on the council, often the human resource officer, or quite frequently a senior line officer, such as a division President. The members offer input to the school regarding how its value-creation processes might be further improved to increase the benefits to the learning partners. Meetings focus the council members on specific topics — feedback on research projects, and teaching programme design in particular — to garner more targeted feedback. The Dean has an important role in making sure the agenda is properly chosen, that the dialogue in and out of the meetings leads to open, constructive feedback, and that the appropriate steps to follow-up are communicated and executed. The Dean must be involved throughout the entire planning process and the meeting itself. The Business Advisory Council must not end up giving advice "off the cuff". Such ad hoc advice can do more harm than good.

At IMD we also have a strong "Foundation Board", consisting again of representatives from the companies that are major clients, major learning partners and key members in IMD's network. Typically, the chief executive officers, or other senior executives of each of these companies, make up the Board. There is only one short formal board meeting each year, but this is in connection with the Chief Executive Officers' Roundtable, which takes up the rest of the day that the board meets. Here, again, a careful agenda is put together, allowing the senior executives to interact with and benefit from each other. In this way, they also send important signals back to the school about the direction they think it should be taking.

While these examples underscore the institutionalisation of the external stakeholder challenge, there will, of course, also be a multitude of one-on-one relationships with key external stakeholders. The Dean will have to play an important role in seeking out those individual stakeholders who are especially useful (not necessarily especially friendly!), and to try to incorporate relevant feedback from them into the school's strategic direction. In short, close links with external stakeholders is key.

Waving the Flag

But the Dean has to do more than manage external stakeholder relationships; another task, by no means less important, is travelling and speaking to publicise the school's vision, waving what I call the "value-creating flag". Consider once again the example of IMD. It is, as noted several times, heavily committed to being a "super-international" institution, a global meeting place. IMD's "Real World; Real Learning" vision is broadly communicated through speeches and presentations all over the world, in communication among various stakeholders, in IMD's brochures, etc. Thus, the positive benefits of learning in such a balanced, global context, with no single home-country bias, has been an important visionary communication point for the Dean and the school.

The Dean also has to publicise the school's commitment to its particular social vision, whatever it may be. IMD, to take an immediate example, has been eager to communicate its commitment to vital societal issues. In this respect, the school has, for instance, undertaken a large research and teaching programme on environmental issues, especially to develop useful business approaches that stem largely from ecologically and environmentally sound business practices, a critical current challenge for leading corporations and academia alike. As an example of our commitment to such environmental courses, the school has also highly publicised this research. Thus, both the school and its stakeholders have mutually evolved, from and through this research, sustainable development and its wide dissemination, which in the long run, can help set new meta-dimensions for better management and governance in society.

Returning to the examples above, it is important that a school be able to convey its leadership in developing critical aspects of business practices, rather than merely being a "me too" adapter of what others propose — or impose. It stands to reason, then, that at IMD one of the Dean's key briefs will be communicating the school's determination to lead the transformation of "international" to "global" in business thinking. Similarly, the Dean will support the school's commitment by "advertising" IMD's leadership role in turning "environmental compliance" into "environmental soundness" and then into "sustainable development".

Social Thought Leader

The Dean *must* take this role as provider of vision and societal leadership seriously. Some US business schools illustrate this well and, we assume, their Deans stand foursquare behind their schools' position on social responsibility. One laudable example is the increasingly wide-spread practice of following non-sexist faculty recruiting and development policies. Similarly, the issue of race has been squarely addressed. Not only does the vigorous handling of these issues imply an unwavering — and praiseworthy — interest, but also effective implementation, with impressive follow-ups, all of which impart a sense of progress in the school's communities, and even more widely in society as a whole.

Alumni

The Dean's interaction with the alumni is also important. They can provide a great deal of word-of-mouth advertising for the school, as custodians of "pride in the school" shown through the activities of the worldwide alumni clubs and magazine. Alumni networks can provide great image enhancement for the school, and nothing is better than happy customers for bringing in new participants. The alumni can also play an important part in fundraising, thus further strengthening the bonds between them and the school. Their activities provide a crucial outlet for alumni members to activate themselves on various substantive issues relating to the latest developments in business practice. As such, an active alumni network is an extension of the school's life-long learning commitment. For the Dean, commitment to alumni activities will be imperative. It should also be clear, however, that he must decide "how much" — alumni activities can take up a lot of the Dean's time. He must, somehow, strike a balance among the seemingly countless demands on him.

Fundraiser

Among these demands is yet another outside activity — fundraising. While a business school's value-creation equation should be such that the school is continually remunerated for what it does on a "going concern" basis, and thus should be able to at least break even based on its operational activities, it may still be difficult for a school to raise sufficient resources from its ongoing teaching activities to launch major research initiatives as well as investments in buildings and grounds, new computer facilities, etc. For these reasons, it is important that the Dean be actively in touch with outside stakeholders who may be willing to support the school for such strategic investments to safeguard and ensure a school's pre-eminence into the future. In my opinion, the Dean should view fundraising as a call for *exceptional* contributions for *exceptional* investments. The usual day-in-day-out academic value-creating activities, which I take to include funding the research necessary for teaching, should not be paid for out of fundraising campaigns. Raising funds for salary increases should be avoided. However, the long-standing tradition of endowed professorial chairs can be justified with the argument that such support can be part of spearheading particular research and teaching initiatives. A select number of particularly important agenda items for teaching and research might thereby be activated through the donations of endowed chairs, matching the particular interests of the donors and the school. In total, one may expect in the future that endowment funds will go towards special research and teaching needs, buildings, and grounds, rather than toward developing a convenient kitty for creating artificial independence for specific senior faculty members. Here again, the Dean is both fundraiser and the custodian of the funds.

The Dean's Process Tasks

Creator of a Positive Team Atmosphere

Deans must be seen as team leaders. Together with the rest of the faculty and the administration, the Dean reacts as a catalyst to help create the school's core academic values. It is essential that the team spirit be positive so that energy can be directed towards value creation instead of political bickering or destructive self-interests. Though this claim is rather intangible — it is certainly hard to define — it still captures what I take to be perhaps the most critical work of the Dean: namely, to create a positive team atmosphere that allows much energy to be unleashed and channelled directly into creating core academic values.

Metaphorically speaking my point is this: in many ways, a strong academic institution can be compared to an effective circulatory system in a healthy human
being. The blood is channelled into purposeful avenues for the benefit of the
organs. In contrast, the blood flow of a sickly person will be less than optimal.
For the school, there will always be great potential danger of energy diversion
into such channels as excessive bureaucracy, unnecessary procedures, unproductive committee meetings and internal disputes. The Dean's role as a facilitator
of a good internal climate based on simplicity is critical.

As a team leader, the Dean will spearhead the team as a whole in meeting one
of its greatest demands: adapting to new realities. A strong internal climate does
not, of course, imply maintaining the status quo, which might well be most
comfortable for all. Anything but! Adaptation is critical for the school to stay
relevant vis-à-vis its learning partners. Adapting with a vision — to lead rather
than be led — is particularly important. The Dean can play an important role in
"positively pushing" the organisation to adapt. As such, the Dean's injection of
energy is necessary to keep things moving. No organisation is indeed stronger
than the weakest link in the team — and the regrettable fact is that the Dean, at
times, can be just that! This he must avoid at all costs.

Keeping things moving will mean, speaking more concretely, keeping all the
school's stakeholders moving. Since the stakeholder mix in academic institutions
is unique, this task may be fraught with difficulty. Remember, the first-row stakeholders are the faculty members-cum-individualists, equal team members in what
amounts to a flat network organisation. Thus, each faculty member will have a
voice, equally strong in a senior or junior professor. Perhaps the tenure process
could somehow modify this, to add more stakeholder voice to tenured faculty.
IMD has a flat, all-inclusive tenureless faculty team of individuals who are the
essential stakeholders. So the roles of the head of such a school are fundamentally different from what one might find for a leader in, say, a typical corporation.
The key difference is that there is no sustainable top-down, hierarchy or posi-
tion-driven base. The school is basically "owned" by its faculty, and it is only
when the faculty is productive that the school excels. The Dean thus manages
more as a catalyst, than a "commander and controller".

Practical Implications

Getting the faculty to accept, even respect top-down leadership input is critical
to the Dean's success. It is by no means a trivial undertaking. Duderstadt aptly
notes that "the concept of leadership encounters a good deal of ambivalence on
the part of faculty. On one hand, faculty members resist — indeed deplore —
the command/control style of leadership characterising the traditional pyramid

organisations of businesses and government". Many faculty strike out on careers in academe believing, at least in part, that in a university they would have no "supervisor" giving direct orders or holding them accountable. "Yet the faculty", says Duderstadt, "also seeks leadership, not in the details of its teaching and scholarship, but in the abstract, in providing a vision for the university, in articulating and defending fundamental values, and stimulating a sense of optimism and excitement." This results in what Duderstadt calls a "widening gap between faculty and the administrational man on campus. The rank and file faculty sees the world quite different from campus administrators" with "significant differences in perceptions and understandings of the challenges and opportunities before higher education".

> The growing epidemic of Presidential turnover is due in part to this absence of faculty understanding of the nature of the modern University and support of its leadership. Of course it is due as well to the stresses on the Universities and deterioration in the quality of their governing boards.[13]

So, what do Duderstadt's insights and all the demands I have described heretofore mean, in practice, for today's Dean? Deans must view their jobs as *collections* of leadership tasks they must carry out in the name of the school's stakeholders. In very general terms, as Mittlehurst says, this means that the Dean must be "brave enough to stand and be counted, yet wise enough to listen and learn",[14] which in many ways summarises the entire essence of the appropriateness and need for top-down leadership in academic institutions, and what the quality of such leadership implies. To illustrate this very important point, take an example from IMD teaching programme management. The demand for the previously mentioned *Programme for Executive Development* (PED) has recently increased, due to the high quality of the programme itself, as well as due to the fact that it has also become the initial building block of IMD's Executive MBA. The school decided to increase the number of PED sessions, from two, then to three and now four per year. This obviously had an immediate "hardship" effect on the faculty teaching in this programme. Still, from an overall portfolio point of view, it was clear that the expansion was in the best interests of the school, securing a strong additional stream of revenue, and also strengthening IMD's position in the market by being able to admit more qualified candidates rather than creating bad will by rejecting too many applicants. The realisation of this advantage for the school took shape through faculty debates, and the decision to scale up was based on broad faculty commitment, rather than fiat from the top.

A second example of a totally different type involves the construction of a major new executive education facility at IMD. This was necessary in order to serve the executives better as the executive programme delivery expanded. Some faculty members felt that this was an inappropriate investment; the funds, they believed, were better spent on research or extra bonuses for individual faculty members. The funds from the school's operations, they believed, should not be used to excessively build up the school's bricks and mortar. Other faculty members, on the other hand, believed that the school needed new classrooms and auditoriums in order to serve the school's learning partners effectively. Of course, there was no right or wrong. What mattered was that the school made the decision following the beacon of what was best for the school as a whole. Again, faculty debate led to the growing agreement that one should go ahead. This decision could not have been reached through top-down "dictum"!

Only if the Dean believes in, and follows, principles and actions that fall under the rubric of "being a catalyst" and of "doing what is best for the school and its members" can he expect to remain effective over the long term. This means being involved and accessible. Even if the Dean resides at the top of the formal organisational hierarchy, his position must not lead to isolation. If the Dean has a false picture of his work priorities and capacity, if he misgauges the time he spends away from the school or over-prioritises what he will need for the routine parts of the job, he may well end up isolated. He may lack the necessary time to open his door to the needs of his faculty. When inappropriate priority setting happens, and the Dean is isolated from faculty, the institution suffers and the Dean becomes a bottleneck.

For me, this means carefully planning my overall agenda, if not necessarily in detail day-by-day, but certainly weekly and monthly. Internally, I need to plan faculty reviews, with one-hour meetings for each professor twice a year. This takes a lot of time, and it will not happen unless it is put into the agenda early on. Faculty and committee meetings also need to be planned, as well as faculty research seminars. I also carefully plan how to be able to review all faculty members' research outputs each year, to be able to integrate my assessment of this into the faculty bonus pay process. Important trips to external stakeholders — especially to far-away continents — will simply not take place if not carefully planned way in advance. In general, to effectively work with the leadership of one's learning partner organisations, one must of course plan well ahead. The result of this planning will be a rather full agenda.

On top of a packed agenda, time will constantly need to be found on the spur of the moment for daily eventualities, such as a request for a short meeting by a faculty or staff member. Small issues will need to be resolved, addressed efficiently, and never ignored. Further, with the advent of the networked society, the daily influx of emails is formidable. The individual expectation is that the Dean will be able to react quickly to those messages, in the spirit of what the active networked society is all about. It is therefore important to have enough slack in one's schedule to have ad hoc meetings and to respond to email. In practice, this involves making sure that one is connected to the school, and answering email, even when travelling. Thus, it is important to have both planning and flexibility at the same time, in harmony, forming one's agenda and activity pattern. If harmony is lacking, the job of the Dean can be a highly stressful and tiring one. This balance should mean the Dean driving the agenda, and not the agenda driving the Dean!

Meeting Both Internal and External Needs: A Dilemma

The most difficult aspect of the Dean's job is to meet both the internal and the external needs of the school at the same time. The hardest part is creating the "links" between the outside and the inside I spoke of earlier. The Dean must look to the outside for directional guidance "from the market place", visiting major customers to maintain key revenue-generating relationships, maintaining the public relations profile necessary for marketing purposes, and paying attention to other external stakeholders, too (regulators, potential donors, board members, etc.). He must make trips to the alumni clubs, and attend conferences to create visibility for the school. These activities are central and legitimate because they keep reinforcing the drive for relevance in its value creation, through the strength of the key links between the school and its environment.

The Dean must equally turn his attention inward, meeting key internal needs I have already outlined. The problem with trying to meet all these internal and external needs is that one person simply will have too little time and too little energy to manage it all. So the Dean has to delegate. But here again complications arise. To what extent can (should) the Dean delegate tasks? If so, which ones? Can the Dean and his office get support to enhance their capacity, to become more efficient? To what extent would such working style efficiencies be dependent on an understanding by and co-operation from the members of the faculty team and from the organisation at large?

Delegation

A typical response to the difficulties of effective delegation is to appoint an associate Dean or a provost to deal with the typical internal academic value-creating issues — the necessary nuts and bolts of running the institution. Perhaps the most natural task for the senior associate Dean will be to focus on workload planning.

This requires a lot of detailed follow-up vis-à-vis all the faculty members, of course in close conjunction with the Dean himself. Internal conflict resolution, especially concerning subsequent modification of teaching loads at the expense of research time, are also perhaps better handled by a senior associate Dean. He may also have a large part in faculty recruiting, given his good sense of what capacity gaps there might be in the faculty team. The Dean can then focus on the more externally-oriented issues. The result of this is a natural split between the external and the internal issues. However, this can unfortunately lead to dysfunctional results too.

Job separation must not lead to a distinct split between the Dean and the associate Dean — with the first more responsible for the vision and the second for the operations — as a potential conflict can easily develop then. It could be for instance that, while the Dean sees clear needs for building up faculty capabilities in certain new areas in order to adapt proactively to a changing executive education market, the assistant Dean may have his eye on covering the immediate teaching loads. Here the two "leaders" have a different — disharmonious — picture of the school's faculty needs.

A more fundamental area of potential conflict is the development of a two-sided perception regarding the external versus internal tasks. While the former includes adapting and serving the clients, from a proactive point of view, the internal tasks involve getting the job done, and delivering on promises to offer programmes that need to be staffed. By splitting the external and internal tasks, dysfunctional perceptions can build up within the faculty and administration, as well as among important learning partner stakeholders, leading to partial views on these two processes rather than seeing them as aspects of the same operation, which they must be.

The Dean and the senior associate Dean may themselves be in conflict on a strictly personal level — a most undesirable situation that should be avoided by all means. It is critical that the senior associate Dean consider himself an extension of the Dean, as part of the Dean's team, rather than following his own agenda. If the latter is the case, and a power conflict ensues between the two, the school's value-creation process is jeopardised. It follows that the Dean should have the privilege to select his own team, rather than having the associate Dean elected by the faculty or by the board.

My view on splitting the internal and external tasks between Dean and some sort of senior associate Dean is this: since the very essence of the role of the Dean is to create a *link* between the outside environment, with its pressures to adapt, and the internal working of the school, which focuses on the steps needed to meet those pressures, splitting the focus between external and internal matters can *only* weaken the adaptive capacity of the school. Consider, for instance, the development of the school's capability to work with emerging corporate universities by developing teaching materials and meta-plans for courses, and by participating in professorial support for virtual learning activities given by a corporate university, etc. All of these activities require the school to innovate and recreate its business model. The internal response challenge to all of this will also be formidable, calling for different ways to work for each faculty member and for different ways to calculate what constitutes a reasonable faculty workload. Thus, it seems to me, environmentally focused adaptation and internally focused response must go hand in hand.

It is necessary to take a holistic view toward external relationships. For instance, at IMD we have recognised the need to develop a holistic relationship with each firm globally, but also to serve the same firms' stakeholders in given key markets. One senior executive from IMD took over responsibility for all activities in each key market. This responsibility included dealing with the various clients, supporting the alumni club, providing inputs on market-based conferences, and advertising. In addition a "global" view regarding each key client had to be established — global account management. Powerful client-focused software (from Siebel Systems) helped us to manage this matrix challenge. Each marketing executive focuses on the overall value-creation activities vis-à-vis a holistically understood set of clients and markets, rather than fragmented kingdoms which can distort how the school perceives its need to adapt. Similarly, it is important to have a holistic view of the internal value-creating activities inside the school. Above all, this means communication.

Communication

One can simply never communicate and inform enough! This is no easy task — at times, so much communication may seem like an unnecessary waste of energy, and may appear to diminish the Dean's ability to complete other, seemingly more important tasks. A highly fragmented faculty department structure might significantly add to the need to communicate, while also providing a barrier to the common reception of a message.

Since IMD does not have a departmental structure, it has fewer silos in which faculty members with the same disciplinary background can "hide" and share a research world-view. Rather, IMD's faculty members are organised around eclectic teams, formed to most effectively serve our learning partners, which requires high levels of communication within each of these customer-focused teams. If communication fails, the intended benefit for the customer orientation might slip. Assuming, however, that this communication works, even more communication is needed for the particular organisational structure the school adopts — that is, communication between people with the same disciplinary and axiomatic backgrounds. The fact that a school is not organised according to functional departments does not mean that the need for communication between people in the same field is any less . . . on the contrary.

To understand this dilemma, imagine Professor X and Professor Y. X and Y are active in the same field — let us say, industry analysis. They have, however, entirely different research agendas, based on their own beliefs that they have powerful ways to see what industry analysis will require in the future. One of them may rely more on the markets, industry structures, and efficient competition within such industries. The other would be more focused on dealing with how to see exceptional opportunities within a particular industry, i.e., what would in fact amount to seeing ways for the industry structure to be efficient, in order to exploit them? Both approaches clearly have merits. It would be highly desirable to have clear communication between the two, so that not only could the two research streams benefit from cross-fertilisation, but also industry analysis is being taught in such a way that it is holistic, not partial, depending on which professor is teaching it in what course.

While each such small group can perhaps develop its own agreed-upon direction, each is unlikely to be adapting, as an isolated unit to the *group of isolated units* that make up the school, in ways that make sense for the school as a whole. Individual, isolated groups or departments cannot be effective, at least from an overall school perspective, in faculty hiring or termination decisions, research projects (particularly if requiring an eclectic base), or teaching programme delivery. Given the school's need to deliver on a holistic cross-functional basis vis-à-vis the typical client it is important that one overall perspective prevails! At IMD the consequence of this realisation is that, as noted, we have abandoned academic departments. Instead we encourage the faculty to organise themselves into research projects and teaching programmes. Self-organisation has thus helped sort out internal communication responsibilities by ensuring, namely, that single "units" are composed of faculty who naturally work together and that the lines between units are based on the clients' needs. Lines of communication among interest groups or functional groups remain blurred, on the other hand.

The overall intention of this IMD strategy is for faculty members to be part of various eclectic teams so as to be better able to serve the particular needs of the learning partners. As strong as this market focus perspective is, there are, unfortunately, potential problems with it too. Given the fact that faculty members tend to develop working relationships, that they tend to develop ways to understand each other, ways to thus cut down on the need for formal communication, there might also be a tendency for teams to form based on long-standing relationships, rather than on what would be emerging and evolving key learning partner needs. I have seen examples of teams of senior faculty members at IMD, for instance, who prefer to work together "come hell or high water", and who thereby even "define" the needs of the clients to fit the capabilities of these well-integrated, mature, stable teams. Not only is this dysfunctional in itself, it also prevents new faculty — in other words, new expertise — from complementing the team. This, of course, makes adapting to the learning partners' needs even more potentially difficult. The need to develop teams for meeting the clients' responses, rather than teams that are comfortable for the participants, must be met. The need to be able to bring in new faculty members, with less proven track records, perhaps with less possibility to score high on the feedback from the course participants, must thus still be enhanced. We have had examples of programme directors who avoid bringing in new faculty members because of their unwillingness to be exposed to "weaker" feedback ratings by the participants in their programmes. Clearly, this is a dysfunctional criterion for putting teams together.

Finding the Balance: Key Success Factors

It is of course important that the academic leader in a business school/academic institution develop an effective management style. Such a management style, in order to be effective, must be partly focused on execution — speed, action, getting things done — but also partly focused on due process — allowing for faculty and staff participation and respect for the organisation's inputs. Both of these two forces are critically important: the key is to have speed and participative governance. What does this mean in practice? It probably means that there must be plenty of room for discussion, analysis, and debate — but that there also must be willingness to take decisions, for moving ahead in the end. Often in academic institutions, there is so much participation, so many fragmented inputs that the execution-oriented decision focus is weakened, or even lost. Both participation and decision making are essential.

The leadership should be patient, maintain a calm, listening stance and, as such, be able to deal with all communication, feedback, even the worst of news, even-handedly. At the same time, the organisation must feel that the leader and his close associates are not afraid to state their own points of view, show their passions. They must not come across as aloof. The Dean needs cool objectivity and spirited, engaged passion at the same time.

The leadership must be willing to empower its organisational members, to entrust them, to delegate to them, to give them "space" to manage their value-creating assignments! At the same time, the leaders must be willing to "get their own hands dirty" by both delegating and being willing to get directly involved, rolling up their sleeves and doing things themselves. As such, the leadership should probably be following the role of leaders in smaller, entrepreneurial organisations, where people at the top actually do things. The Dean should probably shed the role of leaders of large organisations, where the leaders typically delegate everything, unable to do anything hands-on, directly themselves. Action and delegation must come together!

Building commitment is equally critical. Leaders in academic institutions can do nothing unless they see themselves as, in essence, representing the members of the organisation. They are effective leaders only as long as the organisation feels that they are effective in providing the power to the leaders on their behalf. There is no sense of power entrusted in an academic leader unless it firmly comes from the organisation itself. This is the inevitable context for building commitment in academic institutions. The academic leader does not dictate, but leads on behalf of the organisation. This is indeed the only lasting workable basis for developing commitment to strategic direction in academia. Still, the leadership also needs to decide, when it senses that it understands what the organisation might want — leading the organisation to learning committed to a new direction, an initiative, a decision. The academic leader must not look for popularity by after-the-fact consensus. He must both lead the faculty, and be led by the faculty!

Finally, the leader must be willing to praise and give positive feedback. Respect is of course linked with commitment, based on the fact that academic leaders can only be effective if they respect the members of the organisation they are set to lead. Praise and positive feedback are part and parcel of this. Too often there is feedback, usually negative, only when there is a problem at hand. When things go well, the members of the organisation often hear nothing. This "ritual" should be broken. The Dean needs to create an atmosphere of positive feedback, which is more important in an academic institution than in most others. Often, academic institutions are "lonely places to be" for their members, with little or no direct feedback at all regarding how things are going. Academic leadership entails both positive feedback and negative criticism. The Dean must be comfortable working with the faculty and staff.

When it comes to managing all these tasks, particularly finding a balance in addressing both the internal and the external needs of the school, the success of the Dean may ultimately rest on an ability to simply follow good management. Sensible judgement includes sorting out ad hoc items when they come up, without delay. Maintaining a consistent and emotionally stable viewpoint over time — no easy discipline when it comes to providing regular feedback — is also key. There are, of course, no neat ways to find this consistency, but a few principles are worth minding. Overall, the Dean must maintain a holistic point of view, which requires:

- seeing the inside need to get the job done *and* the outside need to adapt;
- seeing the viewpoints of the senior members of an existing faculty team *and* the need to involve new members with new capabilities;
- understanding the present challenges to "deliver" *and* the future needs to reorient and leapfrog the delivery;
- expressing emotion, non-aloofness, passion and striving for a stable, predictable behavioural style.

Clearly, the Dean needs to willingly invest a lot of his own energy to keep things moving. Without this "walking the talk" the insistence on the school maintaining speed, the dynamic workings of the faculty team and the school may grind to a halt. The Dean is the key catalyst in keeping things going forward, the key custodian of speed. As I have stressed several times already, the guiding light must be for the Dean to ask himself, "What is the best decision given the overall school context?" "How can I focus all that I have to give of energy coexistent with this?"

It should be said that a good managerial style also heavily depends on the attitude of the rest of the organisation. It may well be that the school's organisation does not "allow" the Dean to take such balanced, holistic decisions. Consider what happens when a programme director simply refuses to admit certain faculty members onto his teaching team. He may unilaterally decide that this is his prerogative: he is, after all, responsible. With such an attitude, it may be difficult for the Dean to encourage a more balanced approach. Similarly, a faculty team, well entrenched as it can be, may refuse to admit more members. Such resistance is real. But the Dean must "choose his battles"; a break here and there, timed appropriately, is better than an all-out war. The organisation cannot afford to waste time on politics.

The fact remains that many organisations — academic as well as others — are highly political, and are riddled with political problems. Be that as it may, what is the Dean to do? In my opinion, the "ownership dimension" (the sense of owning the school) of each faculty member must be strengthened to counteract the tendency towards politicking. The faculty members must firmly believe that they "own" the school, as earlier illustrated, by sharing in the benefits of successful operations, through exceptionally high salaries, high profit sharing, and high individual bonuses. Thus, someone who wastes organisational time by politicking must be seen as wasting the owners' and the teams' time, and the teams' group norms must be brought into play to ameliorate such politicking. Faculty members should see the benefits of operating in a straightforward manner, of being fully committed to pure academic value creation, of enjoying the "owner's prerogative" of success in the form of added take-home salary. Academic institutions are not salary optimisers. Still, sharing of a strong bottom-line result will give the faculty members-cum-"owners" the positive satisfaction of benefiting from the value-creation process in the school, and from the benefits of a healthy, non-political climate.

Envision a faculty member who is unable to work along such lines. Professor X is highly focused on politics — one might almost say that he has a hyper-propensity towards politicking. It almost looks as if politicking is *the* driving force behind Professor X's behaviour. He professes to be highly committed to research, but delivers nothing. Research is all talk and promise for him; his time and energy are given to politicking instead. In the end, the school's leadership has to act, and the upshot is that the faculty member is asked to leave. It should be the *colleagues* who see the benefits of this severance. It should remind them — demonstrate — the value of value-creating energy use. The Dean's actions are thus in line with the faculty's wishes — well understood and accepted. Of course, this is not merely a hypothetical story. Professor X was real, and his departure turned out to have clear, positive effects: for one thing, corridor politics virtually disappeared.

So again, the Dean does have a role in safeguarding against politics; he himself must be as non-political as he can be. He must not succumb to side deals, agreeing with whoever happens to be standing in front of him, or making under-the-table, non-transparent deals, etc. Due process, full openness, transparency, and full commitment to what is best for the school — these are the sine qua non for the Dean. In this manner, he can clearly show the way towards pragmatic, non-political behaviour.

As the above example also illustrates, the Dean must also be able to intervene in extreme cases of politicking. As a shared ownership organisation, the business school cannot abide excessive value degeneration; it hurts the owners. If the Dean can ensure this maturity, the school will have a better chance of adapting to, and delivering, exactly what the marketplace seeks. With flexibility and adaptive ability, the organisation will be able to close the gaps between supply and demand — the subject of the next chapter.

Chapter 12

Structure, Hierarchy, and Incentives

Executive Summary

If a business school aims, above all else, to be a learning partner to its clients, then, despite its advantages — common, discipline-based language, and manageability — the traditional departmental structure must go. And despite its disadvantages — the complexity, and strain of managing programs and research, the lack of commonalities among teams of faculty from widely different disciplines — abolishing academic departments may well be the optimal organisational structure. Only by adopting a more open (less departmentalised) structure will the business school be flexible and agile enough to adapt to the needs of its learning partners. If, however, research and publication are a school's main mission, then the more departmentalised structure may serve better. Business schools that wish to be flexible and adaptable should also consider doing away with hierarchies and tenure. A business school without a formal hierarchy and tenure will need to establish an incentive scheme (reward system) that compensates for the lack of the traditional rewards. The example of IMD illustrates one set of successful incentive policies. Overall, financial rewards, coupled with the option of dismissing under-performers, are a principal condition for managing a business school strategically, by helping to create a performance-driven culture.

It should be clear by now that, for any business school, organisational flexibility is a key to delivering what its learning partners demand. Only with organisational agility will the school be able to close any gaps between supply and demand. The structures of the organisation must, therefore, not be allowed to make the school rigid or hamper its ability to adapt. This is true for all business schools; nevertheless, IMD can once again serve as a good example of how to protect institutional flexibility.

IMD's recent success attests to its agility and suggests that its lack of departmental structure may well serve as a model for tomorrow's business schools. Recall from Chapter 8 that, although IMD receives no government support, its turnover per professional rivals that of other high-performing consultancies and business schools. All too often, typical business schools build academic departments in order to develop discipline-based strength and focus, and optimise teaching and research assignments. Each discipline will typically be built around its own paradigms, and these usually determine more or less explicit preferences for teaching and research, thus perhaps decreasing responsiveness to demanding learning partners. Let me give an example from my own field, strategy. A strong paradigm dominating this academic field for several decades now has been industrial economics, spearheaded by economists such as Richard Caves,[1] and brought to research-based prominence within the strategy field by Michael Porter[2] and others.[3] Research on this paradigm has had a profound effect on the field, and has led to many publications in leading journals, most notably the *Journal of Strategic Management*. Similarly, strategy courses have, to a large extent, focused on various aspects of competitive strategy. This paradigm-based discipline structure undoubtedly optimises teaching and research; however, in providing value to the customer along multidisciplinary, cross-departmental lines, it often falls short.

Consider the body of strategy implementation knowledge. It draws on organisational science, perhaps most notably when it deals with how teams of individuals function. Further, in dealing with *who* should be involved in *what*, and *when*, strategy implementation would probably need to draw on the strategic *process* body of knowledge. It may even draw further on certain aspects of organisational psychology, perhaps primarily from the field of individual motivation and incentive. A human competence-based view of strategy may build on insights from the field of human resource management and so on. Strategy implementation may even draw on other relevant areas of knowledge. The point here is that often the current research and teaching challenges call on rather eclectic, multidisciplinary, multi-paradigmatic approaches. Strategy implementation, if it is going to serve clients well, may thus be far more than "mere" industrial organisation, far more than what can be offered via separate departments organised along functional lines.

IMD faced this challenge not long ago. It recognised that, to be an effective learning partner, it needed an alternative to the traditional, discipline-based departmental structure. It needed to find a "structure" that would afford maximum agility and flexibility.

To avoid organisational rigidity, and to ensure as fast an adaptation as possible to a given customer's needs, the faculty and leadership of IMD committed themselves to three critical decisions, all intended to keep internal structural formality to a minimum. First, IMD has no academic discipline-based departments. Finance, Marketing, Accounting, Organisational Behaviour, Strategy or General Management, for example, don't exist. The school emphasises sole focus on one academic resource: its single all-faculty team. The professors organise themselves into teaching programmes (typically cross-functional and multi-disciplinary) and/or research programmes. Starting, for example, with a typical open teaching programme, say, the three-week programme *Managing Corporate Resources* (MCR), the programme director has a strong background in industry analysis. His core teaching team includes a professor with a finance background, another in organisational behaviour, a third who is strong in leadership and motivation. A series of "mini-electives" runs in parallel over one of the three programme weeks, and draws on an even wider range of faculty members, including accounting, marketing, and operations management professors. All told, the participants get broad exposure to the critical challenges faced by executives who are about to take on, or have recently been appointed to, the leadership of strategic business units, i.e., managing a business unit or division. The objective of MCR is to provide integrated knowledge to the participants.

IMD's tailored, in-company programmes, say, one that the Lausanne Institute delivers to a large, leading multinational corporation in telecommunications, is another case in point of the advantages of a "departmentless" structure. The objective of the in-company programme may be to expose the participants to working with a dynamic concept of strategy, indeed to get them to "see" a rapidly evolving strategy, which may well amount at IMD to creating a learning process for identifying new business opportunities early, and learning how to map out the most critical implementation challenges for delivering on such opportunities. The faculty team could consist of a leader in the strategy field who also has a strong background in learning theory; he might be backed up by a finance professor, who happens to have a second discipline in accounting; a third professor comes from human resource management; and the fourth, key professor is a marketing expert. All in all, this team provides an *integrated* value proposition to the participants.

I can speak personally for the advantages of the "open" structure, for IMD's departmentless organisation has had a positive impact on my own work, too. As mentioned in Chapter 10, I am much involved in a research programme that is exploring the critical factors behind stimulating effective internally generated growth. A number of the research team members come from the strategy field; others come from organisational behaviour and marketing. This research is an informal umbrella over more specific research into developing radically new businesses, either with acquisition driven growth, or internally generated growth. This research is based on building on one's already established business strengths, say, by "exporting" an already successful business concept into new markets, and/or adding new technology. The organisational implications for a business trying to develop a more growth-oriented strategy would most likely be explored best by faculty with various competencies (from various "departments"). And so, the research is enriched, the various competencies best covered by a multidisciplinary, eclectic ("non-departmental") approach.

Implications of a Structure Without Departments

What are the everyday consequences of having no academic departments? All faculty members will see what it means, in practice, to work with real flexibility. This can be highly demanding. To organise a school around ad hoc teaching and/or research projects, without the stability and discipline-based focus of an academic department, can be both time-consuming and enervating. The traditional disciplinary base can lead to significant co-ordination gains. The professors who share a particular discipline typically have a common language, so communicating will be relatively easy for them. They usually share a common research methodology. Tooling up for a new research study can, therefore, happen very quickly. In contrast, however, developing a multidisciplinary research methodology can be quite complex. Researchers may have to learn a lot. The writing format within disciplines often tends to be of a particular ilk. It is thus, again, time and energy efficient to write in specific, discipline-oriented journals. A disciplinary department can truly represent a community of scholars who can comfortably stick together because of common interests, values, and norms for what constitutes quality research. Thus, the more a business school is structured in clearly delineated academic departments, each with a rather homogeneous internal focus, the easier it may be to manage, at least in the short run. But — and this is a serious drawback — the ease of management typically comes at the cost of relevance to the learning partner. The ability to provide cutting-edge integrated value of the type demanded by today's executives and corporations is reduced. For this reason the departmental structure must go, despite all its apparent advantages.

But eradicating the old departmental structure may be even harder than it sounds to those who know the modern business school well. Consider two schools that tried to meld several of their departments into one large team — but in the end failed. At the Wharton School, one of the largest departments is the Department of Management, with approximately 45 professors. This department was organised into five sub-departments: Strategy, Organisational Behaviour,

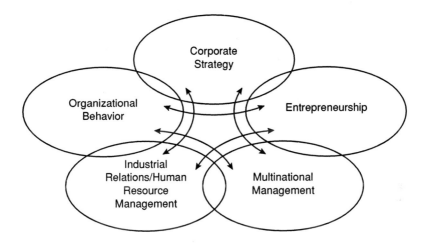

Figure 12.1: Wharton School's management department's vision.

Labour Relations, Entrepreneurship, and International Management. Wharton tried to "dismantle" the sub-department structure, driving for value creation that would build on the eclectic mix of competencies of its various sub-groups, when taken together and applied to cross-disciplinary research and/or teaching. Figure 12.1 above depicts the management department's attempt to find synergies among its diverse departments and faculty.[4]

The internal energy requirements to manage all of this were, however, so large that, after only a few years, Wharton went back to the free-standing sub-department structure. At least in the short run, internal considerations probably diminished the department's ability to adapt to new customer needs, and may thus have jeopardised the alignment with customers in Wharton's environment (though the management task may have been simplified). The main emphases at Wharton were on teaching MBA and Ph.D. students, and research. At the time, relatively little emphasis was put on executive development teaching so the relative lack of alignment with executive needs was clearly not a crippling Achilles heel. The faculty promotion process put great emphasis on publications in refereed journals. It thus turned out to be more time and energy efficient to re-establish an axiomatic set of lenses, providing for more specialisation in teaching and research. Professors could concentrate more directly on their more readily defined research agendas and focus their energy on more axiomatic, conventional research results. The most immediate measure of success for the school —

namely, to provide superior axiomatically driven research, as manifested by publications in refereed, discipline-based journals — was better served by the more departmentalised structure.

A second reason for the return to the multi-departmental structure may have had to do with leadership implications. It took a lot of effort on my part, as the then department chairman, to hold a department like this together. It was easier to run the department as a collection of sub-departments, with more focused internal operations, built around more specific disciplines. This was the tack chosen by my successor as department chairman.

At the Norwegian School of Management, eleven departments existed at the time I arrived as the school's President. Each was small and independent. I took the initiative to combine the eleven departments into three large ones. The school wanted to gain flexibility and be better able to adapt to its customers' demands. Combining small departments into larger ones was also intended to make faculty staffing easier. The idea was to add new faculty members in areas where the school anticipated growth. The school, for instance, saw growth potential in the area of petroleum economics, largely based on a symbiosis between academia and the burgeoning Norwegian oil sector. Both research and a masters programme specialisation within petroleum economics were thus being pursued. Undertaking any academic staffing for this initiative was much easier when the departmental structure was large and flexible enough to allow hiring within such a large, "broad" context, rather than have to fit this hiring into the smaller, incremental context of smaller academic departments. Thus, because of the school's slack in faculty, recruiting thereby could be combined, and since recruiting was no longer split into many mini-departmental sections, with each focusing on extending its own directions, it was easier to find new faculty who would "fit" the new directional agenda. Without such flexibility, the school ran the risk of simply replenishing its faculty along the more or less incidentally delineated staffing patterns of the past. Each small department would simply work to prolong its own life.

The internal energy constraints in managing this loose structure at the Norwegian School of Management were, however, again so large that the school eventually returned to what might largely resemble its old structure. It created nine new departments, but tried to follow a middle road: departments large enough to keep a realistic alignment with the needs of the school's learning environments, but also small and homogeneous enough to allow for reasonably energy-efficient management.[5, 6]

Hierarchy: Academic Titles

Along with abandoning departments, IMD has abandoned the hierarchy of academic titles. All members of the faculty are simply called "professor". The alternative is, of course, the classical hierarchy structure, with a large number of assistant professors, some associate professors and a few full professors. The classical hierarchical organisation associates a certain amount of power and status with each level in the hierarchy. A professor is typically seen, rightfully or not, as a more important and competent person than an assistant professor. Putting together teams of people with different ranks or titles can be difficult. Clients may be put off, or even feel slighted, if they aren't provided with teams of full professors. They may well consider a team of junior faculty less resourceful, even resist them even though they may have the most relevant, up-to-date know-how. Organisational hierarchy can compound internal frictions as well: senior professors may, for example, insist on leading the team, even if a more junior professor is obviously the best qualified. While these perceptions and problems may lie at the extreme of possible reactions, hierarchy and titles *are* associated with faculty members of various ranks. If a key client will not accept faculty members lower than full professor on the teaching team, then the school is going to have a tougher time putting together flexible teams, and adapting.

Another negative effect of such hierarchies is the senior faculty having to spend an inordinate amount of time and energy evaluating colleagues for promotion and tenure. The energy "misappropriated" for such evaluations, as well as the concomitant political "dysfunctionalities", make a strong case for abandoning titles. The evaluation process easily raises political tensions in the organisation. Faculty members may go against each other, rather than working together, and a win/lose atmosphere may ensue. The organisation can use this energy better to create academic value. The modern business school can circumvent these energy-depleting, dysfunctional activities by doing away with these evaluations of colleagues. But this, again, implies the abrogation of tenure.

Tenure

IMD has decided against tenure. Either you are *in*, or you are *out*! The school is unwilling to accept the burden of carrying a faculty member who does not perform acceptably in the longer run. Relinquishing tenure does not seem to have hurt IMD. Perhaps this is not surprising in light of the fact that Rowley *et al.* report that none of the few institutions that have given up tenure — among them,

Evergreen State College in Olympia Washington, and Hampshire College — have experienced severe faculty morale problems as a result.[7]

Perhaps the most typical performance deficiency is lack of ability to deliver in the classroom. A professor must be, in IMD's language, "billable". If the professor is unable to teach in a way that allows him to be accepted by the demanding executive, the feedback is usually clear (low ratings are the result). And relatively soon this will mean that this professor is no longer sought-after. The professor may be technically strong, but will perhaps not be able to get his points across. He just can't package his knowledge effectively for teaching purposes. If such a situation prevails, then there will be little room for this professor at IMD, and the consequence is that he/she might be asked to leave. Interestingly, such departures often tend to come at the initiative of the professors themselves.

As noted previously, faculty members may also be asked to leave because of inappropriate behaviour vis-à-vis outside consulting. Faculty members must stick to the norms, on paper as well as in spirit. If they are drawn too much to the outside, there is no room for them at IMD. No faculty member can be allowed to compete with his own institution!

Another example is breach of value norms, such as plagiarism, a case covered earlier. Suffice it to reiterate that the school has no choice but to ask offending faculty members to leave. Occasionally, a faculty member may be so heavily involved in internal politicking, in excessively challenging the leadership, and may become so dysfunctional, that he will have to suffer the consequences and leave.

The crux of successful academic value creation is having faculty who are able to develop their competencies in line with the school's direction and values, so that both the faculty and the school remain as relevant as possible. Faculty members who produce less than cutting-edge, state-of-the-art academic value will easily become a liability, above all because they tend to slow down the adaptive value-creation process and block positions that could be filled by others who are better able to provide cutting-edge value. Interestingly, the IMD faculty team seems to appreciate the positive benefits of not having tenure. They appear to accept the clear message that IMD is one faculty team working together to help IMD progress through regular, continuous adaptation. They have the maturity and self-confidence to see this as natural.

Without Tenure, What Incentives?

Probably the most obvious and visible reward in most academic settings is promotion to a higher rank, eventually leading to tenure. Promotion to higher academic rank can signify not only progress, but collegiate approval by the other members of the institution. Promotion goes hand in hand with appreciation for contributions to academic value creation. It is an academic handshake that says, "you are welcome to stay on as part of our academic team". The tenure process — in essence, granting life-long job security as a member of a given institution — thus serves as a particularly powerful expression of appreciation for one's efforts — "you are now a member of the club"! The need for job security is legitimate, since it enables faculty to focus on creating value with sufficient depth and long-term focus. However, the down side of rank and tenure may be complacency and lack of flexibility, as we have discussed. For more senior faculty members who cannot be promoted to higher ranks than full professor, tenure may amount to a life-long sinecure, less commitment, rather than more. While IMD does not have much ability to provide incentives through promotion, arguably a weak point relative to many other business schools, pay incentives are particularly important.

More specifically, without a tenure process, it is indispensable to set out a clear contractual arrangement that both protects the faculty member and safeguards the institution. This agreement must be specific and clear, and understood by all. All parties have to agree on how the school will be allowed to terminate the contract of a faculty member who is performing under par: steps, conditions, requirements, and expectations.

A new faculty member typically joins the IMD team with a three-year contract. At the end of the first two years, this contract is renewed for another three years by the President, in conjunction with the Senior Associate Dean for Academic Affairs. Data from the teaching evaluations is key to this. Also, inputs from three professor colleagues are solicited. The two administrators orchestrate an even more thorough review when one year remains of the second three-year term. This time, they also call on outside collegial references, complementing the written inputs from three professorial colleagues. They review the entire dossier of published research and teaching materials. They scour the ratings. If a strong, forward-looking picture does not emerge, IMD asks the professor to leave. In practice, this does not happen very often — say, in one or two cases out of ten.

It is remarkable how well the IMD culture assimilates new faculty members, an ease of integration that can be attributed to its eclectic team culture. This team-based approach provides a lot of support to new faculty members, allowing them to receive backing from their colleagues, mostly ad hoc, and informally. Perhaps the most typical reason a faculty member leaves will have nothing to do with his job-related performance. It might have to do with his family situation. Often, professors want to return to their home country for the children's schooling. This is an issue for the American faculty members in particular.

After the successful completion of the second three-year review, a professor enters into an "open contract". From this point, IMD can ask the professor to leave at any time, but with one year's notice, and only after a thorough review. If there is strong indication of dissatisfaction about the performance of a professor, the President, working with the Senior Associate Dean for Academic Affairs, may at any time ask for a review of the weak performer. This review will of course be even more comprehensive than the one at the end of five years. A representative from the faculty advocates the viewpoint of the faculty member in question, and is a key figure in the deliberations and dialogue around the question of contract renewal. Thus, the due process procedure is intended to fully protect the professor in question. At the same time, it is also clear that due process must not stand in the way of decisions that might end up in the departure of a professor. Often in academia, due process is taken to such an extreme that no faculty member will, in practice, be asked to leave. At IMD, this is not the case.

Still, in reality, very few faculty members leave IMD because of problems associated with various aspects of their performance. The very fact that this option exists, however, has a major impact on the faculty members' behaviour, in my view. They are aware of the fact that they must continue to provide value, in some form or another, re-earn their right to remain on the IMD faculty team every year! And this tends to breed a positive attitude, be it in the form of trying to deliver exceptional pedagogical learning contributions, produce relevant research, self-policing in avoiding excessive consulting, or avoiding excessive politicking, which adds up to more constructive faculty behaviour. Because we do not have a situation where a certain group of faculty members almost "gets away with murder" because they're tenured, highly disruptive and dysfunctional behaviour is uncommon.

Rewarding Performance

An important precondition for managing a business school strategically is a meaningful reward system for faculty. This reward system must link constructive academic value creation and performance to remuneration. The importance of adequate faculty compensation has been stressed by several scholars, including Rosowsky, former Dean of the School of Arts and Sciences at Harvard University. "Faculty compensation also needs to be mentioned in connection with accomplishing institutional goals: inadequate salaries lead to lack of commitment and excessive outside activities. Even adequate salaries may not prevent 'moonlighting'. The point is that the most efficient faculties are reasonably compensated, work full-time, and are subject to control of their outside activities."[8]

While I agree with Rosowsky, I believe it is important to note that it is not only faculty who thrive under an effective reward system. A meaningful reward structure is of course of critical importance for staff members as well. One must recognise, however, that it is typically only a small percentage of the staff — mostly senior staff — who can have a significant impact on the school's performance. So at IMD, the staff with direct marketing responsibilities receive particularly substantial additional performance-based rewards. All members of IMD's organisation do receive some form of bonus, however, if the school is doing well financially.

Allow me to make a more general observation regarding the role of the staff in academic institutions such as IMD. On the one hand, it is clear that it is the entire team — the faculty *and* the staff — that brings value to the learning partners. The latter experience all aspects of the "IMD experience", whether it concerns what is happening in the classroom directly, or in the coffee shop. It is all equally important, in one sense. Dysfunctional performance, whether in classroom teaching or in programme administration, will stick out and lead to negative reactions. Still, the critical success factor for a business school will, after all, be its faculty. One can say that having a good, high-performance staff is a necessary condition for the school's success, but it is not discriminating. The true, decisive success factor is the quality of the faculty. Without this, it doesn't matter very much if the rest of the institution performs well. This book has — and will — take this as a major fact-of-life and will thus not cover the role of the staff very extensively.

To attract — and retain — the best faculty is thus critical. An aggressive, competitive pay structure is one of the keys to this. Base pay must be good. But the variable pay component is also very critical. It is becoming more and more common for individual faculty members of an organisation to expect some sort of direct recognition of, and reward for, exceptional performance. In academia, to do this in a fair way is a particularly difficult challenge. And as the case of IMD shows, performance-based rewards are a radical departure from the more typical seniority-based collegial rewarding of faculty members, with salary and rewards tied strongly to seniority and tenure.

Business schools should grant most of their faculty rewards on the basis of delivered performance. Still, a too highly individualistic reward structure can make the critically important team-based elements of academic value creation potentially more difficult. It goes without saying, therefore, that rewards must be

298 New Vision for Management Education

balanced, based not only on a number of individual academic contributions, but also on contribution to team efforts.

Individual Compensation as a Reward

Basic Remuneration

As noted, an aggressive policy to pay very competitive salaries is at the heart of IMD's success. IMD bases individual compensation on four criteria. The first is *basic remuneration*. The base salary would be set at a level dictated by what is needed to be more or less competitive in the market for strong academicians. While we put some emphasis on seniority, the salary scale is, by design, rather compact, with intentionally relatively little difference between faculty members, who — after all — are all expected to contribute equally anyway. Similarly, given the great team emphasis on IMD's academic value creation, academic "stars" get relatively little extra in fixed salary.

The level of pay must ensure economic comfort for faculty members. This should enable faculty to focus on academic value creation without fear of financial difficulties. If salaries are too low, in order to secure a minimum standard of living, faculty may have no choice but to sacrifice significant amounts of time to outside consulting. The institution needs a big enough resource base to provide sufficient faculty pay. In the end, this is a stakeholder value exchange issue: the customers of the academic institution must be willing to pay what it takes. The funding stakeholders must feel that they get fair benefits in return. Incidentally, relative to the pay levels in other parts of society, salaries for academicians in many schools in many countries have suffered a serious decrease over the last few decades. It is not clear that this can continue, in the age of the human resource-based knowledge revolution.

A business school is, in essence, a modern brain-driven service sector organisation. The attractions for the members are similar to what one finds in other brain-driven service sector organisations like consulting firms, investment banks, and other high-paying institutions. Relatively low faculty salaries can represent a serious threat to the business school. In the longer run, in fact, they will mean that the best and brightest, feeling that many of the intellectual benefits of their work can be achieved in other work-related contexts, elect other professions. After all, a career in consulting or through membership of the management teams of progressive corporations may mean interesting jobs, professional growth, and heavy earnings as well — indeed potentially attractive alternatives to an academic career!

Economic Bonuses

Rewarding research   The second pay element is individual economic bonuses. Pay for performance is commonly seen as a key determinant for success. In academia, pay has often largely been a function of seniority and rank, and not pegged to performance. An element of pay for performance must exist. The stronger, the better. The fixed pay should merely represent a "security blanket" for faculty members, a significant part of the rest of the pay might come as performance-based bonuses. Such bonuses might be a function of one or more aspects of the academic value-creation process, depending on which of these aspects one may wish to strengthen. Some schools may want to focus predominantly on research; others more on teaching quality. Regardless, such criteria must drive pay. Those responsible must apply them in a balanced way, consistent with the school's objectives. If the modus operandi are tempered by inconsistency, the academic value-creation process might well become unintentionally biased. At IMD the criteria for performance-based bonus include academic output, teaching, and citizenship.

The school must emphasise and weigh out *demonstrated* academic output, such as articles, books, working papers, etc. It should also put a premium on the quality of the output. Rewards should go to those who, for example, get their articles into refereed journals. In fact, at IMD the *bulk* of the recognition and credit for academic output — 50 percent of the weight of individual bonus — will go to rewarding research leading to publications, say, in refereed journals and/or scholarly monographs. But the school must also recognise more practitioner-oriented outputs as part of the research. This includes developing and publishing cases. IMD encourages research and development mainly to safeguard the faculty members' self-development process. We want our faculty to stay "fresh", and we want all programmes to be built on cutting-edge knowledge. Contribution to scholarly progress is important, of course, but at IMD it does not represent an end in itself.

The actual assessment of the research output is critical here. In order to safeguard the integrity of the process, this assessment must be objective. It can probably best be made by individuals who themselves have a strong research reputation. Further, it probably means that not too many individuals can be involved, thereby safeguarding that more or less consistent judgements and criteria are used vis-à-vis all of the research and thus, vis-à-vis all of the professors. At IMD I carry out these assessments myself in my capacity as President of IMD. This takes a lot of time, I estimate approximately three full weeks of work per year, every January. However, it is critical that the faculty members feel that I put in this time and commitment, to uphold the integrity of the process.

So far I have received no questioning regarding my assessment of the research by any faculty members. They realise that by applying one's best effort this is perhaps the best process one can get. It is not possible to be entirely objective in an "objective" sense. Just judgements must still be provided. The key therefore is that these judgements are made by one person, also seen as having a reasonable reputation as a researcher himself.

Rewarding teaching   A business school does not thrive on research output alone. It needs top-quality *teaching*. The riddle, however, is how to measure and reward the myriad activities we commonly call "teaching". Criteria may include teaching ratings or pedagogical innovations. Exceptional contributions — *truly exceptional* contributions — to teaching and pedagogical development merit recognition and deserve reward. At IMD, each professor is asked to name what he/she considers the significant pedagogical innovation that he/she has contributed in a given year. This may be an exceptionally good case, a new programme design, or a new multidimensional teaching innovation, say, involving virtual technology in an action learning context. The faculty member must also submit a statement explaining why he/she feels that his/her teaching performance was exceptional. These materials are reviewed by the President and Senior Associate Dean, and are ranked subjectively into three categories: outstanding, solid contribution, and the rest. This approach is of course complemented by the more straightforward teaching ratings, carried out in every programme at IMD and systematically reviewed as part of the incentive process. The teaching performance dimension counts for 30 percent of the overall individual bonus allocation.

The result of this system is that the faculty members themselves will be largely asked to bring forward positive examples regarding what *they* consider truly exceptional in their own teaching performance, since they decide what examples of teaching innovations they wish to put forth. Typically, if teaching ratings based on feedback from the participants is the only criterion, faculty members might well be conservative, only willing to expose their classes to well-tested materials. Without an incentive to innovate, some faculty members might even make use of "old silver bullets", tried-out cases, old lecturettes, etc. Self-nomination of innovative efforts counteracts this tendency. Interestingly, teaching ratings are not taken into consideration at all in the faculty promotion process at Harvard Business School, presumably due to the strong desire to avoid this type of conservatism/showmanship in the classroom. Innovative teaching and the development of new teaching materials is a part of the job — it is what we expect — and should, as such, receive additional bonus or reward. It is a key part of the academic value creation.

Rewarding citizenship The third individual bonus reward criterion is citizenship. Rewarding faculty for their citizenship reinforces the fact that the school's success depends on the professors participating in the governance of the school. In addition to teaching and research, the school must be linked with its major stakeholders. Seeing visiting executives to help bring in new clients, being involved in the design of brochures and marketing plans, but also helping recruit new faculty, including interviews of the prospects, being part of faculty assessments and evaluations, participating in faculty meetings, serving on committees — all are part of the citizenship task. It follows, therefore, that citizenship includes faculty spending time initiating and cultivating "commercial" links with the executives, corporations, and students who pay for the academic services — as well as contributions to the governance of the school.

Citizenship thus also includes internal tasks. These include serving on committees, being involved in faculty assessments, interviewing prospective faculty members, participating in school governance, seeing visiting executives, and helping with brochure design and marketing plans. There are several potential problems with incorporating the citizenship dimension into a faculty incentive scheme. With so many factors representing possible "contributions", the total may seem excessive, providing a rather fragmented picture of what the institution may want to motivate its faculty members to do. In an extreme example, one might find that the myriad citizenship criteria provide incentives for rather minute, non-decision issues. It is perhaps useful, therefore, to put major emphasis on one or a few citizenship dimensions each year, in light of what is particularly critical at a given point in time for the school.

For instance, there has been serious talk for a number of years of expanding IMD's faculty in a measured way. Citizenship in the form of supporting the recruiting process has therefore been emphasised, whether in the form of participation in the seminars where new prospective faculty recruits present their research, interviewing candidates, or more involvement in the process of identifying new candidates. At present, the citizenship focus at IMD leans more towards greater involvement of the faculty in the marketing of IMD's services, as "key account managers" vis-à-vis large learning partners. The specific citizenship criteria must of course be communicated to the faculty members well in advance. A good way to do this is to clarify what would be the school's expectations for each faculty member in terms of citizenship focus during the particular individual faculty planning and review meetings.

Can — and should — the citizenship dimension be measured and "objectively" quantified to the same extent as the other aspects of the faculty incentives? At IMD, we have gone back and forth on this issue. For some years, it was felt that a clear quantification would be desirable, making the process less "subjective". But, over time, it was recognized that, with certain issues such as citizenship, it may be more functional to have this judgementally assessed by the school's leadership, as long as the broad criteria are clear. After all, a certain element of judgement will always be present in providing incentives.

Group Bonus Profit Sharing

The third major pay element is group bonus, or profit sharing. If the business school has an exceptionally good year, it may make sense to distribute some of the surplus as such profit-sharing. This may strengthen the feeling of *all* members of the *team* that they have contributed to the overall success of the school. This further accentuates the sense of a team! What better way to show the faculty that it is in their best interest to work together to contribute to the school's enduring success. The school's entire population, faculty and staff alike, do indeed fall into this team category. All staff members at IMD are usually given a stipend for their contributions to the overall performance of the school. This stipend is the same for all. One could argue that it should be a percentage of an individual's annual salary — reflecting the staff member's position at IMD. We have however chosen to make the granting of the profit-sharing stipend as simple as possible — hence, the same amount to all staff members. For the faculty members however, the profit sharing is provided as a percentage of their fixed salaries. It should be kept in mind that the fixed salary range is relatively narrow, reflecting the fact that all team members are paid more or less similarly for doing essentially similar jobs, with less importance on seniority than one would find in most other academic institutions. What is important is that, by having all members of the school's organisation share in the profits, a general sense of ownership is reinforced within the team. The group bonus thus reinforces the expectation that all will need to work together!

Extra Pay for Extra Workload

The fourth element of the faculty pay equation is extra pay for extra work. It is a matter of fairness for the school to give a faculty member extra compensation for putting significantly more time and effort into teaching than the norm. In addition to rewarding an individual's performance, this also has a trickle-down effect on the team: it generates more faculty capacity, which in turn can be utilised to meet more demand without having to employ more faculty members, i.e., maintaining a sense of control over fixed salary costs. Thus more workload can be covered by the same faculty. The effect is higher figures on the bottom line for all to share.

At IMD, faculty members can "sell" some of their consulting time back to the school, and be compensated at a given fixed rate per day for each day of extra teaching. It may be in their interest to do so, given the fact that they may then be able to spend more time at IMD, with colleagues and family. Further, they may be able to draw on teaching materials that have already been prepared, thus achieving quite some efficiency in use of time. But still, there are a few critical issues involved in this.

First, the expected normal teaching load must be clearly defined. At IMD, this is 90 "days". By a day, we mean a composite measure of not only days (actually half-days) in class, but also days for programme administration and background research preparation. The extra teaching compensation then comes into effect only after the normal teaching load has been covered. A maximum level for this extra teaching must however also be set, so that no faculty member can be tempted by the carrot of extra pay to such a degree that they burn themselves out. After all, each faculty member represents *the* major asset of the school. It is neither in the school's interest nor in the individual faculty member's to let him burn his candle at both ends. For this reason, the extra teaching at the school also means less possibility to do outside consulting. At IMD, one day of additional teaching leads to a "deduction" of half a day of potential outside consulting. In practice, few faculty members, if any, utilise their outside consulting allowance to the fullest. Most of them end up having quite a lot of slack to use for extra work at the school, thus contributing to IMD's success — both by allowing the school to be responsive to additional demands from its learning perhaps and by adding to the school's financial viability.

Time as a Reward

Time is another reward. Granting time to write a book, or an article, or to carry out a major piece of empirical research can be worth a lot to an individual faculty. Often, a tight teaching schedule, together with other institutional commitments, can make it a Herculean effort just to carve out the smallest blocks of time for important research or writing. Sabbaticals can help. But we assume that these are not meted out as an automatic "right" that goes with institutional membership. A lighter teaching load buys time for research, frees up time for doing a major study, or completing that long-dormant book manuscript. Such time should be granted to a faculty member when he/she truly needs it, based on clear documentation in the faculty member's research plan. Typically, such project-based sabbaticals will be quite short, yet still effective, particularly when effectively planned.

Fundamentally, though, an academic institution must be able to assign workloads that allow academic value creation to go on day in and day out, without automatically rewarding sabbaticals and granting reduced teaching schedules. This pragmatism vis-à-vis faculty is a key requirement to long-term institutional sustainability. Thus, workload allocation and assignment planning must be both fair to all faculty members in the team *and* laid out with enough time blocks available to carry out the academic value creation as part of the normal workload.

Total Compensation Packages at IMD Compared to Other Schools

So what does the total compensation package of a typical IMD professor look like? How do all these criteria add up to a compensation package? For 2000, an average faculty member with a fixed salary of SFr 250,000 would receive an additional 18 percent of his/her fixed salary, i.e., SFr 48,000 from the surplus-sharing pot. He could further receive a significant amount in individual bonus (the overall pool for individual bonuses was equal to 18 percent of the fixed salary pool, too, i.e., equal to the group bonus pool). Finally, an additional significant amount in buy-back compensation is added. The total compensation might therefore be significantly increased, with up to 100 percent or even more, for a productive faculty member in a good year.

Benchmarking faculty compensation vis-à-vis other schools is critical, but difficult. At IMD, we undertake systematic benchmarking against a few other leading European schools, as well as a somewhat more cursory benchmarking vis-à-vis approximately eight US business schools. The problem of exact benchmarking is difficult, due to several factors.

What is paid-for workload at each school as opposed to what represents extra work, compensated for on an extra basis? It is, in practice, hard to find a good basis of comparison between the schools, due to the fact that their "standard" workloads tend to differ so much.

Also, the way schools treat executive development from a compensation point of view differs quite a bit. At London Business School, for instance, faculty are paid extra for what they do in executive development programmes; this is not part of their normal workload. This practice is also common among leading US business schools.

The belief in incentives also differs widely among schools. Most of them seem to follow a policy of extra pay for extra work, but not to go so far into extensive profit sharing and individual incentives as IMD has done. When I was at Wharton, for instance, there was no additional variable individual financial incentive, nor any group profit sharing. This also seems to be the case at most leading US business schools. IMD is different. We feel that the basic pay must be competitive with the leading schools with which we compare ourselves.

We also believe that profit sharing and individual incentives should be liberal, so that the faculty — and, to a lesser extent, the staff — are compensated for behaving as "owners". After all, the faculty — and the staff — can have a strong impact on the school's performance. They should be compensated for this. In particular, "ownership" means a relatively increasing degree of participation in the "upside" when it comes to improved performance. This is at the heart of the compensation policy at IMD. And most at IMD — faculty and staff — feel very good about this policy — it works!

Once the institution has figured out what it will reward regarding the individual performance of its faculty members, then the weighting of each criterion according to its express vision and mission will be key — at IMD, as noted, this means 50 percent on research outputs, 30 percent on teaching innovations and 20 percent on citizenship. One hopes, with the school's stated strategy, that the individual rewards will support the implementation of the strategy — even accelerate it! It is thus vital that individual performance be judged on an ongoing basis. This should be true for all faculty members, whether they have tenure or not. (Since we do not have tenure at IMD, it is not an issue here; everyone is reviewed systematically semi-annually, once as part of the annual incentive process and once to ensure that the general focus is maintained.) At many schools, the issue of dealing with the tenured faculty members is contentious. At INSEAD, for instance, the systematic annual review concerns all non-tenured faculty members, but not those who have received tenure. Needless to say, this can easily create a community of two citizenship groups.

Regardless, the criteria should compel faculty to perform year after year. Rewards should follow strong, ongoing performance. If a professor can't perform over time, the rewards should be reduced. Reduced rewards, though they may appear draconian, will signal to the faculty member that he or she should perhaps find other ways of contributing. Implicit here is the subliminal message that those who can't perform well enough to be well rewarded should leave. Equally critical is avoiding individual rewards that become "institutionalised" in the sense that they appear automatic every year. This breeds complacency. Not being able to ask a professor to leave is a serious drawback. With rapid change, and with the constant demand to perform, the modern business school needs to be able to individually award each of its people for stellar performance and sanction others for falling short.

Rewards: How Much Transparency?

Should the rewards be made public to everyone? Should they be fully transparent? Proponents of transparency argue that this has the salutary effect of recognising the top performers and exposing the weaker performers to healthy group pressure for improvement as well. As such, transparency would be good. On the other hand, full transparency taken to the lengths of meticulous detail could easily lead to a confrontational interfaculty culture, where the focus would be on more "win-lose" behaviour in a zero-sum sense. Faculty members might easily end up haggling over their bonuses rather than working on creating more academic value, taking on new challenges. If they're "good" strategists, they may well set conservative targets year-to-year too, in order to guarantee that they reach them early, and clear them easily. The bonus system must provide "stretch" for the individual, in contrast.

An effective way to address the question of transparency is to let individual faculty members know how their rewards compare to the average or even the *distribution* of all rewards, in general, as well as for how he has performed within each major category of criteria. Professors should receive enough feedback that will inspire them to do better the next year. At IMD, this approach has helped build a strong sense of group fairness and school loyalty.

Balanced Overall Reward Structures

The reward structure should represent a true handshake for a job well done. A good job, of course, can take many forms. The school must work to make its reward structure flexible enough so that the leadership extends a hand to any faculty member who has done an extraordinary job. Sole emphasis on one criterion, particularly if it is rather narrowly defined — as "quality research", for example — can lead to a rather strong bias in the school's value-creating activities. The school may want exactly that. (Though it is doubtful that a sole focus on a scholarly research agenda is sustainable today, where the market is likely to insist on a more balanced set of outputs.) I predict that academic value creation will typically have to be reflected by a broader, multidimensional set of criteria, rather than by purely narrow, research-based criteria.

Overall, academic rewards, coupled with the option of dismissing under-performers, represent a principal condition for strategic management of a business school. These two alone go a long way to creating a performance-driven culture. Admittedly, institutional traditions, legal traditions, and attitude traditions can be hard to overcome. Even if the formal conditions are in place for performance-based rewards, the organisation may be too immature to cope, or the school's leadership may be unprepared to put in the time and efforts needed — or simply unwilling to! In some academic cultures, rewards imply — indeed even state outright — that some faculty members have contributed more than others. In many academic circles, this is all too easily dismissed as "elitism", and thus as "inappropriate". After all, argue the dissenters, the ivory tower should be one of the last bastions of freedom to indulge in professorial pursuits without the overbearing pressure of performance ratings. This argument has some elements of truth. Taken to its excess, a system of rewarding individuals may very well cause dysfunctional behaviour among team members — jealousy, back-biting, resentment, and even mobbing in its various forms. Hence, also, a sharp need for group bonuses, too!

Nevertheless, ways exist to counter these arguments. The school can, as noted, offset the possibly negative effect individual rewards may have on teamwork by building team performance assessments into the reward criteria (an across-the-board profit-sharing scheme, for example). Nevertheless, there is no skirting the fact that, in any given year, some contribute more than others. By shining a spotlight on the high-flyers, the rewards should inspire the top contributors to continue and the laggards to strive to "make good [even] better".

Chapter 13

Organisational Reputation and Pride

Executive Summary

A business school's reputation is a very important factor in its ability to succeed in the long run. Reputation can make or break the school. Reputation may shape how stakeholders see it from the outside. A good reputation will attract — and retain — strong faculty and students. It will also help the school attract and develop relationships with corporations that wish to become its learning partners. Rankings and word of mouth are key reputation indicators. The Dean must be concerned about the school's reputation, and the faculty must speak up on behalf of the school whenever possible. The leadership must not focus primarily on reputation, but rather on mission, vision, and delivering to the needs of the learning partners. Reputation has much to do with outside perception; organisational pride is what members of the organisation feel about their school and team. The Dean must worry about the level of organisational pride, and can measure it in regular feedback from students and learning partners. He can ensure that the school has a simple, honest (not inflated) reputation that it can easily communicate. The reputation must be based primarily on the school consistently delivering what it promises.

Organisational reputation is a key, arguably critical, variable in the strategic success-formula of any academic institution. The school's reputation dictates how stakeholders on the *outside* see it. Reputation is important in attracting and retaining faculty members in all academic institutions, not just business schools, and it plays a central role in attracting the best students. But for the leading business school, reputation is even more important in developing relationships with corporations-cum-learning partners. As such, business schools face the challenge of establishing a reputation vis-à-vis a relatively small number of corporations that are typically very demanding and extremely sophisticated.

Depending on how clients perceive the school's reputation, it can experience success and growth, or failure and stagnation. Corporate learning partners typically show little loyalty if they sense that a school's reputation is waning — they will go with the reputed winners! Choice of institutional affiliation for faculty members, as well as their decision to *switch* institutions, depend largely on the institution's reputation. Potential faculty's perception of whether a school is on the go or stagnant, will influence their decision to come — or not. The difficulty for the business school here is that this "perception" of its reputation — arguably the reputation itself — is subjective. So how is the school to measure — or at least get some feeling for — its own reputation among its most important stakeholders?

Rankings

To some extent, rankings in leading journals — *Business Week, US News & World Report, Forbes* and the *Financial Times* — can give some indication of the school's "worth". Of course, these rankings are often somewhat imprecise; they can also be muddied by subjectivity. (For a critical review of ratings, see Zimmermann.[1]) Word of mouth also carries weight: when professors speak highly of their own school, stakeholders are likely to listen. It is incumbent on faculty members to speak up *on behalf* of their school when the occasion arises. Positive testimonials are essential, yet only if genuine; insincere or false support will easily backfire and be meaningless, or even worse than saying nothing at all. For prospective MBA students, reputation criteria such as the GMAT score, yearly rankings (or the change in rankings over the years), the number of applicants compared to those actually accepted, as well as the salary levels of graduates, give indications of reputation, and therefore play a role in the best candidates' choices. For corporations-cum-learning partners, word of mouth is a major determinant of reputation. Leading executives do talk to each other often; their favourable opinion will carry great weight in making the school's reputation.

Reputational Recruiting

Even specific elements of reputation, linked to the school's vision and mission, can be important in recruiting faculty, for example. IMD is quite attractive to faculty members who may be disenchanted with the common academic system as practised in most academic institutions. At such institutions there may be outstanding professors who, for a number of reasons, may not qualify for tenure. They may, for instance, have chosen to emphasise a certain path in their creativity that does not meet the common criteria for tenure, notably that of publishing a large number of articles in refereed journals. In addition, tenured full professors in such institutions may, at some point in their careers, eventually come to believe that the classical academic value system holds little interest for them. They may thus actively seek a different context, like IMD. The fact that IMD's reputation paints the school as different from its more traditional counterparts may thus be an important inducement for some faculty to switch to IMD.

Similarly, learning partners may switch to IMD for its reputation as the most international and the most practical institution, and for its eclectic blend of faculty members who tailor their teaching to support a given learning partner. This will of course create — and enhance — a particular reputation for IMD. A good reputation can be particularly effective if it positions one's institution as "positively different".

Reputation and Focus

A good reputation can enhance the school's potential for success by contributing to a further sharpening of its focus. What a school is known for, what its reputation is built upon, can also be seen as manifestations of the school's environment and its outside stakeholders. As such, these *reputational signals*, if you will, reinforce the recipes for the school's success and academic value creation. There is nothing more stimulating to a school's organisation, including the faculty, than outside feedback. Why not continue a winning strategy by focusing more on what the outside seems to appreciate? The focusing unleashes organisational energy. By being successful, the school also typically puts more energy into sticking with its winning formula. Unleashing energy to follow up on success is a matter of positive reinforcement. Pride plays an important role, too; the more pride an organisation has in its reputation, the more energy it is likely to invest in shoring it up, and to contribute to its sustainability. It will be a positive cycle to "make good even better".

A good reputation also motivates external stakeholders to pep up their support for the institution. There is nothing more satisfactory to a learning partner than being part of a winning team. Working intimately with a leading school can add major value to the learning-partner organisation itself. It is a positively reinforcing, mutually strengthening symbiotic relationship.

These realities can, at times, seem ironic, especially in the case of a weak school that needs outside support. A school in financial difficulty needs support from outside learning partners. In practice, however, if the school's learning partners know about the school's fiscal plight, they are unlikely to bail it out financially. Institutions and individuals alike rarely put their money behind what they perceive to be a losing business school. On the contrary — and here's the rub — the more successful a school is, the easier it tends to be for it to raise additional outside funds, even though the successful school may actually need them less than the laggard. Without a doubt, a good reputation leads to additional support from outside stakeholders.

Reputation, Not Misleading Public Relations Efforts

Building reputation is *not* to be confused with manipulation and public relations efforts that might throw a spotlight on programmes that the school cannot deliver and make promises the school cannot keep. A leading European educational consultant, for example, publishes rankings of schools. It is well known that these rankings are highly subjective; if you sign up for the consultant's services in your broader public relations efforts, your ranking tends to go up. One school in particular, which in fact does not even have its own full-time faculty but draws on visiting faculty from other schools, has come out year after year as one of the leading European MBA schools in this ranking. It seems clear that this type of activity should be called into question. Is it an attempt to manipulate the perceptions of the quality of the school's reputation? Needless to say, not only do such efforts create questions about how to interpret quality, they also have a negative effect by misleading individuals who might otherwise not have grounds for suspicion. Rankings must be built on realities!

On the contrary, a solid reputation and organisational pride come from focusing on achieving tangible progress, concrete developments, and displaying unique competencies. This is again why it is so important that the school be built on a few specific, *distinguishable* features — it needs to be known for a particular set of strengths. The more such features are linked with what one's stakeholders actually appreciate and are looking for, the better. IMD's reputation is tightly linked with our extreme degree of internationalism, our practical approach, and the ability to tailor-make the programmes to the learning partners' needs. A reputation such as this is based on fact, and we can build on it without deception or embarrassment.

Reputation: The Leadership Implications

Given that reputation and success seem to correlate, how can the leadership enhance its own school's reputation? The leadership should not try to influence the reputation of its own school as an end in itself, but only by following the avenue of stimulating solid academic value creation. To elaborate: the school's leadership can do much by helping the school to focus on a clear, positive vision and mission which is also consistent with what its major learning partners seek.

Thus, the school's leadership can do much to articulate and develop such a focused, communicable vision and mission. In addition, the school can focus on external relationship support, by having a press officer who works systematically with the various media, by proactively sending out summaries of one's research (in the case of IMD, the "Perspectives for Managers" publication, issued 10 to 12 times per year, and reproduced in approximately 20 publications around the world), and by inviting journalists to the school to develop further links between the press and the faculty members. But all such communication efforts must be based on incontrovertible realities. In all of these important efforts the school's leadership can play a role, both by being involved with the press and other media, and, by its own example, setting (and enforcing) the highest standards regarding thoughts and realism.

In my view, managing the school's reputation beyond these factual efforts is dubious. There is little value in flaunting the illusory qualities of a school. A good reputation is the result of the hard, steady work of building superior academic value; it comes as a bonus at the end of the long, uphill road. I feel that there is nothing that can be done to bypass this need for honest substance as the way to create a reputation. Anything else would smack of dilettantism.

Organisational Pride

Organisational pride is what the *members* of the organisation feel about their own team and school. Key opinion leaders on the faculty team and the organisation at large will be particularly critical in shaping the school's own view of itself. There will always be some faculty members who have a stronger say than others in articulating what the school's basic values might be. At IMD, these values would include relevance in teaching for the learning partners, strong commitment to pedagogical excellence, and an emphasis on team behaviour in support of the school. The way the faculty members feel about the school hinges on how they internalise these values. There is, no doubt, pride among the members of IMD's team because of the high quality of teaching, the valuable messages and lessons that come out of the teaching sessions with many learning partner organisations, and the fact that, overall, the school is doing well.

Building pride (and reputation) must be based on the school's *real* value. The consequences of the merger between IMI and IMEDE in the early 1990s that formed IMD support this point. The new faculty brought together from the two schools varied quite a bit. Not only did the various faculty members have different profiles, competencies and abilities to contribute, they also had radically different pedagogical backgrounds. This no doubt led to a difficulty in establishing the real pedagogical qualities of the new, combined institution, IMD. The school may well have been riding the leading edge of content, but the quality of the teaching methods was highly disputable. The already robust reputation of the two schools helped the merged one through this difficult period, allowing it to embark on a process of rebuilding its pedagogical competencies.

Perhaps the best way to measure the development of such a quality dimension is in feedback from the students and learning partners. At IMD, we have instituted a system to collect regular feedback from participants of open and tailored programmes, as well as from the member firms of IMD's Partner and Business Associate network. Systematic monitoring of the users' perceptions is critical to maintaining real quality.

Excessive Pride

Unfortunately, the market for management programmes is flooded with "propaganda-like" claims from teaching institutions that hawk their offers to their "lucky" participants. Almost every school today trumpets itself as the "the most international" and offers the participants the chance to work closely with a "designated faculty" — often with little substantiation. Many schools have embarked on exchange relationships with other institutions across the globe, some going so far, as I've already noted, as to have "satellite" campuses around the world. The problem here is that, despite the school's worldwide presence, at each campus, especially the "home" or "core" one, there may not be much internationalisation. The satellite campuses become local or regional meeting places for learners, not global meeting places. And the learners typically prefer to learn at the main campus — to experience "the real thing"! Faculty members tend to shy away from spending time at these satellite campuses. Harvard Business School made an important experiment with this some years ago when it established a satellite campus in Mont-Pélerin, Switzerland, with its own resident faculty. In practice, it turned out to be difficult to assign faculty members to stay at this campus, as they felt de facto that they became sidelined from Harvard's main research and teaching activities. The students, too, preferred to go to the "real Harvard Business School" in Boston.

Recently, Harvard has embarked on developing a network of research satellite campus sites, in South America, East Asia, Europe, and on the US West Coast. These arrangements are meant to bring Harvard's faculty closer to the local action by having local support more readily available and by thus making it easier for the school's faculty to be more effective in their research in various local settings. The faculty members do *not* leave the Boston campus for prolonged time periods, however. Having these research satellites broadens the international perspective of those faculty members who temporarily stay at these regional research campuses.

The fundamental question, however, is still how to internationalise the home base, the "home" campus, how to bring a broader cross-section of students and faculty members together face to face to create a global meeting place. The regional research campuses cannot possibly substitute for the value of the meeting place; they can, at best, merely complement the internationalisation *process*. *All* the members of the team must, in essence, develop an organisational pride in internationalism.

Many leading business schools assign executive education teaching to their faculty members as an extra, a way to earn more money — a consulting activity, in effect. For the school, this can lead to a loss of control over staffing, which may amount to a loss of some control over its own intellectual resources. Even leading schools often hire teachers from outside their own faculties — freelances and even consultants. These "faculty" are, however, often not part of the regular faculty team, and are not contributing to the base of research required to provide top-flight programmes. Staffing an executive programme with what amounts to an "appendix" faculty will lead, in all likelihood, to lower quality and less consistency in the delivery of executive development programmes. Again, it will probably be hard to develop a broad-based organisational pride in such programmes!

All too often, the excessive claims of business schools will portray the schools as not much more than empty shells: many schools don't bother — or perhaps can't — document their haughty claims. I can think of two examples that do *not* fall into this category, but which easily *might* have, and which demonstrate the ease with which today's business schools can fall into the trap of making claims they can't support. And this downward spiral, I maintain, may lead not only to a tarnished reputation, but to a weakening pride in the school among its own faculty and learning partners.

Building an "Honest" Reputation: Two Examples

The Norwegian School of Management offers two types of undergraduate programmes. One is at the main campus outside Oslo, which offers a four-year bachelor's degree for a relatively small number of participants, selected from a large number of applicants. It is structured along rather conventional academic lines, with full-time teaching by research-based faculty members as the norm. The full-time resident students typically receive a lot of attention from a high quality faculty, and also learn from each other through colloquium-based student teams, an integral part of this programme. The other undergraduate programme takes place at 15 regional campuses. Here students can enter freely, as long as they have a high school diploma. The curriculum of these schools is developed by the full-time research-based faculty at the main campus, but the delivery of the programme is carried out largely by practising local business executives. They have been "trained" to deliver the teaching based on the standardised course design, and they also draw on their own managerial experience. Many of the students are enrolled part-time.

These programmes are thus totally different. It would be wrong to claim that one programme is equivalent to — and could substitute for — the other. The full-time programme at the main campus offers the benefits of learning from the resident faculty and learning from fellow students — a fairly conventional, high-quality undergraduate learning experience. The programme offered at the regional campuses, on the other hand, has the benefit of perhaps being more closely linked to real life, perhaps being more practitioner-oriented, and often geared to a greater extent toward the individual student's agenda and career. Both programmes thus have their pluses and minuses. And it is the school's prerogative to communicate the pluses honestly. The school's organisation should be able to take pride in both.

IMD, to offer a second example, went through a long debate figuring out what, exactly, we should claim are the aims and objectives of our new Executive MBA programme (you will remember that the EMBA complements our long-standing full-time MBA programme).[2] We have been offering our MBA programme for over 25 years and have built up a reputation of elitism and excellence, based on intensive full-time learning and learning from other students. There is great quality among the 85 students, due to the highly-controlled admissions process that handles over 1,000 applicants. One might justifiably say that this is an elite, niche programme. The Executive MBA programme, in contrast, rests on the platform of IMD's *Programme for Executive Development*, a ten-week programme open to almost all qualified applicants. After finishing the PED programme,[3] the student must go through a further application step to qualify for the Executive MBA programme, take an admissions test (GMAT), and meet other criteria. The formal application requirements are not as stringent in an academic sense as they are for the full-time MBA. But these students bring broader managerial experience to the table, and often have impressive careers on their résumés. Further, since the participants are expected to keep their main jobs while studying, they definitely have strong drive and motivation. The programme also allows them to link their formal EMBA learning to activities back at work.

Thus, important ingredients of *this programme* are relevance to current work experience, project work, and virtual learning with ongoing feedback. Students can obtain an MBA from both programmes. But they are dissimilar, and have different strengths and weaknesses. It would be wrong to portray the Executive MBA as "another MBA". It represents an *alternative* to a full-time MBA degree, with different "pluses", not lesser quality than a full-time MBA. For us to claim that they are the same would, however, be inaccurate: each programme should be advertised for what it really is. Wild or inaccurate assertions are not likely to lead to sustainable pride and an improving reputation. Honesty and real content are the most effective routes to pride and reputation over time, since they enable members of the school and their stakeholders to associate themselves with their real strengths. This provides programmes that one can be really proud of.

Pride Built on a Simple, Communicable Profile

To set itself apart from the others, the modern business school must develop a simple, communicable profile that distinguishes itself. Pride must be built on this profile! Harvard Business School certainly comes to mind here, with its emphasis on an outstanding MBA programme and a focus on the general manager, and the "administrative point of view". In its executive development, the school can be further characterised as emphasising general management from a "teachable" point of view. A strong sense of pride in these values has emerged. The Wharton School is also characterised by strong commitment to its MBA programme, but perhaps with a more analytical bent, keeping finance and banking at the centre. As such, Wharton has a reputation for providing outstanding executives to the financial sector, and is proud of the fact. At MIT's Sloan School of Management, perhaps the accent on technology management is the distinguishing mark. The school's symbiosis with the rest of MIT is of great value, and definitely a source of pride. At IMD, as has been discussed, the exceptional internationalism, the practical orientation, and the team-based approach towards tailored learning partnerships are essential characteristics of our profile, and we take pride in it. These examples illustrate that there has to be a simple and communicable key value proposition that one can build one's pride on. Developing a simple, communicable profile to differentiate the school from others is thus essential.

Build Pride by Delivering What You Promise

The most effective way to bolster organisational reputation is simply to deliver what you promise. Sounds easy, perhaps, but it entails going way beyond merely delivering a number of disjointed programmes and running an ad hoc portfolio of activities. As you will recall, IMD is primarily focused on developing general management, senior executive education, at the IMD campus, with it being the global meeting place. Despite this clear vision and mission, IMD still offers a one-week programme in Singapore, the *Job of the Chief Executive* (JOCE),[4] and I shall want to elaborate on this experience to illustrate how it could create lack of focus and portfolio stress. If you believe general opinion, the JOCE programme is excellent. Still, it presents several dilemmas for IMD. It draws participants from Singapore as well as neighbouring countries such as Malaysia, Thailand, and Indonesia. It does not offer, therefore, a global student mix, but a regional one. Further, by offering such a teaching activity away from IMD, one might argue that IMD is actually leading potential participants away from its global meeting place in Lausanne. The JOCE programme does act as an introduction to IMD, and as such, as a catalyst, so that the participants may later want to enrol in programmes taking place at IMD. Still, one can see that it is not easy to argue for the JOCE programme as part of IMD's rational vision or mission. Pragmatically it makes good sense, however. For the broader IMD constituency, it is not clear that the programme creates much of an explicit pride effect — it is seen by most as being too much "on the side". The faculty members directly involved can — and should — take pride in a good programme, however.

Another successful IMD reputation-enhancing programme is the *Building on Talent* (BOT), targeted at executives in their late 20s.[5] The programme is excellent, according to the feedback, and its reputation is building up, as evidenced by the great increase in applications. Still, one can perhaps question whether such a programme fits within IMD's vision and mission, which is primarily to serve more senior executives. One can question whether BOT in this way helps IMD communicate its *clear* vision/mission to serve the more senior management segment. I would argue that this programme helps broaden the school's mission and vision — it represents connectedness — not a disconnection. In total, I believe that IMD is much more focused than many of its counterparts. Others give the impression of offering a little of everything: undergraduate, MBA, MS, part-time Executive MBA, doctoral, and shorter executive development programmes. One leading business school offers seven different masters programmes. Is this focus?

With a focused approach, the business school can more easily measure progress partly through internal assessments, and partly through feedback from its partnering organisations. These measurements boost organisational reputation. Systematic feedback from the participants during and after a programme is of course essential. This "echo" keeps professors and support staff striving for excellence. While an occasional poor rating is perhaps less critical than one might think, a typical faculty member takes this seriously and the internal feedback process is a major norm-setter at places like IMD. As indicated, it is, however, essential to complement the internal feedback with feedback from the marketplace. One can, for instance, ask the participants, after they have been back at work for a time, what they think they got out of a given programme. It is interesting to see, thus, how much they recall, and what type of information they value most after being back on the job for some time. IMD does exactly this with one of our major learning partners.

We ask each participant from this company a number of questions approximately six months after their participation in the company's programme with IMD. Interestingly, these students often say that "learning to learn" was the greatest benefit. Learning from fellow students, from other companies, from many worldwide settings is also mentioned as key. The specific materials that the students have been exposed to at IMD seem to be relatively less important criteria, except to help them to analyse new situations and learn from them, so that they become better at speeding up their own development.

Such collection of systematic participant feedback should be ongoing. It should be made in such a way that consistency is established in how one looks at all these types of data, to allow for more cross-sectional and broad-based assessment of what would be the *real* contribution that the school provides, seen from the learners' points of view. And this can be a *real* source of pride!

How Pride Can Improve a School's Progress

The institutional pride I've been describing is uniquely tethered to reputation. The better the internal stakeholders feel about the school because of its good reputation, the more pride they are likely to feel. This pride, then, can be seen as the well-spring of a "can-do" attitude. Consider once more the development of IMD's *Orchestrating Winning Performance* programme.[6] Its unique design initially created a lot of scepticism at IMD. Above all it was felt by some that the programme's large participant size might become a liability. There were those who voiced the fear that IMD's unique pedagogical reputation could suffer from such an activity. Nevertheless, over five years, the programme has developed a strong reputation and turned into a source of pride to all at IMD. This has demonstrated the benefits of bringing a large, diverse group of executives from all over the world together, allowing for exceptional networking, and, at the same time, allowing these many participants to regroup into smaller streams, thus also giving them the benefits of learning in the more typical smaller classes. Every faculty member is not only involved, each one benefits from working with colleagues as one large team. This team pride is further enhanced by the fact that a large number of the school's staff is involved, instilling a widely-shared sense of team-spirit. The various teaching materials offered, all developed specifically for this programme each year, provide an inducement to pedagogical innovation and add a further sense of accomplishment. Judging from the innovations coming out of this programme — new teaching approaches, research that leads to new cases, interesting cases often incorporating virtual technology, the inclusion of Web pages and other aspects of the virtual world — it seems safe to say that it is a good example of the power of pride, built on concrete value creation.

A strong sense of success, backed up, indeed generated, by a strong reputation, will easily push the members of the organisation to stretch themselves beyond their limits. Building on success, one good thing leads to another, which leads to an ever-increasing release of energy and initiative, can-do risk-taking, so that the organisation rises in a positive upward spiral. This also happened at the Norwegian School of Management, which, like IMD, worked itself out of a crisis. During the crisis, it was interesting to see how much energy was spent, with few tangible results. Positive momentum was initially missing. Only when the reputation started to build, and when pride began to manifest itself, did the positive spiral effect kick in.

In the case of IMD and the Norwegian School, pride and energy needed to be coached along. Building a healthy dissatisfaction with the status quo got the momentum going. In these cases, and in general, the leadership of the school must play an important role in setting new standards, encouraging new risk-taking, and new initiatives. The leadership thus needs to manage pride, build on it, and stimulate it. As in our *Orchestrating Winning Performance* programme example, the leadership needs to encourage new initiatives, set new standards, keep the door open for further evolution, as if the school is starting from scratch each year. The leadership must thus act as a catalyst — to maintain speed and momentum!

"Pride-generating" activities do not, of course, have to be associated with the programme side only. They can also be manifested even by perhaps seemingly trivial steps toward progress, which can still have a formidable effect on pride and dynamism. Consider the decision to erect a large tent on the IMD campus to house all of the 400+ participants in the OWP programme in plenum. In previous years, participants had to move to the nearby auditorium of the Polytechnic of Lausanne, but with the tent they had a much better feeling of being welcomed to IMD's own campus, indeed to IMD. The tent led to a lot of activity at the school, involving the staff perhaps even more than the faculty. A sense of pride was clearly developed with the manifestation of the tent project, an example of how new actions and innovations are necessary and welcome to manage pride and to unleash organisational energy.

Pride and reputation thus clearly power the ambition for excellence. The better you feel about the institution, the more positive energy you'll have to go the next mile. Consider a somewhat different example, namely an interesting in-company programme for a leading key company, which involved a small group of IMD faculty members who developed an approach towards strategy articulation at a well-known toy company. Labelled as "serious play", the new approach created contexts which would free senior line executives from their entrapment in present jobs, and open up new hierarchical and vertical relationships. This led to an outburst of creativity around the strategies that were being proposed, and thus to a significant repository of new, fresh strategic thoughts. This success, with a considerable amount of satisfaction on the part of the professors who drove the process, then led to the launching of a research programme on serious play, underwritten by the toy company itself. This, in turn, has led to interesting insights regarding how creative strategies might be formulated, and again, an added source of pride in the faculty members, with a clear outpouring of energy and drive on their part. From a capacity point of view, one can safely conclude that there is no such thing as absolute capacity limitations for inspired, pride-driven faculty members. In other words, a strong sense of pride inspires further effort; the feeling of pride and the commitment it entails should be a positive source of "fuel" for the members of an organisation. In the toy company example, therefore, one can say that the success of, and pride in, the teaching programme fuelled further commitment to path-breaking research; this in itself has led to even more involved research into the development of novel strategies to enhance internally generated growth.

Caveat: Overbearing Pride

I make my previous argument about the importance and value of the school's reputation and pride with a caveat: the school and its constituents must beware of *overbearing* pride. By this, I mean that it would be dysfunctional for the school to develop so much self-satisfaction that the pride actually leads to stag-nation, reinforcement of the status quo, and a tendency to discontinue systematic innovation. In such a case, the energy unleashed through pride might well be channelled into unrealistic, myopic marginal improvements that would hardly be worth the benefits. The story of one of IMD's well-established open programmes serves this point. The feedback from this programme was always strong, and generated a great sense of pride among the participating faculty members. The pride, however, made it perhaps difficult for the team to consider whether the length of the programme was optimal for busy senior executives, or whether a shorter, more topical design would be more desirable. Success in this case — and the concomitant pride — had led to resistance to re-examining the programme's length and design. In the end, important innovations in the form of reduced length and more intense topical coverage were delayed for several years.

Another example of the handicap of overweening pride concerns a faculty team that has developed a series of outstanding cases, several of which have won prizes for the best case in their categories at European competitions. These professors consequently found themselves continually revising some of their more recent cases, in the end coming up with marginal improvements at best, certainly not ones that would justify the considerable amount of time and resources spent. Again, one could argue that overbearing pride in this stream of case research led to an over-extension of the key ideas, an entrapment preventing further substitutive improvements.

Even with a healthy sense of pride, the organisation may be hampered by having dyed-in-the-wool sceptics among its members. These people simply cannot, and will not, let themselves be carried by positive organisational drive. Let us once more return to the *Orchestrating Winning Performance* programme experience. Interestingly, the few negative comments about this programme did not come from the participants — it was amazing to see how informed the positive feedback was from the 400 paying participants. The few critical voices came instead from *faculty members*, who basically thought that the course's design would not allow for sufficient in-depth "mining" of a given topic. They would not be able to do what they do in other programmes, they felt — spend several sessions and several cases on a given topic. Of course, they were not wrong in these objections, but their criticism, had it prevailed, would have pre-vented them — and their colleagues — from reaping the positive benefits of the OWP exercise, namely, the unleashing of all this energy from the exchange between faculty members and participants, all in a big, interactive, positive network. If too many sceptics fill the ranks, the organisation will stall. Willingness to experiment is key.

Sanction by the school's leadership is not the antidote to sceptics and negativists. For instance, the Dean cannot, of course, invite a professor to leave simply by calling his "negativity" a "performance deficiency". Healthy scepticism of the status quo can be a plus. Healthy scepticism can also easily flip over into unhealthy scepticism — being sceptical for scepticism's sake. Such scepticism, and even negativity, will neither help the school move forward, nor promote the necessary experimentation for innovation and regular growth. A "can't-do" attitude dampens the innovation and experimentation drive. Too many such sceptics in a faculty organisation can be devastating. This can be a larger problem than one might at first think; after all, academic institutions have always been built around healthy scepticism, in the form of hypothesis testing and consequent rejection. The key is to make sure that the word "healthy" is driving this process, and not negative scepticism, not entrapment in the past.

An effective way, however, to at least partly neutralise such negative forces is to accumulate positive organisational pride that the majority of the team and the colleagues will work to bolster. What can the school's leadership do to make this happen? All positive developments must be highlighted, celebrated and "paraded". The leadership must bring positive examples forward. A language that talks about "opportunities" rather than "problems" must be instituted — "can do" instead of "can't do". This positive approach is crucial for the entire school, ideally in such a way that positive thinking becomes contagious. Positive momentum can effectively overwhelm the sceptics and the cynics. The team will "isolate" such members of the faculty and diminish their "power". At IMD, we have a faculty member, for instance, who constantly looks for the negative side of things, pointing out problems, voicing his concerns — and never "smiling". Unfortunately, this highly competent professor, though a gifted teacher and researcher, is virtually impossible for most to work with. And since most people prefer working with those who have a positive outlook (too much negativism makes interaction a burden), the negative professor has grown gradually and increasingly isolated. This is too bad for him, but at least his marginalisation will mean that he is unable to slow down the school.

Organisational pride allows the members of the organisation to ask themselves and each other: "Do you want to be part of it or not?". Faculty members who do not want to join will pay the price of isolation. Pride and reputation thus lead to internal sharing and bonding among the progressive members of the faculty team. Symbolism is the key to positivism — to the fighting of entrapment in the status quo.

Chapter 14

The Governance Challenge

Executive Summary

Business schools are traditionally governed by a group of interested people. There are many names for this governing body, but the business school, perhaps its leadership, must define its role and tasks. The governing body — here called the board — has two responsibilities. It must ensure that the generation of resources exceeds the use of resources. But it must also contribute to the nature and content of the school's academic value creation itself. Board members must represent clients and key stakeholders. Three possible roles for the board seem relevant here: watchdog, pilot, and trustee. For a school that wishes to set a strategic direction that best serves the needs of its learning-partner clients, the trustee role seems most appropriate. The school needs clear policies — and reasons — that guide the selection of board members. The school may put in place various organisational structures (committees, regular meetings) to facilitate effective board governance.

Governance Structures: University-Owned or Free-Standing

Most business schools are either "owned" by a university or they are free-standing and self-owned. Rarely are they owned by independent investors, who infuse capital and expect a return. The Arthur D. Little business school was an example of the latter, but even it has now become a free-standing organisation. Even though the school started as a training branch of the consulting firm, Arthur D. Little, it soon grew into a full-fledged business school, with programmes that granted degrees. For a number of reasons, including relatively low returns, the school was then converted and transformed to self-owning status, and affiliated with Boston College's business school, which now grants the degrees. Generally, however, business schools come under the legal and financial wing of a university, or they stand alone, independent and self-supporting.[1]

Unlike the many business schools that do reside under the auspices of a larger institution of any kind, IMD is a free-standing, independent foundation. As a for-profit organisation, IMD owns itself. There are no investors to consider in the governing of the school. The main stakeholders are IMD's major corporate learning partners! Because it is independently owned, IMD is totally independent in resource generation and utilisation, and it controls all its resources. But the school still faces a fairly big governance challenge, particularly in the disposal of its financial resources. More specifically, how can the learning partners' needs for immediate, pragmatic value and efficiency be reconciled with faculty members' need for slack, freedom, and longer-term focus?

Business schools in a university structure face a different challenge. They often have to support other parts of the university financially. This can, indeed, weaken their net financial muscle and limit the amount of new research they can undertake. It also limits funds for new programmes. The result may perhaps be a too heavy reliance on "easy" cash flows such as an established MBA programme, which may in turn ultimately stunt adaptability. This could all too easily lead to not enough new challenges, and not enough new thinking because the financial situation would not permit this!

For some universities, most notably Harvard, it has been a tradition for each entity — each school — to stand entirely on its own. Harvard Business School, for instance, is entirely independent from other schools at Harvard University. Attractive as this is, it seems however to be the exception among business schools. Harvard provides an interesting example of how strategic direction-setting can be helped, but not dictated, from the top.[2] The President of Harvard University undertakes a thorough review of one of his professional schools each year. The Harvard Business School is reviewed thoroughly by the President and his central administration approximately once every ten years. This entails a thorough re-examination of the school's strategy, helping the school, above all, to keep focus on its more fundamental strategic innovation leaps, while not interfering in business-as-usual implementation.

Regardless of ownership structure, business schools are traditionally governed by a group of interested persons. Call this body what you will — *visiting committee, overseeing committee, executive committee, board* — the school still needs to define its role and its tasks.[3] It needs to be steered, or governed. And this is often the job of what, in this chapter, we shall call the board. But how should the board add value? How can it best serve its governing function?

The Two Roles of the Board

The essential roles of the board are usually twofold. First the board ensures that the *uses of resources* at the school do not exceed the *generation of resources*. A strong budgetary process is necessary to facilitate this control. The board must guarantee that realism and prudence are in place and followed. At IMD, for instance, during the period immediately following the merger between IMI and IMEDE to form IMD, it turned out that the cost structure of the new school was unrealistically high: with the two schools simply added together with overheads and other concomitant expenses, no merger benefits were initially realised. An extensive cost reduction programme was initiated, backed and heavily controlled by the board, which involved significant staff lay-offs and deep-reaching cost-cutting in all aspects of the school's operation. To underscore the seriousness of the situation, the board asked the then Dean to leave, and appointed a new acting Dean to carry out these difficult measures. Normally, the board will not have an ongoing active role in making sure that the school's financial ship is on an even keel. The board usually satisfies itself that the budget is healthy and that expenses are not higher than revenue. In exceptional situations, however, an important role of the board is to react, and stand behind, difficult restructuring measures.

Many academic institutions have fallen into an unenviable economic situation by excessive borrowing, and thus leveraging their futures. They seem to fall to the typical temptation of financing the construction of new physical facilities through loans that can be relatively easily got from the market, and at reasonable rates. Of course, there can be compelling reasons for building new facilities. Some Deans, however, simply like to see new building activity. Overbuilding can result, and so, also, overborrowing! The underestimation of a problematic burden on the school's operational budget can result, if financing costs are added to it. A competent, responsible board is essential to safeguard against this.

The second essential role of the board must be to contribute to the nature and content of the academic value creation itself. Board members should represent the various customers and/or key external stakeholders. They should be in a position to encourage necessary change and more effective adaptation to emerging customer needs. For example, the IMD board regularly encourages the President and the faculty to develop an updated vision for the school. This process, highly participative in nature, leads (and has led, at IMD at least) to extensions of the school's revenue-generating activities. The classical offerings of open programmes, tailored in-company programmes, and IMD's learning network were maintained. In addition, two interrelated new activities were proposed: developing support for corporation universities, with much use of virtual technology, and developing a visioning, benchmarking, and think-out service, where IMD would play the role of catalyst vis-à-vis executive teams that would like to work on their strategies at IMD. This vision was then put to the board, and approved. After all, the highly participative, bottom-up process that characterises the strategy-setting within a business school will not give a board much of a pro-active impact in this respect, unless it totally disagrees. The important lesson to draw here is that the board can call for the development of a revised vision. A longer-term view by the board can be particularly beneficial here.

What does this mean in practice? I have argued that the professors in fact "own" the business school, that they can therefore be seen as partners. The conse-quence would be that a governance structure might be put in place that would look after the interests of the "partner" faculty. There might, for example, be strong representation from the professor-partners in the governance process. Perhaps an argument could be made for an increased role of the customers of IMD in the governance process. The customers-cum-learning partners do, of course, provide the bulk of the financial means for the school, not only for its operations, but also for the renewal of intellectual capital and build-up of new knowledge via research and development activities.

The business school can, perhaps, be seen as analogous to a mutual insurance company. Each client puts in resources initially in order to have the right to draw on them later on. As such, the learning partners and other users of the school "invest" in it. They would, thus, also have an "ownership" claim in the know-how of the school. Taking this reasoning one step farther, key clients of the school, to a larger or lesser degree, would clearly also have a legitimate role in governance. The heavy users of the school would perhaps have a stronger claim for representation. The key challenge would be to see that the school is governed in a way that safeguards the long-term quality of its human capital and its ability to deliver. Drawing the "mutual insurance company" analogy, both a faculty perspective *and* a learning partner perspective would be legitimate.

Neubauer and Demb: Three Archetypal Roles for the Board

What would be the role of a board in a business school then, for it to contribute meaningful governance? Perhaps it is useful to draw on an analogy from busi-ness research. Neubauer and Demb identified three major archetypes of roles for a board:[4]

- The board can act as "watchdog", with the primary interest in monitoring and evaluating performance. In this case, the board is be primarily concerned with issues after-the-fact.
- At the other extreme, the board can be a "pilot", attempting to steer the organisation in a hands-on fashion. "Piloting" involves setting strategic direction proactively and monitoring and evaluating post-action steps.
- Neubauer and Demb have also identified the so-called "trustee" board option that offers a compromise between the first two types: involving both direction-setting and post-performance monitoring and evaluation.

For a business school like IMD, the "trustee" board role seems to be the most meaningful, both for satisfying the needs of the professor-partner stakeholders and the needs of the customers/learning partner stakeholders. Consider, in contrast, the pilot board option, for instance, with its heavy emphasis on setting strategic direction. This would run counter to the natural working interest of the school's professors, who typically consider direction-setting their domain. If the board tries to set the school's direction, it will likely clash with faculty, who, appropriately, may see themselves as running the school academically. When it comes to the school's strategic direction, faculty are rightfully unwilling to be thrust into the position of order-taking employees.

The watchdog board also, by solely focusing on the post facto monitoring and evaluation sides of its potential roles, may be unacceptable, too — but now for the customers/learning partner stakeholders. These need a better understanding of the school's direction so they can reconcile it with their strategic learning needs. Fitting the needs of the customers/learning partners-cum-stakeholders with the school's ability to adapt to these needs has been a major argument of this book.

Trustee governance is, consequently, perhaps the most appropriate mode for the board. This would involve some role for the board in setting the school's direction, as well as in the post facto control and implementation follow-up. Three major areas of "trustee" direction-setting have been identified by Neubauer and Demb.

The board would have some role in setting path and vision. I have already alluded to the role of IMD's board in stimulating the development of a revised vision for the school. It is especially important that the board sees itself as playing a role in maintaining the focus and a unified sense of direction for the school. The issue of developing and maintaining a logical portfolio dimension in a school's strategy, in contrast to this being merely an additive function of a number of free-standing activities, is particularly critical. Here, the board can play an important role in supporting the school's leadership; it can take some of the pressure off the school's leadership by supporting, sometimes difficult, decisions, by supporting the leadership in its need to say "no" to certain bottom-up initiatives proposed by the faculty, which may be attractive in themselves, but not dovetail with the school's vision.

The board would also *analyse options*, particularly, perhaps, with major investment projects, such as erecting a new building, acquiring a new major information system to enhance the networking capability of the school, and so on. In this case, the board would not be expected to analyse smaller strategic options, like the choice of which programme alternatives to pursue, but rather to focus on the larger investment options.

The third area is *implementation*. The board might ask for feedback on progress, when it comes to implementing a performance-based compensation system for the faculty, for instance. At IMD, the board played a major part in proposing that not only should the faculty compensation package be strongly competitive — to represent a take-home value for the faculty that would have to be among the best in the industry — but the package should also be made to *vary* with the school's performance, so that the faculty members take part in the benefits when the school does well. This also implies smaller benefits when the school does not perform as hoped. The board wanted the school to keep its break-even point under some control and the faculty to be motivated to act as owners. This scheme was implemented under much prodding from the board. To further underscore this, a sub-committee of the board was formed, the Compensation Committee, that increased positive pressure on the school's administration to implement the new compensation system. The result was highly positive.

The IMD board was also eager to see a more systematic review of the hiring process of new faculty members. IMD's faculty recruitment committee would adopt a process that would focus on assessing prospective faculty members, highlighting the importance of giving offers to those people who showed the most promise of becoming productive. Academic quality — as researchers *and* pedagogically — would be key. The board, on the other hand, asked other questions: What are the overall needs? In what areas do we need strengthening? What are the major shortcomings? In order to follow up on the school's portfolio of faculty — present and anticipated — another sub-committee of the board was formed, the Appointments Committee, which prodded the school's administration concerning the developments of these overall patterns. The result was a smoother, more effective recruiting process.

Neubauer and Demb note two post facto roles of the board, both of which might turn out to be somewhat heavy. The first is *monitoring* the financial performance against budget, after having set clear budget targets. These targets would, above all, focus on the revenue side, levels of resource generation within the major categories of business that the school is in. At IMD, the revenue budget is broken down to open programmes — including a separate accounting for the MBA programme — in-company programmes, and the revenues from the Partner and Business Associate network. Specific research grants for undertaking paid research are also accounted for separately. Finally, the income from the school's endowed chairs, and the school's investment in general, is accounted for. It would also focus on the cost side, with particular emphasis on head-count cost, and on making sure that the break-even point is under control. This monitoring would therefore have a strong emphasis on the cash flows of the school. The key would be to ensure the financial stability and robustness of the school.

Finally, the role of the board could be *evaluation*. Above all, the board would evaluate how the performance of the school could lead to changes in the compensation of the school's faculty and staff. This could include approving annual bonuses. The bonuses for the faculty and the staff would typically be proposed by the school's leadership and then approved by the board after a thorough discussion. By not allowing the fixed compensation proportion to get out of control, the school will be better able to maintain a reasonable break-even point.

IMD's board sees the fixed compensation side as essentially a safety net for each faculty member, and then emphasises the variable component — bonuses and profit sharing — as a reward for extraordinary effort and demonstrated performance. Consequently, increases in variable compensation as it relates to performance are likely to be on the agenda of the board. The compensation for IMD's President is handled more directly by the chairman of the board himself. He comes up with an annual evaluation of the President and, after consultation with other members of the board, sets the variable components of the President's compensation package, which again is meant to reflect the actual performance of the school. In a typical year, but not always automatically, the President's total compensation package will be the highest in the organisation.

Overall, the board should be concerned with supporting the school's plans for strengthening its revenue side through better programme offerings. It should also insist on efficient management of the school's resources so that costs can be controlled, spending levels be kept within reasonable norms, etc. When it comes to adding fixed costs to the school's cost base, such as, for instance, approving a new building that requires fixed interest payments from financing, agreeing on scaled-up hiring of new faculty members with a resulting long-term commitment for salary payments, and the like, the board should play a central approval role. When the school faces expenditures that might put a strain on its resources, the board should be concerned with assessing the risk. More specifically, it should ask: How can a prudent break-even fallback point be re-established relatively quickly?

Some organisations are more advanced than others in their ability to see future trends. It is key to listen to those executives and companies who are likely to provide such robust future-oriented advice. It would, of course, make sense that board members be recruited from such proactive companies. Still, can even the most resourceful executives from the most reputable firms always know what would be the best advice? It will be the board as a collegium that should function well to distil out any essential directional shifts that should be acted on. Individual board members must not be allowed to divert energy and resources by providing advice for the sake of advice. They should help stimulate and encourage the basic directions that have been set. Needless to say, sensitivity to the marketplace must prevail.

At IMD, for instance, a series of executive programmes focusing on doing more effective business in China was initiated, upon the suggestion of executives on the board who represented some of IMD's major customers/learning partners. It turned out, however, that it was difficult to get enough market support for these programmes after they were established. Executives who were close to the decisions to make use of these specific programmes in the companies were not the same as the board members who'd made the suggestion. They did not necessarily share the viewpoint that IMD should be their chosen provider of such services. After all, IMD was not generally known to have a particularly deep competence-base in this area; this hurdle was hard to by-pass, even though IMD certainly did have a strong competency in Chinese affairs. As I noted earlier, the result was difficulty gaining market entry, due to a lack of market support, including from the very sources where IMD would have expected it. It is, perhaps, particularly difficult to know when to take the board's advice about new business directions, and when to further seek out companies and people on whom to test the advice.

To carry on from my previous point about the faculty setting strategic direction, the board's role in contributing to the internal academic value creation directional issues within the school might thus be somewhat limited. Rather, as I have already noted, it would normally be the domain of the faculty to drive the value-creation as part of its interaction with the Dean/President. Still, directional advice from the outside can be essential too, not least to avoid internal myopia and entrapment in the status quo. Normally, it can, however, be difficult with situations where the board becomes heavily engaged in the specifics of the academic direction-setting, including staffing, such as faculty hiring/firing decisions, academic promotions, particularly when judging the substantive merits of such a promotion, and so on. Here the faculty and the Dean/President must clearly be the drivers; of course with a sensitivity to new competence needs that might have to be built up in order to realistically adapt, thus indeed also welcoming gentle prodding from the board!

Board Membership

Who then should be the members of the board? Perhaps each of the school's partner firms has the right to nominate a board representative. This can either be the chief executive officer or another senior officer of the partner firm. The presumption is that the partner firms, in all likelihood, would represent a cross-section of the major customer groups of the firm. In addition, one representative from the school's professors is on the board. Given the size of the partner population, the board at IMD would thereby be quite large, say, now around 40 executives. As noted also, as a matter of practicality, the board meets only once a year in plenary. An *executive committee* has therefore been established, consisting of six to eight executives who typically meet two to three times a year and, as such, can be seen as the de facto board. The President of IMD is also part of the board and executive committee.

Given the legitimate needs of the professorial stakeholder group, why are there not more professors on the board? The professors-cum-"partners" in a school would be most interested, relatively speaking, in the various direction-setting issues the school is facing. The board would, as mentioned, typically ask the *faculty* to initiate its own review of the vision and direction setting. Recall that the faculty will usually be the direct driving force in coming up with the various bottom-up initiatives that shape the content input of a school's vision and mission. The faculty must, of course, also be heavily involved in setting the general portfolio dimension-criteria for the top-down strategy of school — i.e., the portfolio vision/mission. This will have to do with how the various activities should fit together, in order to maintain an overall balance among the various chosen focused directions. The professors will, therefore, be very much involved in this process, which, after all, must be internally generated in a brain-driven organisation such as a business school. They would thus play a key complementary role to the board. It is simply impossible for a board to pro-actively develop its own vision of what such a highly talented, specialised brain-driven team of professionals might want to pursue strategically. This has to be left to the participating professors themselves. Only they can be motivated — and committed — to make such choices. Such issues would thus *not* occupy the dominant part of the agenda of the board, which would thus be run in the "trustee" way. Thus, all the board can and *should* do is stimulate the internal stakeholders to work out a clear vision and mission, but then to critically assess how realistic it is and how exposed to risk. In other words, the board needs to take what I call an indirect, catalytic approach. Instead, one would expect that the key direction-setting issues would be dealt with in other forums within the school.

Board-Related Governance Structures

The *faculty meeting* is an important forum for dealing with the strategic direction at any business school such as IMD. This meeting typically takes place monthly and focuses on discussing — not deciding on — major directional issues. Perhaps the most valuable part of the faculty meeting is making sure that everyone is informed about major developments and that every voice can be heard on the various directional options available. The faculty meeting creates a heightened sensibility of the prevailing sentiments concerning the directional options.

Similarly, the so-called *Co-ordinating Committee* of the faculty meets regularly to work on strategic directional matters. This committee comprises six faculty members, as well as the school's chief financial/administrative officer, and is chaired by IMD's President. Most of the directional issues under review have to do with ongoing activities in the school. One such ongoing activity, for instance, is the research and development programmes of the school. Here, one particular faculty member is in charge, and brings major directional issues to the committee, and then reports progress back to the committee. For example, the faculty member in charge of overseeing research proposes the overall R&D budget to the Co-ordinating Committee, and then elaborates on the criteria for allocating R&D support. Finally, he might discuss with the Committee how some particularly difficult allocation decisions concerning specific subsets of professors might be handled. The discussion in the Co-ordinating Committee will primarily deal with principles and policies, however, not with specific execution of the R&D activities. These will be undertaken by an administrative staff following up on the management of the R&D implementation in light of the broad guidelines given by the Co-ordinating Committee. The faculty member responsible for R&D thus works out the policy issues vis-à-vis the Co-ordinating Committee, and then takes these policies back to the operating organisation and supervises their implementation.

A second area of strong directional importance has to do with the activities focused around in-company programmes. Again, the responsible faculty member brings proposals to the committee that have a more policy-oriented nature.

Typical questions might be: should a particular in-company programme be pursued, in light of the fact that it would have to be given elsewhere than on IMD's campus and, if so, why? Would there be something special for IMD to learn from running this programme? What would be an appropriate policy regarding the financial side of such an arrangement? In general, the faculty member in charge is keenly concerned with ensuring that the various in-company programme activities truly represent unique cutting-edge firms for IMD to learn from — i.e., an optimal cross-section of learning relationships for IMD's own learning, too. Again, the execution of all of this would then be for the faculty member in charge of the in-company programmes to carry out with the school's operating organisation. His role, alone and in conjunction with the Co-ordinating Committee, would be to have an impact on the general direction and the policies. The school's administration carries out the operating implementation. In order to safeguard the proper learning partnership focus in the school's value-creation activities, the quality of the "business mix" in in-company programmes is particularly important as a focus of the Co-ordinating Committee.

A third professor might cover open teaching programme activities, reporting back to the committee on a regular basis on the progress of IMD's portfolio of these. Here again, the committee discusses policy-related issues associated with the open programme portfolio. Typically, it asks: should IMD become more involved in this specific programme, given its potential fit, or not, within the overall programme portfolio? This might, for instance, be a programme specifically for junior executives, such as IMD's aforementioned *Building on Talent* (BOT) programme. Further, should the length of the programmes be changed? Should, for example, the *Breakthrough Programme for Senior Executives* (BPSE) be shortened from three to two weeks? What are the learning implications and the policy issues regarding the commercial implications of such decisions? The faculty member in charge serves as a catalyst for focusing on the policy side of the open programme activities. Decisions about adding or dropping specific programmes are particularly critical to the Committee. The school's administrative staff, on the other hand, implements the portfolio, the marketing, the brochures, the programme scheduling, etc., from an operational point of view, guided by the policies set by the Co-ordinating Committee under the leadership of the particular faculty member.

Some decisions may lead to a temporarily higher degree of involvement in the direction-setting for the Co-ordinating Committee. It could happen, for instance, that the school is pursuing a major new open programme initiative, such as implementing an executive MBA programme as a major revision of the full-time MBA programme. A member of the Co-ordinating Committee would then oversee this implementation. Another example would be a major effort that might take place in "investing" in various aspects of IT hardware and software for more effective academic value-creation networking. When this activity has been successfully put into motion, the function of the Co-ordinating Committee member would shift. The member on the committee dealing with these issues would also be changed when this particular initiative has been completed.

Finally, as noted, the head of finance is also a member of the Co-ordinating Committee. His participation ensures full alignment between the school's financial reality regarding the implications of various policy decisions.

Another "governing" committee at IMD, the *Faculty Recruiting Committee*, guides the hiring of new faculty members, since the hiring of new faculty members is a particularly sensitive issue, and since changes in the collegial team clearly go to the heart of the faculty's role as a stakeholder group. From the point of view of current faculty members, it is crucial that new faculty fit well in the team, that they can become productive new parts of an already well-oiled machine. In a school where particular value goes to eclecticism and tailored teamwork, and less emphasis goes to hierarchical control, titles, and academic discipline-based departments, it is especially important that the Faculty Recruiting Committee work actively to make sure that new faculty members fit in. Their personal values must not create unnecessary stress and disruption. And they must have substantive and pedagogical competencies that make them "billable". The recruiting committee screens those candidates who have shown interest in the school, but it also takes the initiative to go after particularly promising candidates. Faculty recruiting visits are arranged, and feedback from all faculty for each given candidate is assessed, before deciding to offer a potential candidate a faculty position. Conceptually, it is felt that every faculty recruit should heighten the overall quality of the faculty as a group.

IMD also has an *Operating Committee* that comprises the senior administrative staff members of the school. They are concerned with co-ordinating operating matters, generally operating within the policy directions from the Co-ordinating Committee and the faculty members specifically in charge of various aspects. The Operating Committee is thus concerned with the hands-on implementation of policies, above all, marketing. Administrative implementation is thus handled by the staff. The faculty is concerned with what they do best — research and teaching — not administration and execution, so that they are not being excessively bogged down in administrative matters. This split between the directional policy making and specific operational implementation roles, and the corresponding faculty seems to work well. A well-oiled, efficient, speedy, results-oriented organisation is the result.

In total, both of the two major groups of stakeholders — the professors-cum-partners and the customers-cum-learning partners — are satisfactorily represented in the governance structure of the school. The professors-cum-partners are actively involved in the direction-setting part of governance through the faculty meeting, the Co-ordinating Committee and the Faculty Recruiting Committee. At the same time, the customers-cum-learning partners are served by the board, which primarily focuses on selective strategic direction-setting and on post facto evaluations and monitoring activities.

There are, of course, other stakeholders. The staff is essential. The alumni are also key. The community at large must also be included — we could go on and create an extensive stakeholders list. Generally, we do not feel that these stakeholders should play a role in the governing of the school, though. At IMD there is, for instance, no formal governance role for the alumni. One could argue, as many schools do, that even though the alumni represent a significant stakeholder group, they have already received their learning. While the alumni are important at IMD, we do not feel that they should be heavily involved in setting our direction. After all, the alumni have already attended the school, and as such, they no longer have an active stake in future value creation. What is important for the alumni, above all, is the maintenance of the overall quality and prestige of the school. Maintaining a strong "brand name" and public relations profile is essential. As such, these stakeholder needs are covered via the public affairs activities of the school and the maintenance of a strong link between the alumni club and the school, and do not call for representation in a formal governance sense.

Chapter 15

New Opportunities in Executive Education

Executive Summary

The modern business school is facing more competition than ever before from corporate universities, professional organisations that offer courses, classic consulting firms, "open" universities (corporate or otherwise), and "networked" business schools. These competitors are a very real, and direct, threat. The new competition mirrors a shift in the value chain. Corporate clients are limiting the modern business school's "space" by taking over roles on which it previously had close to a monopoly. The business school can make itself, in various ways, an invaluable resource to the corporate university, though it must guard against having its faculty "cherry-picked" away and its research "borrowed". The two entities can be strategic partners. Networks, a serious threat to non-members, may nevertheless represent a potential opportunity for the business to expand its space by organising itself in alliances and reaching out with networked distance learning, among other strategies. This chapter looks in depth at each of these sources of competition, where they compete with the business school head-to-head, and how the modern business school can respond to them, with a focus on the possible ways the modern business school can work with them to its own best advantage. At the same time, the school will need to create and enforce guidelines for the outside work of its faculty, whether consulting or "for the competition". All of this requires visionary leadership — and here we come back to the Dean.

The modern business school, no matter how well it meets its clients' needs, still faces stiffening competition from several potential "rivals". As observed by van Baalen and Moratis:

The change in competitive landscape, both in qualitative (and natural) competition and quantitative (number of competitors) terms, poses business schools with different opportunities and threats . . . their traditional educational environment has ceased to exist and is increasingly penetrated by other providers of education. These providers originate not only from countries all over the world, they also spring from new traditional educational sectors, like business . . . competition in the market for management education will increase, not only between public institutions, but also between public and private initiatives, like corporate universities.[1]

One such rival is the newly-emerging "corporate university". Much of the development of the Corporate University movement can be attributed to Janne C. Meister, President of Quality Dynamics in New York, which issues the *Quality University Xchange Newsletter*. Her book (1994) is also fundamental.[2] The very companies that in the past came to the business school might well be organising free-standing in-house programmes, and — herein lies the most serious threat — "cherry-picking" the best professors from the ranks of the school's faculty. Further, a wave of new entries — top-of-the-league players — is churning up the management education market, among them, the potentially powerful, classic consulting firms. Another competitive initiative is the so-called "networked" business school: single business schools trying to compete more effectively by organising wholly-owned or franchise-based networks of affiliated organisational entities. For the stand-alone business school, these networks, rich as they are in faculty, research, and new teaching ideas, represent another real danger to lasting success. Slaughter and Leslie characterise these new situational settings for business schools as:

an environment full of contradictions, an environment in which faculty and professional staff expend their human capital stocks increasingly in competitive situations. In this environment, university employees are simultaneously employed by the public sector and increasingly autonomous from the public, corporate body. They are academics who act as capitalists from within the public sector; they are state subsidized entrepreneurs.[3]

This new competition mirrors a shift in the value chain. Corporate clients are taking over many of the roles that were previously the domain of the traditional business school. They are effectively *diminishing* the school's "competitive space". Networks, though a potential threat to those not hooked into the loop, present a chance for the business school to *expand* its competitive space. By organising itself through alliances to enrich its offerings, even under different labels, it can thus strengthen its position in the value chain.

Business Schools and Corporate Universities: Real Synergy![4]

Over the last few years, corporate universities have come into full blossom. They take many approaches to executive development; however, they all speak loudly of a particular company's wish to strengthen its executive development, based on the assumption that human resources are a weighty factor in the equation of strategic success — and this is good. Both the corporate university and the business school, thus, have the same fundamental objective. But some of these corporate universities are merely clones of traditional business schools. They may have their own buildings, or even their own campuses. They may even have full-time teachers ("professors"). They may offer their own syllabi of courses, although these frequently tend to be repeated every year. Typically there is no original research behind these courses; they therefore also tend to focus on the basics.

Some leading corporate universities, such as GE's Crotonville, Nestlé's Rive-Reine, and the Motorola University, have had a significant impact on the trends of corporate university approaches in the business society at large. These corporate university models have set the example for many corporate universities around the world. One reason is that the companies developed tailored curricula through these wholly-owned entities. Motivated by the need to be relevant and to bring learning more firmly to employee agendas, they cater directly to the specific needs of their own corporate settings. Successful corporate universities also allow the companies themselves to "indoctrinate" their employees with their own corporate values and cultures. The effect is that employees learn from each other, and thereby reinforce a common *esprit de corps*. Chief Executive Officers such as Welch, Brabeck, and Galvin see their corporate universities as a vehicle for implementing their strategies, through the development of a strong corporate culture. And this is all legitimate, as well as positive. A strong corporate culture is indeed essential, and only the firm itself is empowered to instil this sentiment. The business school cannot deliver a corporate culture, nor should it try.

At the other extreme are the corporate universities without buildings, with not one cent invested in bricks and mortar. They have no professorial teachers on the payroll. What they do have is a small cadre of executives who run the university, essentially orchestrating the various programmes that "subcontract" to outsiders. These are indeed networked organisations that heavily emphasise the outsourcing of pedagogical value creation. The overall programme calendar for these corporate universities is often fluid. They change every year, according to the needs of the corporation. Both company employees and professors from various external universities (on a subcontracting basis) teach these programmes. Herein lies a most serious threat to the traditional business school — "cherry-picking" the best professors from the ranks of a school's faculty. This new competition mirrors a shift in the value chain. Corporate clients are taking over many of the roles that were previously the domain of the traditional business school, and by so doing, they are effectively diminishing the school's "competitive space".

What then should be the key roles of the business school? I see several roles in the marriage between business school and corporate university. Providing a teaching partnership is the first. The business school can provide various in-company programmes, or modules of larger programmes, not only on a sub-contracting basis, but as true partners. This means carrying out meta-planning around a given programme or sub-programme, allowing the school to bring forward its pedagogical capabilities, so that the design of a particular programme might be as pedagogically effective as possible. With virtual learning, where large numbers of students will typically be exposed to a given programme, this is particularly important.

The business school can also apply its faculty and research staff to developing particular teaching materials, such as virtual cases, technical background presentations, and topical briefings. The classical case development know-how that resides in a business school will clearly be helpful here. The key challenge, however, is to make sure that the virtual cases are, indeed, pedagogically sound.

At IMD, we are in discussions with several corporations that are not directly competing with us, about the possibility of sharing such virtual teaching materials developed for their corporate universities. There is quite a large investment in the development of such materials: the cost per unit of material is high, though the cost per student may be quite low (the costs are spread over many students). The corporate university has a much larger capacity to serve many more students than the traditional classroom-based university. In fact, speed of dissemination of learning is one of its great advantages. By sharing materials among several non-competing corporations, dissemination is not only faster, but the overall richness of the corporate university might be even greater. Further, a multi-corporate network can develop, serving an even larger population of executives, with even richer materials at even greater speeds of dissemination. Clearly, today, one of the bottlenecks in a virtual corporate university is its ability to develop appropriate teaching materials quickly and on time. Yet, with consortia of non-competing firms working in co-operation, we may see considerable progress.

The business school can provide professorial resources in a mentoring capacity. This means giving students access to the professorial resources as needed — for questioning, feedback, even discussions. The faculty resource can thus serve both as learning catalyst and as support. Here again, distance-learning technology will be critical for faculty members' ability to effectively "deliver".

As already mentioned, it can be beneficial to have ad hoc, shorter, get-together learning sessions, which could be held on the business school's own premises, giving the corporate university participants the chance to learn in a neutral-to-the-company, efficient facility. This type of learning, complementing the virtual learning, can reinforce the learning process positively, above all by bringing executive students together in a learning partnership context. This begins to look a lot like offering programmes to in-company clients. The design of such offerings, as it would be with any in-company client, is a matter of working not only with one corporate university, but with several. "Discovery events", for example, are excellent "vitamin pills" for keeping the vitality and dynamism in corporate universities. This might thus be achieved by creating a learning partnership network between the business school and several corporate universities working together.

Individual faculty members can also teach in corporate university programmes. But this arrangement has hidden risks. The corporate university may want to hire faculty members on their own "consulting" time. For the corporate university, this is doubtless attractive. But if the corporate university is free to hire whomever they want, and as many of a business school's faculty as they wish, the business school may find itself seriously disadvantaged. Its position will quickly become untenable. For what school can survive having its best faculty hired away? And what school will put up with bearing the costs of developing and maintaining each faculty member's intellectual competence by funding of his/her research and research-based teaching, only to have that intellectual capital migrate to the competition?

This is a tangible threat. How is the business school to respond? Some business schools have developed contracts with corporate universities: the professors teach, and in return the school reaps a royalty fee. Other corporate universities are allowed only to use individual faculty members from business schools on a limited basis, typically as single individuals fitting into programmes that are otherwise staffed by the corporate university itself. Sensibly, many business schools have policies that prevent corporate universities from "borrowing" faculty members wholesale. At IMD, for instance, we regulate this with strict faculty guidelines, and thereby ensure that the faculty members do not end up, in essence, competing with their own institution.

There is, thus, a definite challenge to creating a win-win situation. Consider again a hypothetical IMD example: Corporation X. With the corporate university of Corporation X, IMD might have a technology contract that involves systematic review on a scheduled, revolving basis of each of the programmes that this corporate university offers. This means that IMD's professors would undertake an audit of the content and pedagogical approach for each of the corporate university's programmes. This audit would ask what new teaching materials are needed, and could consider the development and delivery of the bulk of these materials by IMD. Finally, IMD faculty might occasionally participate in the programmes. All in all, this arrangement would lead to a more flexible, easily evolving, more adaptive value-creation activity mix at this corporate university. In essence, IMD could thus "guarantee" the appropriate content of the Corporation X university programme.

This hypothetical example, and similar arrangements, essentially make the business school and the corporate university strategic partners. But the partnership must be built on clear complementarities. This challenge is providing exceptional executive human capital value — not to save costs, but to invest! So long as all concerned parties have this clear premise in mind, positive symbiosis can result. Not a question of "either/or", meeting this challenge successfully depends on leading firms realising that they would need both the corporate university and the business school!

If we start with the assumption that corporate universities are here to stay, and that they offer opportunities for the modern business school, not just challenges, it is worth exploring further the differences between the integrated, institutionalised corporate university and the more loosely organised, network-based corporate university. What are the pros and cons of each approach? One benefit of the closed corporate university is a more consistent "indoctrination" of the corporate culture among the students. Under strict control, the corporation can essentially design and run the programme, picking the teachers from inside the company, which further assures a strengthening of the party line. Such a corporate university is a potent source for enhancing the common company culture. The potential negatives are, however, also obvious. A clear danger exists that such a closed corporate university can develop into a vehicle for corporate in-breeding. All too easily, it can become a mill for fostering inward-looking thinking, rather than remaining a proponent of open, adaptive, change-oriented ideas, especially those that go against the corporate "grain". As such, even the use of the word "university" can be misleading, which is ironic, since the university is traditionally associated with freedom, openness, and the discovery of new ideas.

Unfortunately, in-bred, closed corporate universities do exist. The physical facilities of such corporate universities can in themselves lead to inflexibility. There is a designated building, designated permanent staff of administrators and teachers (who may, in the face of change, naturally keep the protection of their own jobs in mind), and a group of designated students, all recruited from within the company. This means little or no cross-fertilisation from other types of corporate settings. In such cases, the corporate university can fall into a static approach to knowledge development, navel-gazing and a "we know best" attitude. In such cases of stasis, students often view attending programmes as a reward, more of a time to relax and enjoy exchange with other colleagues, than pushing themselves toward discovery. My experience, thus, is that developing a permanent, physical structure can easily lead to dysfunction.

The basic idea — to make a stronger, even more visible manifestation of the corporation's commitment to life-long executive development — is laudable. Still, its institutionalisation, and the accompanying development of what might easily become an inflexible physical infrastructure, might lead to the opposite of what was intended — preservation of the status quo, rather than the facilitation of learning that emphasises adaptation, speed of change, and aggressiveness. This can lead quickly to the propagation of unintended signals throughout the organisation.

The *open* corporate university, by contrast, has several attractions. When you draw on outside resources — business schools, consulting firms, and individuals, you can develop a more eclectic approach, with more variety in teaching and in ideas exchanged. Over time, such open arrangements typically afford a better opportunity to change, which, over time, fosters more dynamic flexibility, and reduces the risk of in-breeding.

An open corporate university has no building. Rather, its "foundations" typically rest on virtual learning technology, which allows for much more flexibility. The open corporate university allows individuals to study wherever they may be, typically while on the job, and learning as they require, which makes relevance more likely. Further, the open university allows more participants to study on an as-needed basis, since they aren't constrained by actually having to bring the participants into the classroom. Such an open corporate university can even more easily take on students from other corporations, by forming consortia with non-competing companies. All in all, I feel more comfortable with the virtual, open university as a vehicle for relevant executive development, sponsored directly by the corporation. This kind of life-long learning can more readily be managed so that it stays on track, provides relevant value, and supports rapidly evolving business needs.

Given all these mutations of the corporate university, what can we expect in the future? What are the trends? First, it should be noted that an already established, closed corporate university in its own facility may turn out to be difficult to reposition. We do not see many closed corporate universities migrating to open forms; the resistance to change associated with any entrenched organisational activity is normal. To go from more formality to less formality is typically hard.

At Corporation X, for instance, the brick-and-stone corporate university calls for the execution of a number of technical and general management programmes staffed by practising executives, and backed up by executives who are semi-permanently on loan to the corporate university for several years. A staff of approximately 20 permanent administrators and trainers support the programme. The bureaucratisation of all of this is cause for concern! Creating curriculum changes, for instance, involves difficult negotiations among the various stake-holders, with the creation of "losers" and "winners" among the executives who teach. The difficulties of the process are further exacerbated by the fact that the various "professors" assigned to the learning centre will, perhaps naturally, try to guard their own jobs. The result has become a rather static institution, with only small changes year after year. In this case, institutionalisation has led to stagnation, perhaps even degeneration. Keeping experiences such as this in mind, when corporations set up new corporate universities these days, they typically seem to prefer the open variety. So it should come as no surprise that labels like "meeting place" are increasingly associated with new corporate universities.

Corporate-Based Course Offerings

Many corporations have found it cheaper, rather than contracting with a business school for a programme, to run specific programmes by employing professors directly and integrating the various practical sides of the offering of the programme themselves. This may mean that the programme can be partly offered at the site of the operation itself, which cuts down on expenses for travel and time away from work. The fee for the professors might be significantly smaller since the professors work on their own, the corporate university is freed from the overhead costs a business school has to factor in.

For the business school, this trend should also raise warning flags. Merely utilising the business school as a source for cheap teaching resources represents a serious danger. It is cherry-picking, nothing less. And it isn't sustainable over time. Cherry-picking cannot be combined with developing new knowledge based on original research and development. In fact, since the modern corporation can be said to live in a symbiosis with the modern business school, particularly when it comes to generating additional knowledge, we have to ask what might be the longer-term rationale for the corporation to follow such cherry-picking habits. Although the company might perhaps benefit from such development in the short term, this might in essence mean that the corporation will be ignoring its responsibility to develop new knowledge. After all, the corporation is likely to feel dysfunctional effects of cherry-picking in the future — today's immediate benefit is tomorrow's liability.

The business school must develop clear strategies against the cherry-picking practices of free-standing corporate clients. For one, such practices violate the spirit of learning partnership. In the value-creation/usage equation, they take resources, without giving enough back. All take and no give. An effective defence is to hammer out clear guidelines for a business school's faculty, making sure to answer such questions about consulting as: For whom? For how long? How many faculty? To limit this involvement to one faculty member, say, per outside client and also limit the number of sessions that a faculty member can do will at least make it more difficult for a firm to develop effective course offerings via cherry-picking practices.

Luckily, such policies mean that a corporation may at least have to hire faculty members from various business schools, which raises the burden of co-ordination. In practice, corporations may find such co-ordination difficult. And they thus risk running relatively weak, unco-ordinated programmes. A tailored, well-run business school programme would have been leagues better. Leading business schools thus have the capacity to offer a more effective, tailored programme. They can, in effect, guarantee quality. They can do a better job than the alternative: a sloppily co-ordinated, less-than-ideally prepared, cherry-picked, shoe-string programme. To play on quality is thus the business school's best defence.

New Competitive Arenas

In recent years, a new breed of players has found a niche in the executive education market. These professional organisations see themselves as co-ordinators of programmatic offerings for corporate clients. Many of them draw primarily on business school resources. Examples are Management Centre Europe in Brussels, and Clariant Corporation in Boston. Management Centre Europe provides short programmes, advertised broadly, open to individual executives from any company. The faculty members come from the traditional business school, and the offerings are typically "silver bullet" presentations that these faculty members can readily give. The Clariant Corporation specialises in offering more tailored programmes to individual firms. It staffs these programmes by drawing on faculty resources from business schools and occasionally from consulting firms. As van Baalen and Moratis state, "the commercialization, or 'marketisation', of higher education, has been subject to blazing discussion and has recently been called "academic capitalism".[5]

Organisations such as these may represent a peril for the modern business school because they usurp the business schools' major value-creating possibilities. They offer similar products, and they draw largely on the same faculty. One could argue that the faculty teams thus assembled are more of a disjointed collection of ad hoc resources than the faculty at a typical business school would be. But still, these two hybrids use fundamentally the same know-how-based resources. Just as for privately offered programmes under the professor's own leadership, the situation is rather paradoxical for the business school, in that *it* will carry the financial burden for allowing the professors to maintain and evolve their intellectual capital, by financing faculty research, putting resources of various sorts behind its professional staff so that they can develop their materials. The result? A professor will now be in a position to offer his know-how to learning partners, but *without* having to charge for the development expenses that have already been incurred by someone else, namely the professor's employer, the business school! The fundamental reason for not welcoming this type of cherry-picking value creation is again the dilemma around who pays for the discovery of new knowledge. A business school that only pays the bill for developing new knowledge, but remains bereft of the benefits, is in an unenviable long-term position, to say the least. Needless to say, it would behove the business schools to attempt to limit such organisations.

As already noted, a business school must have in place various guidelines for outside work of its faculty, which could actually prohibit professors from engaging in competitive activities. The school's leadership must be willing to actively enforce these strictures. At IMD, for instance, we set a certain minimum length of a teaching activity, as well as a maximum number of faculty members involved, which allows corporations to have access to individual faculty members only for shorter programmes. For more substantial programme offerings, the IMD team, however, is off limits. Probably even more important, the school can create an atmosphere of ownership-thinking among its faculty members, and this is perhaps easiest if the school is doing well financially and the professors are thus sharing significantly in the financial gains. Particularly, if this is the case, the professors may not find it in their interest to engage in activities that, in essence, quarry their own gold mine. Last, but not least, professional pride and a sense of ethics can, one hopes, also guide the professors.

Should the business school take seriously the threat of its own faculty doing consulting? Should the business school itself engage in such consulting activities? Consultants typically offer analytical support: they find problems and formulate solutions. For example, they may undertake some sort of industry analysis, then assess the various players within this industry, and focus on the options of the given firm relative to its competitors. Having come up with a recommendation, the consultant may then outline steps for implementation, for putting the new approach into practice, suggesting the involvement of its own organisation as well as of outside resources in the extension of the project. The consulting firm undertakes valuable services that, in theory, the corporation might have done itself on its own, if it had the necessary resources and expertise. Needless to say, the consulting firm typically has highly specialised, cutting-edge competence that few corporations could match.

So, the consulting firm provides a useful value creation, and is therefore a meaningful complement to the business school. Some faculty members in business schools have the competence and are interested in providing problem-oriented consulting on their own. As such, *they*, but not the business school as an institution, can compete with consulting firms. Typically, however, what an individual faculty member can do relative to a well-established consulting firm, is rather limited. Faculty consulting is typically highly specialised. As an alternative to an offering by a consulting firm, individual faculty can also offer process-oriented consulting activities. Here again, competition between school and consultancy is minimal.

Where do business schools and consulting firms compete head to head? Student-based consulting projects are one arena. Such action-learning efforts are becoming a fixture of more and more MBA programmes. Corporate clients hire teams of MBA students to undertake a strategy implementation project. These projects typically involve extensive analysis, leading in turn to recommendations. Under the auspices of the MBA programme, IMD offers the services of ten to 12 consulting teams per year. The projects are typically a combination of problem formulation, solution, and implementation. The first is usually heavily based on an industrial analysis approach, understanding the competitive realities that the client firm is exposed to, and seeing the solution to its business problem in light of how to create a strategic advantage for an operator within an industry. The implementation side is usually heavily based on an attempt to clarify who does what and when, in a competent, motivationally committed manner. The student teams make interim reports and presentations to the clients, and present their final reports, not as a lengthy tome, but as a managerially relevant document.

Thus, in all aspects, this value creation resembles closely what the client organisation would have got from a full-blown consulting organisation. Faculty members support and coach the students. Although it could be argued that the business school is infringing on the consulting firm's activities, it would still be hard to see this competition as significant. After all, student-based consulting has only a limited scope, and is neither ongoing, nor sustainable.

Some teaching activities at the business school are also quite similar to management consulting. Consider a so-called *visioning process* approach, which involves the top management of a learning partner organisation getting together at the business school for a number of days, under the tutelage of a professor who acts primarily as a catalyst in a review of its top management's own vision and in a reconfirmation of this and/or a revised vision. Such a visioning approach is arguably a kind of consulting activity. It is, however, more academic to argue what it actually is: essentially, such a visioning process represents meaningful value creation for the learning partner organisation. One can actually imagine "think-outs" where the faculty plays a catalytic role with groups of executives on other issues, too. Again, this might be a legitimate extension of a business school's activities.

The business school might also think about conducting special benchmarking activities for a learning partner. Identifying best practices might be particularly useful for corporations, say, in the designing of their in-company programmes. Indeed, it may be useful for the faculty of the business school to carry out the benchmarking in its own right as background research for the design for an in-company programme.

Engagement in action learning to put together a new business development project might also draw on consulting-type capabilities. IMD's *Venture Booster Programme* does exactly this, by supporting creative teams who come to IMD to speed up potentially highly significant projects![6] All in all, we can therefore see extensions of a business school's value creation that can be thought of as "consulting". This type of consulting builds on the school's capabilities, notably both pedagogical catalytic as well as substantive insights regarding particular industry settings, i.e., capabilities of its professors. Still it is hard to see the business school evolving into head-to-head competition with the mainstream consulting firm.

Consulting firms may, however, provide specialised teaching offerings that might compete directly with the business school. One could imagine a consulting firm running specific, limited workshops, say, for board members. Many business schools can, in principle, offer the same, and so, direct competition exists. In general, most consulting firms have, however, restricted their entrance into executive teaching activities. If they are active at all, they concentrate on shorter, specialised programmes. The recognition among most consulting firms has probably been that it is generally difficult for their consultants to combine problem-solving consulting activities with teaching. This might also be a consequence of potential differences in fee structures. Teaching could easily be seen as an opportunity loss for leading, highly billable consultants!

Why don't consulting firms establish their own business schools as self-contained separate divisions? This has indeed happened! The most prominent example is the Arthur D. Little business school, which has developed over time into a full-blown business school. The business proposition equation for Arthur D. Little has been such that the activities of the school have also had to support the new knowledge generation necessary to support the school in a longer-term sense. Because teaching activities need to support research and development activities, the economics of the Arthur D. Little business school and most other business schools are more or less the same. For Arthur D. Little, the fact that business school life does not automatically lead to additional profits has become a valuable insight — this way is certainly not golden! Consequently, as noted previously, the Arthur D. Little business school was eventually turned into a not-for-profit, free-standing institution. The school has also moved into close co-operation with Boston College, a traditional business school. In general, one might assume that, taking into consideration that the necessary research and development activities have to be paid for, there simply would not be enough room for private capital to profit as owners of a business school.

The Business School as a Network Organisation: Achieving Scope

In the modern business school, funds are typically generated only when a professor faces students. When a particular class is given, the school collects a fee from the learning partner and/or the individual student. Simply put: the school charges a fee for a programme. The school's revenue stream is a function of the professors teaching in the various programmes — obviously, the more programmes offered, the higher the revenues! Outside the cumulative effect of professor teaching in classrooms, the business school has little leverage in generating resources. For a typical business school there is thus little economy of scale. Further, the revenue generated per professor would be more or less the same, perhaps with some variations depending on the school's reputation. A business school with fifty professors thus tends to be able to generate more or less half of the revenues of one with one hundred professors. Economically speaking, size (within certain minimum or maximum) is neither an advantage, nor a disadvantage.

If we accept the above as true, the only way for the business school to modify its value chain to create more value per head is to create more of a scale effect. But how can it restructure its delivery function in order to create more economic value per professor? Two approaches seem to work well. One is the wholly-owned, franchise approach developed by the Norwegian School of Management (NSM);[7] the other utilises distance learning.

The Norwegian School of Management has established an extensive network organisation. This allows for a considerable leveraging of "professorial time". It works as follows. There is a main campus in Sandvika, outside Oslo. At this campus, there is a full-blown academic staff organised along functional lines — more than one hundred professors, at all ranks. The central campus offers mainly a bachelor's degree in management ("civiloekonom"), as well as a number of master's degree offerings, including an MBA, and several specialised Master of Science offerings. A doctoral programme also exists. The school has established a network of fifteen regional campuses all over Norway. At these campuses, students can earn a three-year bachelor's degree. The professorial staff at Sandvika develop the materials for these regional offerings. At each of the fifteen satellite schools, business executives from the local communities teach the materials on a part-time basis. The central staff at Sandvika trains each of these executives, i.e., provides them with the necessary background, supports them as executive teachers, helping them with grading their students. Using respected local business people as professors lends considerable legitimisation to business as a field of study in each local community. At each of the satellite campuses, a small core of full-time professors complement the part-time "business person teachers"; this full-time group safeguards the quality of the offerings. This network approach brings considerable scale benefit in the use of Sandvika professors' time. By having them spend some time on developing teaching materials, some time on teaching/coaching the part-time business people, and some time on supervising grading, the Norwegian School of Management business school can deliver more to more students than it otherwise could — at a lower price. For executive education activities, NSM has put a similar programme in place. The school offers programmes for managers not only in Oslo, but at the other regional campuses throughout Norway. Here too a notable scale effect occurs.

Distance learning technology can also have a scale-enhancing effect. The modern professor can develop "canned lectures" that the school can thus distribute throughout the world. Needless to say, distance learning activities often take the form of direct tutorials, with professors working with students either one-on-one or in small groups. Scale effects will, of course, be absent here. If however, the school can use Internet technologies to offer outstanding lectures to many more students than could possible sit in a lecture hall, scale effects may kick in.

I imagine a future in which business schools might think in terms of "networked" distance learning. Business schools may encourage the very best professors in given fields worldwide to develop their very best lectures. The schools may co-ordinate them into a logical course-design, and thus make them available to all students with a PC and an Internet connection. In this vision of tomorrow, students will "receive" lectures from a wide variety of professors, all the very best in the world in their own narrow fields. For this vision to become reality, business schools may well have to co-operate in a network fashion, "sharing" professors and lectures.

Several examples for this development already exist. First, consider the international MBA programme involving INSEAD, McGill, and other well-known business schools. Students commute from institution to institution, drawing on the separate faculties' capabilities. Thus, a broader faculty population is thereby created, with more resources and capabilities. A similar arrangement exists for MBA programmes offered by a number of leading business schools, such as Northwestern's Kellogg, Sasin Graduate Institute of Business (Bangkok, Thailand); Recanati Graduate School of Business (Tel Aviv, Israel); Otto Beisheim Graduate School at the Koblenz School of Corporate Management (Germany); Australian Graduate School of Business; Copenhagen Business School; ESSEC and the Institut Superieur des Affaires (France); Hong Kong University of Science & Technology; KEIO University; IPADE (Mexico); IESE International Graduate School of Management (Spain); Rotterdam School of Management; and London Business School.[8]

Taking this line of thinking one step further, even though it turned out that it was not initially as successful as hoped, Wharton's attempt is worth consideration. Wharton tried to create a network of leading business schools from all over the world — one in Europe, one in Asia, one in South America, etc. — all offering an MBA programme with a similar curriculum. The idea was to draw the best professors from each school, who would give lectures, lead teaching initiatives and programmes, all of which would be available over a virtual network. The plan foresaw students and faculties migrating back and forth among the network schools. The students would receive a degree from Wharton and from one of the other network schools. This initiative, though too ambitious to be realistic, points towards possible scale effects available through the pooling of educational resources in new ways. We may see more of this in the future.

A similar trend is apparent in executive development. At IMD, for instance, we are co-operating with other schools to offer particular programmes for given learning partners, typically, the result of preferences of the learning partners so they can benefit from a combination of leading schools' faculty resources. For instance, there is an in-company programme for Bertelsmann offered jointly by the Harvard Business School and IMD, which allows both schools to utilise their faculty more effectively. Deloitte Touche Tomatsu, another example, has subscribed to an in-company programme offered by Northwestern's Kellogg School, Columbia Business School, and IMD. Again, the effect of such co-operation will be the pooling of academic resources, representing new ways to create value by activating such a network, thereby increasing the revenue per faculty member.

It is especially important that a business school consider the domain of its business as dynamically evolving, its vision as temporary — on the move towards something else. The analogy with strategic business unit thinking and core competence thinking of the corporate world comes to mind. A static view of strategic business units and core competencies is often blinkered to interesting new business developments, which can come about by seeing new opportunities between well-defined business units, by combining established core competencies in new ways. While the business school must build on its core competencies, it must still allow for the evolution of the core competencies in a rather free, opportunistic manner, inspired by the spirit of scientific discovery. The result will be that the business school of the future will embrace new types of academic value-creation activities. It may reformulate what it is presently doing. It may draw more heavily on networks. It may base its new value creation more heavily on emerging technologies. But evolutionary vision requires leadership support. Again, a school's leadership must *lead*, not only be led by its present customers.[9] The school's leadership is responsible for stimulating an evolutionary development of its vision. Evolution means what the word says — not revolution! The business school must develop its core competencies in such ways that they hang together in some sort of dynamic pattern, offering cutting-edge value to its clients. These core competencies should not be generally accessible, so there should be no temptation for outsiders to "cherry-pick"! In this sense the school's know-how should be seen as a "closed" system.

Chapter 16

Final Words

Ask the Dean or President of a business school for a succinct list of the truly critical success factors for the school, and you may well get an inconclusive one. The task, as you now appreciate, is remarkably complex. No wonder so many business school leaders are often unable to give a sufficiently focused answer. Several times, I have myself been asked — even pressured — to come up with a list of the "ultimate" factors for managing a business school such as IMD. After the hours of reflection and revision that have gone into this book, I have managed, at the risk of over-simplification, to reduce the complex challenges described in the previous pages to six "ultimate truths" — six critical points.

Many others points are doubtless also important for maintaining a school's success. But still, focusing on the six factors here can take the business school a long way. For the President (or Dean), the old dictum that "strategy means choice" applies too: the Dean needs to be focused, and the six following points can serve as useful managerial guidelines.

First, the school's strategy must remain *simple* and *focused*. For IMD, this means sticking to being "the global meeting place for executive learning", convening executives from around the world to learn together at IMD in Lausanne. Simple and focused means networking these executives into *one* learning community by exposing them to knowledge that is, above all else, immediately relevant for practitioners, with a strong focus on their experience. IMD is *not* the place for the less experienced learning segment, for whom global networking would, perhaps, be less critical.

Second, a school like IMD must cultivate a strong *climate of innovation*. It must expect of its faculty that they will undertake ongoing *cutting-edge research*. For the faculty members, such research activity is important in several ways — it keeps them fresh, and it keeps them working regularly to transform their research into teachable points of view in the classroom. While supporting cutting-edge, innovative research, the school must also make room for, and visibly support, advances in pedagogy. Learning executives must feel they are benefiting from innovative thinking all the time.

Third, and this goes almost without saying, the faculty must, of course, be the best the school can get. The school must be able to attract and retain the best faculty possible. The basic salary package must be highly competitive, and the bonus scheme — rewarding team as well as individual performance — is just as important. Further, the school must make sure its reputation is sterling; it must be generally seen as a "prestigious place to be". The environs and living conditions for the faculty members and their families must also be attractive. Above all, and perhaps most critical, the school must provide a truly stimulating intellectual milieu — with engaging colleagues and top students. It must be a "happy place". Productive. Rich in intellectual capital. Inspiring. Enjoyable. A good team to join.

Fourth, it is essential that the school maintain *speed, flexibility,* and *relevance* in serving both corporate clients and individual executives-cum-learning partners. Being fast, flexible and relevant will have several impacts on the school. It can get away with only a minimum level of internal formal organisational structure, with no departments or formal hierarchy. Faculty members can organise themselves ad hoc around teaching programmes or research projects, according to the specific needs dictated by a particular programme and/or project. Customer orientation will mark the school's "attitude". Very often, though, the prevailing attitude runs counter to speed, flexibility, and relevance, with introversion and a "me, me, me" self-centredness setting the tone. This is unfortunate and does not bode well, since the business school, like any academic institution, must see itself as a *service* organisation.

Fifth, strict *cost control* must be in place. Of course, controlling costs and actively managing the break-even point is a never-ending challenge. It is very easy to lose a realistic focus; once it is lost, it is hard to re-establish. One beneficial way to encourage cost control and break-even management is to create an "ownership attitude" among faculty and staff. The school is made up, after all, of "their" resources. At IMD, for instance, faculty and staff receive reasonable, but not extremely high, fixed pay that the school sees as a kind of "safety net" salary. On top of that, when IMD's economic conditions allow it, they receive aggressive group and individual bonuses. When IMD is doing well, IMD team members do equally well. Everybody shares in the economic ups and downs! In this way, faculty and staff, much like actual owners of the organisation, help keep the break-even point for the school better under control.

Sixth, the *physical* facilities, buildings and grounds, must be in good shape. Often, academic institutions are allowed to be rather shabby, giving the impression that it is practically a cultural dictum that academic institutions should be like this, a little dull-walled, with hints of dilapidation, and certainly not five-star hotels. My feeling, which is implemented at IMD, is that *good learning* takes place in *outstanding physical facilities*. Maintaining the physical facilities at a high level is, indeed, part of developing a proper set of conditions for good executive learning.

You can, of course, think of a business school's strategy in many ways. You can see it analytically, perhaps focusing on the school's strengths and weaknesses, and its opportunities and threats. You can analyse your own school relative to other leading schools. Both views are valid. But I believe we must delineate strategy such that it allows for broad organisational ownership, a wide sense of comfort through participation in the decision making and a strong sense of freedom to undertake *speedy* implementation and an orientation to action. What does this imply for the members of the organisation? The faculty and staff of the school must actually *understand* the strategy and *internalise* it. Team members must have an *active* view of what the school's strategy means. They must be able to work with it every day, taking decisions, in the large *and* in the small, and consistent with the strategy that they so well understand.

The upshot is this: a strategy for an academic institution can perhaps best be delineated in terms of a relatively small set of guidelines that, taken together, delineate some "limits" within which the organisational members of the school must stay. By conceiving of the strategy as, in a sense, defining the "space for decision action/implementation action", the school should be able to move faster, while also giving the organisation's members a sense of true involvement and ownership. Throughout this book, I have tried to show in some detail how a business school can be managed with these six precepts at the centre of its strategic universe, and so it seems fitting to bring it to a close with a recap of the most important examples from the business school I refer to most frequently, IMD.

IMD is fundamentally engaged in the executive education segment. The school offers a learning context to experienced executives from all over the world. IMD also has built a network of leading corporations-cum-learning partners (our "partners/business associates network"), the very existence of which further cements the executive learning tasks inside these partner companies. Not only do individual executives come to programmes at IMD to support the development of their strategic human resources portfolio, but also for support for what we call their "life-long learning". IMD serves its learning network companies with Web-based briefings, discovery events in which executives can get research briefings on current topics, tailored Web-based learning updating for those who have already been to IMD, and many other complementary offerings.

IMD also offers a niche-MBA programme with a focus on quality, intentionally small, and meant for practising executives in their early thirties, "on their way up" and with exceptional qualifications. Gaining admission to this elite

MBA programme is tough. In terms of "value for money", it represents a logical extension of our executive education mission. IMD also offers a small EMBA programme, similarly positioned at the high quality end. Except for the small MBA/EMBA programmes, IMD offers no degree programmes, including no doctoral programme. IMD does co-operate with a few leading institutions so that some members of the organisation can do specialised graduate work at the doctoral level (thesis supervision, for example).

From this understanding of IMD's strategy, the members of IMD's organisational team will, therefore, need to accept that the school's product focus is not about to change — no large expansion of the MBA programme, for instance, no establishment of an undergraduate offering or a Ph.D., for example.

The main set of target "customers" for IMD are large, successful multinational corporations (IMD's *major* customer base), companies that most readily see the need for services of a school such as IMD. They are probably the companies most capable of developing their own action plans for using IMD in their own human resource strategies. This might typically entail the delineation of a joint, tailored action plan that further supports the development of the company's strategic executive development activities. In addition, joint development can, however, be extended to smaller, primarily high-growth companies, ideally within interesting hi-tech areas, and leading family firms.

IMD serves the individual executive primarily *through* their corporations. Hence, the bulk of the tuition fees also come from company sponsors. The exception would be the majority of the MBA participants as well as a few individuals signing up on their own for our executive programmes. Normally, however, most of IMD's "clients" would be "sponsored" by their corporations. This fact has a profound effect on IMD's marketing activities — it being "B2B" not "B2C", to use the Internet argot. Again, IMD's organisation would sense that this provides valuable strategic direction — the School would *not* embark on a large advertising campaign focused on the young, individual executive, for instance.

So far as geographic scope goes, IMD is "the global meeting place": executives from all over the world physically get together at the IMD campus in Lausanne, to learn together. The value of this is a truly diverse, cross-cultural eclectic learning network. Typically, we have several dozen nationalities represented in a given programme at a given point in time. For a typical year, we have between 65 and 70 nationalities represented.

As such, IMD is not interested in offering local or regional programmes, not interested in becoming No. 1 on the local or regional scene. The global mix of participants is critical to our strategy, and provides guidelines for our organisation. There is no point, for example, in proposing free-standing local programme offerings away from IMD. Selectively, however, IMD has a number of alliances, to further strengthen its presence in particular geographic markets. These alliances can be seen as "feeders" for generating more participants to ultimately come to our "global meeting place" in Lausanne.

Behind IMD as a "business system" is the understanding that IMD must be seen as a distinctive, high image brand. The offering — our value proposition — must be something the clients/customers are willing to pay for, worth a premium for them, not a commodity they feel they can get anywhere. The focus is thus on exclusivity, quality, and upscale. So IMD takes a strong marketing approach, based on serving the customer — the learning partner. A field force is in place for this. IMD aims to provide exceptional value, and thus create a high quality image of exclusivity. The school invests in providing exceptional servicing as the major generator of revenue. Since all IMD programmes must be "fresh" and faculty must always present themselves as cutting-edge (not burned out or backward looking), strong investments flow to R&D. The Institute focuses on customer value.

The school does not pursue fundraising along classical avenues, it does not try to tap everyone for typically smaller amounts (thereby avoiding the typical — and often unintended — friction/noise). Rather, fundraising is based on securing a select number of endowed professorial chairs from key individuals and/or corporations that can truly identify with what IMD is doing, underscoring that they want to associate themselves more closely with IMD's value proposition, existing research, high quality and high image.

Last but not least, the school makes heavy investment in information technology, not driven by the need to be more efficient internally, but above all to serve the learning partners better, as corporations and as individuals worldwide. For the school, information technology is a key quality enhancement vehicle vis-à-vis the learning partners, providing networking support, creating an even stronger value proposition (not as a cost saver).

In sum, the "business systems" create a strong *value proposition* for learning partners. IMD is ready to undertake aggressive funding. IMD's strategy depends on active support of these value-creating activities for its learning partners with funds and human resources. We spend frugally on administration, keeping it lean, and rein in our fixed costs. Strategically, the organisation knows that strategic spending to enhance the value proposition for the learning partners is up; other spending is not!

IMD's policies and behaviours have developed over time. Typically, they are not written, but have shaped themselves as a manifestation of the values the IMD team wants to subscribe and aspire to. As such they are equally critical in shaping strategy. Transparency is the first, above all when it comes to faculty workloads, compensation packages (including bonuses), outside consulting activities, etc.

It would be inconsistent with IMD's strategy for individual faculty members to push for special deals. The merit of a narrow base load for compensation for all is broadly accepted: the school sets more or less the same base salary for all, uncoupled from seniority and individual faculty prestige. The school compensates seniority and individual performance/prestige as part of the individual bonus. Creating a cache of "star professors" with widely higher benefits would be irreconcilable with IMD's strategy.

IMD strongly encourages new initiatives, as long as they are commercially viable in the sense that they offer value to the school's learning partners that they are willing to pay for. "Celebrating" these new value initiatives — praising not criticising — is critical, too. Risk taking is encouraged and celebrated. Team members realise that they are free to try new initiatives, as long as they fit IMD's value proposition.

The school holds internal structure to an absolute minimum. Without academic departments, silos, or kingdoms, delivery teams form around the specific needs of given teaching programmes and/or research projects. Seniority among professors should not give them a privileged standing. The members of IMD's organisation understand that to prepare and instigate excessive new routines, controls, procedures, etc. would *not* be consistent with the strategy!

Faculty members' membership within specific key committees of the school rotates, so that everyone gets the feeling that he/she is responsible and has to do a job at certain points of time. Freeloaders are frowned upon. Everyone can be tapped to serve, younger or older, and the strategy implies that those tapped are expected to say "Yes".

Every new faculty recruit should be good enough to raise the average quality of the overall faculty team. No new faculty members should merely fill a need. The faculty recruitment strategy must not be based on friendships, on bringing in disciplines, on attempting to strengthen certain academic disciplinary areas. A business school such as IMD must simply go for the best.

Life-long tenure does not exist; everyone has to earn their keep by contributing year after year. Providing value to the school and the learning partners on an ongoing basis is a basic requirement and those faculty members who do not provide such value will be asked to leave. IMD does not ask anyone to stay on simply for the sake of nicety, or as a reward for previous service. Our dynamic, customer-service strategy demands strict adherence to performance.

Teamwork is the focus of IMD's culture, not individual faculty stars. We believe that academic value, relevant for our learning partners, both companies and individuals, springs from teams working together, not "high entertainment stars" or soloists. IMD does not bring such high-flyers on board, either, even though they may have many apparent strengths that they could bring.

The Institute encourages its faculty to do private consulting, but within clear guidelines. Above all, no individual faculty members should be allowed to engage in activities that compete, in any way, with IMD. They are not allowed to become targets for "cherry-picking" by corporations who might want a certain IMD faculty member for a "less expensive deal". Individual faculty members are expected to make their consulting activities totally transparent. Many educational initiatives "on the periphery" of broader network organisations of typical business schools would be off limits at IMD.

IMD discourages corridor politics. A faculty member with an issue should raise it immediately, not leave it simmering on the back of the stove. The school's culture and strategy encourage self-policing. No one has the time, nor the tolerance, to spend energy on such activities.

The working environment — the final set of "strategic shaping issues" — may, in fact, look rather like the policy and behavioural issues raised before; they are, however, even more "emergent", shaped more by actions than by specific decisions. They contribute equally, however, to IMD strategy. IMD must be a " fun place", a "happy organisation". Positive thinking should hold sway over criticism and negativism. In terms of strategy implementation, this implies that the school tries to steer clear of organisational members who do not fit the organisation, or do not seem to have a good potential for developing such a fit. There is indeed a predominant IMD way.

That way also includes ethical considerations. Every member of IMD must think of its learning partners as stakeholders and treat them entirely fairly. Everyone is part of creating a positive value proposition for the learning partner. Those who shrink from this ethical stance, by choice or not, should ultimately leave. Every member of the IMD community is expected to do what is good for the learning partner, to conduct every single external transaction as though each individual of the organisation is the "owner". The strategic guideline here is this: you should not commit resources on behalf of IMD that you would not have committed if you owned IMD.

The Institute encourages an atmosphere of creativity and innovative risk-taking. It tolerates failure, which it sees as the inevitable, occasional outcome of risk taking, and strongly rewards success, including celebration. The strategy is thus one of supporting each other — in success *and* in failure. Here, too, speed and non-bureaucratic drive, in a non-political atmosphere, are critical. Discussions and analysis ad absurdum are not being encouraged. To get things done *fast* is one of IMD's core values. The organisational strategy would *not* call for tolerance for faculty members who want to debate everything and re-open every issue. The school cannot accept high "transaction costs".

Finally, what emerges from all of this is a collegial, productive, effective organisation. The strategy calls for behaviour from all the individuals in the organisation that would make them part of a true team — a professional one! The set of six broad guidelines introduced at the opening of this chapter and illustrated with examples from IMD seem to be rather effective in pointing the direction for IMD's strategy. Based on the belief that strategies *happen* through individuals' choices and commitments within the context of some broad constraints, it represents an indirect way of delineating the strategy. IMD's organisation seems comfortable with this way. Above all, it allows for people to take initiative and for action to take place, and does not allow the setting of strategy to become a "slowing down process" — the latter being the case in many organisations, where a more formal, analytically driven view of strategy prevails.

Notes

Preface

1   Platt, L. E. (1998). *Rules for Survival in the Brave New World of Total Connectivity*. Remarks given at the IDC European Forum; H-P Pictures the Future. In: *Business Week* (pp. 100–109), July 7, 1997. Nee, E. What have you invented for me lately? In: *Forbes*, July 28, 1997.
2   Argyris, C., & Schön, D. A. (1978). *Organizational Learning*. Reading, MA: Addison-Wesley.
3   van Baalen, P. J., & Moratis, L. T. (2001). *Management Education in the Network Economy: Its Context, Content, and Organization* (p. 53). Dordrecht: Kluwer Academic Publishers.
4   Lorange, P. (March 2000). Developing an internally driven growth strategy in network organizations: The Nestlé Friskies example. In: Bolko von Oetinger (ed.) (of the Boston Consulting Group), *Unternehmer im Dialog: Zu Gast bei Helmut Maucher, 1992-2000* (pp. 38–47). Munich: Walter Biering GmbH.
5   Cyert, R. M. (1983). In: G. Keller, *Academic Strategy* (p.vi). Baltimore: Johns Hopkins University Press.
6   Tyson's London Corner. *The Economist* (p. 50), August 18, 2001.

Introduction

1   Gordon, R. A., & Howell, J. E. (1959). *Higher Education for Business*. New York: Garland; Porter, L. W., & McKibbin, L. E. (*c.* 1988). *Management Education and Development*. New York: McGraw-Hill; Schlossman, M., Sedlak, M., & Wechsler, H. (1987). *The "New Look": The Ford Foundation and the Revolution in Business Education*. Los Angeles: Graduate Management Admission Council.

2 Mittlehurst, R. (1993). *Leading Academics* (p. 1). Buckingham, UK: Open University Press.
3 Friedman, M., & Friedman, R. (1979). *Free to Choose: A Personal Statement.* New York: Harcourt Brace & Co.; Friedman, M., & Friedman, R. The next big free-market thing. In: *The Wall Street Journal.* July 9, 1998. New York: Dow Jones & Company, Inc.
4 Tjeldvoll, A. (1998). The idea of the service university. *International Higher Education*, 13.
5 Tjeldvoll, A., & Holtet, K. (1998). The service university in a service society: The Oslo case. *Higher Education, 35*, 27–48.
6 Clark, B. R. (1998). *Creating Entrepreneurial Universities: Organisational Pathways of Transformation.* Oxford: Pergamon.
7 Hedberg, B. (1981). How organisations learn and unlearn. In: P. L. Nystrom and W. H. Starbuck, *Handbook of Organisational Design* (Vol. 1, pp. 3–27). Oxford: Oxford University Press.
8 Piaget, J. (1968). *Le Structuralisme.* Paris: Presse Universitaire de France.
9 Descartes, R. (1994). *A Discourse on Method.* New York: Everyman.

Chapter 1

1 Abell, D. (1993). *Managing with Dual Strategies — Mastering the Present; Preempting the Future.* New York: Free Press.
2 Lorange, P. (1985). Tailormaking of strategic management systems design: Matching systems capabilities to strategic needs. In: R. Lamb and P. Shrivastava, *Advances in Strategic Management* (Vol. 4). Greenwich: JAI Press.
3 Cohen, M. D., & March, J. G. (1973). Leadership and ambiguity. *The Carnegie Commission on Higher Education* (p. 33). New York: McGraw-Hill.
4 Op. cit.
5 March, J. G., & Olsen, J. P. (1976). *Rediscovering Institutions: The Organisational Basis of Politics.* New York: Free Press.
6 Dahrendorf, R. (1995). *A History of London School of Economics and Political Science 1895-1995,* Oxford: Oxford University Press.
7 Op. cit.
8 Cohen, M. D., & March, J. C. (op. cit.) (p. 33).
9 Keller, G. (1983). *Academic Strategy* (p. 152). Baltimore: Johns Hopkins University Press.
10 Blau, P. M. (1994). *The Organisation of Academic Work* (p. 279). New York: Wiley-Interscience.

11 Blau, P. M., ibid., (p. 280).

12 Clark, B. (1998). *Creating Entrepreneurial Universities: Organisational Pathways of Transformation*. Oxford: Pergamon.

13 Duderstadt, J. (2000). *A University for the 21st Century* (p. 104). Ann Arbor, Michigan: The University of Michigan Press.

14 Bain, G. S. (2000). Balanced excellence (private correspondence).

15 Simon, H. (1967). The business school: A problem in organisational design. *Journal of Management Studies*, 5(1).

16 Kumar, N. *et al.* (2000). From market driven to market driving. *European Management Journal*, 129–142.

17 van Baalen, P. J., & Moratis, L. T. (2001). *Managing Education in a Network Economy: Its Context, Content, and Organisation* (pp. 161–163). Dordrecht: Kluwer Academic Publishers.

18 Cyert, R. M. (1983). In: G. Keller, *Academic Strategy* (p. vii). Baltimore: Johns Hopkins University Press.

19 Norwegian School of Management (B. I.). Governor's Report, Sandvika, 2000.

20 Thompson, J. D. (1967). *Organisation in Action*. New York: McGraw-Hill.

21 Gibbons, M., Limoges, C., Nowotny, H., Schwartzman, S., Scott, P., & Trow, M. (1994). *The New Production of Knowledge*. London: Sage; Simon, H.A. (1991). Bounded rationality and organizational learning. In: *Organizational Science*, 2(1), February 1991.

22 Norwegian School of Management (B.I.). Governor's Report, Sandvika, 2000.

23 Amdam, R. P. (2000). *For Egen Regning — BI og den Økonomisk Administrative Utdanningen 1943–1993*. Oslo: Norwegian University Press.

24 Revang, Ø. (2000). *Med BI fra Aftenskok til Vitenskapelig Høyskok*. Oslo: Fasbokforlaget.

25 Sarvary, M. (1999). Knowledge management and competition in the consulting industry. *California Management Review*, 41(1), 41.

26 Gibbons, M. *et al.* (op. cit.).

27 Stabell, C. B., & Fjellstad, O. D. (1998). Configuring value for competitive advantage: On chains, shops, and networks. *Strategic Management Journal*, 19, 413–437.

28 IMD's *Orchestrating Winning Performance* programme brochure 2001/2002. Lausanne, Switzerland.

Chapter 2

1 Lee, C.-M., Miller, W. F., Hancock, M. G., & Rowen, H. S. (2000). *The Silicon Valley Edge: A Habitat for Innovation and Entrepreneurship.* Stanford, CA: Stanford University Press.
2 Chandler, A. D. (2001). *Inventing the Electronic Century.* New York: The Free Press.
3 Collins, J. (2001). *Good to Great.* New York: Harper.
4 Simon, H. (1967). The business school: A problem in organisational design. *Journal of Management Studies, 5*(1).
5 Barsoux, J.-L. (2000). *INSEAD: From Intuition to Institution* (p. 216). London: MacMillan.
6 Bok, D. (1986). *Higher Learning* (p. 128). Cambridge, MA: Harvard University Press.
7 IMD's *Building on Talent* programme brochure 2001/2002. Lausanne, Switzerland.
8 Interview with Peter Brabeck. *Harvard Business Review*, February 1, 2001.
9 Heisenberg, W. (1971). *Physics and Beyond.* New York: Harper & Row.
10 Kumar, N., *et al.* (op. cit.).
11 Lorange, P. (1988). On stimulating strategic direction in an academic department. In: R. Lamb and P. Shrivastava, *Advances in Strategic Management* (Vol. 5). Greenwich, CT: JAI Press.

Chapter 3

1 Pounds, W. (1969). The process of problem finding. *Sloan Management Review, 11*(1).
2 Towl, A. R. (1969). *To Study Administration by Cases.* Cambridge, MA: Harvard Business School Press.
3 Porter, M. E. (1980). *Competitive Strategy.* New York: The Free Press; Porter, M. E. (1985). *Competitive Advantage.* New York: The Free Press.
4 Vancil, R. F., & Lorange, P. (1977). *Strategic Planning Systems.* Englewood Cliffs, NJ: Prentice-Hall.
5 Caves, R. E. (1982). *Multinational Enterprise and Economic Analysis.* Cambridge: Cambridge University Press.
6 Boscheck, R. (2001). The governance of global market relations. *World Competition* (Vol. 24, no. 1, pp. 41–64). Dordrecht: Kluwer.
7 Raffia, H. (1982). *The Art and Science of Negotiation.* Cambridge, MA: Harvard University Press.

8   Kerr, C. (1966). *The Uses of the University*. New York: HarperCollins.
9   Bok, D. (1986). *Higher Learning* (p. 1). Cambridge, MA: Harvard University Press.
10 Andrews, K. R. (1971). *The Concept of Corporate Strategy*. Homewood, IL: Dow Jones-Irwin.
11 Kaplan, R. S., & Norton, D. R. (1995). *The Balanced Scorecard: Translating Strategy into Action*. Boston, MA: Harvard Business School Press.
12 IMD case DM 653, Hewlett-Packard (HP): Competing with a global IT infrastructure (1997).
13 Hedberg, B., & Wolff, R. (2000). Organizing, learning and strategizing. In: M. Dierkes, J. Child and I. Nonaka (eds), *Handbook of Organizational Learning*. Oxford: Oxford University Press.
14 Descartes, René. French philosopher and mathematician. Gaarder, Jostein (1997). *Sophie's World: A Novel About the History of Philosophy* (pp. 229–240). London: Phoenix.
15 Gilbert, X., & Lorange, P. (1997). A strategy for more effective development. In: T. O'Neal and M. Ghartman, *Strategy, Structure, and Style* (pp. 301–310). Chichester: Wiley.
16 Gilbert, X., & Lorange, P. (2001). The difference between teaching and learning: Does executive education really improve business performance? *European Business Forum*, 7–8.
17 Source: Chakravarthy, B. S., & Lorange, P. (1991). *Managing the Strategy Process: A Strategy Framework for a Multinational Business Firm*. Englewood Cliffs, NJ: Prentice-Hall.

Chapter 4

1   IMD's *Building on Talent* programme brochure, 2001/2002. Lausanne, Switzerland.
2   IMD's *Orchestrating Winning Performance* programme brochure, 2001/2002. Lausanne, Switzerland.
3   IMD's *Orchestrating Winning Performance* programme brochure (op. cit.) (pp. 5–6).
4   IMD's *Corporate Sustainability Management* brochure. Lausanne, Switzerland.
5   IMD case GM 610 Nestlé in ASEAN (1996).
6   IMD case GM 716 Alcon Laboratories (A) (1998).
7   IMD case GM 543 Innovation and Renovation: The Nespresso Story (2000).
8   IMD case GM 840 Managing Internal Growth: The Story of LC-1 (2000).

9 IMD's *Partnership Network* brochure. Lausanne, Switzerland.
10 IMD's *Programme for Executive Development* brochure. Lausanne, Switzerland.
11 IMD's *Managing Corporate Resources* programme brochure, 2001/2002. Lausanne, Switzerland.
12 IMD's *Breakthrough Programme for Senior Executives* brochure, 2001/2002. Lausanne, Switzerland.
13 IMD's case GM 840 Cokoladovny, A. S.: Nestlé /Danone Partnership in Czech Confectionery (1998).
14 IMD's *Executive MBA* programme brochure, 2001/2002. Lausanne, Switzerland.

Chapter 5

1 Rowley, D. J., Lugan, H. D., & Dolence, M. G. (1998). *Strategic Choice for the Academy: How Demand for Lifelong Learning Will Recreate Higher Education* (p. 23). San Francisco: Jossey-Bass.
2 Lorange, P., Scott-Morton, M., & Ghoshal, S. (1986). *Strategic Control*. St Paul, MN: West Publishing.
3 Chakravarthy, B. S., & Lorange, P. (1991). *Managing the Strategy Process: A Framework for a Multibusiness Firm*. Englewood Cliffs, NJ: Prentice-Hall.
4 Lorange, P. (July 1998). The internal entrepreneur as a driver of business growth. *Perspectives for Managers* (no. 8). Lausanne, Switzerland: IMD.
5 Kumar, N. *et al.* (op. cit.).
6 Note that I borrow here from a two-dimensional model developed by Chakravarthy and Lorange (1990).
7 Chakravarthy, B., & Lorange, P. (op. cit.).
8 *World Competitiveness Yearbook*. Lausanne, Switzerland: IMD.
9 IMD Nestlé LC-1 case (op. cit.).
10 Baghai, M., Coley, S., & White, D. (April 1999). *The Alchemy of Growth: Practical Insights for Building the Enduring Enterprise*. London: Orion Books. US: Perseus Books.
11 IMD's *Venture Booster* programme brochure, 2001/2002. Lausanne, Switzerland.
12 Piaget, J. (op. cit.).
13 Hedberg, B., & Wolff, R. (op. cit.).
14 Levitt, H. J. (1986). *Corporate Pathfinders: Building Vision and Values into Organizations*. Homewood, IL: Dow Jones-Irwin.
15 Abell, D. (op. cit.).

Chapter 6

1 Duderstadt, J. (op. cit.) (pp. 224–225).
2 Rowley, D. J. *et al.* (op. cit.) (pp. 241–245).
3 IMD's *Executive MBA* programme brochure, 2001/2002. Lausanne, Switzerland.
4 IMD's *Building on Talent* programme brochure, 2001/2002. Lausanne, Switzerland.
5 IMD's *World Competitiveness Yearbook.* Lausanne, Switzerland.
6 *Building on Talent* programme brochure (op. cit.).
7 *Training Magazine* (Oct. 1998), *35*(10), 43.
8 Piaget, J. (op. cit.).
9 Interactive adventures: Learn by doing. *Where Learning Lives.* (1999) San Francisco: Ninth House Network.
10 Games and activities: Testing your knowledge. *Where Learning Lives.* (1999) San Francisco: Ninth House Network.
11 E-Mail Nation. *US News & World Report* (p. 54). March 11, 1999.
12 IMD's Hewlett-Packard case (op. cit.).
13 The former President of ABB, Sweden, Mr Bert Swanholm, is quoted as saying this in several presentations — no written reference.

Chapter 7

1 IMD's *Executive Learning* brochure 2001/2002. Lausanne, Switzerland.
2 IMD's brochure for the CEO. Lausanne, Switzerland.
3 IMD's *Senior Executive Forum* programme brochure, 2001/2002. Lausanne, Switzerland.
4 IMD's *Orchestrating Winning Performance* programme brochure, 2001/2002. Lausanne, Switzerland.
5 Marchand, D. (2000). *Competing with Information: A Manager's Guide to Creating Business Value with Information Content.* Chichester, NY: J. Wiley & Sons Ltd.

Chapter 8

1 Rowley, D. J. *et al.* (op. cit.) (p. 31).
2 Op. cit. (p. 31).
3 Op. cit. (p. 31).

4   Munitz, B. (1995). *Never Nake Predictions, Particularly About the Future.* Washington, DC: American Association of State Colleges and Universities.
5   Quoted from Rowley, D. J. *et al.* (op. cit.).
6   Clark, B. (op. cit.).
7   Grønhaug, K. (1999). Forskning og nyttig Kunnskap. In: K. Friedman and J. Olaisen (eds), *Underveis til fremtiden: Kunnskapsledelse I teori og praksis: Handelshøyskolen BI Årbok 1999* (pp. 55–70). Bergen: Fagbokforlaget. Petz, B. C. (1978). Some expanded perspectives on use of social science in public policy. In: I. M. Yunger and S. J. Cutler (eds), *Major Social Issues: A Multi-disciplinary View.* New York: Free Press.
8   Kumar, N., *et al.*, *From Market Driven to Market Driving* (op. cit.).

Chapter 9

1   Duderstadt, J. (2001). Fire, ready, aim? University decision making during an area of rapid change. In: W. Z. Hirsch and L. E. Weber (eds), *Governance in Higher Education: The University in a State of Flux* (pp. 30–31). London: Economica.
2   Rhodes, F. H. (1999). The new university. In: W. Z. Hirsch and L. E. Weber, *Challenges Facing Higher Education at the Millennium* (p. 168). Phoenix, AZ: Oryx Press.
3   Schwarzkopf, H. N., with Petre, P. (1992). *It Doesn't Take a Hero: The Autobiography.* New York: Bantam.
4   IMD's *Orchestrating Winning Performance* programme brochure, 2001/2002. Lausanne, Switzerland.
5   Samson, A. T. S. (1973). *Sovereign State: The Secret History of ITT.* London: Hodder & Stoughton.
6   Lorange, P. (November 1983). Implementing strategic planning: An approach by two Philippine companies. *Wharton Annual* (Vol. 8).
7   Glaser, B., & Strauss, A. (1967). *The Discovery of Grounded Theory: Strategies of Qualitative Research.* London: Weidenfeld & Nicolson.

Chapter 10

1   IMD's *Programme for Executive Development* programme brochure, 2001/2002. Lausanne, Switzerland.
2   Lissack, M., & Roos, J. (1999). *The Next Common Sense: The E-Manager's Guide to Mastering Complexity.* London and New York: Nicholas Brealey Publishing.

3   Strebel, P. (ed.) (2000). *Focused Energy: Mastering the Bottom-Up Organization*. Chichester: J. Wiley & Sons.
4   Marchand, D. (ed.) (2000). *Competing with Information: A Manager's Guide to Creating Business Value with Information Content*. Chichester: J. Wiley & Sons.
5   Rosenzweig, P., Gilbert, X., Malnight, T., & Pucik, V. (2001). *Accelerating International Growth*. Chichester: J. Wiley & Sons.
6   Swanholm, Bert (op. cit.).
7   Schwarzkopf, H. N. (op. cit.).

Chapter 11

1   Barry, J., Chandler, J., & Clark, H. (1 January 2001). Between the ivory tower and the academic assembly line. *Journal of Management Studies*, 38.
2   de Boer, H. (1996). Changing institutional governance structures. In: P. A. M. Maassen and F. A. van Vught (eds),. *Inside Academia: New Challenges for the Academic Profession* (p. 89). Utrecht: De Tijdstroom.
3   Bok, D. (op. cit.) (pp. 158–160).
4   Cohen, M. D. & March, J. (1974). *Leadership and Ambiguity: The American College President* (p. 151). New York: Nakro Hill.
5   Kerr, C. (1982). *The Uses of the University* (p. 38). Cambridge, MA: Harvard University Press.
6   Cornford, F. M. (1964). *Microcosmographia Academica: Being a Guide for the Young Academic Politician* (p. 10). London: Bowis & Bowis.
7   Rhodes, F. H. (1999). The new university. In: W. Z. Hirsch and L. E. Weber, *Challenges Facing Higher Education at the Millennium* (p. 168). Phoenix, AZ: Oryx Press.
8   Leslie, D. W., & Fretwell Jr., E. K. (1996). *Wise Moves in Hard Times: Creating and Managing Resilient Colleges and Universities* (p. 109). San Francisco, CA: Jossey-Bass.
9   Duderstadt, J. (op. cit.) (pp. 252–253).
10 Bok, D. (op. cit.) (p. 191).
11 Mittlehurst, R. (op. cit.) (pp. 99–101).
12 Bok, D. (op. cit.) (pp. 193–194).
13 Duderstadt, J. (op. cit.) (pp. 254–255).
14 Mittlehurst, R. (op. cit.) (p. 196).

Chapter 12

1   Caves, R. (op. cit.).
2   Porter, M. (op. cit.).
3   Boscheck, R. (2000). The EU policy reform on vertical restraints: An economic perspective. *World Competition* (pp. 3–49).
4   Lorange, P. (1988) (op. cit.).
5   Amdam, R. P. (op. cit.).
6   Tjeldvoll, A. (1998). The idea of the service university. *International Higher Education* (no. 13).
7   Rowley, D. J. *et al.* (op. cit.) (p. 180).
8   Rosowsky, H. (2001). Some thoughts about university governance. In: W. Z. Hirsch and L. E. Weber (eds), *Governance in Higher Education: The University in a State of Flux* (p. 100). London: Economica.

Chapter 13

1   Zimmermann, J. L. (2001). Can American business schools survive? Rochester: The Bradley Policy Research Center, Financial Research and Policy, Working Paper No. FR 01–16.
2   IMD's *Executive MBA* programme brochure, 2001/2002. Lausanne, Switzerland.
3   IMD's *Programme for Executive Development* brochure, 2001/2002. Lausanne, Switzerland.
4   IMD's *Job of the Chief Executive* programme brochure, 2001/2002. Lausanne, Switzerland.
5   IMD's *Building on Talent* programme brochure, 2001/2002. Lausanne, Switzerland.
6   IMD's *Orchestrating Winning Performance* programme brochure, 2001/2002. Lausanne, Switzerland.

Chapter 14

1   van Baalen, P. J., & Moratis, L. T. (op. cit.) Chapter 6.
2   Bok, D. (op. cit.).
3   Barsoux, J. L. (2000). INSEAD: *From Intuition to Institution*. Basingstoke: MacMillan.
4   Neubauer, F. F., & Demb, A. (1997). *The Corporate Board: Confronting the Paradoxes*. Kiev: Ochobe.

Chapter 15

1 van Baalen, P. J., & Moratis, L. T. (op. cit.) (p. 53).
2 Meister, J. C. (1994). *Corporate Quality Universities: Lessons in Building a World Class Work Force.* Alexandria, VA: American Society for Training and Development.
3 Slaughter, S., & Leslie, L. (1997). *Academic Capitalism: Politics, Policies, and the Entrepreneurial University* (p. 210). Baltimore, MD: The Johns Hopkins University Press.
4 Based on: Opportunity — and a threat: corporate universities and business schools learn to cohabit, commentary by Peter Lorange, *Financial Times*, March 26, 2001.
5 van Baalen, P. J., & Moratis, L. T. (op. cit.) (p. 120).
6 IMD's *Venture Booster* programme brochure, 2001/2002. Lausanne, Switzerland.
7 Norwegian School of Management (B.I.), Governor's Report. Sandvika, 2000.
8 van Baalen, P. J., & Moratis, L. T. (op. cit.) Chapter 6.
9 Kumar, N. *et al.* (op. cit.) (pp. 129–142).

Author Index

Subject Index